Carl Young's

Adobe® Acrobat® 6.0: Getting Professional Results from Your PDFs

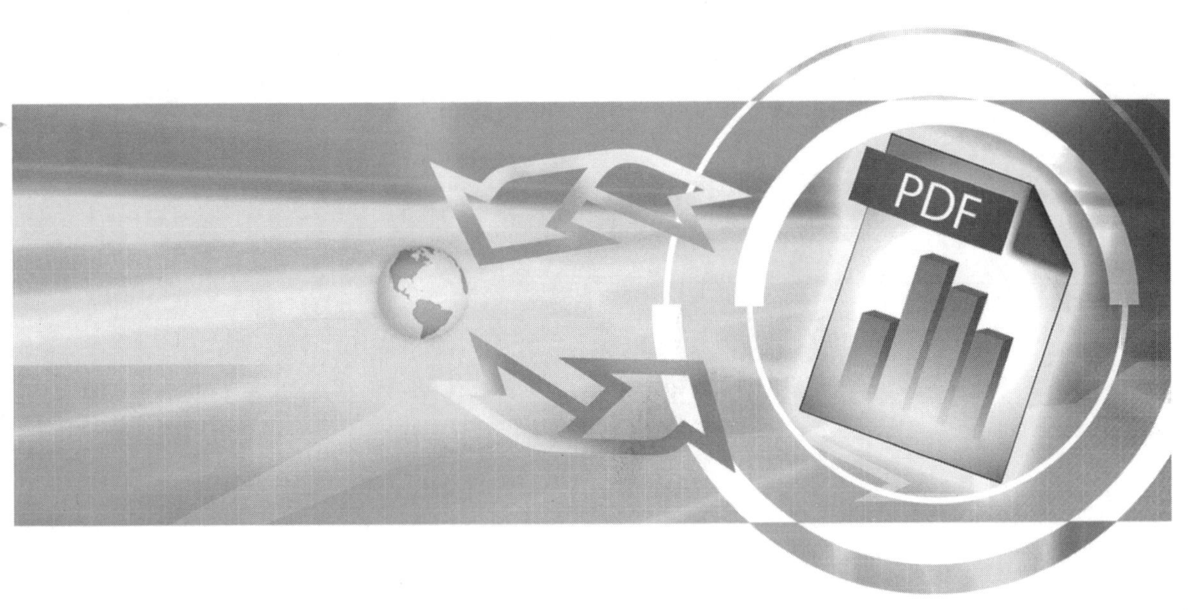

About the Author

Carl Young is president of DigiPub Solutions Corp., the producer of the PDF Conference. Carl is an ACE (Adobe Certified Expert) in Adobe Acrobat 6 Professional and Adobe FrameMaker 7 and a CTT (Certified Technical Trainer). He performed his first PDF consulting job with Acrobat 2 and has been a beta tester for every release of Acrobat since version 3.

He is past president of the Phoenix Chapter of the Society for Technical Communication and is founder of STC's Arizona FrameMaker User Network and Acrobat special interest groups. Carl often presents on Acrobat on behalf of Adobe at trade shows and seminars, including the introduction of Acrobat 6 at the FOSE trade show in Washington D.C.

He has spoken at many S7TC, National Science Foundation, Seybold, BookTech, and IPA events. In addition to producing his own PDF Conference, he has spoken at the Asia-Pacific PDF Conference in Australia and at PDF Conference Korea.

Carl regularly conducts public Acrobat classes in the Phoenix and Washington, D.C. areas and private, on-site classes around the United States. For more information, see **www.pdftrain.com**.

About the Technical Editor

Shlomo Perets of MicroType (**http://www.microtype.com**) has focused primarily on developing online documentation applications since 1993. He trains technical communicators to get the most out of FrameMaker and Acrobat and the combination of these tools. He is developer of the FrameMaker-to-Acrobat TimeSavers/Assistants and author of the ongoing "PDF Best Practices" series. Shlomo has worked in electronic publishing since 1983—in production, training, and consulting.

Carl Young's

Adobe® Acrobat® 6.0: Getting Professional Results from Your PDFs

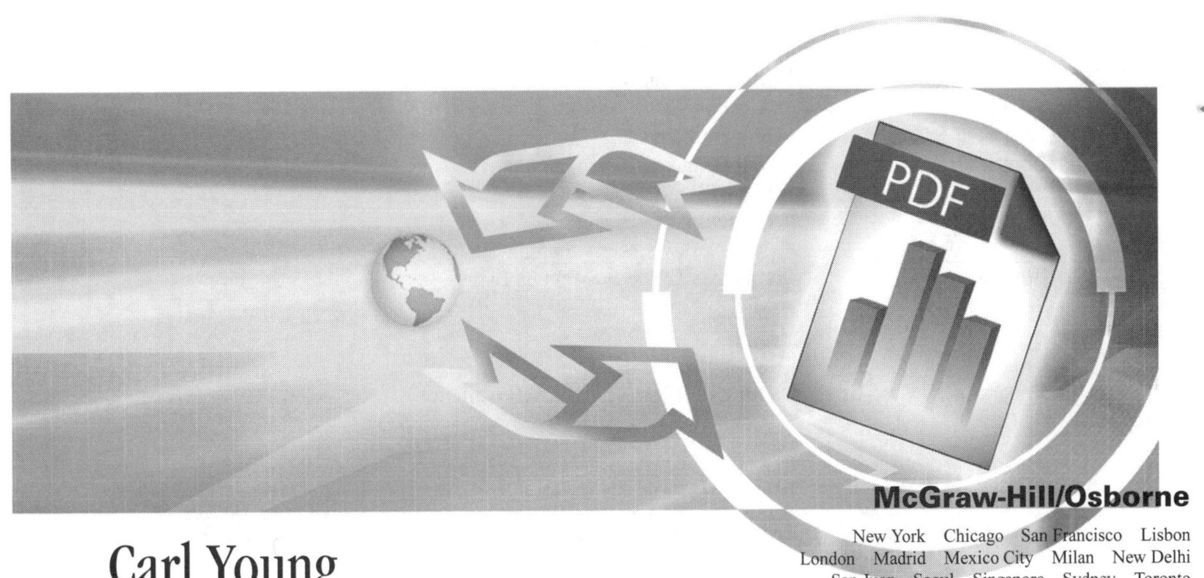

McGraw-Hill/Osborne

New York Chicago San Francisco Lisbon
London Madrid Mexico City Milan New Delhi
San Juan Seoul Singapore Sydney Toronto

Carl Young

The McGraw-Hill Companies

McGraw-Hill/Osborne
2100 Powell Street, 10th Floor
Emeryville, California 94608
U.S.A.

To arrange bulk purchase discounts for sales promotions, premiums, or fund-raisers, please contact **McGraw-Hill**/Osborne at the above address. For information on translations or book distributors outside the U.S.A., please see the International Contact Information page immediately following the index of this book.

Carl Young's Adobe® Acrobat® 6.0: Getting Professional Results from Your PDFs

1234567890 FGR FGR 01987654

ISBN 0-07-223138-6

Publisher	Brandon A. Nordin
Vice President & Associate Publisher	Scott Rogers
Editorial Director	Wendy Rinaldi
Project Editor	Mark Karmendy
Acquisitions Coordinator	Athena Honore
Technical Editor	Shlomo Perets
Copy Editor	Marcia Baker
Proofreader	Susie Elkind
Indexer	Claire Splan
Composition	Tara A. Davis, Kelly Stanton-Scott
Illustrator	Kathleen Edwards, Melinda Lytle
Series Design	Mickey Galicia

This book was composed with Corel VENTURA™ Publisher.

This book is dedicated to my wife, Jo Lou, and son, Marcus.
Thank you for your patience while I spent hundreds of hours in
front of the computer researching and writing this book.

Contents at A Glance

PART I PDF Standards for Everyone

1 What's New in the Acrobat and PDF Universe 3
2 Why Quality Matters 29
3 Creating the Best PDF for the Job 43
4 Making Onscreen PDFs 67
5 Making a PDF Everyone Can Read 91

PART II In Business with Acrobat

6 Putting Acrobat to Work 109
7 Working Together: Acrobat Collaboration 131
8 PDF from Corel WordPerfect 155
9 Working with Acrobat Security and Digital Signatures 167
10 The Wide World of Acrobat 191
11 Moving Beyond One-Document-at-a-Time Creation 201
12 PDF Forms 223
13 Introduction to Adobe Acrobat JavaScript 247
14 A Short Course for System Administrators 273

PART III Acrobat for Creative Professionals

15 Adobe Products 295
16 Corel Applications 327
17 PDF from QuarkXPress 341
18 Preflighting and Color Printing 357

Index 383

Contents

Acknowledgments xix
Introduction xxi

PART I **PDF Standards for Everyone**

CHAPTER 1 **What's New in the Acrobat and PDF Universe** **3**
How to Adopt the Right Member of Adobe's Acrobat Family 4
Acrobat Elements 5
Acrobat Standard 6
Acrobat Professional 6
Reader Linguistically No Longer Part of Acrobat Family 7
Extended Acrobat Family Members 7
Acrobat Capture 7
Adobe Distiller Server 8
Adobe Document Server 8
Adobe Document Server for Reader Extensions 8
Adobe Form Designer 9
What's New in Acrobat Professional 9
Print and Creative Professionals 9
Preflighting 10
PDF/X Creation and Support 11
Creative 12
More Multimedia Support 12
New Viewing Options 12
Enhanced User Aids 13
Editor's Marks 13
The Review Process 15
Integration with Word XP 15
Forms Creation 16
Engineering Drawings 16
Improved UI 17
Task Buttons 17
Items Below Menus Reorganized into Logical Groups 17
Docking Toolbars 18
Better Help 19
Only One Set of Navigation Buttons 19
Much More Like an MS Office Application than an Adobe One 20
More Compression Without Loss of Image Integrity 20
Better Security 20
What Adobe Means by Certified PDF 21
New Functionality 22
Layers 22
Headers and Footers 23

Watermarks and Backgrounds 23
Right-Click Combine in Adobe PDF 24
Better Accessibility Options 24
Read Aloud 25
Auto Scroll 25
More Options for the Visually Impaired 25
Reflow 25
Creating Accessible PDFs 26
Win Versus Mac Differences 27
No Browser Plug-in Until Safari 28
No Round-Tripping of Comments into Word for the Mac 28

CHAPTER 2 **Why Quality Matters** **29**
What's the Matter with PDF? 30
Creation Is Easy, but Getting It Right Is Not 32
Start with a Thoughtful Mind Set 32
Classifying the Types of Problem PDFs 33
The Types 33
Diagnosing Problem PDFs 36
Start with Document Properties 36
Font Information 38
Checking for Problems 38

CHAPTER 3 **Creating the Best PDF for the Job** **43**
Good PDF Creation Is for Everyone 44
Four Fundamental Ways to Create PDFs 44
Adobe Acrobat Distiller 45
What's in the Acrobat Box 45
Suggestions for Improvement 47
Changing Adobe PDF Settings 47
Modifying the Standard Settings 48
Modifying the Smallest File Size Setting 49
What About File Size? 53
Acrobat 6 Compatibility 53
Create Settings for High-Quality PDFs 53
What About PDFWriter? 54
PDF Directly from an Application 54
Third-Party PDF Creators 54
Desktop Alternatives 55
Server-Side PDF 55
Paper to PDF 55
Alternatives to Capture 57
Strategies for Creating Efficient PDF Workflows 58
Working with Fonts 58
Font Handling 101 58
Subsetting and Embedding 59

An Urban Legend 60
Preparing Graphics for PDF 60
Working with TIFF Images 61
PDF Optimizer 63

CHAPTER 4 **Making Onscreen PDFs** **67**
Common Problems in Onscreen PDFs 68
Fixing Problem PDFs 69
Zombie PDF 69
Lost in Space PDF 69
Fix the Page Numbers in a Labyrinth PDF 73
Betrayal PDF 75
Preserving Links and Bookmarks 75
Fat Albert PDF 76
Waiting Game PDF 77
Wrong Turn PDF 77
Honey, I Shrunk the Kids PDF 79
Beauty and the Beast PDF 82
Searching for Bobby Fischer PDF 82
Alternatives to Capture 85
Good Examples of Onscreen PDFs 85
A Financial Report 86
An Interactive Brochure 86
An Onscreen Book in PDF 89

CHAPTER 5 **Making a PDF Everyone Can Read** **91**
Why It Matters to You 92
New Accessibility Features in Acrobat 6 93
Why Accessibility Matters in the PDF World 94
General Considerations 97
An Illustration of the Problem 98
Creating a Tagged PDF 99
Microsoft Word 99
Adobe Applications 100
Editing Tags 105
Testing 106

PART II **In Business with Acrobat**

CHAPTER 6 **Putting Acrobat to Work** **109**
Matching Acrobat to Office 110
Acrobat Integration with Other Applications 111
Viewing PDFs Inside Web Browsers 111
Web Capture from Microsoft Internet Explorer 111
Microsoft Outlook Integration 113
What About Microsoft Publisher? 113

Microsoft Office Applications 114
Enable Tagged PDF for Accessibility in Word 115
Setting Up PDFMaker for Microsoft Word 116
Prepping Microsoft Word for Conversion to PDF 117
Styles and Fields 117
Create a Table of Contents 118
Setting Up Bookmarks 119
Settings 120
Running PDFMaker 121
Troubleshooting PDFs Created from Word 122
Repurposing PDFs 123
Acrobat Export Options 125
Tabular Data 127
Creating from Microsoft Excel 127
Troubleshooting Excel Spreadsheets 127
Creating PDFs from Microsoft PowerPoint 127
Why Use a PDF Presentation? 128
Create from Multiples (eBinder) 129
Creating from Microsoft Visio and Autodesk AutoCAD 129
Open Office 1.1 130

CHAPTER 7 **Working Together: Acrobat Collaboration** **131**
Onscreen Reviewing with Acrobat 132
Types of Onscreen Reviews 133
Review and Markup Tools 133
Commenting Tools 134
Insert a New Acrobat Note Comment 136
Using Editor's Marks 136
Working with Comments 138
Sorting and Filtering Comments 139
Reporting on Comments 140
Reviewing with Acrobat 140
Using Acrobat to Duplicate a Paper-Based Review Cycle 141
Using E-mail–Based Reviews 142
How It Works 143
Starting an E-mail–Based Review 143
Participating in an E-mail–Based Review 144
Receiving and Reconciling Comments from Reviewers 146
Browser-Based Reviews 146
Using Browser-Based Reviews 147
Setting Up WebDAV for Browser-Based Reviews 148
Importing Comments into Word XP/2002/2003 150
Checklist for Integrating Acrobat and Word Comments 151
Review Tracker 152
Comparing Documents 153

CHAPTER 8 **PDF from Corel WordPerfect** **155**
Searching for a Perfect PDF from WordPerfect 156
Terminology 156
Publish to PDF 157
Setting Up Your Document 158
Create a Table of Contents 159
Create WordPerfect PDF 162
Publish to PDF 162
Finish the Job 163
Making a WordPerfect PDF Accessible 163

CHAPTER 9 **Working with Acrobat Security and Digital Signatures** **167**
Why Secure a PDF? 168
Acrobat Security Types 170
Displaying Security Settings 170
What About eBooks? 170
Password-Protected PDFs 171
Which Security Level Is Best? 172
Compatibility 172
Document Open Password 172
Permissions Password 173
Printing Allowed 173
Changes Allowed 173
Enable Copying of Text, Images, and Other Content 174
Enable Copying of Text, Images, and Other Content and Access for the Visually Impaired 174
Enable Text Access of Screen Reader Devices for the Visually Impaired 174
Enable Plaintext Metadata 174
Adobe Policy Server 175
Digital Identities 175
About Digital IDs 176
Creating Your Digital ID 176
Sharing Your Digital ID 177
Requesting Digital Certificates 177
Assembling a List of Trusted Identities 178
Configuring Identity Search Directories 180
Encrypting a Document for a Group of Users 180
Using Digital Signatures 181
About Acrobat Digital Signatures 182
Using Your Signature 182
Applying an Invisible Digital Signature 183
Displaying an Invisible Signature 183
Creating a Digital Signature Form Field 184
Signing a Digital Form Field 184
Configuring the Appearance of Your Digital Signature 185

Certifying a Document 186
Steps to Certify a PDF 187

CHAPTER 10 **The Wide World of Acrobat** **191**
PDF Covers the Map 192
New Features in Acrobat 6 194
Multilingual PDFs 194
Different Languages on Separate Layers 196
New Features for Japanese 196
Bookmarks in Non-Western Languages 196
Creation Is the Key 197
Font Terminology 197
Application Support for Unicode 199

CHAPTER 11 **Moving Beyond One-Document-at-a-Time Creation** **201**
Introduction 202
Acrobat Batch Processing 203
What Is Batch Processing? 203
Running a Sequence 204
Adobe and Non-Adobe Server Solutions 210
The Development of Non-Adobe PDF Products 210
The Server-Side PDF Opportunity 211
PDFs from Web-Based Products 212
PDFs from Big Iron and UNIX and Windows Servers 212
Examples of Server-Based PDF Creation 213
What Is Not Legal 216
Converting File Cabinets of Paper to PDF 216
Adobe Acrobat Capture 217
Capture "Lite" 218
Alternatives to Capture 221
Company Information 222

CHAPTER 12 **PDF Forms** **223**
Why PDF Forms? 224
How PDF Forms Can Benefit Your Organization 225
Moving Up the Food Chain 225
PDF or HTML Forms? 226
PDF Forms from Acrobat Professional 227
Create a Simple Form 228
Where Do PDF Forms Come From? 228
Start with an Image 228
Combo Box and List Box Fields 234
Submitting Data 239
Receiving Form Data 242
PDF Forms from Other Applications 245
If You Really Enjoy Creating Forms 246
Company Information 246

CHAPTER 13 **Introduction to Adobe Acrobat JavaScript** **247**
About Acrobat JavaScript 248
Acrobat JavaScript and HTML JavaScript 249
Where Acrobat JavaScripts Can Be Used 250
Folder Level Acrobat JavaScript 250
Document Level 250
Field Level 250
Page Actions and Links 253
Naming Fields 254
Terms 254
Inputting JavaScript into Acrobat Professional 255
Syntax 255
Objects 256
An Example JavaScript 256
Display the Date in a Field 257
What Just Happened? 257
Using the JavaScript Console/Debugger 258
Useful Acrobat JavaScript Examples 259
Performing a Calculation 259
Perform Another Calculation 261
Automatically Tab from One Field to the Next 261
Alert Box 263
Make Acrobat Bark Like a Dog 264
Add Voice to the Alert 265
Pop-Up Menus 266
Specify a User Preference 268
Add a New Menu Item 269
E-mail and Version Sniffing 270
E-mail Form Data 270
Check the Version of Acrobat 271
Acrobat 6.0 Software Development Kit 272

CHAPTER 14 **A Short Course for System Administrators** **273**
An Acrobat on Every Desk 274
Incorrect Acrobat Installations 274
Order of Installation 275
What to Install 275
Components of Acrobat Professional 276
Where Is PDFMaker? 278
PostScript Driver Setup 279
Windows 2000/XP/2003 280
Font Issues 285
Distiller Can't Find My Fonts 286
Fixing Phantom Font Problems 286
Mac OS X Issues 288

Installing Acrobat Across the Enterprise 288
Microsoft SMS 289
IBM Tivoli 289
Keeping Up-to-Date 289
A Checklist for System Administrators 291
The List 291

PART III **Acrobat for Creative Professionals**

CHAPTER 15 **Adobe Products 295**
Adobe Illustrator CS 296
Illustrator File Formats 297
Creating a PDF from Illustrator 297
Illustrator Presets Compared 298
Suggested Changes to the Illustrator Presets 301
Printing to Adobe PDF 301
Adding File Information for Acrobat 303
PDF and Photoshop CS 304
Photoshop PDF Format 304
Save As PDF 304
Placing PDFs in Photoshop 305
Opening a PDF in Photoshop CS 306
Importing Images from a PDF 306
Automating PDF to PSD Creation 307
Creating a PDF Presentation 308
Layer Comps to PDF 309
Importing and Exporting PDF Text and Audio Comments 309
Transferring Photoshop Metadata to PDF 310
Importing PDFs into InDesign CS 310
Exporting to PDF 311
Changing Presets 313
Creating Interactive PDFs with InDesign CS 313
About InDesign Buttons 314
The Button Tool 314
Converting Objects to Buttons 314
Button Options 315
Button Behaviors 316
Creating Rollovers 316
Adding Hyperlinks and Bookmarks 317
Adding Hyperlinks 318
Adding Bookmarks 319
Considerations for Creating Interactive PDFs from InDesign 319
Adding Movies and Sounds 320
Creating Tagged PDF 321
Adobe PageMaker 321
Adobe FrameMaker 7.1 321
Importing PDFs into FrameMaker 322
Creating PDFs from FrameMaker 322

Setting Up FrameMaker for PDF Generation 322
Generating a PDF from FrameMaker 324

CHAPTER 16 **Corel Applications** **327**
Corel Ventura 10 328
Ventura Publish to PDF Capabilities 328
Online PDFs from Ventura 329
Creating PDFs for Specific Uses 331
PDF for Document Distribution 332
PDF for Editing 332
PDF for Prepress 333
PDF for the Web 333
PDF/X-1 334
Fonts and Publish to PDF 334
CorelDRAW 11 336
Creating Online PDFs with CorelDraw 337
Creating Prepress PDFs from CorelDRAW 338
Creating PDF Forms with CorelDRAW 339
Corel DESIGNER 10 340

CHAPTER 17 **PDF from QuarkXPress** **341**
Overview 342
QuarkXPress 4 and 5 342
Adobe's Recommended Solution 343
Printing to Adobe PDF from QuarkXPress 4 or 5 345
Creating the PDF 347
Quark's PDF Solution 348
Using the PDF Filter QuarkXTension 349
Exporting the PDF 351
A 100-Percent Non-Adobe Solution 351
Print Driver Configuration 353
PDF Export Options 354

CHAPTER 18 **Preflighting and Color Printing** **357**
Color Printing and PDF 358
PDF/X: The PDF Publishing Standard 358
What Is PDF/X? 360
Creating a PDF/X-1a 360
Advantages of PDF/X 361
PDF/X Resources 362
Quality Assurance 363
Preflighting in Acrobat 6 Professional 363
Previewing Color Separations 365
Previewing Transparency Flattening 367
Preflight Profiles 367

- Creating a Preflight Profile 368
- Exporting and Importing Preflight Profiles 369

Preflighting with PitStop Professional 370

- PitStop PDF Profile Control Panel 370

Printing from Acrobat 372

- Print Options 372
- Advanced Printing 374
- Output Settings 375
- Marks and Bleeds 376
- Transparency Flattening 377
- PostScript Options 377
- Printing Layers 378

Measuring Tools 378

Cropping Pages 379

Job Definition Format (JDF) 380

Imposition 380

Index 383

Acknowledgments

This book would not have been possible without the hundreds of students and PDF Conference attendees who have provided countless insights into the world of Acrobat. My thanks, too, to the experts who bring their skills and knowledge to the PDF Conference. They have broadened my horizons and inspired me to dig deeper into the PDF world.

A particular thanks to Shlomo Perets of MicroType, the technical editor of this book. Shlomo has pioneered the use of standards in the general PDF world, and he has done much to educate the technical writing community in the proper way to create electronic user manuals. Shlomo's Acrobat expertise was invaluable in the creation of this book.

Many others in the PDF world were generous enough to review portions of the book. Among them are Lori DeFurio, Dov Isaacs, and Greg Pisocky of Adobe Systems, Inc.; Tim Sullivan and Gina O'Reilly of activePDF; Thomas Merz of PDFlib; Douglas Hanna of Hewitt Associates LLC; Leslie Greenberg; Catherine McCarthy of Enfocus; and Paul Showalter of IRS. Any mistakes in the text are my mine, not theirs.

The publishing team at McGraw-Hill/Osborne has been wonderful to work with. A particular thanks to Editorial Director Wendy Rinaldi, who understood the concept behind the book and supported it through the approval and publishing process. This book would not have been possible without Acquisitions Coordinator Athena Honore, Executive Project Editor Mark Karmendy, and Copy Editor Marcia Baker. They held my feet to the fire when deadlines loomed so the book actually was finished, and they fixed countless editorial mistakes.

Introduction

Welcome to *Carl Young's Adobe® Acrobat® 6*. It is my hope that this book will enable you to produce better PDFs and save your organization some time and money. While there are lots of how-tos and time-saving tips in the following pages, the purpose of this book is to raise the quality of PDFs you produce.

What's wrong with the PDFs you are generating now? Maybe nothing. Maybe a lot. Most people don't even know how to tell. Read this book and you will.

It is my experience that many PDF creators don't put enough thought into what end users will go through when they open a PDF. Will they see exactly what you intended, or will they see something entirely different? Are the colors true and the fonts exact? Will it open to the right page and at a zoom level they can use? Can you go to sleep at night after you've attached a PDF and hit the Send button from your E-mail tool or posted the file to a Web site? Or are you restless, worried that your PDFs will not perform as you hoped?

If you produce a PDF intended to be read on a computer screen, can users easily navigate through the document? Can they get to the right page?

If you are creating a PDF for commercial printing, how can you be sure that it will reproduce correctly? Will your PDF increase or reduce your overall bill?

I work in a world where proper PDF creation is saving organizations thousands, or even millions, of dollars in reduced printing bills and staffing levels. How about you and your organization? Are you getting the most out of your investment in PDFs, or are you overlooking some hidden capability that will solve a business issue?

Acrobat, and the free Adobe Reader, have become the premier solutions for electronic document publishing. But there is more to PDFs than Acrobat. Adobe is expanding the Acrobat franchise to include form processing, XML, and other key businesses processes. Third-party vendors, such as activePDF, Ad Lib Document Solutions, Appligent, and PDFlib, produce server-based applications built on the PDF specification. This book can open the PDF world for you and your organization.

About this Book

Both Acrobat 6 Professional and Standard are covered in this book, but many of the advanced techniques are possible only with the Professional version. However, you can produce excellent PDFs with the Standard version of Acrobat. Most of the screen captures are from the Windows version of Acrobat, but the keyboard shortcuts for both Mac OS X and Windows are included in the text. The chapter on color printing uses screen captures from Mac OS X.

This book is divided into three parts. The first part outlines what's new in the PDF world, what the most common mistakes creators make are, and how to avoid making a faulty PDF. The second part focuses on using Acrobat in business and government. The last part focuses on PDF for creative professionals.

Part I: "PDF Standards for Everyone"

In Part I, you'll get a tour of what's new in Acrobat 6, a look at the expanded Acrobat family, and who some of the major third-party PDF providers are. You'll also be introduced to quality standards for Acrobat, how to diagnose typical problems, and how to avoid making mistakes.

Part II: "In Business with Acrobat"

You'll find the chapters in Part II focus on typical business applications of Acrobat. Included in this part are ideas on meeting U.S. government Section 508 requirements for accessibility, working with Microsoft Word and WordPerfect, and using Acrobat security, PDF forms, and server-based PDF applications.

Part III: Acrobat for Creative Professionals

Part III is for graphic artists, designers, and prepress and commercial printing professionals. There is information on creating PDFs from Adobe applications such as Photoshop and Illustrator. In addition, there are chapters devoted to QuarkXPress, Corel products, preflighting, and color printing.

In Closing

Like other computer books, this one is not designed to be read cover to cover (although you are free to do so!). You can read the chapters on quality, see what mistakes you might be making, and then skip to the chapter that covers your favorite creation tool. Or, if you want information on advanced topics such as forms creation, you can absorb that information and then use a creation tool to create a background image for the form. The JavaScript chapter can help you add intelligence to your form or add more functionality to your electronic documents.

Part I

PDF Standards for Everyone

Chapter 1

What's New in the Acrobat and PDF Universe

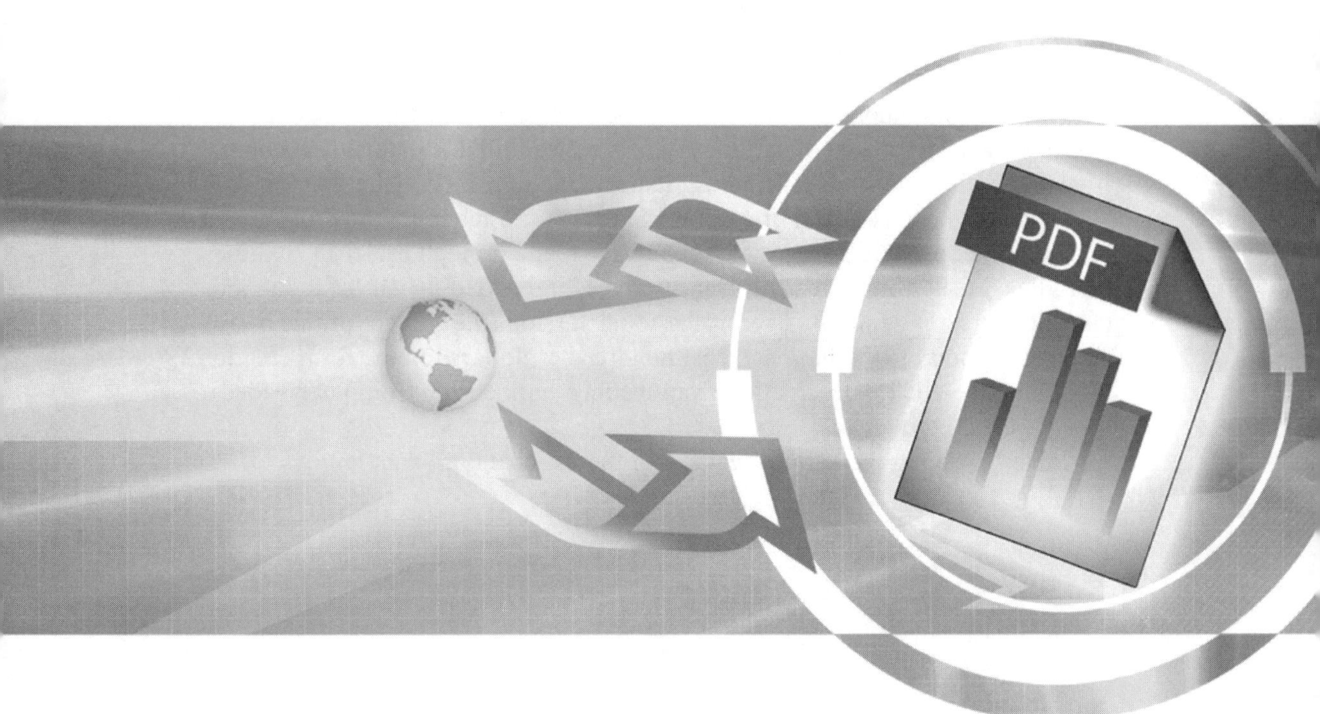

Most people encounter Adobe Acrobat when someone sends a PDF file via electronic mail, or a PDF shows up on the corporate intranet, or when they download a form from a government agency. The free Adobe Reader comes preinstalled on a large majority of computers today, and many people in government and private business even have access to a PDF creation tool, such as Adobe Acrobat.

While end users will likely employ Adobe Reader 6 to view files, PDF creators will need a tool to produce a PDF. Although we discuss alternatives in this book, by far the most widely used creation tool is Adobe Acrobat. In this chapter, we look at the various Acrobat family members, so you can choose which is best for you.

How to Adopt the Right Member of Adobe's Acrobat Family

To celebrate ten years since the launch of Adobe Acrobat 1, Adobe Systems Inc. had a public birthday party—the company launched version 6 of its primary product, Adobe Acrobat. Instead of lighting candles on a cake, Adobe launched a commercial broadcast television campaign to promote Adobe PDF—a first in corporate history. The company had never put on a television ad campaign before, not even for Photoshop. By all accounts, Acrobat 6 is off to a very strong start.

The arrival of Adobe Acrobat 6 brings new choices to customers. Gone is the one-size-fits-all approach of earlier versions. Instead, PDF creators can choose from one of three versions: Elements, Standard, and Professional.

Inside the boxes of each product is the most significant upgrade to Acrobat in years. The software wizards at Adobe have made it much easier to create PDF files, greatly improved the user interface, and added dozens of tools to the document creator's toolkit. The Professional version (the subject of this book) includes prepress tools that once cost hundreds of dollars to buy, form creation tools, and one-click PDF creation from leading engineering Computer Aided Design (CAD) tools.

Table 1-1 shows the various features of the Acrobat 6 product family.

	Adobe Reader 6	Adobe Acrobat 6 Elements	Adobe Acrobat 6 Standard	Adobe Acrobat 6 Professional
Navigate, view, and print PDF files	X	X	X	X
One-button creation from Microsoft Office applications		X	X	X
One-button creation from Internet Explorer and Outlook				X
128-bit encryption and password protection		X	X	X
Review-management and commenting tools			X	X
Capability to combine multiple document types into one PDF file			X	X
One-button creation from AutoCAD, Microsoft Visio, and Microsoft Project for Windows				X
Enhanced tools for printing, viewing, and navigating large-format documents				X
Support for document layers in technical drawings				X
Built-in validation and preflighting tools				X
Capability to verify and output PDF/X-compliant files				X
Capability to preview and print color separations				X
Electronic forms creation				X
Accessibility optimization and accessible forms authoring				X
Catalog for creating searchable indexes				X

TABLE 1-1 Adobe Acrobat 6 Product Comparison. Source: Adobe Systems, Inc.

Let's take a look at each Acrobat family member.

Acrobat Elements

Elements is a simple creation tool designed to be sold in bulk to large organizations. It inserts Adobe PDF buttons in Microsoft Office applications, which allows one-click PDF creation. Think of Elements as utility software. You can't buy a single copy of Elements. You must buy it in a quantity of 1,000 or more. The viewer for Elements is the free Adobe Reader. Reader users can't perform PDF document assembly or editing tasks.

Acrobat Standard

Adobe has positioned *Standard* as the version for the typical office worker. Standard users get all the features in Elements, which include right-mouse click PDF creation and Adobe PDF buttons in MS Office products. They also get a button added to Internet Explorer that lets them search for PDFs on the Web and to turn a web page—or a web site—into a PDF.

The viewer for these PDF creators is *Acrobat Standard. Acrobat Standard* includes features to remove and extract pages, add links and bookmarks, and a paper-capture feature to convert paper into PDF. What Adobe calls "knowledge workers" can use Standard to perform the tasks required of most PDF creators and document assemblers.

Acrobat Professional

What do graphic artists, civil engineers, and form designers have in common? Acrobat Professional, that's what. Adobe souped up the new version of Acrobat with new features for designers and engineers, and upgraded the tools for form designers.

Creative types and printing professionals will find a host of new tools waiting for them in *Acrobat Professional.* Adobe licensed the Acrobat prepress tools from callas software gmbh of Berlin and included those tools in Acrobat Professional. Acrobat can check to ensure a PDF meets certain industry standards, such as PDF/X. It can even fix some problems to try to bring the file into compliance.

For engineers who use CAD tools, such as AutoCAD, Professional adds one-button file creation. In addition, Acrobat 6 does a much better job of displaying fine line weights, formerly a common complaint from engineers. Engineers—and, of course, everyone else—also can split the screen to display two different views of a PDF simultaneously. One screen can show an area in detail and another a larger view to help the engineer navigate through an oversized drawing.

For form designers, Adobe has divided what was once a single form tool into parts and grouped all the parts on a toolbar. Instead of editing all form fields at once, a designer can now only edit the check boxes. The text fields and radio buttons can't be edited at the same time, reducing the risk that a change to one type of field could accidentally reposition another field type.

Professional also includes *Catalog,* a tool for creating full-text indexes. Searching through files indexed by Catalog is generally faster than using the Search tool to look through groups of unindexed PDFs on the Web or on a network drive. Catalog indexes are often found on PDFs collected on compact discs.

Reader Linguistically No Longer Part of Acrobat Family

If you point to a PDF file on someone's computer screen and ask them what application they'll use to open it, the most common response is "Adobe." Because Adobe gives the Reader away free, the Reader has become synonymous with Adobe. That caused a problem, however. Many users were confused about the free Adobe Acrobat Reader that came with their computer and the *not-free* Adobe Acrobat sold in stores. For version 6, Adobe decided to drop the Acrobat family name from the Reader. One reason is to help distinguish between what software users pay for and what they don't.

There's a clue in the name, as well. *Adobe Reader* views PDF files and files from Photoshop Album. It also includes the *Acrobat eBook Reader,* which was formerly a separate product.

Extended Acrobat Family Members

Adobe has realized the value of PDF, and it has produced a wide variety of PDF-based products for enterprise and government users. Too many exist to include here, but some of the most important are discussed in the following sections. You should know about these because you might see files produced by these applications. Nearly all are Windows-only products designed to work as department or enterprise-wide solutions, and they're priced accordingly. Some of these tools arrived at Adobe with the 2002 purchase of Accelio, formerly known as JetForm. Many products have gone through one round of name changes during the Accelio acquisition and they might change again in the future.

Many companies compete with Adobe in these arenas. Some directly compete in the PDF forms area and others, like Microsoft, compete indirectly with InfoPath. The market is vast. If you think about it, PDF and HTML, the language of the Web, are time- and money-saving replacements for paper. We all know how much paper still sits on desks and in filing cabinets!

Acrobat Capture

Capture turns paper into PDFs. The Standard and Professional versions of Capture include something called the *Paper Capture Plug-in*, or more commonly as *Capture lite.* The stand-alone version of Capture is designed for those organizations that have years of paper documents stowed away in filing cabinets and cold storage. Optimized for use with high-speed scanners—the kinds that can zip through a ream of paper in a minute—Capture can pull those paper documents out of storage and into a corporate intranet where they can be electronically stored in a searchable format.

Adobe Distiller Server

Tucked way in an Acrobat installation is an application called *Distiller,* which is the creation engine inside Acrobat.

Many companies need to automate the production of PDFs. For example, a financial institution might need to generate hundreds of thousands of statements each month. That's too much work for someone sitting at a desktop computer.

Distiller Server uses what are known as *watched folders*: any time a certain file type, say, the print file of a customer's monthly statement, lands in the watched folder, Distiller Server turns the print file into a PDF.

Distiller Server comes in 100-user and unlimited editions for Windows and UNIX servers. This is probably the arena where Adobe faces the most competition from companies such as activePDF, AdLib Systems, PDFlib, and many others. For a comparison of Distiller Server and the watched folder feature in Acrobat Professional, see Chapter 11.

Adobe Document Server

Adobe Document Server can create PDFs from PostScript files or from XML data. In addition, it can manipulate PDFs in the following ways:

- Combine PDFs
- Split PDFs
- Add TOCs and bookmarks
- Extract form data
- Flatten forms for archiving

Adobe Document Server for Reader Extensions

Tucked away inside the free Adobe Reader are some amazing capabilities. For example, the capacity to save form data, digitally sign documents, add markup to review materials, and highlight text. Only special PDFs produced by Document Server for Reader Extensions can turn on these hidden functions.

Adobe produced this product because government agencies, banks, insurance companies, and others like PDF-based forms. PDF-based forms can look like the original paper documents, making it easy for users to make the transition from paper to online forms. Until this product was released, the only way for users to save data to their hard drives, or to review a document, was to buy a version of Acrobat. Large organizations with many customers say this business model doesn't work for them. How long would you be a customer if your bank required you to sign each check with a special pen that costs more than $200? Not very, I'm sure.

Buying Document Server for Reader Extensions shifts the cost from the end user to the form creator. The free Reader is all customers need—they needn't buy anything. And large organizations can usually justify buying Document Server for Reader Extensions because they can save a tremendous amount of money by not having to print paper forms.

Adobe Form Designer

While Acrobat Professional includes form creation tools, *Adobe Form Designer* is a complete authoring environment. Users design an XML-based form in a What You See Is What You Get (WYSIWYG) environment, and can then output the form as an intelligent PDF or as an HTML form.

The form design environment is rich, as you would expect in an Adobe product. Form fields and labels can be easily formatted for shape, fill, border, and font. It also contains a library where form designers can store commonly used components, such as address fields, for reuse in other forms. Form Designer also is great for producing forms that meet United States government accessibility standards, and it has a feature for linking PDF forms to databases.

Now that you've had a quick look at Adobe Acrobat and its relatives, let's turn back to our main topic: Adobe Acrobat 6 Professional.

What's New in Acrobat Professional

Professional is the top-of-the-line product in the Acrobat family. Everything in Adobe Reader, Adobe Acrobat Elements, and Adobe Acrobat Standard is included in Professional. In addition, Professional has its own set of tools for power users.

Print and Creative Professionals

Adobe Acrobat 6 Professional gives print and creative professionals a powerful set of tools for moving a project through the print production cycle. A graphic artist, for example, can create a press-ready PDF from QuarkXpress. A prepress service provider can use Professional to check the work of the artist for adherence to industry standards. A print production house can use Professional to view separations of each color used in the job or for *soft proofing*. Soft proofing uses an image format such as PDF instead of paper "hard copy" in the review and markup cycle of a publication. For example, a PDF of a four-color brochure can be reviewed by a customer via e-mail or the Web, drastically reducing approval times and saving printing and delivery costs.

In many ways, the new tools for print and creative professionals are a logical extension of Acrobat's functionality. The PDF created by Acrobat is the deliverable required by many magazine and book publishers, and having the capability built into Acrobat to check PDFs for accuracy and quality is reasonable.

Preflighting

Preflighting is a printing industry term for checking files for mistakes before the files are printed. Incorrect fonts, image quality, color model used, and inks can often delay a print job.

Professional makes checking files and generating reports easy. Choose Document | Preflight and select a prebuilt preflight checker, or build your own from the 400 possible options. See Figure 1-1 for an example. The number of items that Professional can check is quite amazing. For example, print providers can check the number of inks required for a job, how many plates are necessary,

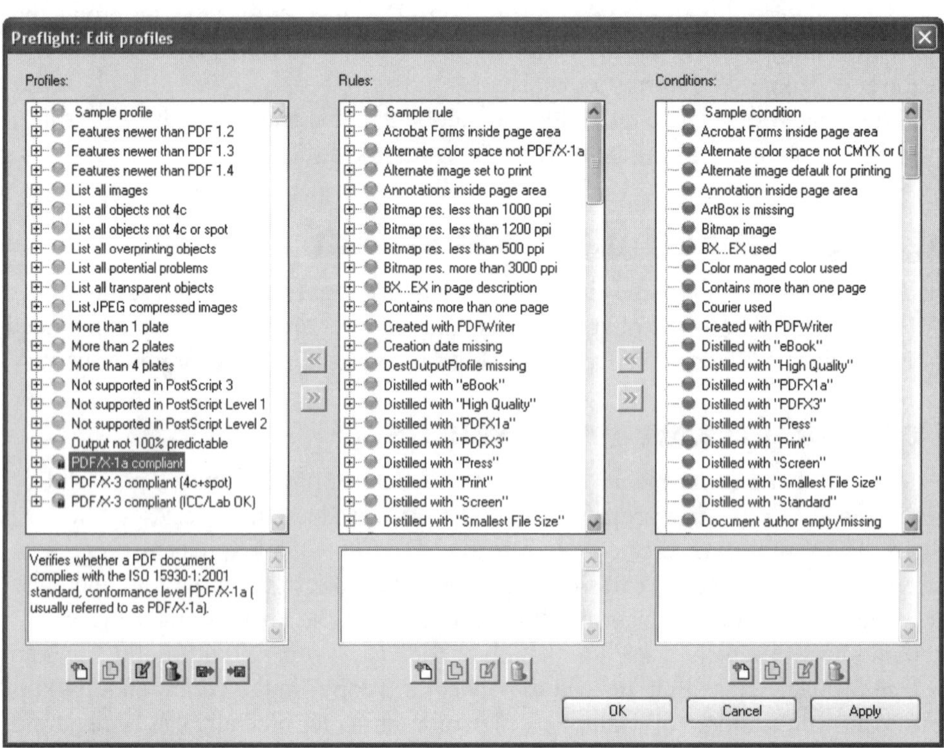

FIGURE 1-1 Preflighting options in Acrobat 6

and whether the fonts have traveled inside the PDF. No extra tools are required; everything is built into Professional.

PDF/X Creation and Support

In an effort to build standards to ease the exchange of PDFs, the print industry has devised a specific kind of PDF called PDF/X. What those in the publishing industry like about PDF/X is it lacks all the fun, flashy stuff that draw so many people to Acrobat.

A *PDF/X* is a static PDF with no JavaScript, multimedia elements, or RGB—onscreen—colors. Think of PDF/X as a pure image format. While many of us enjoy dynamic PDFs, a printer doesn't want a PDF to start playing a movie just as the printer tries to use the file to print a million-dollar press run! PDF/X keeps that from happening. There's much more to a PDF/X, and it comes in several variants. We discuss this topic in more detail in Chapter 18. Figure 1-2 shows PDF/X creation options in Acrobat 6 Professional.

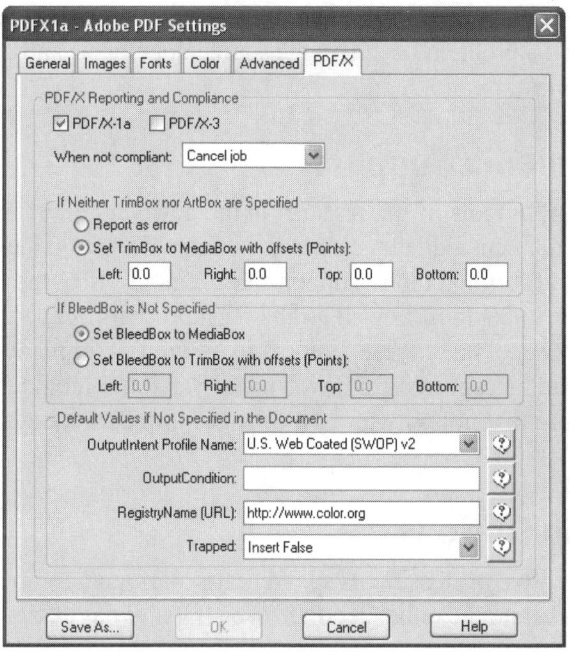

FIGURE 1-2 PDF/X creation options

Professional comes with PDF/X output as an optional setting. Do you need to send an ad to *Time* magazine? This requires a specific type of PDF/X and, with Professional, you can create one with a touch of a button.

Other tools for the print/prepress industry inside Professional include the following:

- Separation preview and printing
- New advanced printing controls similar to other Adobe applications
- Common transparency flattening controls with other Adobe applications
- JDF Job Ticket Creation

Creative

In the printing industry today, it's sometimes hard to know when the role of a creative professional, such as a graphic artist, ends and the job of a prepress specialist begins. Professional helps by providing support for both job functions.

For example, a graphic artist can prepare an ad for *Sports Illustrated* and bypass the prepress shop. How so? If the designer is using QuarkXpress, the artist can print to the Adobe PDF virtual printer set to output a PDF/X. A PDF/X-compliant file will appear (or won't, if a problem occurs in the source document) and can be sent to the magazine for publication.

More Multimedia Support

Creative types can find lots of fun features in the new version of Acrobat. For example, there's more embedded multimedia support. For some inexplicable reason, previous versions of Acrobat didn't support the common MPG and MPEG audio and video formats. Version 6 does, as well as adding support for RealAudio and Flash.

Not only can creators add these features to a PDF but, in many cases, these dynamic media can be captured from web sites. Version 6 includes a beefed-up web capture feature that not only turns web pages into PDFs, but also includes Flash animations.

New Viewing Options

Because many creative professionals spend hours staring at computer screens, they'll likely appreciate the enhanced PDF viewing and navigation features in Professional.

There are new tools specifically for those people who need to examine a PDF page in detail. The *Loupe* tool works just like a loupe used by a jeweler or photographer. Grab the Loupe tool, click on an area, and then zoom in and out for a closer view.

If you ever zoom way in and need a sense of perspective, the *Pan & Zoom* tool works the opposite of the Loupe. Choose Pan & Zoom and get a thumbnail view of the entire document.

If you've ever used a zoom lens on a camera, you'll like the *Dynamic Zoom* tool: click-and-drag up over an area and zoom in; click-and-drag down to zoom out.

In both Standard and Professional, you can split the screen. For example, in the top-half you might have zoomed in to enlarge an area. In the bottom-half. you can have a one-up view of the document to help you navigate through complex drawings.

New to version 6 are rulers and a toolbar for measuring graphics. The measuring tools can also calculate an area of an object, a handy tool for engineers. The *Info* tab shows the size of an object as you resize it.

Enhanced User Aids

Spread throughout Acrobat 6 are enhancements for interacting with a PDF. Take the Hand tool, the most basic of Acrobat's tools. The *Hand* tool is used for moving pages around the screen, selecting form fields to be filled in, and so on.

Users can now optionally turn on a feature in Preferences to enable text selection with the Hand tool. Need to copy some text from PDF? Enable this feature, click, drag-and-copy, and then paste away. How do you do this? Choose Edit | Preferences | General | Selection | Enable text selection for the Hand tool.

Another example can be found in the Bookmarks tab. Open the Bookmarks tab in a document that contains bookmarks and choose Options | Wrap Long Bookmarks. Any bookmarks that extended beyond the bookmark pane are wrapped. No more guessing about which bookmark you want to select!

Also in the bookmark tab are options to change the size of the display text. The choices are small, medium, and large. Medium is the default. Users can choose what size of bookmark text they want to see.

Many more user aids exist—more than can be listed here. I seem to stumble across a new one every time I use Acrobat. Go exploring for yourself and see what the software wizards in San Jose have come up with.

Editor's Marks

Every industry has its traditions, and the printing industry is no exception. When editors review paper copy submitted by writers, the editors indicate changes in a certain way with specific symbols, such as a caret (^) to indicate text insertion. And, while previous versions of Acrobat included sticky notes and other ways of specifying changes, the results looked nothing like the traditional way editors direct writers to make changes.

Both Standard and Professional include a basic set of editor's marks. For example, the traditional way of calling for a word or phrase to be removed is to draw a line through it with a red pen. Substitutions are requested by placing a caret at the point of insertion, and then writing the text to be inserted above the line. See Figure 1-3 for an example.

Here's how the process works in Acrobat 6.

1. Choose Tools | Commenting | Show Commenting Toolbar, or click on the Review & Comment button in the toolbar.
2. Click on the Text Edits tool.
3. Click-and-drag over text you want deleted.
4. Once the text is highlighted, press the BACKSPACE key.
5. Type the replacement text.

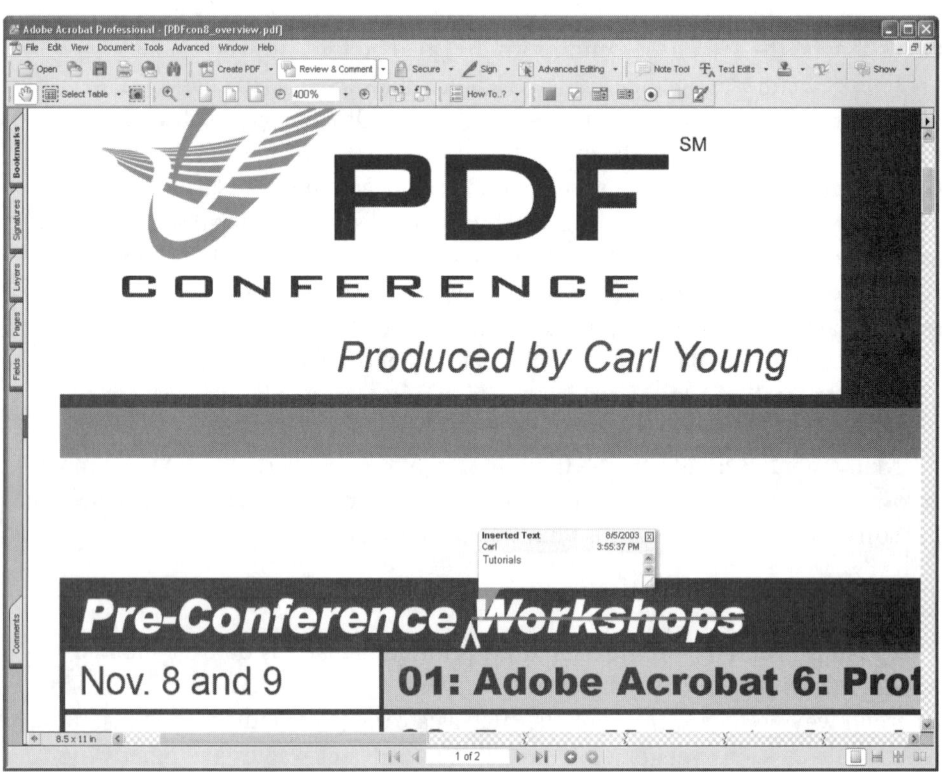

FIGURE 1-3 Acrobat editor's marks, including a strikeout and a caret

This process places a strike mark through the highlighted text, inserts a caret where the strike ends, and places the replacement text above it. It works just like old-fashioned editor's marks, except these are always legible!

The Review Process

Disputes often come up during the editing process. For example, in commercial, academic, or legal publishing, authors might disagree with an editor's decision. In technical publishing, subject matter experts reviewing documents might differ on the steps in a procedure.

In many situations, an author makes one paper copy of a document for each reviewer, and then sends the copies via interoffice mail or express delivery. Each reviewer marks up their copy without knowing what the other reviewers are doing. Then, when the copies land back on the writer's desk, the author must go through each copy of a document, a page at a time, looking for comments. When two reviewers request conflicting changes, the author has to contact each reviewer and hash out the differences.

Both Standard and Professional allow all reviewers to see the Editor's Marks and other comments simultaneously. Not only can reviewers make their own comments, but they can also remark on the comments made by other reviewers.

No special software is required to implement Acrobat review and comment. To conduct these discussions, Standard and Professional use e-mail, network drives, or web sites—computer services that nearly every company has today. Version 6 has greatly eased the implementation of Acrobat reviews.

Acrobat 6 introduces a new term for the person in charge of reviews and gives this person the capability to use e-mail to invite reviewers to participate. This person is called the Review Initiator. The *Review Initiator* can use new tools to greatly simplify the process of starting a web-based review. The *Review Tracker* lets the Initiator keep track of who is participating in reviews and can automatically send e-mails to remind reviewers to keep to the project schedule.

Users of Professional also get reviewing tools that Standard users don't get. A *cloud* tool, a favorite of engineers, and *arrowheads,* often used in technical fields, are included in the Advanced Commenting | Drawing toolbar of Professional.

Integration with Word XP

Adobe realizes that Acrobat will be a companion product for millions of Microsoft Office users, and it has taken great steps to make Office and Acrobat compatible. While integration exists between Excel and PowerPoint, the deepest levels of interoperability are in Microsoft Word XP and 2003.

NOTE *Adobe released Acrobat 6.1 in December 2003. It includes integration with Office 2003, including Word 2003.*

With the newer versions of Word, comments from Acrobat can be integrated into a Word document. Again, this feature is only available for Word XP and 2003.

Here's how the process works. The author writes in Word XP or 2003, and then creates a PDF for review by using the Adobe PDF menu in the Word Menu bar. The PDF is then distributed for review. Once the review cycle is finished, comments are consolidated into a single PDF. The author then reopens the source Word document and chooses Acrobat Comments | Import Comments from Acrobat. As the author works through the import process, he or she can selectively import comments or import all of them.

Acrobat comments can be directly inserted into the Word document. Skipped or unintegrated comments appear as Word comment bubbles. Right-click to delete individual comments or use the Acrobat Comments menu to delete all unused comments.

Forms Creation

Inside Professional is a whole new look for PDF forms creation. Gone is the single form tool. In its place is a *form toolbar,* which displays separate tools for creating each type of form field.

Once a form is deployed, users can now enter richly formatted text. When a text field is set to accept rich text formatting, users can apply styling information to the text, such as bold or italic. The purpose of this option is to allow long entries, such as a biography in a job application form, to be more attractively presented and readable.

Engineering Drawings

A new area for PDF growth is in engineering departments. Engineers use specific drawing packages, such as AutoCAD and Bentley Systems' MicroStation, to create highly complex drawings. Printing these drawings on plotters, or oversized printers, is costly and time-consuming. Each CAD application provider has its own, proprietary viewer, so exchanging drawings electronically can be clumsy. The obvious solution is to create PDFs from engineering drawings.

NOTE *Adobe is launching a major marketing campaign in 2004 focused on the engineering market. Adobe has dropped Autodesk AutoCAD as a partner and is working with Bentley MicroStation.*

Creating PDFs from engineering drawings can save tremendous amounts of money. For example, a company could design a large machine in the United States for manufacture in China. Instead of printing the drawings on huge sheets of paper, and then shipping the paper to China, PDFs of the drawings could be e-mailed to the factory in China. The Chinese would print the PDFs on oversized paper or simply view the drawings on their computer screens. The time and expense of shipping large drawings could be eliminated or at least greatly reduced.

One complaint about earlier versions of Acrobat is that it did a poor job of reproducing small line weights, or thicknesses. A typical engineering drawing is made up of thousands of small lines of varying weights, so these display issues were frustrating. Fortunately, display of small line weights has been improved in Acrobat 6. Text in AutoCAD drawings created with Acrobat 6 is now searchable, too. Adobe worked closely with CAD software developers such as AutoDesk, maker of AutoCAD, to improve PDF output.

In addition, Professional inserts an Adobe PDF button into AutoCAD, Microsoft Visio, and Microsoft Project. Layers are also supported as output from these technical applications. For example, a Visio file converted to a PDF could display the flow of a liquid processing plant. One layer could show the piping, a second, the electronics, and, a third, the various kinds of liquids moving through the plant. We discuss layers in more detail in the section "New Functionality."

In Acrobat 6, each layer can be shown or hidden, making it much easier to see one process separate from another or to see only certain elements in a Project Gantt chart. And, because Acrobat includes a set of reviewing tools, engineering drawings can be electronically circulated for comments.

Improved UI

Adobe spent a lot of time working on user interface issues in preparation for Acrobat 6. For the first time in the product's history, a team of interface designers was available to improve the look and operation of the software. For users who were familiar with earlier versions, Acrobat 6 has a radically new look.

Task Buttons

Gone are the tiny icons that littered the screens of earlier versions. Instead of icons, Acrobat 6 has bigger objects called Task Buttons. Some *Task Buttons,* such as Search, fire off a process as soon as it's clicked. Others, such as Create PDF, reveal more choices.

Items Below Menus Reorganized into Logical Groups

The organization of items below the main menus in earlier versions was a bit haphazard. Menu items have been rearranged in a logical sequence. For example, under the Document menu, there's a submenu for Pages, which, in turn, has the various functions for working with pages—inserting, removing, and so on.

Docking Toolbars

In Acrobat 5, users could move groups of tool icons off the menu bar and onto the document screen in floating palettes. Unfortunately, there was no command to reset the toolbars back to their starting positions.

Acrobat 6 still lets users move toolbars around the screen and dock the toolbars in new positions in the menu area. The toolbars can also be docked on the sides of the document window or at the bottom. There's also a command to reset the toolbars to their starting positions.

Because the Task buttons on the toolbars are so large, you probably won't want to work with all the toolbars open. If you do, you won't have much screen real estate left for your work. See Figure 1-4 for an example.

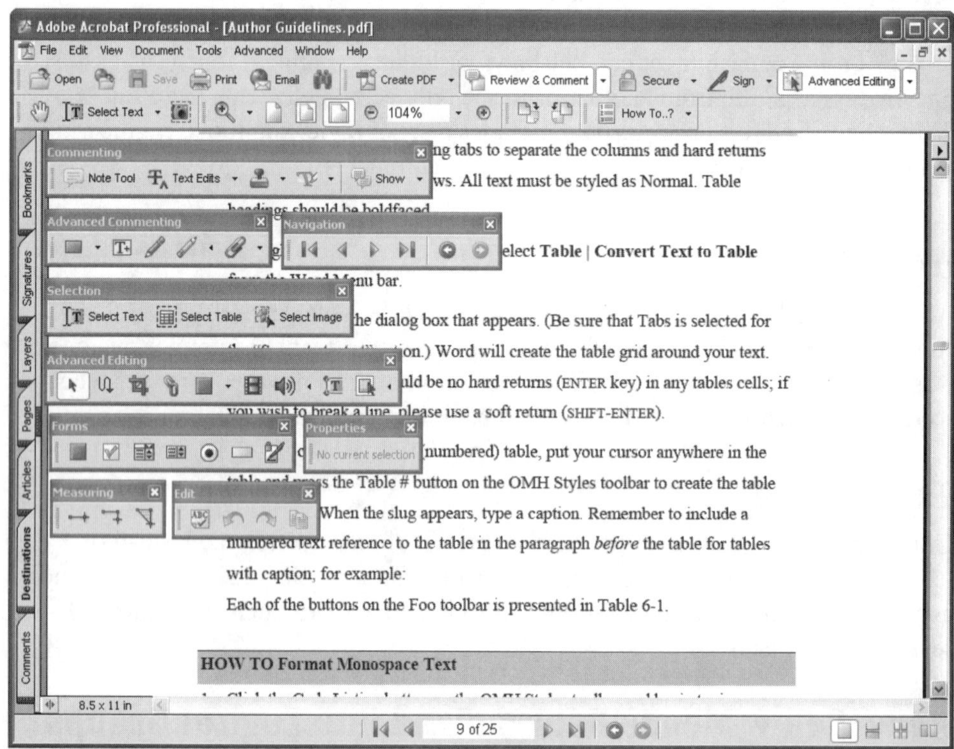

FIGURE 1-4 Adobe Acrobat 6 Professional with toolbars open

Better Help

Acrobat 6 includes task-based help. When a document opens in Acrobat, a How To..? pane appears on the right side of the screen. See Figure 1-5 for an example. You can click on a task listing to see detailed steps showing how to perform an action, such as creating a PDF.

Only One Set of Navigation Buttons

Previous versions of Acrobat had page up, page down, and first page/last page buttons at the top and the bottom of the screen. This dual look has been replaced with a single set of larger, easier-to-see buttons in the status bar at the bottom of the screen.

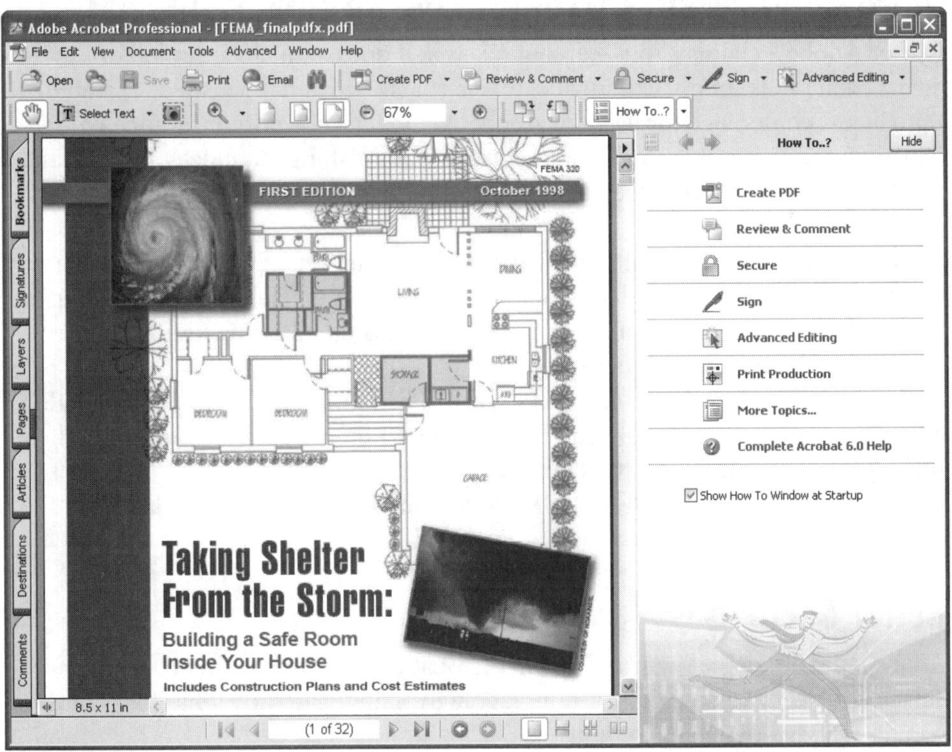

FIGURE 1-5 A How To..? pane in Adobe Acrobat 6 guides users through many common tasks.

Much More Like an MS Office Application than an Adobe One

Overall, the idea is to make Acrobat look like the applications users are most familiar with. In the business world, that means applications from Microsoft, specifically, members of the Microsoft Office family.

If you've used Adobe Photoshop or Adobe Illustrator, you know Adobe gives its applications a certain look and feel. Photoshop and Illustrator cluster tools in floating palettes that photographers and graphic artists can move around the screen and customize.

While Microsoft lets users customize the menus, add buttons, and so on, the look is generally linear. Unlike most of Adobe's other products, Acrobat has adopted this look and feel to make new users feel as comfortable as possible.

More Compression Without Loss of Image Integrity

One of Adobe's claims about Acrobat 6 is that it does a much better job of compressing files. In my experience, this is exactly what happens. For example, I produce a conference for users of Adobe Acrobat (**www.pdfconference.com**). Although the conference is all about electronic publishing, attendees still demand paper copies of speaker presentations. We print these in advance as part of the conference program.

When we finished assembling the program for the June 2003 show, the file was 80 megabytes. I decided to put Adobe's compression claim to the test. I ran the 80 megabyte program through the Acrobat 6 Professional PDF Optimizer and shrunk the file to 12 megabytes.

Not only was the file smaller, but it printed beautifully. We shipped the PDF off to the printer on a Tuesday and had 500 copies delivered on Friday. Other than scaring the pants off the printer (Acrobat 6 hadn't been released yet—he didn't know what to do when his Acrobat 5 told him his viewer was out of date), the file printed just fine.

Better Security

Adobe bumped up the security level in Acrobat in version 5 and made some nice enhancements in version 6. To begin, let me explain that Acrobat has two kinds of security: password and everything else.

Password security is used most often. It's the same kind of security you use to log on to a computer or sign in to a web-based merchant's account. Everything else is just that. Acrobat has a software architecture that supports nearly any kind of security measure you can think of, including card readers, eye scans, and special pads that record your handwritten signature. This security support was carried over into Acrobat 6, plus Adobe added some new twists as the result of increased public awareness of the need for better security.

First, Acrobat 6 supports the digital security certificates issued by Verisign, Entrust, and other companies that specialize in public key infrastructure (PKI) security. You obtain a digital certificate from one these companies, install the certificate on your computer, and then use the certificate to sign PDF documents digitally.

Second, Adobe introduced the concept of the Certified PDF. A *Certified PDF* is one that's been digitally signed and whose signature can be verified by a third party. The idea is to establish the identity of the signer of a document, so the receiver can trust the information the document contains. For example, imagine an agency of the Homeland Security Department wants to send a PDF to the Department of Justice. How can the Justice Department know if the Homeland Security PDF is real or a fake? If the two departments set up a file of trusted identities using PKI certificates, the two departments can exchange PDFs, and then verify the authenticity of a document. Adobe calls one of these digitally authorized documents a certified PDF or a certified document. When a document is certified, a small blue ribbon appears in the status bar at the bottom of the Acrobat screen.

What Adobe Means by Certified PDF

Adobe's choice of terms for its new, "trusted" PDF is causing some confusion. For many years before Adobe announced Acrobat 6, a company called Enfocus was using the term "Certified PDF" to mean something completely different.

Enfocus specializes in PDF-based software tools for the printing industry. Because a single mistake can costs a printer thousands, or hundreds of thousands, of dollars, Enfocus developed the concept of a Certified PDF. By using Enfocus tools, a printer can check a PDF for proper colors, resolution, and so on before running the job on a press. If a PDF meets the Enfocus Certified PDF test, it's ready to print. If not, something must be fixed. When Adobe talks about a Certified PDF, it's speaking about security issues. When Enfocus talks about a Certified PDF, it means a file that will print correctly.

New Functionality

Acrobat 6 includes some helpful new tools, such as the capability to add watermarks, backgrounds, and headers and footers, but the most dramatic change is the addition of layers.

Layers

Layers have the potential to be the most significant addition to Acrobat since forms were introduced in the mid 1990s. The layers in Acrobat work just like the layers in other applications, such as Photoshop or Illustrator. To show a layer, you click a small eye icon. To hide a layer, poke the eye icon again and you make the layer disappear.

Why are layers important? Consider these possibilities. Let's say an international company wants to place advertisements in magazines in the United States, Spain, Brazil, France, and Germany. The company could design a single ad that has text for each country's main language in separate layers. For publication in the United States, a magazine would turn on the English layer. For publication in Brazil, a magazine would turn on the Portuguese layer, and so on.

Tremendous possibilities exist for business and technical publications as well. In another example, a manufacturer might want to distribute a product in the United States, Japan, and Korea. The quick reference guide could be written with illustrations on one layer, with the text explaining how to use the product in separate layers for each country. If the guide were a multilayer PDF on a CD, each user could click on their own language and see those instructions onscreen.

PDF maps have marvelous potential. Imagine a map of New York. When you view all of Manhattan, you might only see major streets and landmarks. Zooming in could trigger the view of a hidden layer that shows secondary streets. Zoom in some more and a third layer could be trigged, showing every street and intersection.

Interestingly, Acrobat 6 can't create layers on its own. The layers must be created in an authoring application, and then transformed into a PDF. The first products to support PDF layers are the latest versions of Photoshop, InDesign, and Illustrator, plus Microsoft Visio and AutoCAD. Adobe has made the details of how to make layered PDFs publicly available, so you can also expect to see layered PDF support from other products.

Headers and Footers

One agony of Acrobat users has been the combined PDF. A *combined PDF* is one made up of files created from different applications. For example, a report made up of a Word document, an Excel spreadsheet, and a Gantt chart from Microsoft Project.

The Word document and the Gantt chart each would have its own page numbering, and the Excel spreadsheet likely would have none at all. While Acrobat let you put these documents together, the result often wasn't pretty. The page numbers in the Word file and the Gantt chart would often conflict, and users would be confused by the lack of page numbers in the PDF that originated from Excel.

While you can combine PDFs created from each of these applications, it was hard to make the combination look like one unit. Acrobat 6 Standard and Professional have the capability to stamp headers and footers, including page numbers, across a single PDF. While this isn't as polished as a document coming from a page layout application, you can at least stamp coherent page numbers on the document, and then add a header that gives a document title. For example, an aerospace company might be required to give a weekly update on a project to a major client. The report would originate as a Word document, an Excel spreadsheet, and a Gantt chart. PDFs would be created from each application, and then combined into a single PDF. In Acrobat 6, you can stamp page numbers in the bottom margin of the document, and then add a document title to a header.

Watermarks and Backgrounds

While authors can add watermarks and backgrounds in most page layout or word-processing applications, many authors don't like to do it that way. They feel they'll have difficulty removing the background after it's inserted or they don't like to look at the background as they work on the document.

One of the most frequently asked questions in my Acrobat classes is this: How can I add a background to my PDF? Until Acrobat 6, the best answer was to place the watermark in the authoring application. With Acrobat 6 Standard and Professional, authors can now keep the backgrounds out of their source documents and simply place them in the PDF. To mark a PDF as a draft, for example, a user just has to create an image file of the word draft, and then insert the image into the document. Acrobat 6 even lets you set the opacity of the background. You can set the opacity of a draft graphic to 20 percent, so it doesn't overwhelm the reader and distract from the text.

NOTE *Adobe defines a background as appearing behind the text and a watermark as appearing on top of the text.*

Right-Click Combine in Adobe PDF

Also part of Standard, a new feature in Acrobat 6 is the capability to convert a batch of files, and then combine them into a single PDF. When users right-click (Windows) or CONTROL-click (Mac OS) a file, they see a menu option for Combine in Adobe Acrobat. Up pops a screen that lets users add more files and set the order in which the files appear in the PDF.

Better Accessibility Options

Section 508 of the Rehabilitation Act requires that federal agencies provide "reasonable accommodations" for employees and members of the public with disabilities. This is generally interpreted to mean that PDFs distributed by federal agencies and contractors should be accessible to the visually impaired. Many visually impaired people use assistive technology to access government information. The most common of these are *screen readers,* which read aloud what's shown on a computer screen.

Here's the issue: let's say you work for a federal agency and you publish a one-page, two-column brochure. If you aren't careful, screen readers used by the visually impaired might be unable to read that document. Why? Because if the PDF is improperly created, the screen reader will read the first line of Column one followed by the first line of Column two, and then read the second line of Column one and the second line of Column two, and so on. Sighted readers, of course, would read the first line of Column one, the second line of Column one, and so on.

A properly created PDF will use either Tagged PDF or an earlier version called Logical PDF. *Tagged PDF* basically is an XML-like structure housed inside the PDF, which tells a screen reader whether to read up and down a column, or all the way across the page. It also reads alternative text to describe the contents of a picture. Because an improperly created PDF can fool certain screen readers, Adobe has embarked on a major campaign to educate users to create better PDFs. And it has inserted some great new technology into Acrobat 6.

Read Aloud

Built into Adobe Reader, Acrobat Standard, and Acrobat Professional versions 6 is *Read Aloud* technology that translates written text into spoken language. The software works with both Windows and MacOS X.

To have Acrobat read to you, choose View | Read Aloud | This Page Only or Read to End of Document. The voice is robot-like, but the rate and pitch of the voice can be changed in Acrobat preferences.

Auto Scroll

Auto Scroll is for those people with disabilities who have trouble using a mouse. Choose View | Auto Scroll and the pages of a PDF slowly move up the screen. No clicking is required to advance pages. The effect is somewhat like a teleprompter.

More Options for the Visually Impaired

To better determine if a PDF is accessible, there's a new command: Advanced | Accessibility | Quick Check. *Quick Check* checks the structure of the PDF to see if it's set up properly. It notifies a reader if a document has been scanned into a PDF and not converted to text, for example.

Increasing the size of text in Bookmarks, Comments, and Signatures is also much easier in the Windows versions of Acrobat 6. More keyboard shortcuts have also been added, so it's simpler to navigate in Acrobat without having to reach for a mouse.

Reflow

Available since version 5, text reflow can be a great help to those people who have some visual impairment. *Reflow* lets readers enlarge text and have the text fit into the screen. By zooming in to 200 or 400 percent, and then choosing View | Reflow, text in a PDF will expand and reflow logically to fit the screen. Figure 1-6 shows text that has simply been enlarged with the Zoom tool. Figure 1-7 shows the same text reflowed. Notice the text keeps its enlarged state, but it reflowed to fit the screen, making it much easier to read. Even multicolumn text will reflow to fill the screen. This feature is especially useful for displaying text on handheld devices, such as PDAs and TabletPCs.

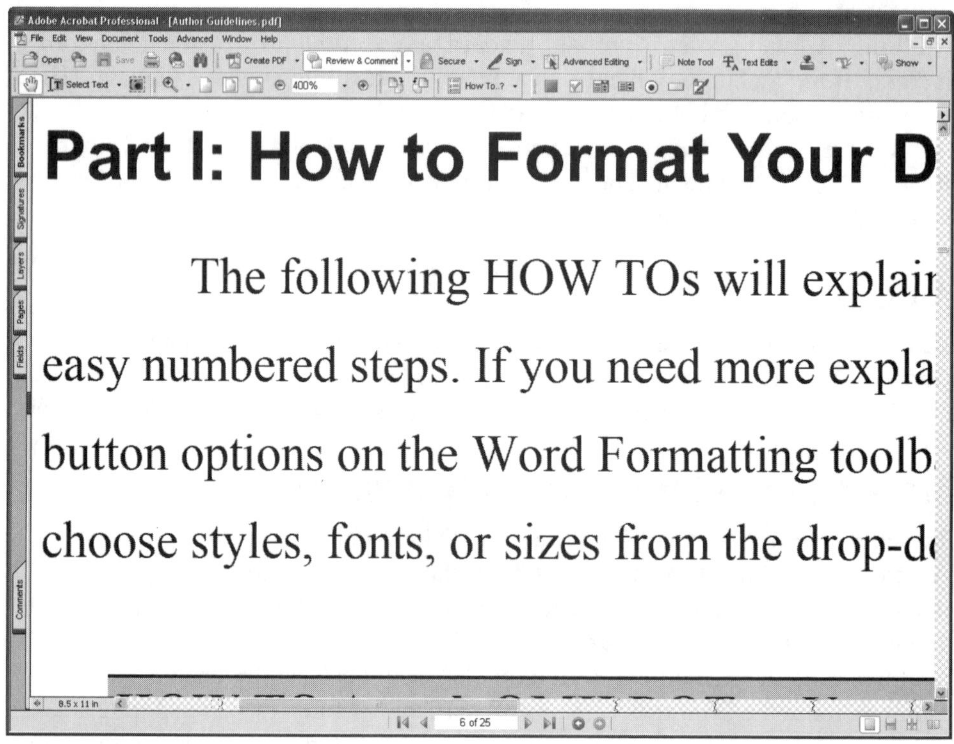

FIGURE 1-6 The text is enlarged at 400 percent. Readers must scroll to the right to read the text. Acrobat 6 users can reflow the text to fit the screen.

Creating Accessible PDFs

The best way to meet Section 508 requirements is to create an accessible PDF to start. An accessible PDF has a logical structure inside the PDF. This can be created by the Adobe PDF button in Microsoft Word. Be sure to turn on the option for Enable accessibility and reflow with Tagged PDF. Most Adobe applications can produce either tagged PDF or an earlier version called logical PDF.

Acrobat 6 includes a way to fix noncompliant files. You can use an automated routine by choosing Advanced | Accessibility | Add Tags to Document. This feature can be run on a large number of files at once using Acrobat's Batch Sequences. You can also manually add tags in the Content Panel of Professional.

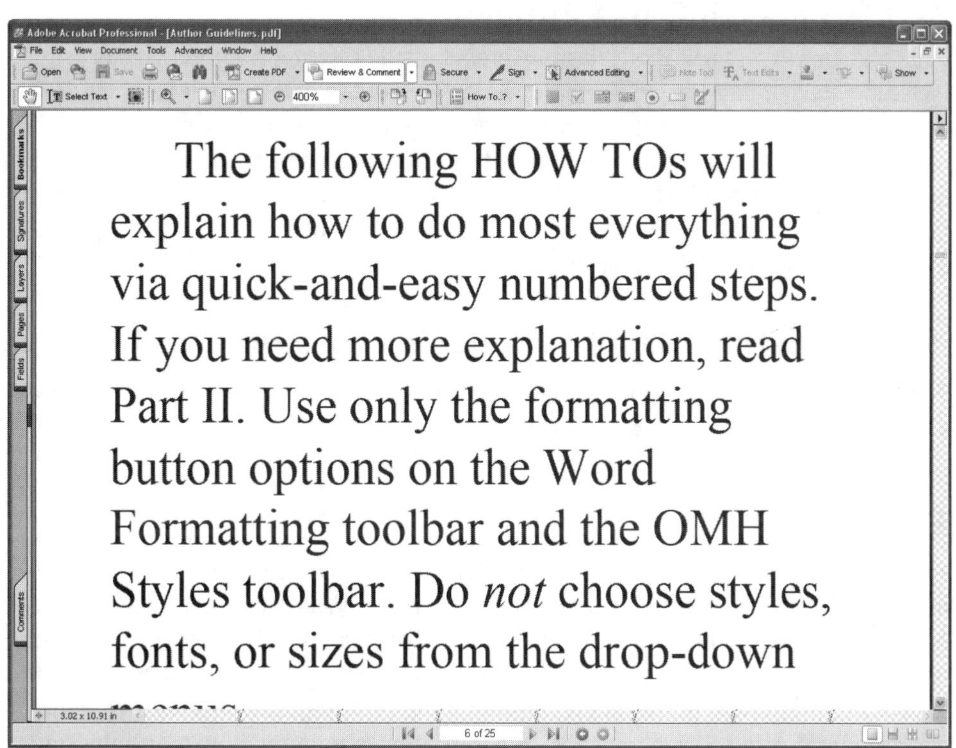

FIGURE 1-7 The same text reflowed to fit the screen. Scrolling to the left and right isn't required.

Adobe added accessibility support for Japanese in the initial release on Acrobat 6. For the latest news on accessibility, see **www.access.adobe.com**. This web site contains the most current information on creating accessible output from Adobe applications, including Acrobat. For a more detailed look at creating Section 508-compliant PDFs, refer to Chapter 5.

Win Versus Mac Differences

Because so many Acrobat users have Windows as their operating systems (OSs), Mac users occasionally gripe about being left out by Adobe. Adobe has brought more parity to the two platforms in Acrobat 6, but some differences still exist.

No Browser Plug-in Until Safari

Windows users can view PDF files in Acrobat inside Internet Explorer (IE) or Netscape Navigator. Mac OSX users must download the PDF to their local hard drive and view it there. Because Apple is developing its own browser, *Safari,* Adobe has no plans to support IE on the Mac. Adobe does promise a browser plug-in for Safari once it's released. However, Mac OS X users can now submit form data from the PDFs they download from the Web. Earlier versions of Acrobat didn't support form data submission from Mac clients at all well.

No Round-Tripping of Comments into Word for the Mac

Adobe does include an Adobe PDF button in Word for the Mac. However, comments can't be exported from Acrobat into Word for the Mac.

Summary

Adobe Acrobat 6 Professional is a major advance in PDF technology. Layers, built-in preflighting tools, better integration with Microsoft Word, and new viewing tools make Acrobat 6 Professional a must-have tool for serious PDF creation work. But just having the right tools isn't enough. You have to know how to use them properly to produce professional-looking results. Anyone can use a saw, but not everyone can use a saw to cut a smooth, straight cut. You have to know how to use the saw properly to get good results, as a skilled carpenter can.

In Part I, you learn what the Acrobat equivalents to a smooth, straight cut are. You learn what separates a poor PDF from one that has a polished, professional look. In Part II, you look at specific tools for creating PDFs and get tips on how to use them. Part III is for creative and print professionals who need to create high-quality PDFs that will print well.

Chapter 2

Why Quality Matters

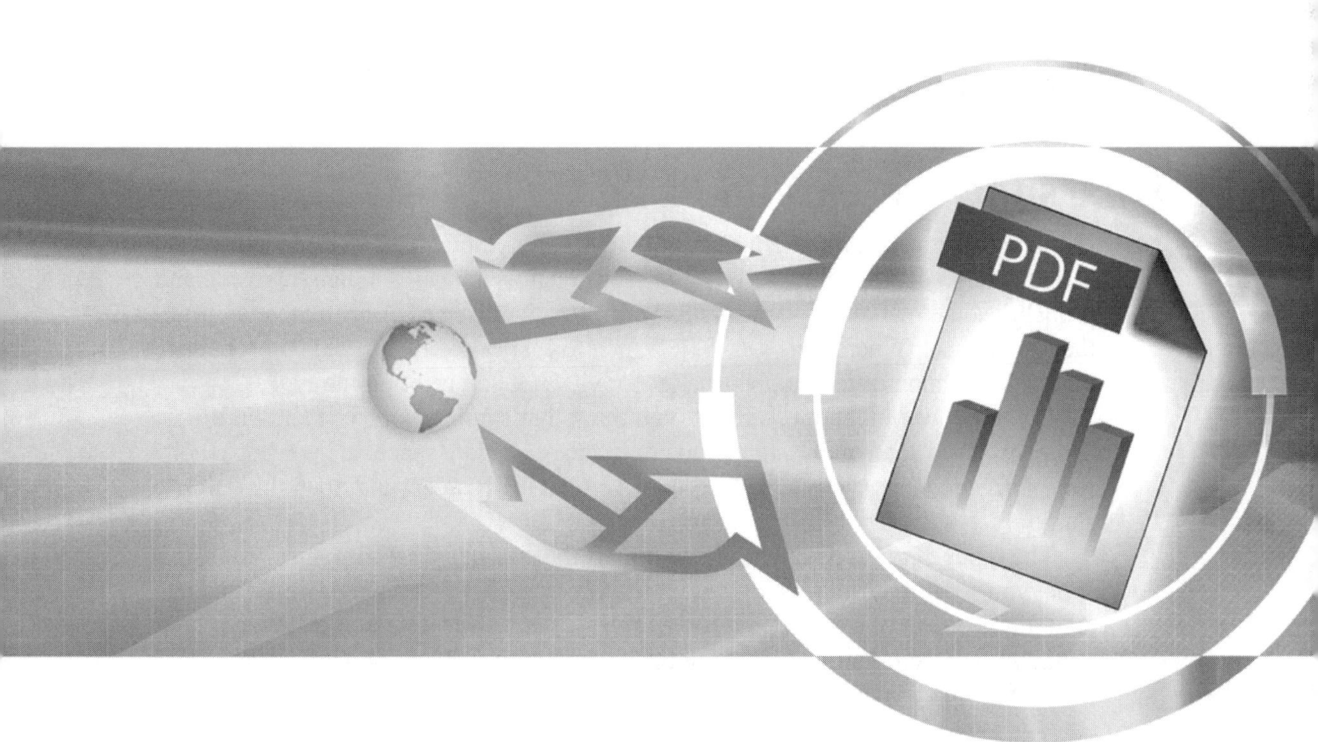

Good PDFs are the identical twins of the original documents—page by page, line by line, character by character. Good PDFs faithfully reproduce the colors and design of the original.

PDFs destined for print production, such as a book, magazine, or product brochure, behave in a logical, predictable pattern throughout the print production cycle. Fonts stay in place, the color model accurately reproduces the colors of photographs and graphics, and color blends and fills are smoothly consistent.

Good onscreen PDFs are even better than the originals, in many cases. There are bookmarks that link to major topics inside the file. There are hyperlinks from a document's table of contents to the relevant information inside. Index entries and cross-references also are hyperlinked, making it easy for readers to instantly go to the information they are looking for. Good online PDFs are searchable, and can be indexed either on the Web or on a CD. Page numbers in the PDF match those of the original, including roman numerals and pages without numbers.

Bad PDFs do none of these things. They don't look like the original, either on a page-by-page basis or a line-by-line basis. The fonts are not the ones in the original. The colors in the graphics are all wrong, and photographs look blurry. Bad online PDFs confuse the reader, and bad PDFs for print can be downright ugly.

In this chapter, you find out how to tell if you have a bad PDF, or a good one. In Chapter 3, you learn how to create terrific PDFs and, in Chapter 4, you learn more about creating good PDFs for onscreen viewing. All of Part III is dedicated to producing PDFs for creative professionals.

What's the Matter with PDF?

If you are like most computer users, you've probably noticed something about the boxed version of software you've purchased. There's a nice-looking CD inside and probably some marketing literature as well. What's missing? A printed version of the user manual. Where is it? On the CD, in a format called PDF. The CD probably includes a version of the Adobe Reader for viewing and printing the PDF.

If you know a bit about Acrobat, you think that's not so bad. The software company saved some money, and you don't have any more space on your bookshelf for a software manual anyway. You start Acrobat (or Reader) and open the quick start guide.

The quick start guide opens and spills off the sides of your computer monitor. What you see is a terrible-looking graphic. After a while, you realize you are seeing an online version of a document that was designed to be printed on oversized paper. As you scroll around, looking for the beginning, the graphics flash and redraw slowly on your screen. Frustrated, you give up and close the quick start guide.

Next, you open the 200-page reference manual. This document slowly opens to the cover, displaying a jagged-looking copy of the graphic on the front of the software box. You open the bookmarks tab in Acrobat and are dismayed to see there aren't any.

You navigate away from the cover, past blank pages and legalese, until you see the table of contents. You find the subject you are looking for and click on the entry. Nothing happens. You sigh, and you see that the information you want is on page 25. You enter 25 in the Acrobat page counter and move to page 25. As you look at the page, you discover it isn't the information you wanted. You look at the page number displayed on the document. It's page 19. You realize that the pages numbers referred to in the text don't match the page counter in Acrobat.

You decide to give it one last shot. You open the Search tool and type in the subject you are looking for. The Search tool says "Total instances found: 0." Puzzled, you click the Text Select tool and drag over some text. Nothing happens. Then you realize: these people printed the document, and then scanned each page as an image into PDF. Because each page is a picture, not text and graphics, it isn't searchable.

Who would produce anything this terrible? Unfortunately, some combination of the previously listed faults find their way into many PDFs.

If you cruise online newsgroups, you can see many complaints about PDF. Users complain about not being able to find information, about PDFs containing extra pages, or about graphics moving around. Adobe's competitors feed this ire by hiring consultants to label PDF as unfit for use on the Web.

The sad fact is all these complaints could be prevented. None of these issues have anything to do with PDF itself. All are creation issues and did not have to happen. These mistakes are made because so few people are expert PDF creators.

As a publishing medium, Acrobat and the PDF format are 11 years old. That's young, especially when compared to the hundreds of years of experience publishers have in learning how to print readable, high-quality books. Because of PDF's relative youth, there are few official standards for new PDF creators to look to. (The only standards are highly technical ones for the publishing industry, which is discussed in detail in Chapter 18. There is nothing similar for the vast majority of PDFs, which are designed for onscreen reading.)

I know how easy it is to make many of the slips described in this chapter, because I've made them all in my nine-year history of producing PDFs. I list as many common errors as possible here so you can learn from my mistakes.

Just because you can make a mistake with a PDF is no reason to avoid it. People mess up web pages with broken links and unreadable text every day, and the graphic artists and writers I know have all made mistakes in print. PDF isn't inherently better or worse than web or print publishing. Like HTML and print, you just need to use PDF correctly.

As a file format, PDF is capable of doing amazing things. It helps companies save money by reducing, or even eliminating, printing costs, and companies can quickly publish design-intensive documents. Created properly, a PDF is superior to HTML pages for high-quality documents, such as marketing collateral, financial data, and annual reports.

Creation Is Easy, but Getting It Right Is Not

PDFs are simple to create, yet powerful and complex. It's the complexity that makes for problem PDFs. How complex is PDF creation? Let's consider that for a moment.

Compare the world of PDF creation to the production of a Microsoft Word document. How do you create a Word document? From Word, of course. How do you create a PDF? From any application that has a File | Print command—Word, certainly, but also WordPerfect, Excel, PowerPoint, QuarkXPress, CorelDRAW!, AutoCAD, Mac OS X, and even the Windows Paint program.

Throw in all the non-Adobe PDF generators and the mix gets even more complex. There are PDFs created directly from QuarkXPress 6 and CorelDRAW!, PDFs produced by Jaws PDFCreator, activePDF Toolkit, RoboPDF, or any of a dozen other products. PDFs created on Linux, UNIX, mainframes and minicomputers. Oh, yes, PDFs from Acrobat 1, 2, 3, 4, and 5 are out there, too, and each version does more than the previous one. The possibilities are nearly infinite—and so are the possibilities for mistakes.

Start with a Thoughtful Mind Set

Although it would be easy to blame bad PDFs on the bewildering number of creation tools, that isn't the problem. Attitude is.

Think about the mind-set required if you are paying to produce a printed software user manual, for example. You likely will be careful that the printed pages look as you intend them to. You will probably take care to make sure the graphics look right, the table of contents refers to the correct pages, and that no missing or extra pages are there.

After all, if you make a mistake, you might have to reprint the manual. Not only would that be embarrassing, but it would be expensive. Reprinting a software manual could cost thousands, or even tens of thousands, of dollars. Make that kind of mistake in a four-color marketing piece and the cost could run into the millions. Jobs have been lost over such slip-ups.

Now consider PDF creation. How much does that cost? Nothing, other than the cost of your creation software. The manufacturing cost is zero. Just push a button and out pops a PDF you can e-mail instantly or post to a web site. My theory is that a no-cost (after buying the software, of course) production line produces stuff that is treated like it costs nothing—little thought goes into the process. This kind of thinking is what produces bad PDFs. Just because the manufacturing cost of a PDF is zero doesn't mean a bad PDF is inexpensive. It's just that the costs of a poor PDF are hidden.

For example, a bad PDF user manual that doesn't contain proper hyperlinks likely means customers can't find the information they need, so they call tech support. More irritated customers on the phone raises the budget of the support department, and can produce lost future sales.

A PDF of a marketing brochure that prints terrible-looking photographs can prompt a customer to say, "Yuk" instead of "I want to buy." Although it costs nothing to produce a bad PDF, the lost sales and increased calls to tech support hurt a company's bottom line.

In my experience, just a little education can lead PDF creators to produce much better PDFs, no matter what creation tool they are using. In the rest of this chapter, you learn about the common kinds of bad PDFs, and some techniques for identifying them. Chapters 3 and 4 are dedicated to creating good PDFs.

Classifying the Types of Problem PDFs

To start the discussion of what constitutes a bad PDF, I've developed a series of 11 problem types. I'm sure there are more—it's just that these are the ones I most often see. Many bad PDFs are a combination of the types.

The Types

The Zombie PDF, where substituted fonts are used. Instead of being the identical twin of the original, the Zombie PDF can be recognized as looking approximately like the original. Unfortunately, the creator of the Zombie PDF used an unusual font and forgot to select the Embed all Fonts option when creating the file. Or, he or she used a common font and decided not to include it.

When the reader opened the Zombie PDF, Acrobat couldn't find the original font. Because the font wasn't available, Acrobat looked on the user's machine for it. If the font wasn't there, Acrobat makes up a font it hopes looks like the original. Sometimes it does, sometimes it doesn't. Frequently, it doesn't, as shown in Figure 2-1. Note that the document in the bottom window contains the special font the author intended to use. The top window shows the result if the font isn't embedded in the document. Embedding the font increased the file size by 3KB.

FIGURE 2-1 When fonts don't agree

The Lost in Space PDF. This most often occurs in a PDF that masquerades as a user manual, as discussed at the start of this chapter. A Lost in Space PDF usually opens to a pretty cover that contains no useful information. When the user turns enough pages to find a table of contents, the contents page doesn't have links to the material inside. When the user opens the bookmarks tab, there are no bookmarks to help out, either. A user in search of information has a choice: hunt through the document with the Search tool, or call tech support. The tech support call is easier and usually wins.

The Labyrinth PDF, a cousin of the Lost in Space PDF. From the outside, the Labyrinth PDF looks unremarkable, but try finding something in it. A cross-reference may say, "For more information, go to page 25." You type 25 in the Acrobat page counter and the information isn't there. You look at the page number in the document. It says page 23. There is a mismatch between the number of pages in the document, which Acrobat counts, and the numbers placed on each document page. An example is shown in Figure 2-2. (The Labyrinth PDF is also known as the *Mo' Money PDF* because the company creating the PDF was obviously just trying to save money by not printing a user manual, and didn't care about usability.)

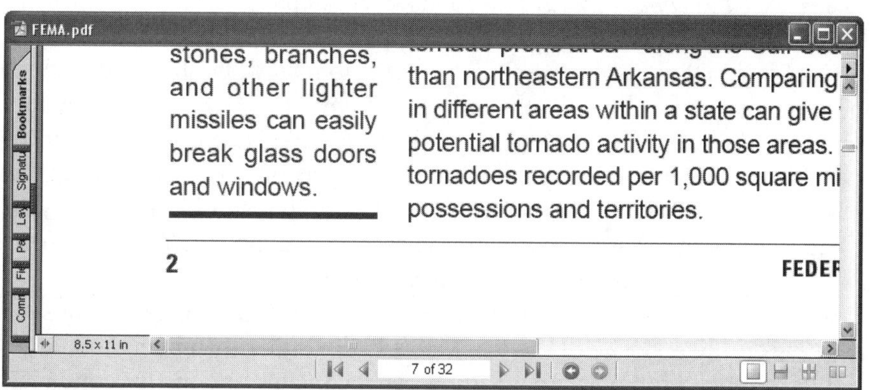

FIGURE 2-2 What page are we on? A Labyrinth PDF contains confusing page number displays.

The Betrayal PDF. Unlike the Lost in Space PDF, the Betrayal PDF contains hypertext links. Unfortunately, some of the links don't go anywhere, and others link to the wrong pages.

The Fat Albert PDF. When you download this PDF, it seems to take forever to load. Bloated by unnecessary information, the Fat Albert PDF often originates in Adobe FrameMaker or Microsoft PowerPoint. PDFs created from scanned documents often are far larger than necessary, as are many graphics-heavy PDFs.

The Waiting Game PDF. This PDF appears on the Web. When a user selects a Waiting Game PDF, Acrobat loads in Internet Explorer but no document appears. You wait and wait, and, finally, the PDF appears. A Waiting Game PDF has not been linearized, or set up for what Adobe calls *Fast Web View.* Instead of appearing in the browser window as soon as the first page arrives at the end user's machine, a Waiting Game PDF must download in its entirety before it displays. If a Waiting Game PDF is also a Fat Albert, you could be in for a long wait.

The Wrong Turn PDF. This onscreen PDF contains pages that are not oriented for humans. Landscape pages appear in Portrait orientation, forcing users to tip their heads (or monitors) sideways, or to go off in search of the page rotation command in their PDF viewer.

The Color Purple PDF. The designer was precise in selecting a certain color of blue, but somewhere along the line the blue was transformed into purple—or some color other than the one specified. This often occurs in PDFs that were designed for printing, but wound up being onscreen PDFs.

The Honey, I Shrunk the Kids PDF. This standard paper-sized PDF opens to Fit Page view, which means an entire page appears in the middle of the screen. The text of this PDF is hard, or even impossible, to read when the document opens. To make the document readable, the user must hunt for a comfortable view level.

The Missing Pieces PDF. This PDF look exactly like the printed version of a paper form. That makes it easy for customers to accept as the "real" thing, but there is a problem. The user must print the PDF form out and fill it in by hand. All the creator of this PDF has done is shift the cost of printing the document to you. You should be able to at least fill it in before you print it.

The Beauty and the Beast PDF. This PDF looks fine onscreen, but prints terribly. This is the opposite of the Fat Albert PDF. Rather than being too large to be useful, this type of PDF is too small. Acrobat contains options for compressing graphics, but some compression methods throw away image detail to save space. These PDFs can look great onscreen, where image resolution is low, but lack enough image detail to print well.

Searching for Bobby Fischer PDF. The elusive American chess genius has become a recluse, reportedly in Asia. He hasn't been seen in public for years. Image-only PDFs fall into the "where is it" category. Hundreds of thousands of paper documents are being scanned into PDF and archived. Acrobat includes a nifty feature called Paper Capture that performs Optical Character Recognition (95 to 98 percent accurate) on the scanned images, turning these PDFs into searchable documents. Nonsearchable, image-only PDFs have few excuses for existing.

Diagnosing Problem PDFs

To determine whether you have a good or bad PDF, you need an examination. It's like you've fallen and have a pain in your ankle. What do you do? You go to the doctor, who orders an X-ray of the ankle to see if it is sprained or broken.

Start with Document Properties

In the PDF world, you don't order up an X-ray when you see a potentially problem PDF. You check *Document Properties,* which describes some basic characteristics of your PDF. Choose File | Document Properties, or CTRL-D, and click on Description to see basic information about the file, as shown in Figure 2-3.

Document Properties tells you a lot about the PDF in front of you. In the *Description* section, there are fields for Title, Subject, Author and Keywords. Although this *metadata* (information about a file) is optional, you should make

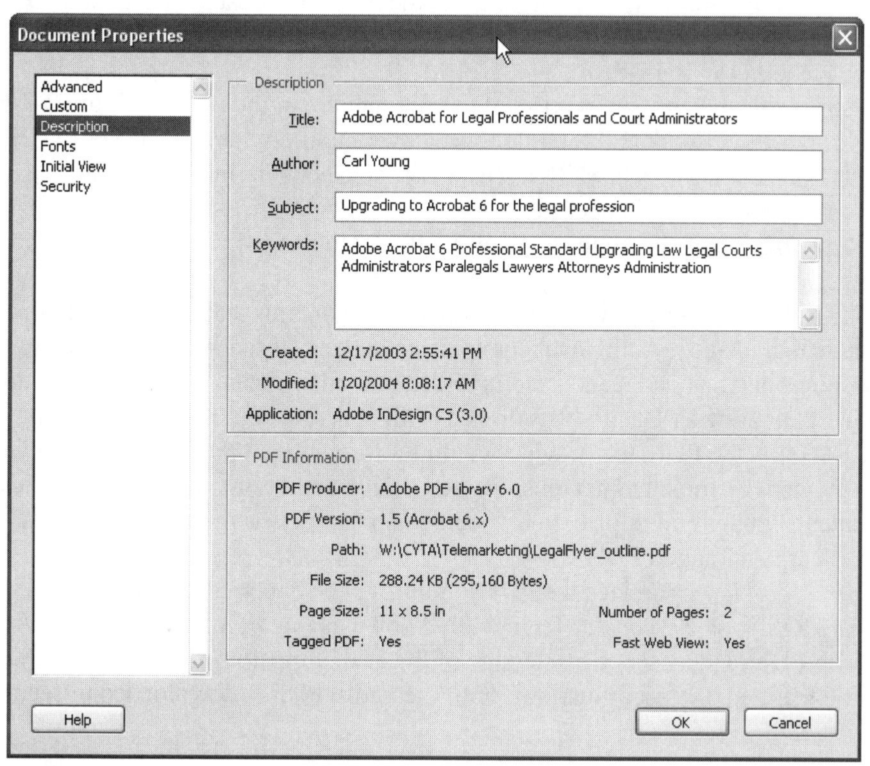

FIGURE 2-3 Document Properties

a point of filling in all the fields. It's especially important if the PDF will be indexed, because these fields can be indexed and searched.

Also in Description are automatically produced fields that provide information on the origination of the PDF. *Created* is the date and time the PDF was produced, *Modified* shows the date and time any changes were made. *Application* can be blank, but often lists the authoring application that the PDF was generated from.

The next section in Document Properties, PDF Information, is often the starting point for troubleshooting. First up in PDF Information is *PDF Producer,* which explains what PDF generator took information from the authoring application and produced the PDF. In Figure 2-3, the PDF Producer is the Adobe PDF Library 6.0, which is built into InDesign CS.

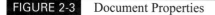

PDF Version shows whether the PDF is the most up-to-date version, or an older type. In Figure 2-3, you can see the PDF is based on the PDF 1.5 specification, which is the *Acrobat 6 version.*

Path shows the current location of the file, which, in the case of Figure 2-3, is on a local area network (LAN). File Size shows (in kilobytes) the size of the PDF. The one in Figure 2-3 is 228KB, a reasonable size considering it includes two high-resolution bitmap images.

Page Size shows the dimensions of the PDF. Number of pages is the number of pages in the PDF.

Tagged PDF indicates whether the document contains an internal, XML-like structure that identifies individual components of the PDF, such as images, hierarchy of headings and text, language, reading order, and other organizational information. Tagged PDF allows PDFs to be reflowed to fit onscreen, eases the repurposing of information in the PDF, and provides helpful information to the assistive technology used by visually impaired persons. Tagged PDF is unnecessary in most technical documents, but public information documents from government agencies should always contain Tagged PDF.

Fast Web View optimizes the PDF to improve the experience of the person viewing a PDF on a web site. Technically known as *linearization,* Fast Web View lets web PDF readers see the first page of the PDF almost immediately. If a PDF is not linearized, the user must wait until the entire PDF is downloaded to see the first page.

Font Information

There is much more to Document Properties, but the only additional area helpful in troubleshooting is the Fonts section in Document Properties, as shown in Figure 2-4. If Embedded Subset appears after the font name, then only the characters used in the document are transferred to the PDF. *Embedded* means all the font characters are inserted into the PDF.

Checking for Problems

Here are some tests to determine whether you have a PDF that falls into one of the problem types. Readers who are creating PDFs for printing should go to Chapter 18 for information on preflighting PDFs.

In surveys on PDF usage, the number one issue concerns fonts. Figure 2-4 shows the font information for the Acrobat 6 Professional Help Guide from Adobe. Notice that Helvetica-Bold was used to create the document, but what is being displayed in this PDF is Arial-BoldMT.

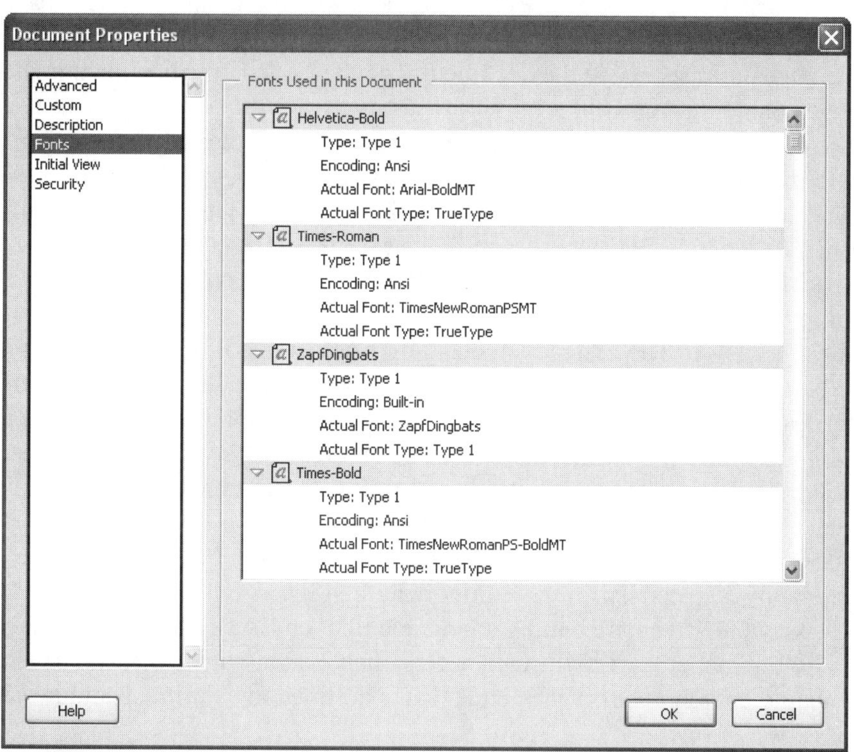

FIGURE 2-4 Document Properties includes a section on fonts used in a PDF.

Why? Because the author at Adobe choose not to embed Helvetica-Bold at the time of PDF creation. Because the computer displaying the PDF doesn't have Helvetica-Bold available, Acrobat performed a font substitution and used a close copy of Helvetica-Bold, Arial-BoldMT. You can see that the same thing happened with Times-Roman and Times-Italic. Although these are close font matches, Arial is not Helvetica. By my definition, the Acrobat 6 Professional Help Guide is a Zombie PDF. It is a close cousin of the original, but it is not identical.

The Lost in Space PDF. This multipage PDF is designed for onscreen reading, and needs a navigational system. Open the Bookmarks tab. Are there any bookmarks? Go to the table of contents. Are there links to the topics inside the document? Find a cross-reference. Does it contain a hyperlink? If the answers are no, then you have a Lost in Space PDF.

The Labyrinth PDF. Open the PDF to a page with roman numerals for page numbers. Then check the Acrobat page counter. Do the pages match? Check Arabic page numbers inside the document—do the ones on the document match the page counter in Acrobat?

The Betrayal PDF. This PDF contains hyperlinks, but the links are dead or point to the wrong locations. You can check these by hand, clicking on every link one at a time. If you produce lots of PDFs with many links, consider a nifty plug-in like ARTS Link Checker, available at **www.artspdf.com**. ARTS Link Checker, shown in Figure 2-5, looks and displays dead links for you, greatly speeding the testing process.

Fat Albert PDF. The first step in deciding whether a PDF is too big is to see what its current size is. This information is available inside the PDF in Document Properties. Choose File | Document Properties | Description look at the file size.

Although you can measure actual size down to the last byte, just what clearly is "fat" or too big is a judgment call. In general, you should make onscreen PDFs as small as possible without jeopardizing the printability of the graphics in the PDF. PDFs designed for printing, CD, or DVD distribution can't be too fat because image quality is generally far more important than file size.

For example, if you are putting a ten-page PDF on a web site, you probably want it to be smaller than 1MB. On the other hand, a ten-page PDF with several high-quality photographs on each page that is destined to be printed could easily surpass 1MB in size.

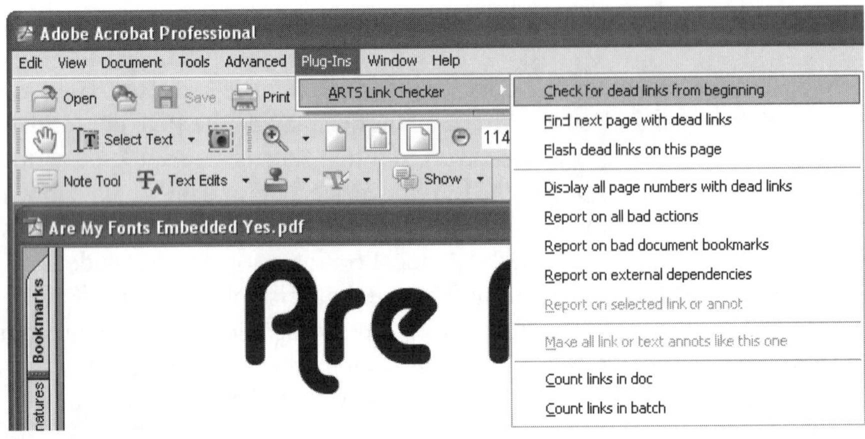

FIGURE 2-5 ARTS Link Checker can check for dead links.

Waiting Game PDF. This is an easy one to diagnose. Just make sure a Yes is next to Fast Web View in Document Properties.

The Wrong Turn PDF. There are a couple of ways to check page orientation. First, open the Pages tab and choose Options | Reduce Page Thumbnails. Then click the ribbed blue divider on the right side of the window and drag to the right. You can then look at the pages tab and check to see if any pages should be turned. The Options fly-out menu in the pages tab has an enlarge/reduce thumbnails option to adjust the size of the miniature pages.

If the thumbnails are too small, set the document zoom level to 25 percent and click the Continuous - Facing Pages button in the lower-right corner. You'll then have a miniature, but highly detailed, view of several pages of your document, so you can see if any pages are oriented the wrong way.

The Color Purple PDF. You can usually tell right away if there has been a major color shift—you'll notice it right away. For more subtle changes, such as a shift in color model, you'll need to use the Preflight commands in Acrobat 6 Professional. (This is a complex subject and is covered in more detail in Chapter 18.)

The Honey, I Shrunk the Kids PDF. You open one of these, and you start to squint. Instead of presenting a page in an easy-to-read manner, this PDF opens at a zoom setting so small, you can't see the type. The user must fumble around with Acrobat's zoom settings to find a comfortable viewing level.

The Missing Pieces PDF. A great idea is to move forms from paper to PDF. An even better one is to make the PDF form fillable. People are becoming familiar with HTML forms on the Web, which they can fill it. Why shouldn't they be able to fill in a PDF they find online? Acrobat 6 Professional includes tools to create form fields.

The Beauty and the Beast PDF. You can diagnose one of these by printing it, or by zooming in to 200 or 300 percent. If bitmap images in the PDF looks good at a high resolution, the file will likely print well. If it looks bad at 200 percent onscreen, it probably won't print well.

Why bother with checking if the PDF is going to be published at a web site? Remember, sooner or later, someone is going to take a PDF from the Web and will print it. The end user will expect the PDF to look good on paper.

Searching for Bobby Fischer PDF. Paper stuffed into file cabinets is hard to find. Scan paper documents into PDFs, and you can store the information electronically. Unfortunately, you can create PDFs from paper a couple of different ways, including a format Adobe calls Image Only. An Image Only PDF doesn't contain any body text, and it can't be searched.

If you are going to go to the bother of scanning paper in the first place, why not make the document searchable? True, you will make the file somewhat smaller by leaving out the text. But you lose the capability to search the text inside the document, so much of the data inside the PDF remains locked away.

Click the Search Icon and look for a common word, such as "there." Or, choose the Text Select tool and see if you can highlight some text. If your search word can't be found, and you know it's in the document, and the text can't be selected, you have a Searching for Bobby Fischer PDF.

Summary

Good PDFs look like the originating document. Fonts are the same, graphics are accurately reproduced onscreen and in print, and the file behaves in a logical, predictable manner. Good PDFs headed for onscreen usage include bookmarks and hyperlinks making the relevant information inside the document easy to navigate to. Good PDFs are well organized and the page numbers even match.

Many users create flawed PDFs unintentionally. PDF is a relatively new format, so standards are just beginning to be developed. Because PDF creation is low cost, some users do not perform the same extensive quality checks on PDF documents that they do for expensive printed documents.

Whether a PDF is flawed depends on its intended use. A PDF intended solely for print production doesn't need hyperlinks and bookmarks, and file size is seldom an issue. An online user manual does need links and bookmarks, and file size generally doesn't matter. A multipage, web-based document probably does need links and bookmarks, and file size is important.

In the next chapter, we look at preventing problems from the start by creating good PDFs.

Chapter 3

Creating the Best PDF for the Job

In the previous chapter, you saw many of the common faults found in PDFs. In this chapter, you will learn how to avoid many of those flaws by creating solid-performing PDFs from the start.

First, a word about these suggestions. They rely heavily on the recommendations of Adobe's Dov Isaacs, who has presented six times at my PDF Conferences on how to create good PDFs, and the work of Shlomo Perets, the technical editor of this book. Like Dov Isaacs, Shlomo is a frequent presenter at my PDF Conferences, and he has an uncanny ability to find and deconstruct some of the worst PDFs I've ever seen.

Good PDF Creation Is for Everyone

I'm a big believer in investing some time up-front to make sure the end result is good, and then using the same process over and over again. Traditional print publishers have been doing that for hundreds of years, and I think it is a good model for PDF creators.

However, by investing some time at the beginning, I am not advocating that mainstream users take heroic steps, such as writing special PostScript code to manipulate Acrobat Distiller. In this chapter, you will learn techniques for producing good PDFs from the Acrobat interface. In other words, producing good PDFs doesn't require programming skills or a hotline to some PDF guru. Everything you need is right in front of you on the computer screen.

(If you would like to learn more advanced techniques, please see the web site of Shlomo Perets at **www.microtype.com**. Shlomo teaches his classes in North America, Europe, and Israel on a regular basis. See **www.microtype.com** for a current list of events.)

Four Fundamental Ways to Create PDFs

To begin the discussion of creating solid, reliable PDFs, let's take a look at the four basic ways to create a PDF:

- **Via Acrobat Distiller/Adobe PDF printer** This is probably the most common method, whether you choose File | Print | Adobe PDF, or the PDFMaker button in Microsoft Word, which indirectly does the same thing, but adds interactive features.
- **Directly from an application** Some applications bypass Distiller/Adobe PDF printer. For example, Adobe InDesign CS includes Adobe's PDF creation

technology, and exports a file as a PDF. QuarkXPress 6 uses JawsPDF Creator technology to produce PDFs, sidestepping Distiller entirely.

- **From a third-party tool** Because Adobe publishes the PDF specification, dozens of companies are making PDF creation tools. Planet PDF (**www.planetpdf.com**) and PDF Zone (**www.pdfzone.com**) have lists of these third-party vendors.
- **From paper** Acrobat 6 Standard and Professional include the capability to turn scanned paper images into PDF. Many scanning applications also include this capability.

Adobe Acrobat Distiller

The primary way of creating PDFs in Acrobat is through Acrobat Distiller. Distiller takes a PostScript file generated by an authoring application and turns that PostScript file into a PDF. Adobe ships Distiller with several specific settings, which are called Adobe PDF Settings or Job Options. (See the following section for a description of Acrobat's Job Options.)

Distiller has been closely linked to the Adobe PDF printer in Acrobat 6, and the Job Options that pop up in the Adobe PDF printer are the same ones available in Distiller. Users can modify these Job Options to create customized versions that will create PDFs for specific purposes, such as distribution on the Web or for printing a four-color brochure.

NOTE *Adobe has changed its terminology for measuring compression. In previous versions, compression was measured in dots per inch (dpi). In Acrobat 6, the measurement unit is pixels per inch (ppi). According to Adobe technical support, ppi and dpi can be used interchangeably.*

What's in the Acrobat Box

In any discussion of creating high-quality standards for creating PDFs, you must start with what Adobe gives you as default settings. Brief descriptions follow.

Standard

The idea behind *Standard* is to create PDFs that can be produced on general office printers where everyone is running Windows. A medium amount of compression is applied to graphics. Subsets of fonts are embedded, except for the standard Windows fonts. Zombie PDF font substitution may occur if the originator uses a standard Windows font and doesn't embed it, and the end user doesn't have a standard Windows font. Most Windows fonts are available for the Mac as well, but there is still a chance that some users would experience the Zombie PDF effect. PDFs produced by Standard are compatible with Acrobat 5.

Smallest File Size

Smallest File Size is conceived as the means of creating PDFs for the Web. Low-quality graphics are produced, which look fine onscreen. However, these low-quality graphics increase the risk that ugly graphics will be printed if end users click the Print icon, producing a Beauty and the Beast PDF. No fonts are embedded, but the subset of fonts used by the creator does get placed in the PDF. These files are Acrobat 5-compatible.

Unfortunately, Smallest File Size does not produce PDFs that can be reflowed for devices that need tiny file sizes, such as the Pocket PC or Palm OS. The General tab setting for Object Level Compression compresses the tagging information required for reflow, and the current generation of viewers for the Pocket PC and Palm OS don't support compressed tags.

Press Quality

Press Quality creates PDF files designed to be printed to an imagesetter or a platesetter. Little compression is applied, and all fonts are embedded and subset. Because this PDF will only be printed, landscape pages aren't automatically rotated into portrait orientation. Adobe has wisely chosen to set PDF creation to fail if a font cannot be embedded. PDFs produced with Press Quality are Acrobat 5-compatible.

High Quality

High Quality is similar to Press Quality. PDFs produced with this setting will have high-resolution images and embedded fonts. Recommended changes are to set Auto-Rotate Pages to Individually, and to change When Embedding Fails to Cancel Job. These settings will prevent Wrong Turn and Zombie PDFs from being created by the High Quality settings.

PDF/X-1a

This is a specialized setting available only in Acrobat 6 Professional. *PDF/X1-a* is an ISO standard for the printing and publishing industry. (See Chapter 18 for more information.) No PDF will be produced if the PostScript file sent to Distiller doesn't contain the features needed for PDF/X-1a compliance.

PDF/X-3

This is another ISO standard for the printing and publishing industry. (See Chapter 18 for more information.) Like the PDF/X-1a Job Option, *PDF/X-3* checks incoming PostScript files for compliance, and produces a PDF only if the incoming PostScript contains the required features.

TIP *The fonts Courier, Symbol, Times, Helvetica, and ZapfDingbats are no longer included with Acrobat or Adobe Reader. You must embed those fonts if you want to prevent font substitution.*

Suggestions for Improvement

The default settings in Acrobat Distiller give you a good starting point from which to produce better PDFs. However, I am going to suggest that you can do better. I use these settings all the time, and I am producing smaller PDFs that generate fewer complaints from my print vendors.

Changing Adobe PDF Settings

To implement these changes, you will need to modify the existing Adobe PDF Settings (also known as Job Options). The following are the steps to modify your settings:

1. From within Acrobat, choose Advanced | Distiller, or choose Start | All Programs | Acrobat Distiller 6.0.
2. In the Adobe PDF section of Distiller, select the Adobe PDF Settings you want to modify from the Default Settings pull-down menu.
3. Choose Settings | Edit Adobe PDF Settings.
4. Move through the General, Images, Fonts, Color, Advanced, and PDF/X tabs, and then specify the settings you desire.
5. When the settings are complete, choose Save As and save the file with a new name with the `.joboptions` file extension.

Modifying the Standard Settings

To help get your feet wet, I suggest you modify the Standard settings to begin. Although you can get better results with the settings discussed in the following section, modifying the Standard settings is a good start.

I have two suggestions for improving the Standard setting. Using the procedure outlined in the preceding section, edit the Standard Adobe PDF settings file and follow these steps:

1. Click the Fonts tab.
2. Change When embedding fails to Cancel job.
3. In the Never Embed: window, select all the fonts listed and click Remove. Your fonts window should look like the one in Figure 3-1.
4. Click Save As…
5. Save the file with a new name, such as `Standard(embedall).joboptions`.

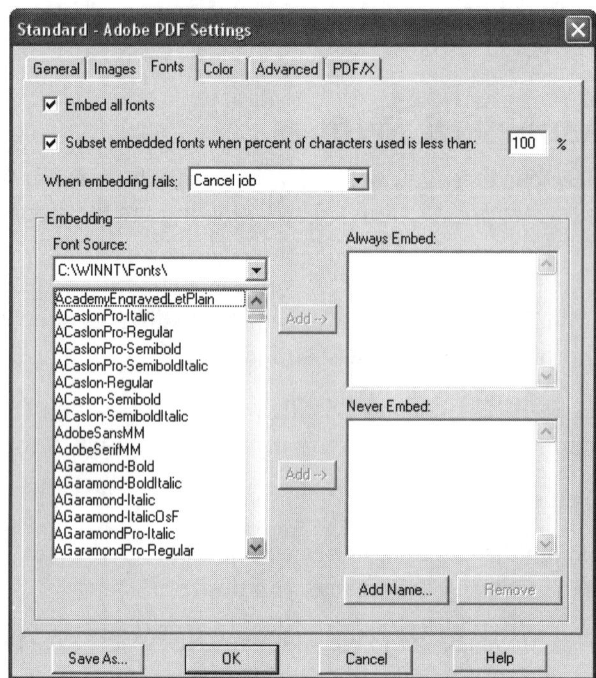

FIGURE 3-1 Clear all the fonts from the Never Embed: window and change When embedding fails to Cancel Job.

You now have a Standard job options file that you can use over and over again. These settings are best for general office PDFs that will be printed. This file has two improvements over the default setting:

- If a font cannot be embedded, the job will fail.
- All fonts, even the standard Windows ones, will be embedded and subset, assuring universal fidelity to the original document.

Modifying the Smallest File Size Setting

The software wizards at Adobe and I have a large philosophical difference when it comes to preparing PDFs for the Web. Adobe recommends this setting for files to be distributed on the Web, or an intranet, or to be sent via e-mail.

I agree with the goal, which is to prevent a Fat Albert PDF so huge that it can't be downloaded in a reasonable amount of time. It also prevents a Waiting Game PDF by optimizing the file for Fast Web View. However, this setting is a recipe for creating Zombie and Beauty and the Beast PDFs that don't look like the original and print terribly.

When creating files for the Web, I believe you should consider file size, but not disregard quality at the expense obtaining the smallest possible size. While my recommendations will increase the file size slightly, you will end up with a much higher-quality PDF that will look like the original and print well.

In many ways, this is the Superman of PDFs. It will display well on the Web and look good in print, too. You won't have to make two different PDFs for each application.

1. To begin, edit the Adobe PDF settings for the Smallest File Size setting. Notice that Optimize for Fast Web View is already turned on in the General tab. This prevents a Waiting Game PDF.
2. In Auto-Rotate Pages, change from Collectively by File to Individually. This prevents landscape pages from being displayed in portrait orientation, creating a Wrong Turn PDF.
3. Set Resolution to 2400. The resolution applies to vector art, and will not enlarge the file more than a few KB. The recommended higher setting will produce smoother grayscale and color gradients.
4. Set Object Level Compression to Off. Object compression is not supported in earlier versions of Acrobat.
5. Click the Images tab.

6. In Color Images, change the Bicubic Downsampling to 150 pixels per inch for images above 225 pixels per inch.
7. Set Image Quality to Maximum. Won't this greatly increase the size of my file? Perhaps. But you will also produce a PDF that someone can download and print reliably. Lower the setting to High or Medium if you must, but be sure to test print your document before sending it out.
8. The Grayscale Images section should already have these settings by default, except for Image Quality, which should also be set to Maximum.
9. Change Monochrome Images Downsample: to Bicubic Downsampling 600 pixels per inch for images above 900 pixels per inch. This setting applies to black and white bitmap images, such as faxes.

When complete, your Image settings should look like the one shown in Figure 3-2. Now it's time to look at changing the Font and Color settings.

1. Switch to the Fonts tab.

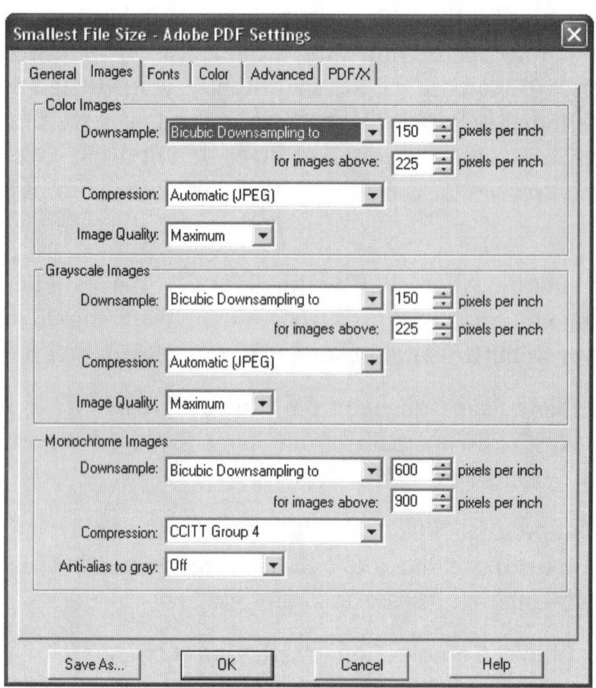

FIGURE 3-2 Settings to produce better images for web-based PDFs

2. Turn on Embed All Fonts. Remember, you don't want to create any Zombie PDFs.
3. Change When Embedding Fails to Cancel Job. Canceling the job means no PDF is produced, so you won't send out a bad one.
4. Move to the Color tab.
5. In Color Management Policies, change from Convert All Colors to sRGB to leave Color Unchanged. This will reduce the chances of producing a Color Purple PDF where unusual color shifts occur.
6. In Device-Dependent Data, enable Preserve Under Color Removal and Black Generation. Useful when printing color.
7. Set When Transfer Functions are Found: to Preserve. Also helpful for printing color.

Your Color settings should look like the ones in Figure 3-3.

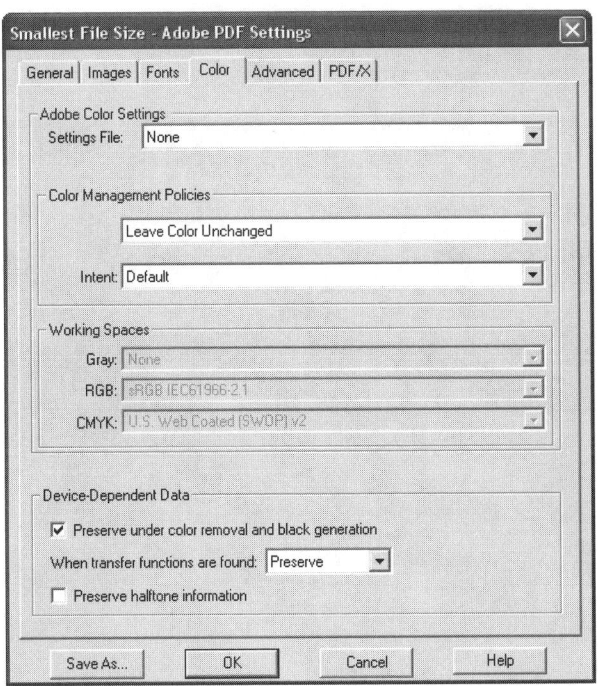

FIGURE 3-3 Color settings

To finish up, you need to set a few things in the Advanced tab:

1. Switch to the Advanced tab.
2. Enable Save Original JPEG Images Inside PDF If Possible. This option processes compressed JPEG files without recompressing them and possibly degrading the image.
3. Add the following Document Structuring Conventions (DSC, information about a PostScript file):
   - Process DCS Comments
   - Preserve EPS Information
   - Preserve OPI Comments
   - Preserve Document Information
4. Your Advanced Settings should look like the ones shown in Figure 3-4.
5. Click Save As and save the options as `GeneralPurpose.joboptions`.

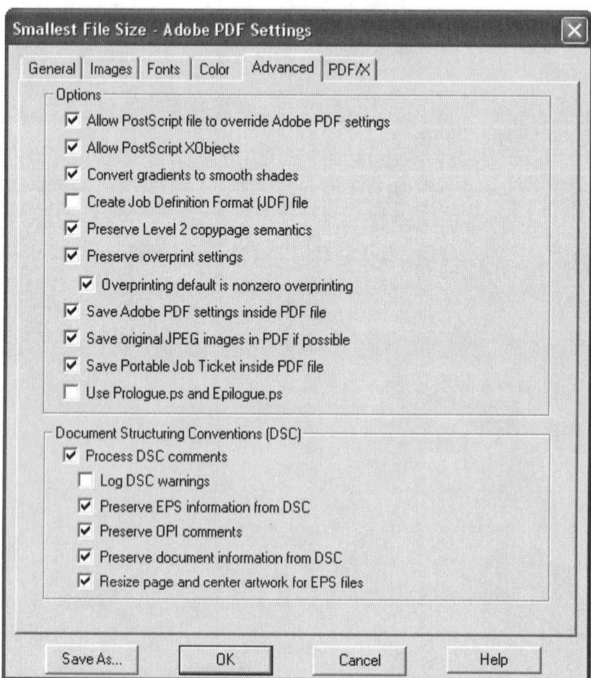

FIGURE 3-4 Advanced settings

You now have a solid Adobe PDF Settings file that will create PDFs that look like the original, display well onscreen, and print like a champ.

What About File Size?

I anticipate hearing some groans coming from people who will object to changing the graphics compression from Low to Maximum. For example, a 14-page, 12.7MB Word file with eight color photographs and one drawing turned into a 2.1MB PDF when processed with the General Purpose job options. This file would print well in color even on the relatively high-quality printers you would find at a "Fast Print" copying center.

The Smallest File size settings produced a smaller file—300KB. However, the Smallest File size PDF was a Zombie and a Beauty and the Beast. The fonts did not look like the original, and a noticeable loss of quality was in some of the photographs.

My contention is that going from a 12.7MB Word file to a 2.1MB PDF is a tremendous amount of compression, and a 2.1MB file is easily managed. You can e-mail a 2.1MB PDF, and even download it from the Web in a couple of minutes at dial-up speeds.

Sure, a 300KB file is smaller, but look at the cost. It doesn't look like the original, and the graphics do not print as clearly.

TIP *If compressing to the smallest possible file size is a priority, I recommend PDF Enhancer from PDF Sages (**http://www.apago.com/enhancer.html**). Enhancer will compress graphics in PDF files even more than Acrobat, and without a loss of graphics quality.*

Acrobat 6 Compatibility

The General Purpose Adobe PDF Settings file created in the preceding section is compatible with Acrobat 5. That's good for people who are using the older versions, but not so good for creators who want to do things like produce layered PDFs.

If you want to use some of Acrobat 6's new features, such as layers, go right ahead. Change the Compatibility settings in `GeneralPurpose.joboptions` to Acrobat 6, and give the `.joboptions` file a new name.

Create Settings for High-Quality PDFs

The `GeneralPurpose.joboptions` file is flexible. Let's say you would like to create a PDF that could be printed on an imagesetter. Just go into the Images tab and change the Color and Grayscale image downsampling to 300 ppi for images over 450 ppi. Also set Monochrome Image Downsampling to 1200 ppi for images over 1800 ppi. Save the file with a new name, and you are ready to go.

This new joboptions file will create PDFs that are larger than those created with the General Purpose settings. On my test document, the higher resolution settings created a PDF of 3MB, nearly 1MB larger than the 2.1MB produced with the General Purpose settings.

What About PDFWriter?

Acrobat 4 and 5 included something called *PDFWriter,* which was Adobe's attempt to create a shortcut for PDF creation. Instead of creating a PostScript file and processing it with Distiller, PDFWriter used the Windows video system to create PDFs.

While PDFWriter was fast and worked well with text-heavy documents, it tended to create jaggy graphics. Adobe has dropped PDFWriter from Acrobat 6. The Adobe PDF virtual printer in Acrobat 6 is basically a shortcut to Distiller, and produces high-quality PDFs.

I've seen PDFWriter still installed at sites that upgraded from Acrobat 4 to 5 to 6. Your system administrator should remove PDFWriter installations.

PDF Directly from an Application

Because PDF has become such an important publishing medium, many software companies have built PDF creators into their applications. All these products except for FrameMaker enable you to create PDFs without Distiller.

You'll learn more about these products later in the book. Chapter 8 gives you information about creating PDFs from WordPerfect, and Chapter 16 discusses other Corel products. Chapter 15 covers Adobe products, such as Photoshop, Illustrator, InDesign, and FrameMaker. QuarkXPress output is detailed in Chapter 17.

Third-Party PDF Creators

Well into 2004, Acrobat was powering Adobe to record growth. For the 2003 fiscal year, Adobe's ePaper group, which is based around Acrobat, had $444 million in sales, a 40 percent increase over the previous year. More than half a billion free Adobe Readers have been distributed world-wide.

Acrobat's popularity hasn't gone unnoticed by other software companies. There are more than 600 third-party products for Acrobat and dozens of alternatives to Acrobat. The PDF Store at Planet PDF lists 43 non-Adobe creation tools.

NOTE *The new OS X operating system from Apple even uses PDF as the graphics display engine. Mac OS X users can use a Save as PDF option from many applications.*

These tools break down into two categories: Desktop PDF creators for individuals, and server-based tools for workgroups, departments, and enterprises.

Desktop Alternatives

For creative professionals, the most popular alternative to Acrobat is the Jaws PDF Creator product family. Quark put Jaws PDF technology into QuarkXPress 6. Like Distiller, *Jaws PDF Creator* turns PostScript files into PDFs. This technique is generally regarded as suitable for high-end commercial publishing. *activePDF,* considered to be Number Two to Adobe in the PDF world, private-brands Jaws PDF Creator under the *activePDF Composer* name.

Other desktop products popular in government and enterprise organizations include *RoboPDF* from the eHelp group at Macromedia, *Instant PDF* from Enfocus, *Rapid PDF* from Amyuni, and *easyPDF* from BCL Computers.

Server-Side PDF

Although Adobe is pouring resources into enterprise products, its initial approach with Acrobat was to sell to desktop users. Lots of companies saw a vacuum for companies who wanted to produce hundreds, or thousands, of PDFs at a time.

activePDF rose to Number Two in the PDF industry by targeting Windows-based server creation. Its activePDF Server product dynamically generates PDFs from Windows NT/2000 server applications.

Other contenders in the server-based field include AdLib eDocument Solutions, Appligent, Amyuni Technologies, and PDFlib. For more information, see Chapter 11.

Paper to PDF

Adobe has a stand-alone product called *Capture,* which is specifically designed to turn paper into PDF. Adobe includes a scaled-down version of Capture in

Professional and Standard. Unlike Acrobat 5, Adobe doesn't put a limit on the number of pages that can be processed in this "lite" version of Capture.

Whether you use the Capture lite version inside of Acrobat or the stand-alone version of Capture depends on your needs. The full Capture runs with minimal manual intervention, and is optimized to run on high-powered workstations or servers. The Capture inside of Acrobat requires the participation of the user to scan every page.

To use Acrobat's built-in Capture, you must either scan documents into Acrobat or convert scanned images created by others.

To scan a document into Acrobat, use the following procedure:

1. Close all open documents.
2. Click the Create PDF button and choose From Scanner, or File | Create PDF | From Scanner.
3. In the Create PDF from Scanner dialog box, select your scanner, and whether you are scanning a single-sided or double-sided document.
4. Choose Open New PDF Document.
5. Turn off Adapt Page Compression to Page Content.
6. Click Scan.
7. When your scanning software appears, make sure you set a resolution of at least 200, the minimum required by Acrobat. A resolution of 300 is a good starting point. The maximum resolution is 600 dpi, but this setting will result in unacceptably large files. Scanning in black-and-white is by far the most common selection because it produces the smallest files.
8. Start your scanning software.
9. When the Acrobat Scan Plug-In appears, either choose Next to continue scanning or click Done when you are finished.

NOTE *Adobe recommends using Adaptive Compression only on documents with a large number of graphics.*

What you now have is an image wrapped inside of an Adobe PDF. Click the Text Select Tool and try to select some text. You will be unable to do so. Try using Search on the document—it won't work. It is time to put Capture to work.

The following procedure will run Optical Character Recognition (OCR) on the image and create searchable text:

1. Choose Document | Paper Capture | Start Capture.
2. Accept the default settings of Searchable Image (Exact) and Downsampling (none).
3. Save the file.

NOTE *Searchable Image (Exact) does not apply any compression to the scanned image. Searchable Image (Compact) does apply compression. Whether to use Exact or Compact depends on the number and quality of graphics of the scanned pages. You'll have to test each type to see which is best for you. The Compact setting will produce the smallest file size, but may result in unacceptable image degradation.*

4. Now use the Text Select Tool again to select text. You can! You can copy-and-paste the text you select, or even choose File | Save As… | Save as Type | Microsoft Word Document to save the OCR text as a *.doc file.

Notice that the onscreen image hasn't changed. We've just added a hidden layer of text behind it. This feature was formerly known as Original Image + Hidden Text.

NOTE *You can turn a scanned page into a regular PDF by changing the default Capture settings to Formatted Text & Graphics. This option almost always requires manual cleanup with Document | Paper Capture | Find First OCR Suspect, and continuing to clean up Suspect words. This file will not look identical to the original document.*

TIP *Fixing Suspect words only works in a Formatted Text & Graphics document. The feature does not work in a Searchable Image Format.*

Alternatives to Capture

As in many cases in the PDF world, there are alternatives to the full Adobe Capture product and the lite version inside Acrobat:

- **AdLib eDocument Solutions eXpress & OCR** Creates Image+Hidden Text searchable PDFs from a wide variety of source files, including TIF images from scanned paper documents. See **www.adlibsys.com** for more information.
- **Image Solutions DocComposer** Creates Image+Hidden Text PDFs from scanned images. Adds bookmarks and page numbers, deskews pages, and can remove punch hole marks. See **www.imagesolutions.com**.

Strategies for Creating Efficient PDF Workflows

While you can go a long way toward producing better PDFs by modifying the default Adobe PDF Settings, you can do much earlier in the workflow. After all, creating a PDF is like anything else in the computer world—if you put garbage in, you'll get garbage out.

In this section, you will learn some techniques for creating better PDFs that can be applied early in the workflow, and head off any problems that might only appear when you create a faulty PDF.

Working with Fonts

In surveys of PDF creators, one problem usually tops all lists: problems with fonts. In discussing this issue with students in my classes, I've concluded that these problems come up because it isn't clear to many users how Acrobat handles fonts. To start, let's take a look at font basics in Acrobat.

Font Handling 101

First, if you want certain fonts to appear in your PDF, those fonts must be installed on your computer and you must have the legal right to place those fonts in any PDF you create.

In addition, some fonts are only available on certain printers. These fonts are "enabled" when you select the printer's driver. However, Distiller cannot access these printer resident fonts.

How do you know if you can legally install a font in a PDF? Your attorney would advise you to read the licensing agreement that accompanies the purchase of a font. Because few people bother to read such agreements, Adobe gives you a visual cue in the Fonts section of the Adobe PDF Settings in Distiller. See Figure 3-5 for an example.

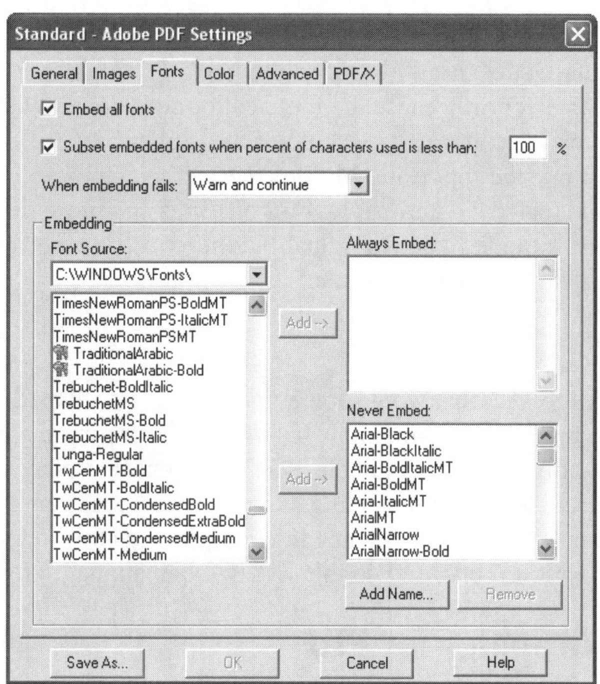

FIGURE 3-5 The keys next to the Traditional Arabic and Traditional Arabic-Bold fonts indicate that the user does not have the right to embed those fonts in a PDF.

Designers of TrueType fonts have the option to place a lock on the font to prevent you from embedding it. Just look for a golden key icon next to a font. This means you cannot embed a font.

Distiller needs access to your computer's fonts to embed them. The fonts can be in folders on your computer, or on a network drive.

Subsetting and Embedding

Subsetting inserts only those font characters used in your document. PDFs with subset fonts generally cannot be edited if the embedded font isn't installed on the end user's computer. You should enable font embedding to ensure that subsetting will take place.

Subsetting also can clear up confusion over font names. For example, if you embed Helvetica in your document, Acrobat creates a custom font name and preserves your Helvetica's font metrics. If your commercial printer has a Helvetica typeface that is different from yours, the font subsetting information will use the font metrics for your Helvetica instead of the printer's Helvetica.

Embedding places the entire font set in the PDF. If a font is not embedded by the choice of the creator or because the font vendor does not allow it, Acrobat will look for the font on the end user's machine. If the font cannot be found, Acrobat will attempt to mimic the font using Multiple Master technology.

The faux font created by Acrobat will fill out lines and preserve page breaks, but it may or may not look like the original. Script fonts are especially difficult for the Multiple Master technology to mimic.

An Urban Legend

Five or six years ago, Acrobat would sometimes struggle to embed TrueType fonts. This hasn't been the case for some time, but a holdover from the old days is a common myth that Acrobat can't handle TrueType fonts. Acrobat can, and does quite well. As discussed in the preceding paragraph, just make sure the TrueType designer has given you the right to embed the font. Acrobat 6 works well with TrueType, Type 1, OpenType, and double-byte (Asian language) fonts.

Preparing Graphics for PDF

After fonts, the issue of graphics quality seems to come up most often. Because graphics frequently take up most of the space in a PDF file, the size, resolution, and type of graphic can often make the difference between a manageable PDF and a Fat Albert.

Vector Art

If you want to minimize the size of your PDFs, then use vector instead of bitmap art.

What's the difference? In the old days, we called vector art "line art" because it is principally made up of lines. Programs like Adobe Illustrator, CorelDRAW!, AutoCAD, and Microsoft Visio produce vector art. Modern *vector art* also contains more than lines—it often has solid colors and gradient fills.

Bitmap art is made up dots, as you might see in newspaper photographs. The most common bitmap art today is digital photographs. Bitmap art is created or edited with programs such as Photoshop or Paintshop Pro.

Acrobat is exceedingly friendly toward vector art. Vector drawings can be compressed significantly with no loss of quality. Earlier versions of Distiller contained an option to compress vector art. This option has disappeared in Acrobat 6—vector art is compressed automatically and significantly. Given a choice, go with vector art to produce the smallest possible PDF.

Bitmap Graphics

Photographs and screen shots seem to make up the majority of bitmap graphics that I see my students use. Marketing collateral is filled with photos, and technical manuals usually contain lots of screen shots.

First a word about bitmap graphics formats. Photographs commonly come in a format called JPEG, which uses a lossy compression format to hold down file size. When *lossy* compression is applied, data is thrown away to reduce the size of the file. The more compression, the more data that is discarded and the lower the quality of the image.

Acrobat 6 supports a new JPEG format known as *JPEG 2000,* which uses non-lossy compression. JPEG 2000 is a relatively new format, and is not yet widely used. Only Acrobat 6 Standard and Professional, and Adobe Reader 6, can view PDFs that use JPEG 2000.

Another compression method is *ZIP compression,* which is a nonlossy format that does not throw away data to achieve high levels of compression. Acrobat Distiller contains both kinds of compression methods.

Because JPEG was developed by photographers, it works great on photographs. It doesn't do so well for screen shots. JPEG-compressed screen shots tend to be blurry. Users will say they have a hard time reading the text in screen shots.

If you are producing documents that are primarily made up of screen shots, you should change Distiller's default compression settings. Go to the Images tab in Adobe PDF Settings, and switch the Compression options in Color Images and Grayscale Images to ZIP, as shown in Figure 3-6.

Another problem I often see is that students choose the wrong format for screen captures. The crispest screen capture format is Tagged Image File Format (TIFF). Unfortunately, TIFFs are big. Because they take up so much space, many end users mistakenly choose JPEG for screen shots.

Screen shots in JPEG can look fine at a low resolution onscreen, but they usually print poorly. If you run an already-degraded image through Acrobat's JPEG compression routine, you are throwing away even more data. What happens when you apply JPEG compression to an already-compressed JPEG? You get a worse-looking JPEG.

Working with TIFF Images

TIFF is a great format for displaying the text in screen captures, but the files do tend to be large. For example, a screen capture of the Distiller Adobe PDF Settings window is 720KB in an uncompressed TIFF format, and 56KB as a high-quality JPEG.

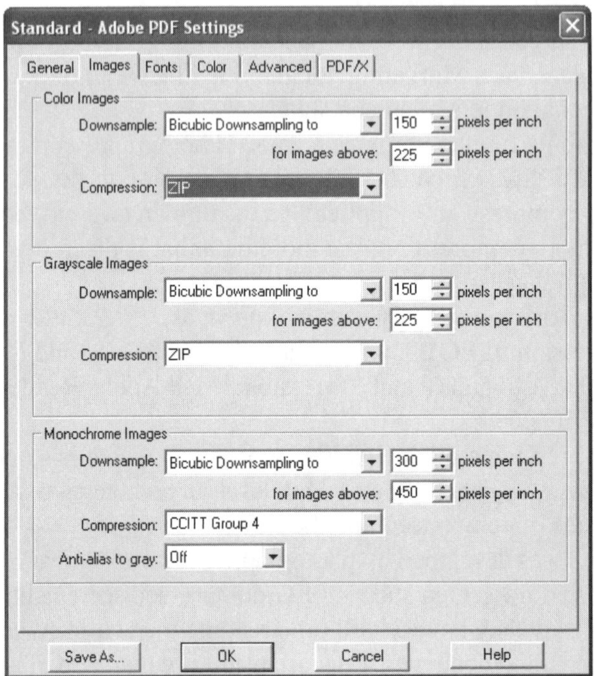

FIGURE 3-6 ZIP compression works well for screen shot images, which often contain text.

Go Black and White

What can you do? If your screen shots are going into a manual that will be printed, convert the color screen shots to black and white. Doing that dropped the file size of the test file to 252KB from 720KB. That's still larger than the 56KB of the JPEG file, but it is a substantial reduction over the original.

Don't Click-and-Drag to Resize

If you are placing a lot of screen shots into a manual or book, you have a good idea of what size you want the image to be when it is placed into your page layout program.

Usually the screen capture, especially if it is of the entire screen, is too large to fit on a page. Many end users place these large files onto a page, and then click-and-drag to resize them.

While that achieves the desired appearance, you are making your document unnecessarily large. Let's say you place the 720KB screen capture mentioned in the preceding section into your document, and then click-and-drag to reduce its size in half. Although the image is taking up less space in the document, it's still taking up 720KB of space.

Now, let's say you take a different approach, and open the 720KB file in an image editor, such as Photoshop, and reduce the size there. For example, if you choose Image | Image Size in Photoshop and reduce the width and height by half, the file size drops to 180KB.

Although clicking-and-dragging to shrink the size of an image on the page may increase the resolution of the image in some applications, you also can control resolution in your image-editing application. In general, you will get better results by working with an image in a bitmap-editing application such as Photoshop, rather than working with it in a page layout application.

PDF Optimizer

This is a new feature in Acrobat 6 Professional, and one that I often use. In my experience, the PDFs coming out of Adobe InDesign CS and Adobe FrameMaker 7.1 tend to be larger than I expect. *PDF Optimizer* will shrink those PDFs, and many PDFs from other applications.

The Optimizer analyzes a PDF and gives you a report. If you think the file could be smaller, give Optimizer a try. The Optimizer consolidates font sets, removes duplicate images, and applies compression to the document's internal structure.

TIP *Optimizer can also make Acrobat 6 files compatible with earlier versions of Acrobat.*

How well does Optimizer work? Put it to the test with one of Adobe's own files. Open the Acrobat 6 Help manual located in the Help folder on your Acrobat 6 installation CD.

Check Document Properties and note the file size. It is 415 pages long and 17MB in size. Now use the following procedure:

1. Choose Advanced | PDF Optimizer.
2. Click the Audit Space Usage button. You should see the report shown in Figure 3-7. Notice that 33 percent of the document is made up of images and 21 percent in structure information. A tagged PDF would be expected to have that much structure information.

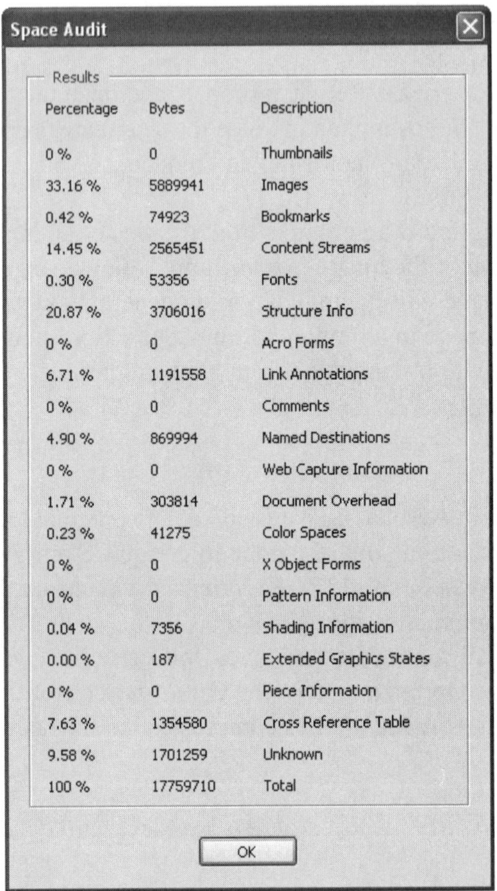

Percentage	Bytes	Description
0 %	0	Thumbnails
33.16 %	5889941	Images
0.42 %	74923	Bookmarks
14.45 %	2565451	Content Streams
0.30 %	53356	Fonts
20.87 %	3706016	Structure Info
0 %	0	Acro Forms
6.71 %	1191558	Link Annotations
0 %	0	Comments
4.90 %	869994	Named Destinations
0 %	0	Web Capture Information
1.71 %	303814	Document Overhead
0.23 %	41275	Color Spaces
0 %	0	X Object Forms
0 %	0	Pattern Information
0.04 %	7356	Shading Information
0.00 %	187	Extended Graphics States
0 %	0	Piece Information
7.63 %	1354580	Cross Reference Table
9.58 %	1701259	Unknown
100 %	17759710	Total

FIGURE 3-7 An analysis of the Adobe Acrobat 6 Professional Help file in PDF Optimizer

NOTE *The PDF Optimizer report doesn't make any suggestions for improving file size. It is simply an audit of the information found in the file.*

3. Click the Images tab. Make sure image compression is set to 150 ppi for images above 225 ppi for both color and monochrome images. Use ZIP compression.
4. Move to the Fonts tab. Move TimesNewRomanPSMT from the Unembed side to the Embedded side.
5. Move to the Cleanup tab. Use the options shown in Figure 3-8.

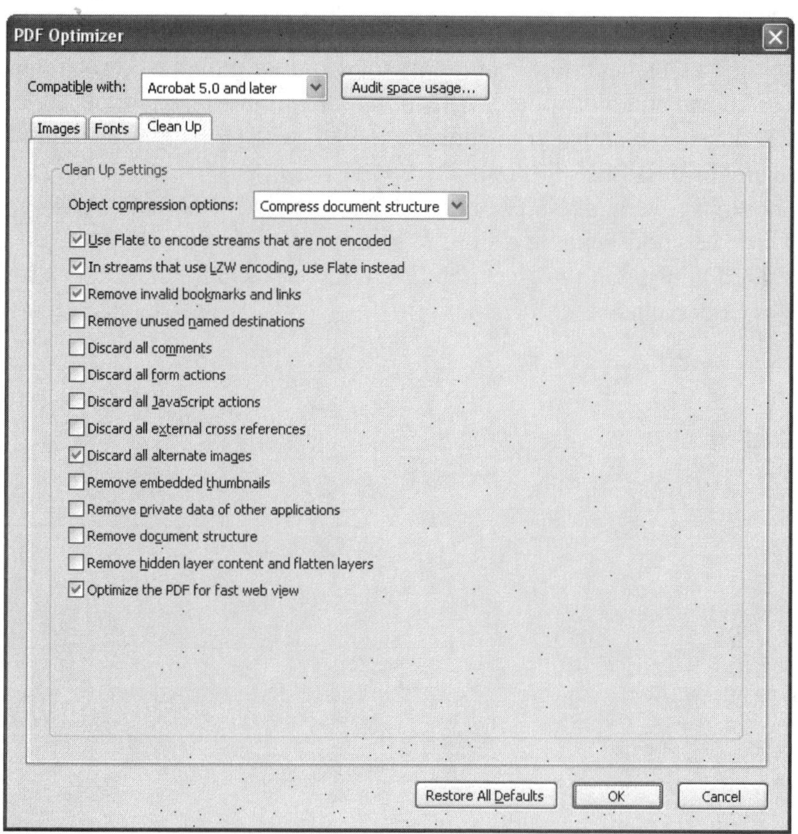

FIGURE 3-8 The Cleanup tab in PDF Optimizer

CAUTION

The "Removed unused named destinations" option is potentially a dangerous setting. Acrobat only checks for destinations used in the current PDF, and does not know about destinations used by cross-file links and bookmarks in other PDFs or in HTML files. Furthermore, Acrobat's analysis of used destinations is limited to links, form fields, and bookmarks, so if you have destinations used by some JavaScript functions, these are deleted.

6. Click OK to optimize the file. Save it from the CD onto a hard drive.
7. Recheck the file size. The file should now be around 12MB, or 5MB smaller than when you began.

Summary

Creating good PDFs isn't hard, but it does take a bit of thought. Acrobat Distiller is the best-known and most popular creation tool, but third-party tools are available as well. You can convert paper documents to PDF with the Capture feature in Standard and Professional.

Adobe ships several default settings for use with Distiller, but you can modify those to produce more reliable results. While appropriate Distiller settings can produce good PDFs, don't neglect good page-layout techniques when putting together your documents.

Chapter 4

Making Onscreen PDFs

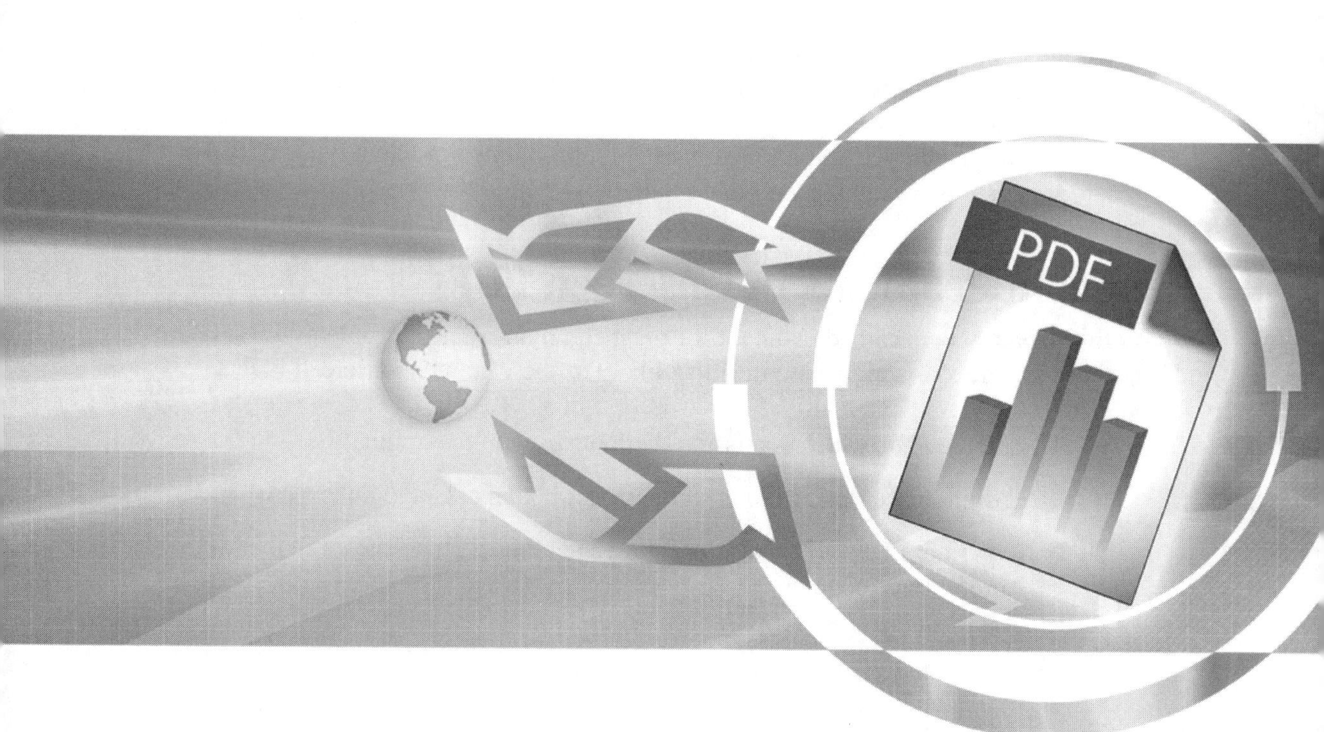

The move from paper to electronic documentation is happening unevenly, and at diverse rates for a variety of products. In some areas, electronic documents already rule. As discussed earlier, many vendors stopped publishing paper manuals for their products almost as soon as Acrobat appeared and made an inexpensive replacement possible. The same thing happened for many massive documents, such as new drug applications in the U.S. pharmaceutical industry and for many large federal government proposals.

Driving down costs is the biggest factor for many organizations in switching from paper to Acrobat. After all, it costs nothing to produce a PDF, and it can cost quite a bit to print a paper manual or to print and ship multiple copies of a 10,000-page proposal.

In other businesses, PDF acceptance has been uneven. Some U.S. courts, such as most bankruptcy courts, require court filings in PDF. Other courts still require paper. In other industries, PDF has hardly made a dent. In marketing, for example, companies will often post PDF product data sheets to a web site, but still print thousands of four-color brochures for distribution by mail or from sales representatives.

I contend that even wider acceptance of PDF would occur if creators would realize they are making faulty PDFs, and if they would take the simple steps outlined in this chapter to fix them. Fewer customers would complain about not receiving a printed manual, for example, and they might even start requesting high-quality PDFs instead of four-color brochures if the PDFs were a more engaging experience than the paper versions.

In this chapter, you learn how to fix the most common problem types of PDFs and see some fine examples of high-quality onscreen PDFs.

Common Problems in Onscreen PDFs

In Chapter 2, you learned about the 11 most common types of problem PDFs. Of those 11, the following 10 are the most likely to show up in an onscreen PDF:

- Zombie PDF, which is missing the fonts used in the original.
- Lost in Space PDF, which lacks Acrobat bookmarks and links.
- Labyrinth PDF, which has different page numbers than shown in the Acrobat page counter.
- Betrayal PDF, which has incorrect hypertext links.

- Fat Albert PDF, which is bloated beyond a reasonable size.
- Waiting Game PDF, which is not set up for displaying quickly on the Web.
- Wrong Turn PDF, which has landscape pages oriented in portrait mode.
- Honey, I Shrunk the Kids PDF, which opens at an unreadable zoom setting.
- Beauty and the Beast PDF, which looks great onscreen, but prints poorly.
- Searching for Bobby Fischer PDF, which contains image-only PDFs that are not searchable.

Fixing Problem PDFs

You may run across PDFs that have combinations of these flaws. Like sick human beings, problem PDFs can have multiple symptoms. It's just easier to see the solutions if the problems are separated into groups. In the following section, you learn the remedies for these problem PDFs.

Zombie PDF

This PDF looks approximately like the original because the creator did not embed the original font. The solution to this problem is discussed in detail in Chapter 3, but the quick answer is to enable Embed all fonts in Adobe PDF settings.

Embedding fonts is like packing for a trip. You don't have to bring your socks with you—you can always borrow some from your host. But wouldn't you and your host be happier if you brought your own?

Lost in Space PDF

Acrobat bookmarks are like an onscreen table of contents, as shown in Figure 4-1.

When a user spots the information they are looking for, they simply click a bookmark and are taken to the appropriate location in the document. A *bookmark* generally is a specific type of hyperlink in Acrobat. Other hyperlinks, commonly referred to as *links,* can take users to web addresses, to other PDFs, or to another page in the same document.

NOTE *Bookmarks can include all Acrobat actions, but the most common use is to use bookmarks to point to a location inside the open PDF.*

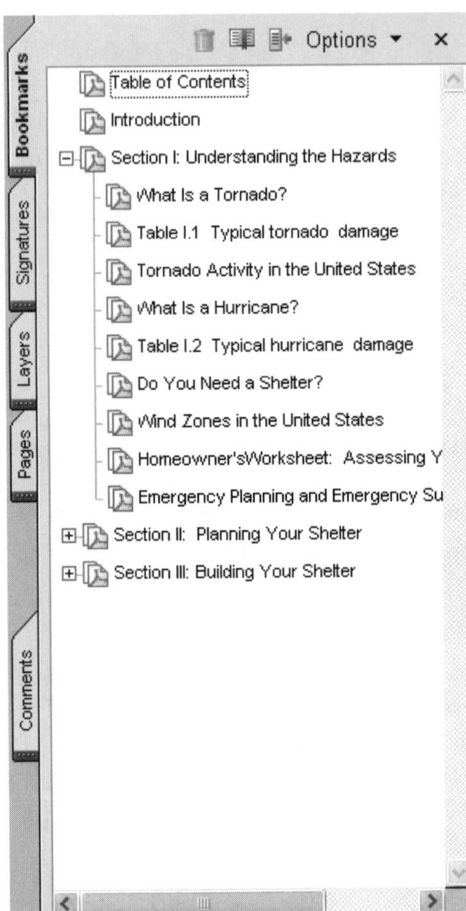

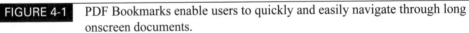

FIGURE 4-1 PDF Bookmarks enable users to quickly and easily navigate through long onscreen documents.

To avoid the Lost in Space syndrome, always make sure documents long enough to have tables of contents include links from the contents page to the appropriate content inside. Hyperlinks in Acrobat are shown to the user as a pointy finger, as shown in Figure 4-2.

Creating Bookmarks

The easiest way to create bookmarks is to use the automation features available in your creation software. For Microsoft Word, see Chapter 6. For Adobe applications,

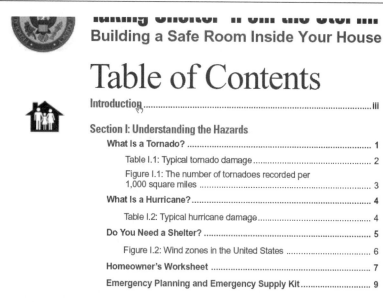

Building a Safe Room Inside Your House

Table of Contents

Introduction ... iii

Section I: Understanding the Hazards

What Is a Tornado? ... 1

Table I.1: Typical tornado damage ... 2

Figure I.1: The number of tornadoes recorded per 1,000 square miles ... 3

What Is a Hurricane? ... 4

Table I.2: Typical hurricane damage ... 4

Do You Need a Shelter? ... 5

Figure I.2: Wind zones in the United States ... 6

Homeowner's Worksheet ... 7

Emergency Planning and Emergency Supply Kit ... 9

FIGURE 4-2 Acrobat provides a visual cue when users come across a hyperlink. The cursor switches from an open hand shape to a hand with a pointed finger.

see Chapter 15. After you create more than a few bookmarks by hand, you'll appreciate the automation features.

Adding bookmarks is not a hard job, but it can be tedious if you have a long document. Use the following procedure to add bookmarks to a PDF:

1. Open the Bookmarks tab.
2. Choose the Text Select tool.
3. Click and drag to highlight the heading you want to bookmark.
4. In the Bookmarks tab, choose Options | New Bookmark (keyboard shortcut: CTRL-B).
5. Navigate to the next heading you want to bookmark and repeat the process until you are done.

TIP *Set the Opening View of a PDF with bookmarks to display when opened. That way, users will know the bookmarks are there. Set the zoom to Inherit Zoom and users will keep their current zoom setting.*

Once you create a set of bookmarks, you may want to show the bookmarks in a hierarchy for ease of navigation. For example, you might want H2s to be nested beneath H1s. Nesting shows a parent/child relationship between bookmark topics. See Figure 4-2 for a set of nested bookmarks.

This nesting operation is the trickiest thing to do in the entire Acrobat world. It requires acute vision, steady nerves, and a good hand on the mouse.

1. Select a single bookmark or a range of bookmarks.
2. Drag the icon of the bookmark to be nested underneath the icon of the parent bookmark. A red line will appear when you are in the correct position.
3. Release the mouse.

NOTE

There is no keyboard shortcut for nesting bookmarks.

If you see a No Go sign, pull back on your mouse. The red line must be visible when you release the mouse.

Once you have created some bookmarks, especially if you use the CTRL-B keyboard shortcut, you begin to see why it is such an ideal job for automation. It is a simple task done over and over again.

TIP

*If you just want to add bookmarks to your PDFs, but your authoring software doesn't support automatic creation, a couple of solutions are worth considering. eDocPrinter PDF Pro (**www.iteksoft.com**) and FinePrint PDFFactory Pro (**www.fineprint.com**) both create PDF bookmarks based on text formatting used in the document. Neither creates links from a table of contents, however.*

*ARTS PDF Bookmarker (**www.artspdf.com**) will create bookmarks after PDF creation. It uses style information to create bookmarks and has many other features.*

Creating Links

Creating links is much like creating bookmarks. It is an easy task, but tedious. Use the following procedure to create a link:

1. Select the Link tool by Choosing Tools | Advanced Editing | Link tool, or click the Link tool icon in the Advanced Editing toolbar.

2. Draw a marquee where you want to have a link or other "hotspot" for your link.
3. The Create Link dialog box appears.
4. In the Create Link dialog box, make sure to select Open a page in this document (or other appropriate option).
5. In most cases, Inherit Zoom is an appropriate zoom setting for onscreen documents. Inherit Zoom preserves the zoom level of the end user.
6. Click OK.

TIP *Compose from Infodata (**www.infodata.com**) does create links and bookmarks from text formatting in the documents. It will create links from tables of contents.*

Fix the Page Numbers in a Labyrinth PDF

As discussed in Chapter 2, a mismatch between the page numbers on each PDF page and the page numbers displayed in Acrobat is one of the leading causes of user confusion. Fortunately, an easy fix is available.

Acrobat's Pages Tab

Acrobat displays page numbers in two ways. Most people never bother to add the second set of page numbers, but these are critical to the usability of a PDF.

To recap the problem, most PDFs start out as printed documents. By tradition, cover and inside cover pages are unnumbered and front matter, such as legal notices and tables of contents, are numbered with roman numerals. You don't reach Page 1 until the first page of the content. For example, the first page of a book, historically, has been Page 1 of Chapter 1.

Move that same document online in a PDF, and users begin to have navigation problems. Acrobat, by default, begins its numbering sequence at the first page of a file–just like a printer would if the printer were charging to publish your document. If your document starts on Page 1, then the default page numbering sequence works.

On the other hand, most documents, especially those of any length, usually follow the pattern of a book—they begin with a cover page, followed by a legal disclaimer page, followed by a table of contents. Which one is numbered Page 1? It could be any one, or none. Your Page 1 could be the third or fourth page of the file.

I cannot count the number of times I have downloaded a PDF manual from the Web and seen a table of contents entry or a cross reference that says something like, "For more information, see Page 55." The entry is not linked, so I have to manually navigate to the correct page.

When I navigate to Page 55, the information isn't there. Why? Because Page 55 in the printed page world is Page 52 in the online world. The PDF author didn't bother to tell Acrobat to correctly display page numbers in the document.

This flaw is easily corrected. You simply use the Pages tab to reset Acrobat's display of page numbers. I like to start at the end of the first range of page numbers and work backward. Here's how you do it:

1. Navigate to the page in your PDF that has Page 1 printed on it.
2. Open the Pages tab. (If it isn't showing, choose View | Navigation Tabs | Pages.)
3. Go to the Options menu and select Number Pages.
4. In the From: dialog box, enter the page number showing in Acrobat's page number display. This number should come up by default.
5. In the To: box, enter the last page of the document.
6. In the Numbering section, select Style | 1,2,3…
7. Click OK.

TIP *You can select a range of thumbnails, and then right-click (*CTRL*-click Mac OS) to access Number pages.*

Acrobat's page number display should now show 1 (5 of *x*). It is now displaying two sets of numbers—the folio count of all pages, and the actual numbering sequence of the document.

If the preceding pages have roman numerals, you do the same thing, except choose the i, ii, iii,… style. If we add to roman numeral pages in our previous example, Acrobat will now show i (3 of *x*) in its page count readout.

TIP *Instead of specifying page numbers, you can use the Pages tab to change page numbers. Select the range of pages you want to number. Choose Options | Number pages and specify the new page numbers you want to use.*

Readers who see you have set up page numbers for them can now navigate your document with confidence. They know that if your text refers to Page 55, they can navigate to Page 55 and find the information you promised.

TIP *Assign a letter to unnumbered pages. You may lose the capability to set a document's opening view and other functionality if you set a page number value to none. The opening view dialog box requires a page number—even a letter qualifies as a number.*

Betrayal PDF

The Betrayal PDF has links and bookmarks, but these navigation elements are incorrect. You can, of course, look for bad ones manually. However, if you have a user manual of several hundred pages, clicking on hundreds or thousands of links is going to become boring quickly.

As mentioned in Chapter 2, ARTS Link Checker (**www.artspdf.com**) is an invaluable tool for managing documents with many links and bookmarks. If your budget allows you to buy only one PDF add-on, I would recommend this one. It can save you hundreds of staff hours.

ARTS Link Checker checks for dead or invalid links and bookmarks in your document. It can display the bad items page-by-page, or in a report. It also can click a batch of PDFs in a folder and subfolders. Its report is a PDF with items linked to the source page.

Preserving Links and Bookmarks

Adding links and bookmarks manually is tedious. Adding the same links and bookmarks to an updated version of your PDF can cause despair.

When your bookmarks and links are created on the fly from your authoring tool, it doesn't require any of your time to create a new PDF that will complete bookmarks and links. You just enable the appropriate settings and out flies a new, fully interactive PDF. It's another story if you've invested many hours in manually inserting bookmarks and links. If you need to create an updated PDF, you may be faced with many hours of tedium redoing your manual linking and bookmarking.

If the updates don't cause information in the document to reflow to other pages, there is a technique you can use to preserve your links and bookmarks. You simply swap out any pages of your fully linked PDF with updated ones. The following technique shows how.

1. Open the Pages tab in the linked and bookmarked document.
2. Select the page that should be replaced.
3. Choose Options | Replace Pages.
4. Select the file containing the replacement page.
5. Make sure the settings are correct in the Replace Pages dialog box.
6. Click OK.

The links and bookmarks in your original document are preserved, but a new page (or pages) will appear in place of the old one. This is as if the links and bookmarks are on an invisible layer on top of the text. You slip the old text out, and insert the new page. Your links also may be incorrect if the content shifted to new pages after the content was edited or rewritten.

Fat Albert PDF

Bloat in PDFs can be caused by a number of things. Images can be disproportionate to the size required, the creation software can insert unnecessary information, or the creator could have selected the wrong Job Options in Adobe PDF Settings.

The best way to prevent a Fat Albert PDF is to use the proper Job Options (for more information, see Chapter 3). You should also use graphics that are appropriately sized, another issue discussed in Chapter 3.

What happens if a Fat Albert lands on your desktop for fixing, and you don't have access to the source file for re-creation? New in Acrobat 6 Professional is the PDF Optimizer, discussed in Chapter 3. Optimizer can do a fine job of reducing file sizes, and is an improvement to the PDF Consultant in Acrobat 5.

Many advanced users will try two other tricks. One is easy and the second is not so hard, but it is unpredictable. The first trick is to simply choose File | Save As and resave the file. Amazingly enough, this simple technique will often reduce the size of the file. To make this technique work most effectively, enable Save As optimizes for Fast Web View in Acrobat preferences (Edit | Preferences | General). For more in Fast Web View, see the following section. The second technique is known as "refrying," and it may have unwanted side effects. Only use this technique with great care. To refry a PDF, you create a new PostScript file from your bloated document, and then run that PostScript through Acrobat Distiller again with more appropriate Job Options.

CAUTION *You cannot refry a secured PDF. Acrobat is designed to prevent users from using this technique to void the security settings of a PDF. Refrying may also render text unsearchable, and you will lose any interactivity you had in the original PDF. Graphics quality may suffer as well. See Adobe Technical Note 321185 for details.*

Space savings in refried PDFs can be substantial. I've seen files reduced by more than 50 percent with this technique. If your Fat Albert is a fully bookmarked and linked document, see the previous section on how to replace pages and keep your links intact.

Waiting Game PDF

A Waiting Game PDF lives on the Web, but it isn't set up for optimal viewing inside a browser. A Waiting Game PDF makes the user wait until the entire PDF is downloaded before it will display. It doesn't have to be that way, at least for users of Windows. (Adobe promises to integrate Acrobat with the Safari browser from Apple when Safari ships.)

Acrobat contains a setting called Fast Web View. Technically known as "linearization," *Fast Web View* organizes the PDF so all the information is in page order. This means the opening page of a PDF will display in the browser, as soon as that information is downloaded to the end user's computer. Fast Web View may also reduce the size of a PDF if Acrobat identifies duplicate graphics on many pages, such as a logo that appears on every page. Acrobat will drop the duplicates, and just keep one to redisplay on each page.

An unlinearized PDF can be set up for Fast Web View by enabling Save As optimizes for Fast Web View in Acrobat preferences (Edit | Preferences | General). PDF Optimizer also will organize a PDF for Fast Web View. Choose Advanced | PDF Optimizer | Clean Up. Enable the Optimize the PDF for Fast Web View option.

Wrong Turn PDF

A *Wrong Turn PDF* means landscape pages are shown in portrait orientation, as shown in Figure 4-3. To read these pages, you must turn your head sideways. The end user's other option is to use the Pages tab to change the orientation.

Some applications, such as Adobe FrameMaker, will keep landscape pages in the correct viewing orientation if you select Auto-rotate pages to Individually.

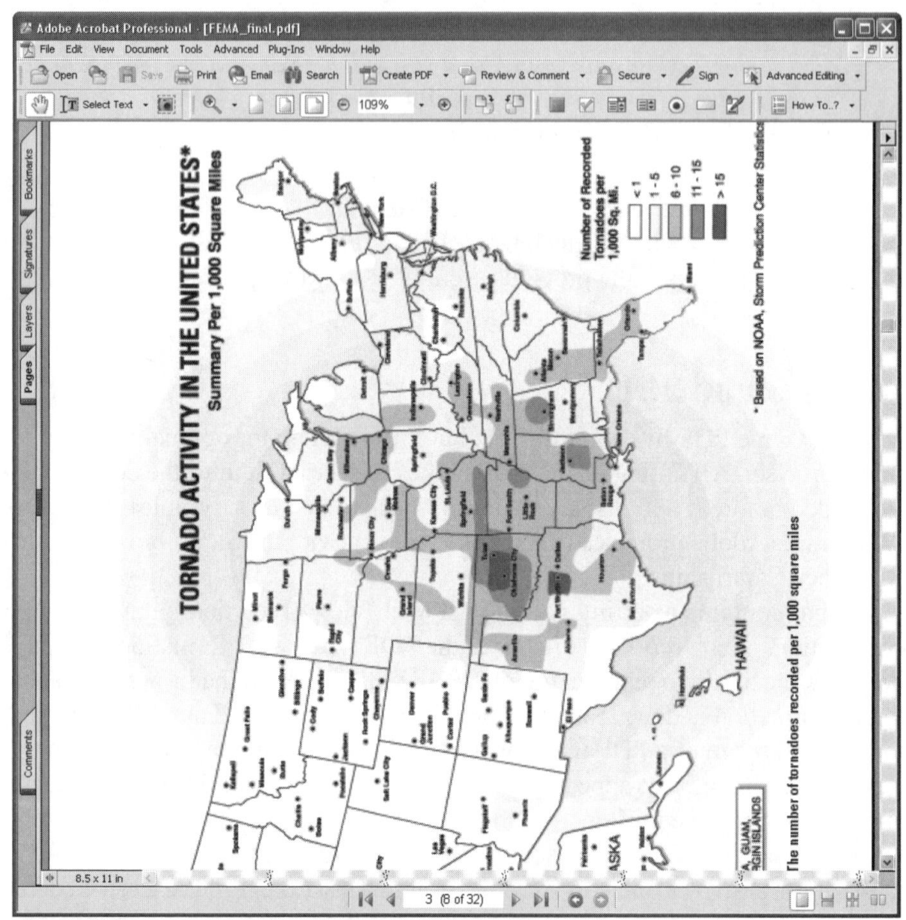

FIGURE 4-3 A landscape page in portrait orientation

With others, you will have to change the orientation yourself by using the following procedure:

1. Open the Pages tab.
2. Select the page to change by clicking the page number below the thumbnail image of the page. (Press SHIFT to select a group of continuous pages.)
3. Choose Options | Rotate Pages.

4. Choose the correct rotation angle. For a landscape page in a group of portrait pages, choose Clockwise 90 degrees.
5. Save the file.

One of the objections I hear to placing landscape pages in their correct orientation is that the landscape pages won't print correctly. This idea is nonsense, as is shown in Figure 4-4. The Auto Rotate and Center option will print the landscape pages in portrait orientation. It chooses the proper print orientation based on the text in the document.

Honey, I Shrunk the Kids PDF

Onscreen PDFs with this problem present themselves at a view level that even the sharpest eyes can't read. This is a particular problem for PDFs that open inside a browser window, as shown in Figure 4-5.

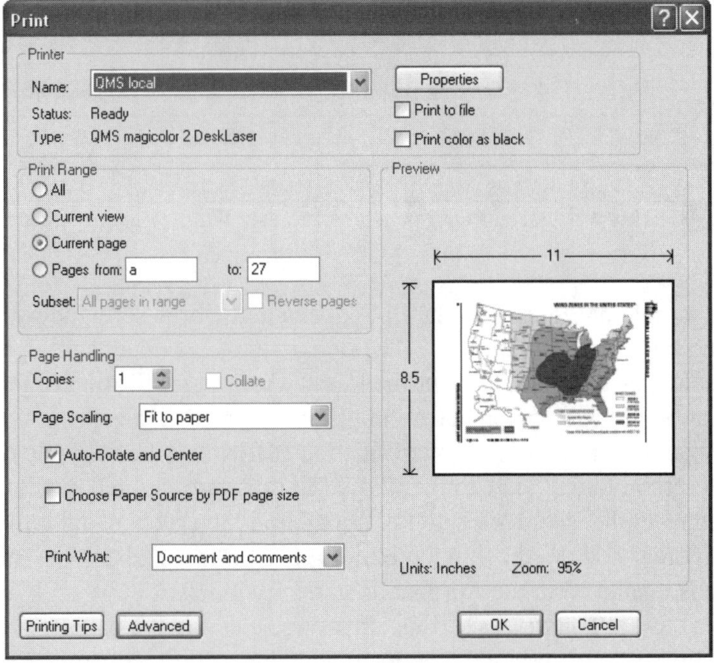

FIGURE 4-4 Auto Rotate and Center print settings are enabled in Acrobat 6. This setting will correctly print landscape pages.

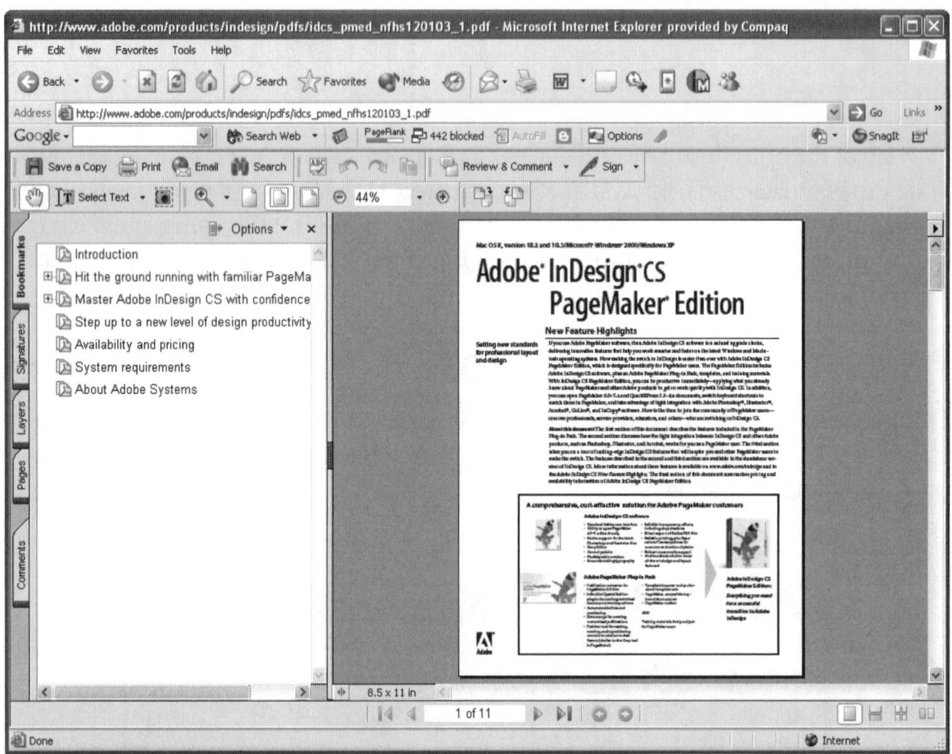

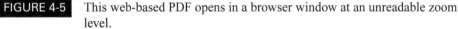

FIGURE 4-5 This web-based PDF opens in a browser window at an unreadable zoom level.

In the example in Figure 4-5, the PDF opens in the browser window of my laptop at the size of a shipping label. The bookmarks expand and are open to let the user know they are available, but the Initial View magnification of the PDF is set to Fit Page. Fit Page zooms out, so the entire page is visible.

In this example from Adobe's web site, the PDF would be readable if the creator had set the Initial View to Fit Width. To illustrate, I saved the PDF to my desktop and reset the Initial View to Fit Width, and then reopened the file in my browser. Figure 4-6 shows how much easier it is to read the text when the width of the page is displayed in the Acrobat document window.

Another flaw, although less serious, involves selecting the page to show when the PDF is first opened. While many documents have pretty covers, a cover page generally won't get the user to information inside the document quickly. You may

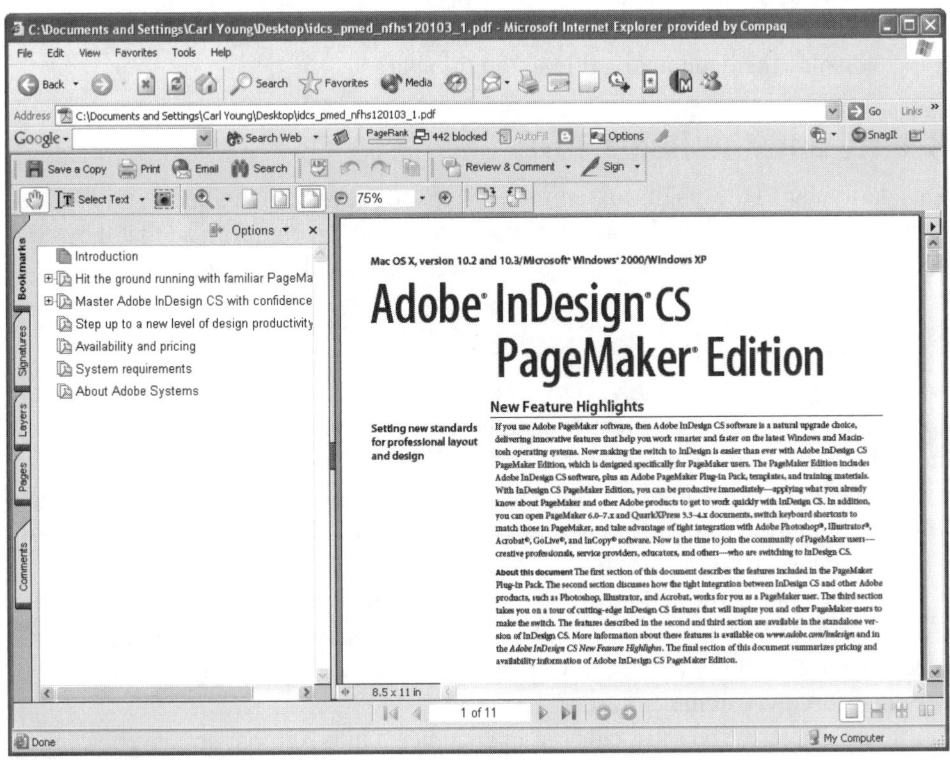

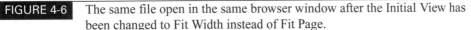

FIGURE 4-6 The same file open in the same browser window after the Initial View has been changed to Fit Width instead of Fit Page.

want to set the Initial View to open to the table of contents, giving the user the choice of bookmarks or the contents page to find the information they are seeking.

Setting the Initial View can be done in some PDF creation tools, but you can always set it from within Acrobat. Use the following procedure to establish a productive opening view for your end user:

1. Choose File | Document Properties (Keyboard shortcut: CTRL-D) | Initial View.
2. In Document Options, enable Show: Bookmarks Panel and Page; set Magnification to Fit Width; and Open to: the page number of the table of contents.

3. In Window Options, enable resize window to Initial Page. This resizes the document window to fit tightly around the page. Change Show: to Title to display the document's title in the title bar.

Beauty and the Beast PDF

This particular PDF was discussed in detail in the preceding chapter. For a PDF to display and print well, make sure the graphics are not so compressed that they do not print well. Be sure to test print your PDF before sending it out.

Searching for Bobby Fischer PDF

A *Searching for Bobby Fischer PDF* is basically a picture of a page wrapped inside a PDF. You can't select any text or search in an image-only PDF. These PDFs are created by scanning paper documents into PDF.

Adobe makes a stand-alone product for turning paper into PDF called Acrobat Capture. *Capture* is designed to work with a high-speed scanner that can zip through a ream of paper in a few minutes.

Adobe includes a scaled-down version of Capture in Professional and Standard. Unlike Acrobat 5, Adobe doesn't put a limit on the number of pages that can be processed in this "lite" version of Capture. However, this lite Capture is definitely designed for low-volume conversion.

To use Capture, you must either scan documents into Acrobat or convert scanned images created by others. To scan a document into Acrobat, use the following procedure:

1. Close all open documents.
2. Click the Create PDF button and choose From Scanner, or File | Create PDF | From Scanner.
3. In the Create PDF from Scanner dialog box, select your scanner, and whether you are scanning a single-sided document or a double-sided document.
4. Choose Open New PDF Document.

5. Turn off Adapt Page Compression to Page Content if your document doesn't have a lot of images.
6. Click Scan.
7. When your scanning software appears, make sure you set a resolution of at least 200, the minimum required by Acrobat. A resolution of 300 is a good starting point. The maximum resolution is 600 dpi, but this setting will result in unacceptably large files. Scanning in black-and-white is by far the most common selection because it produces the smallest files.
8. Start your scanning software.
9. When the Acrobat Scan Plug-In appears, choose either Next to continue scanning or click Done when you are finished.

NOTE *Adobe recommends using Adaptive Compression only on documents with a large number of graphics.*

What you now have is an image wrapped inside an Adobe PDF. Click the Text Select tool and try to select some text (you will not be able to). Try using Search on the document—it won't work. This is the time to put Capture to work.

1. Choose Document | Paper Capture | Start Capture….
2. Accept the settings of Searchable Image (Exact) and Downsampling (none). This format was formerly called Original Image Plus Hidden Text.

NOTE *Searchable Image (Exact) does not apply any compression to the scanned image. Searchable Image (Compact) does apply compression. Whether to use Exact or Compact depends on the number and quality of graphics of the scanned pages. You'll have to test each type to see which is best for you. The Compact setting will produce the smallest file size, but may result in unacceptable image degradation.*

3. Now use the Text Select tool again to select text. You can! You can copy-and-paste the text you select, or even choose File | Save As… | Save as Type | Microsoft Word Document to save the OCR text as a *.doc file. See Figure 4-7 for an example of selected text in a Captured PDF.

Notice that the onscreen image hasn't changed. We've just added a hidden layer of text behind it.

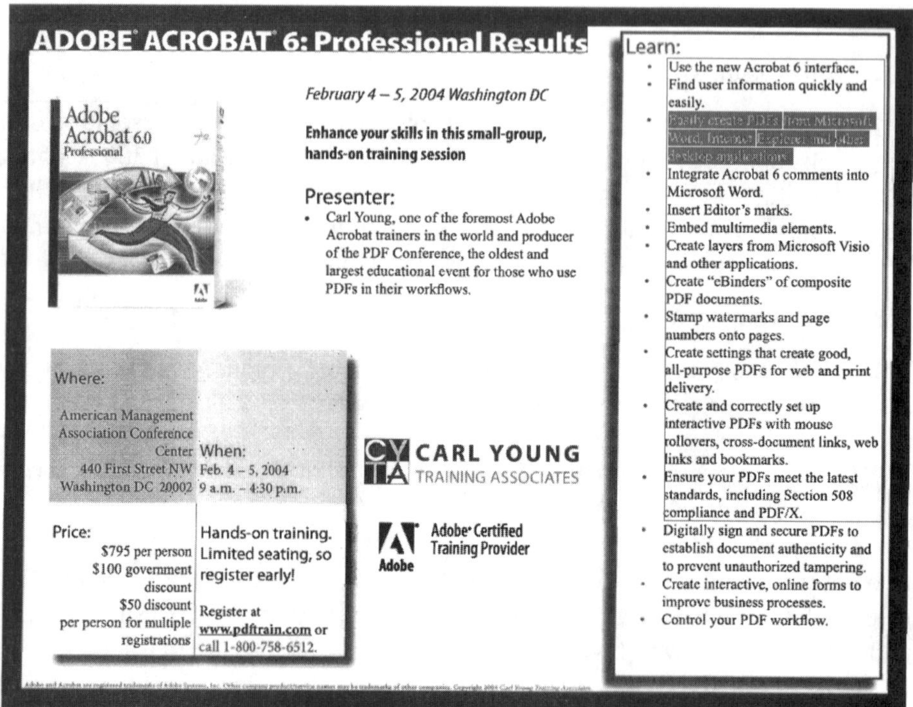

FIGURE 4-7 Paper Capture turns image-only PDFs into documents that can be searched or even repurposed.

NOTE *You can turn a scanned page into a regular PDF by changing the default Capture settings to Formatted Text & Graphics. This option almost always requires manual cleanup with Document | Paper Capture | Find First OCR Suspect, and continuing to clean up Suspect words. This file will not look identical to the original document.*

Nearly everyone I have met who uses Capture chooses the Searchable Image format (previously called Image+Hidden Text). The image you see is an exact replication of the paper document. The text created by Capture is on an invisible layer. Although you cannot see the layer with the text, it can be searched.

Your results with Capture will depend a lot on the quality of the original document. A document written in the 1970s on an IBM Selectric typewriter and photocopied a dozen times since then will produce many errors. The type will have become blurry after being copied so many times, and the OCR engine in Capture will have a difficult time reading the text.

A more modern document with crisp type will produce fewer errors, but some will occur. Even if the OCR is 98 percent accurate, that means 2 of every 100 words will be misspelled. To a human reader, that seems like an unacceptable amount of errors.

By using Searchable Image, you avoid seeing the errors in the OCR. Many organizations like this format because they can be assured that the picture presents the original document. Unlike paper, this kind of electronic document can be searched from a desktop computer.

Are these documents 100 percent searchable? No, because the OCR isn't 100 percent accurate. With care, these kinds of PDFs can be 95 to 98 percent searchable, which is acceptable for many organizations. This is certainly faster than filling out a request form and submitting it to a filing clerk, who then has to hunt through file cabinets to retrieve the correct document.

Whether you use the Capture Plug-in inside Acrobat or the stand-alone version of Capture depends on your needs. The full Capture runs with minimal manual intervention, and is optimized to run on high-powered workstations or servers. The Capture inside Acrobat requires the participation of the user to scan every page.

Alternatives to Capture

As in many cases in the PDF world, alternatives exist to Adobe Acrobat Capture. Some suggestions:

AdLib eDocument Solutions eXpress & OCR creates Image+Hidden Text searchable PDFs from a wide variety of source files, including TIF images from scanned paper documents. See **www.adlibsys.com** for more information.

Image Solutions DocComposer. Creates Image+Hidden Text PDFs from scanned images. Adds bookmarks and page numbers, deskews pages and can remove punch hole marks. See **www.imagesolutions.com** for more information.

Good Examples of Onscreen PDFs

Whether a PDF is a technical manual, a book, a presentation, a catalog, a financial report, or a marketing brochure, it can be a good PDF that avoids the flaws listed in the preceding sections. In the final section of this chapter, you will see some examples of high-quality onscreen PDFs and learn what makes them outstanding examples.

A Financial Report

Adobe produced this example for its 1998 annual report when Acrobat was just starting to take off. Adobe produced two versions of its annual report that year: one was just an electronic copy of its paper annual report and this one, which was produced specifically as an onscreen PDF. See the contents page of the onscreen PDF, as shown in Figure 4-8.

The document was reformatted to landscape orientation to fit onto the screen. Adobe turned off the task buttons and window controls in the Initial View settings of Document Properties, forcing users to use the document's built-in navigation buttons. (Use the F8 key to restore the task buttons and F9 to restore the menus in documents such as this.)

This onscreen PDF is easy to use, and shows how to create a good-looking, useful financial report that takes advantage of being an online document.

An Interactive Brochure

I think the next big area of growth for PDF is going to be in the area of interactive brochures and catalogs. While earlier versions of Acrobat could contain links to movies and sounds, Acrobat 6 enables authors to embed Quicktime, Flash, RealAudio, and other multimedia formats into the PDF.

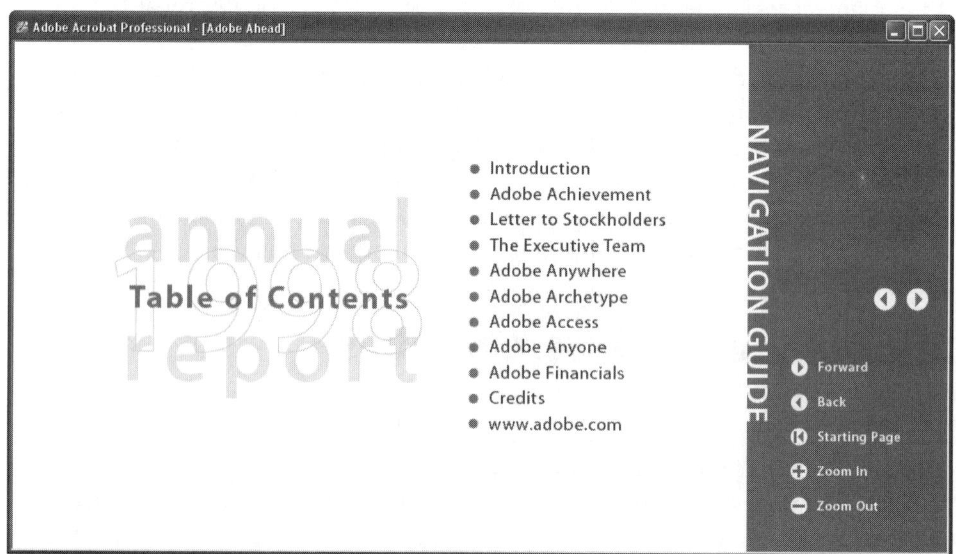

FIGURE 4-8 The annual report has been reformatted to landscape orientation to fit better on a computer monitor.

This makes PDF a multimedia container and simplifies the creation of interactive PDFs. A growing number of businesses and consumers have high-speed Internet access as well, so previous barriers to placing large PDF files with embedded multimedia elements are giving way.

Leading the way into the world of electronic brochures is Bob Connolly of **www.pdfpictures.com**. If you download the samples from the www.pdfpictures .com web site, you will see bright, easy-to-use, and interesting PDFs filled with multimedia elements. For example, the La Cabana brochure about a resort in Aruba, shown in Figure 4-9, opens in Full Screen mode. Simple controls advance the page or play a Quicktime movie.

During his presentation at the November 2003 PDF Conference, Bob explained his process for making electronic brochures for high-end auto manufacturers.

He takes regular, four-color brochures developed in QuarkXPress and reformats the documents for the screen in Adobe InDesign. Navigation buttons and basic page layout elements, such as photos and text, are laid out in InDesign. Bob shoots the Quicktime Virtual Reality (VR) of some auto interiors and adds those as multimedia elements. See Figure 4-10 for an example.

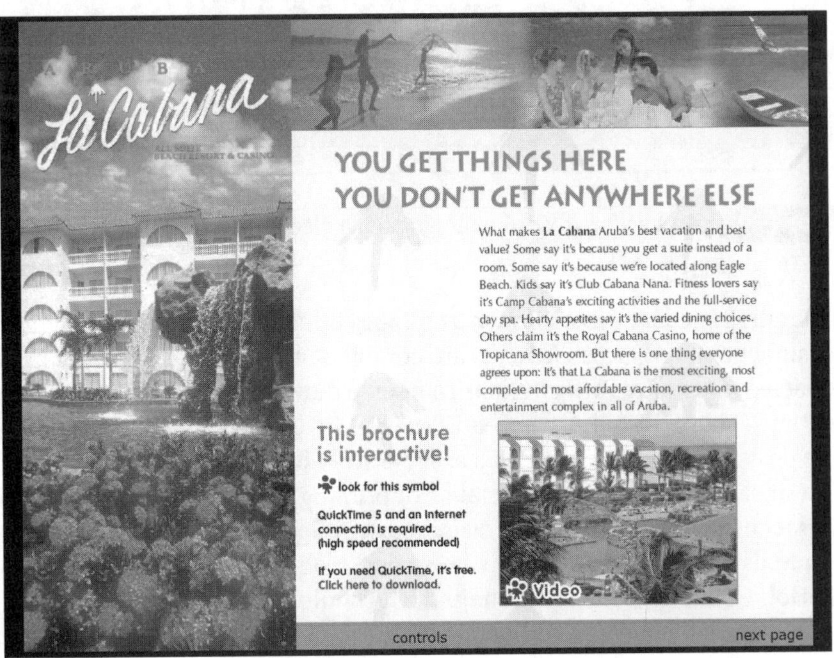

FIGURE 4-9 The leading edge in PDF marketing brochures is shown in this example from PDF Pictures.

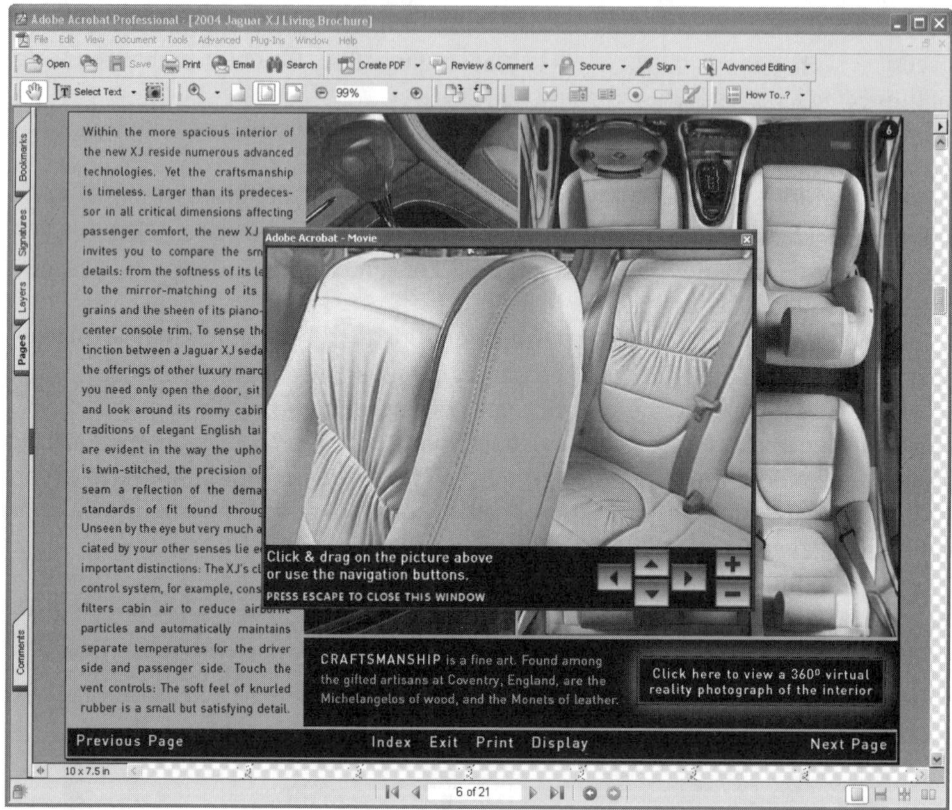

FIGURE 4-10 A Quicktime VR file running in an electronic PDF brochure

Other multimedia elements, such as movies of cars in motion, are supplied by the manufacturer. All these elements are combined into the PDF either in InDesign (see Chapter 15) or after PDF creation. To insert a movie or other multimedia element into a PDF, choose Tools | Advanced Editing | Movie tool.

The costs of these kinds of PDFs are relatively inexpensive when compared to the cost of shooting a TV commercial or of printing tens of thousands of 16-page color brochures. While Bob won't disclose exact figures, the price is well below the hundreds of thousands of dollars needed to produce a TV commercial.

As Bob Connolly is demonstrating, the technology to produce these kinds of PDFs is available today. The biggest hurdle to overcome will be the fear of Madison Avenue advertising agencies, who make millions of dollars from printing commissions.

An Onscreen Book in PDF

The final example is the interactive book *How to Read a Film,* by James Monaco. Shlomo Perets, the technical editor of this book, provided his PDF expertise in producing this book. *How to Read a Film* is not an eBook. eBooks are generally thought of as textual books designed to fit on small screens, such as a Palm Pilot or Pocket PC device. Unlike an eBook, *How to Read a Film* is a regular PDF set up as a series of linked files and is meant to be viewed on a computer screen. See Figure 4-11 for the opening view of the book.

The book's "pages," illustrations, photographs, and movie clips are stored on a DVD. Pages of the PDF document have navigation elements built in for going to the top item, or for going from page to page.

Unlike the printed version of this book, the Acrobat version contains links to the movie clips discussed in the book. For example, if you want to see what a "roll shot" looks like, click a link and you get to see Fred Astaire dance on walls and

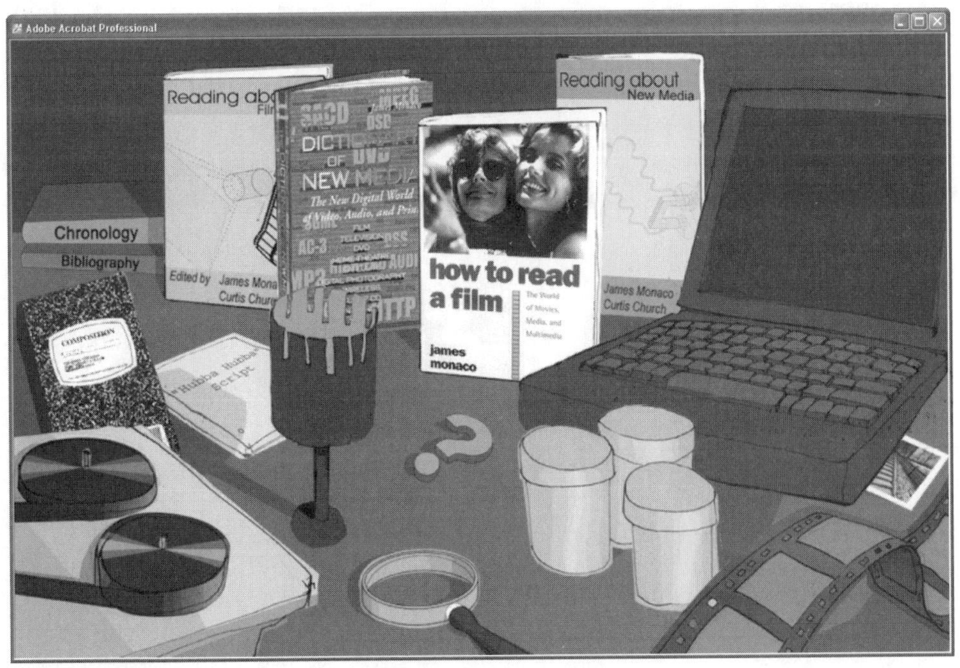

FIGURE 4-11 The opening page of *How to Read a Film* is a graphic with a series of linked hot spots to content inside.

ceilings. All the document are searchable, making the document a wonderful reference.

The movie clips, photos, and illustrations are not unthinking, gratuitous insertions of material just because they can be shown on a computer screen. Each image, either still or moving, is included to help the reader better understand how movies can be "read," just like a book, if you know the right language. Because the language is made up of pictures, seeing those images is vital for understanding. For more information, you can go to the book's web site at **http://readfilm.com**.

Summary

Onscreen PDFs are probably the most common form of PDF in use today. Companies place PDFs on web sites, on CDs, or on DVDs instead of printing manuals or marketing collateral.

A good onscreen PDF is an excellent replacement for a paper document, if the PDF is produced correctly. By avoiding the pitfalls outlined in Chapter 2, you can create a PDF that can be better than the paper document it replaced.

As PDF usage grows, you will begin to see more marketing materials converted to PDF. Acrobat 6 includes the capability to package multimedia elements, such as movies and sound files inside the PDF, something a paper-based, four-color brochure cannot do.

Chapter 5

Making a PDF Everyone Can Read

In many ways, computers are a wonderful gift to people with a visual impairment or a reading disability. Unlike a paper book, computers can read out loud. The voice likely will be harsh and robot-like, but it is still a wonderful advancement for leveling the playing field between those who can read and those who cannot.

In the eyes of the U.S. government, and other governments around the world, making online data accessible to the visually impaired is a civil rights issue. Cataracts, glaucoma, macular degeneration, and other causes create 10 to 11 million blind and visually impaired people in North America, according to the American Foundation for the Blind. This number includes 5.5 million elderly Americans, and 1.5 million computer users.

Section 508 of the Rehabilitation Act of 1988 passed by the U.S. Congress mandates that federal information be accessible to people with disabilities. For the PDF creator, this means making sure information inside your PDF is available to visually disabled persons.

At this point, Section 508 is only being applied to federal executive agencies, but many expect the requirements to be expanded to include state and local governments, and private businesses, as well as voluntary adoption by the legislative and judicial branches. A similar path was taken to reducing architectural barriers in the United States for people with physical impairments. Adding entrance ramps, elevators, and other physical accommodations started with the federal government, and then spread to state and city governments, and, finally, to private businesses through local building codes.

Why It Matters to You

You might know someone like an acquaintance of mine I will call Bob. Bob is a successful businessman, but he has a reading disability. It is so severe that Bob cannot even read street signs. Street numbers are perfectly clear to Bob, but the letters in a street name are just gibberish to him. A computer with screen-reading technology has been a great help to Bob. Now the computer, rather than his secretary, can read Bob's e-mail to him (although it won't help him read street signs yet).

As the world's population ages, so do the cases of macular degeneration. This condition impacts 10 million Americans a year. Macular degeneration is an incurable eye disease that affects the central portion of retina, leading to a loss of sight. It is the leading cause of blindness in those aged 55 or older. Many afflicted with macular degeneration have some sight, but they see at a reduced level. They may be able to see large items on a computer screen, but not small type. Screen magnifiers will assist many of those individuals.

New Accessibility Features in Acrobat 6

Adobe has included many new features to try to improve the creation of PDF files that are accessible. Some of the features are built into Adobe Reader 6, Acrobat Standard, and Acrobat 6 Professional.

New accessibility features in the software include the following:

- Read Out Loud. Choose View | Read Out Loud | Read This Page Only to have Reader and Acrobat 6 recite text in a PDF to you. To change the rate, speed, and pitch of the voice, use the settings in the Reading section of Preferences.

NOTE *Keyboard shortcuts are essential for people who are blind or who have visual disabilities. They often have difficulty directing a mouse. Useful keyboard shortcuts for Read Out Loud are the following:* CTRL-SHIFT-V *(Read this page) and* CTRL-SHIFT-B *(Read entire document).* CTRL-SHIFT-C *(to pause reading).* CTRL-SHIFT-V *or* CTRL-SHIFT-B *(to resume either).* CTRL-SHIFT-E *(Ends the reading.)*

- Automatically Scroll. This moves the text up the screen. Choose View | Automatically Scroll to activate. (The keyboard shortcut is CTRL-SHIFT-H.) Speed and direction are controlled by the up/down arrow keys.
- Support for making Japanese language documents accessible has been upgraded.
- Acrobat 6 will reflow text more easily than previous versions, although tagged PDF is still required. (The keyboard shortcut is CTRL-4.)
- This version integrates better with many of the most popular assistive technology applications, such as MSAA-compliant screen readers.
- An enhanced accessibility checker,
- Documents can be secured, but remain accessible to assistive technology applications.

Why Accessibility Matters in the PDF World

One of PDF's main attractions is this: it can present information in a visually complex and compelling fashion. Unfortunately for those who rely on assistive technology, visually complex documents are often the toughest to understand.

Adobe has recognized the needs of the visually impaired community to be able to navigate through complex PDFs and has created an internal structure called Tagged PDF. Among other things, *Tagged PDF* tells screen readers something about each element on a page, such as the graphics, number of columns, and the locations of headlines.

Most of the assistive technology available today works with Tagged PDF. For the purposes of PDF creators, the technology falls into three categories: screen readers, which read text and menus out loud; text to speech synthesizers (TTS), which read the text in a PDF file, but do not verbalize menus and dialogues; and screen magnifiers, which enlarge text.

You can tell if a document is a Tagged PDF by looking at the Description in Document Properties (File | Document Properties | Description). In the PDF Information Section, you will see an item that says Tagged PDF. Tagged PDF: Yes means the PDF contains Tagged PDF structure, as shown in Figure 5-1. Another simple test is to open the tags palette and check for the presence of a tags tree.

For example, think of a photograph of a man and child sitting at a table that appears in a PDF. What does the screen reader say about that?

With Tagged PDF, you can include text describing the contents of the photograph that the screen reader can recite. This is just like the text that you might see on a web page before an image loads. Think of alternate text as an audio caption. Text describing a graphic is known as alt text, or alternate text. *Alt text* is vocalized by screen readers or the Read Out Loud feature in Acrobat and Reader.

Acrobat Standard and Professional and Adobe Reader include a feature called Read Out Loud (View | Read Out Loud) (The keyboard shortcut is CTRL-SHIFT-V or CTRL-SHIFT-B) that can read a single page or an entire document. Users do not have to buy screen-reading software to take advantage of this feature, which works on both Windows and Mac OS X.

It is not sufficient to simply provide alternate text for graphics. Most accessibility standards require meaningful alternate text descriptions. For this reason, providing adequate alternative text can be challenging, especially if the graphic presents complex information. For example, a detailed graph showing hundreds of plot points cannot realistically be fully reproduced as alternative text. Instead, a description of the main points would be helpful to the visually impaired.

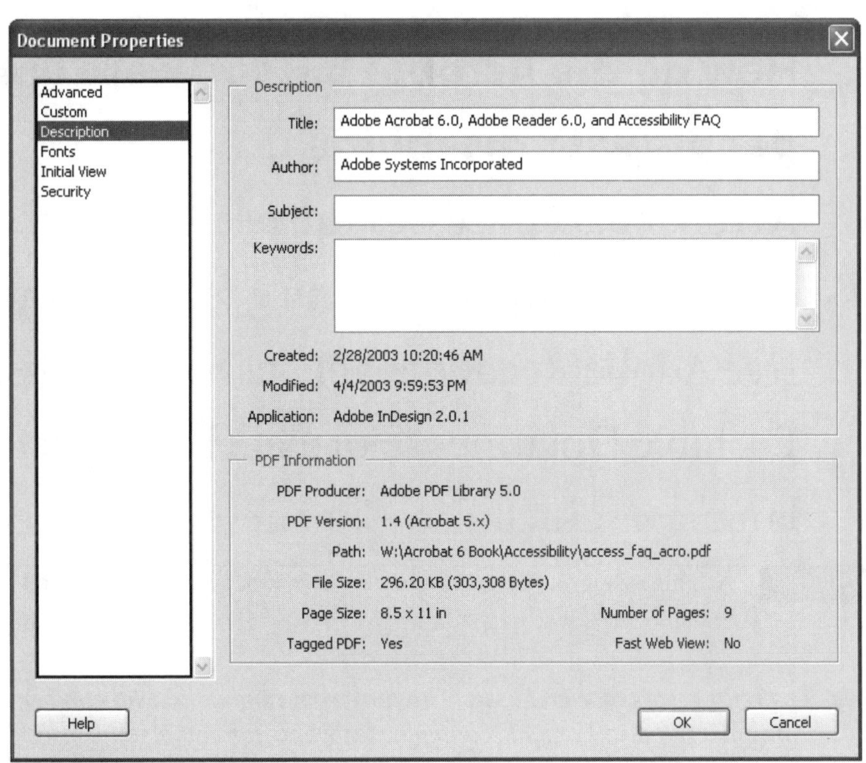

FIGURE 5-1 Whether or not a file is a Tagged PDF is shown in the document description.

Now consider a two-column document. How does the screen-reading application know where Column 1 ends and Column 2 begins? Tagged PDF explains the structure of the document to the screen-reading application in a process known as *logical reading order.*

Tagged PDF also enables text reflow. In a Tagged PDF, the end user can zoom in to a high level, such as 400 percent. Screen magnifying software works in a similar fashion. However, at a 400 percent zoom setting, the user has to scroll left and right to read a single paragraph. See Figure 5-2 for an example.

By choosing View | Reflow (CTRL-4) in Acrobat or Adobe Reader, Tagged PDF will reflow the text to fit onto the screen and the text will wrap. No longer will a visually impaired person have to constantly scroll left and right to read a page. See Figure 5-3 for an example of text that has been reflowed.

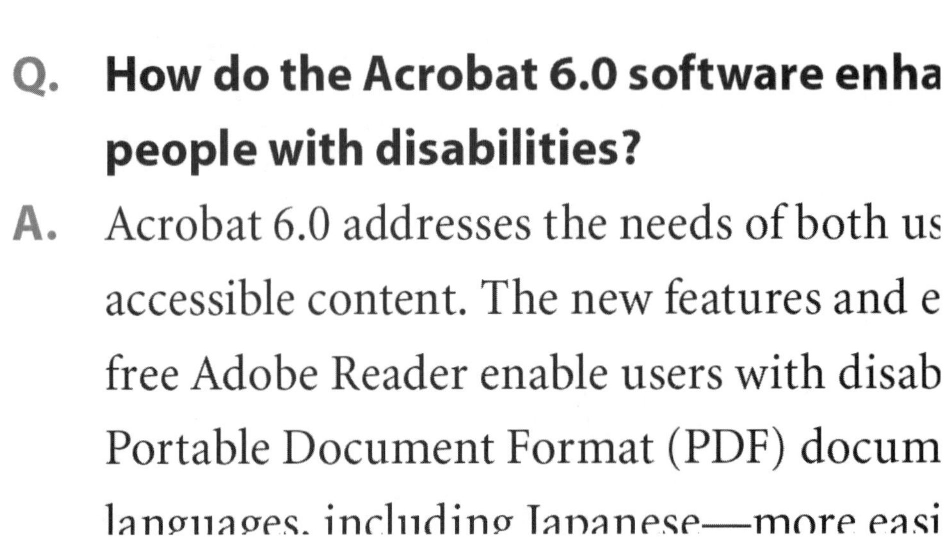

Q. How do the Acrobat 6.0 software enha
people with disabilities?

A. Acrobat 6.0 addresses the needs of both us
accessible content. The new features and e
free Adobe Reader enable users with disab
Portable Document Format (PDF) docum
languages, including Japanese—more easi

FIGURE 5-2 At a high-zoom level, text can be easy to see, but users have to scroll left to right to read it.

NOTE *Text reflow works for end users who have some sight, but who can benefit from enlarged text. Logical reading order works for completely unsighted end users who rely on assistive technology to read text aloud. Both make use of Tagged PDF.*

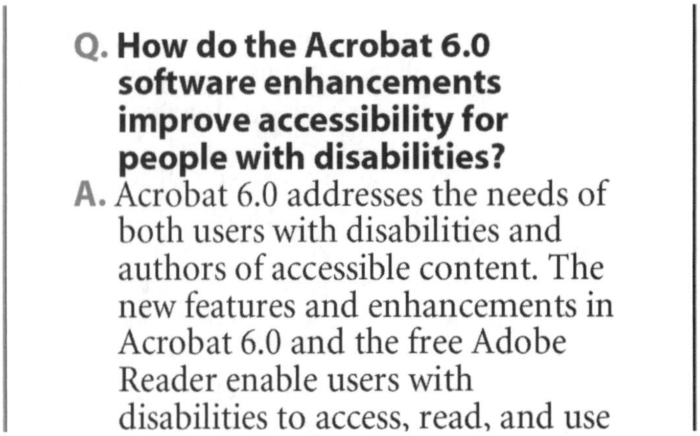

Q. How do the Acrobat 6.0 software enhancements improve accessibility for people with disabilities?

A. Acrobat 6.0 addresses the needs of both users with disabilities and authors of accessible content. The new features and enhancements in Acrobat 6.0 and the free Adobe Reader enable users with disabilities to access, read, and use

FIGURE 5-3 Text reflowed to fit on the screen at a high-zoom level.

General Considerations

Preparing documents to be decoded by screen-reading software is a relatively new requirement. Few organizations or individuals have much expertise in the area, and most tools are still in the early stages of development.

While each application has its specific method for producing Tagged PDF, every author should consider some common considerations. Sighted end users can scan a complex graphic and pick out the details important to them. Visually impaired ones cannot, and they may rely entirely on a screen reader to tell them about the graphic.

When designing for accessibility, keep these points in mind:

- Simple, one-column designs are easier to make accessible than multicolumn ones. Newsletters and magazines with multiple stories sharing space on the same page and continuing on different pages may be especially difficult to make accessible.
- Text elements such as headlines, subheads, and text should be logically organized.
- Every paragraph in a document should be consistently formatted with a style. In most cases, the logical use of styles will be transformed into a hierarchy when the application produces a tagged PDF.
- PDF Bookmarks, which are like an interactive table of contents, will help users navigate quickly to the information they are looking for.
- PDFs created from scanned paper documents should contain searchable text, and should not be in an image-only format. See Chapter 4 for more information on using Paper Capture to transform scanned images to searchable text.
- Graphics, such as photographs, illustrations, logos, maps, charts, and graphs should contain alternative text that can be read aloud to a visually impaired end user.
- Acrobat form fields should contain a description in the field's Tooltip section. For Form fields created in Adobe Designer, enter the text in Object Properties | Help | Accessibility | Speak Text.

An Illustration of the Problem

To help you, as a PDF creator, understand the needs of those who use assistive technology, let's examine how well the Acrobat 6 Accessibility Frequently Asked Questions document performs as an accessible PDF. You can download this file from **http://access.adobe.com**, or **http://www.adobe.com/products/acrobat/access_faq.html**. An example is shown in Figure 5-4.

The accessible FAQ is simpler than many documents, but it is still relatively complex. One column of main text is below the headline, and table of contents entries are below a subhead in a second column. You could even say this is a three-column document if you consider how the *Q* and *A* are floating in a sidehead alignment with the text.

This document is a Tagged PDF, as shown in Figure 5-1. Here is the reading order I hear when I choose View | Read Out Loud | Read This Page Only:

1. The main headline.
2. The first question or, perhaps, the first item in the table of contents.

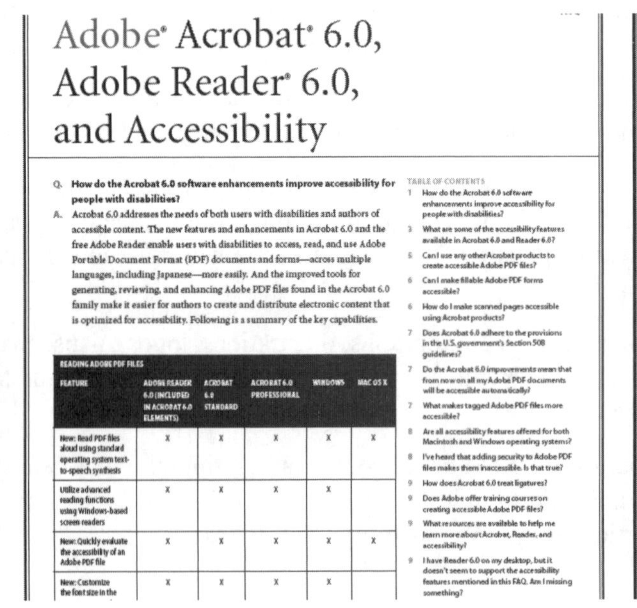

Adobe® Acrobat® 6.0, Adobe Reader® 6.0, and Accessibility

Q. **How do the Acrobat 6.0 software enhancements improve accessibility for people with disabilities?**

A. Acrobat 6.0 addresses the needs of both users with disabilities and authors of accessible content. The new features and enhancements in Acrobat 6.0 and the free Adobe Reader enable users with disabilities to access, read, and use Adobe Portable Document Format (PDF) documents and forms—across multiple languages, including Japanese—more easily. And the improved tools for generating, reviewing, and enhancing Adobe PDF files found in the Acrobat 6.0 family make it easier for authors to create and distribute electronic content that is optimized for accessibility. Following is a summary of the key capabilities.

READING ADOBE PDF FILES

FEATURE	ADOBE READER 6.0 (INCLUDED IN ACROBAT 6.0 ELEMENTS)	ACROBAT 6.0 STANDARD	ACROBAT 6.0 PROFESSIONAL	WINDOWS	MAC OS X
New: Read PDF files aloud using standard operating system text-to-speech synthesis	X	X	X	X	X
Utilize advanced reading functions using Windows-based screen readers	X	X	X	X	
New: Quickly evaluate the accessibility of an Adobe PDF file	X	X	X	X	X
New: Customize the font size in the	X	X	X	X	

TABLE OF CONTENTS

1 How do the Acrobat 6.0 software enhancements improve accessibility for people with disabilities?
3 What are some of the accessibility features available in Acrobat 6.0 and Reader 6.0?
5 Can I use any other Acrobat products to create accessible Adobe PDF files?
6 Can I make fillable Adobe PDF forms accessible?
6 How do I make scanned pages accessible using Acrobat products?
7 Does Acrobat 6.0 adhere to the provisions in the U.S. government's Section 508 guidelines?
7 Do the Acrobat 6.0 improvements mean that from now on all my Adobe PDF documents will be accessible automatically?
7 What makes tagged Adobe PDF files more accessible?
8 Are all accessibility features offered for both Macintosh and Windows operating systems?
8 I've heard that adding security to Adobe PDF files makes them inaccessible. Is that true?
9 How does Acrobat 6.0 treat ligatures?
9 Does Adobe offer training courses on creating accessible Adobe PDF files?
9 What resources are available to help me learn more about Acrobat, Reader, and accessibility?
9 I have Reader 6.0 on my desktop, but it doesn't seem to support the accessibility features mentioned in this FAQ. Am I missing something?

FIGURE 5-4 The first page of the Adobe Acrobat 6 Accessibility FAQ is a two-column document with a table.

3. The item numbered three in the table of contents.
4. The rest of the items in the table of contents.
5. The answer to the question.
6. The table heading row.
7. Each table row. Marked items in the table are pronounced as *X*.

Not read are the FAQ label, the subhead over the table of contents, and the first entry in the TOC. What went wrong? Although this document is Tagged PDF, it is improperly tagged. Fixing the tags is possible, but creating a good Tagged PDF at the time of creation is much easier. Fixing the tags after creation can take hours or days. Creating proper tags at the time of creation takes a little preparation and the click of a button, depending on the capabilities of the application.

NOTE *I am not singling out Adobe for ridicule. Many federal government documents on accessibility are not accessible, either. The reason is this is a new area, and the tools are relatively new. Making accessible documents will improve as the creation tools mature and users become more expert at meeting accessibility standards.*

Creating a Tagged PDF

Tagged PDF is easiest to produce within the authoring application. And the best applications to produce Tagged PDF are Microsoft Word, Adobe FrameMaker 7.0 and higher, Adobe PageMaker 6.5 and higher, Adobe InDesign 2.0 and higher, and forms produced in Adobe Acrobat Professional and Adobe Form Designer.

Microsoft Word

In this section, you will learn how to prepare Word documents for output to Tagged PDF.

Because it is so widely used in private businesses and government, more PDFs are probably created from Word than anything else. Fortunately, Adobe has made great strides in making it easy to create Tagged PDFs from Word 2000/XP/2003 with PDFMaker. For details on creating PDFs from Word, see Chapter 6.

To make a Tagged PDF, be sure to use Word's capability to produce PDF bookmarks and links. In addition, you should use good word-processing techniques, such as formatting headings with styles, creating tables with Word's table tool (not using tabs and spaces), and creating columns with Word's column toolbar. Using all these techniques will lead to the production of better PDFs for everyone, including the visually impaired.

If you follow the recommendations in Chapter 5 for creating an onscreen PDF, then adding alternative text to graphics is the only additional step you need to take in Word.

Word Graphics

Graphics can be placed into Word documents in a variety of ways, but the only method that works well with accessibility is to place images as an inline graphic.

NOTE *When you insert a graphic into Word, remember that a screen reader will read a description of the graphic at the point of insertion. For that reason, be sure to insert graphics in a logical place in the text.*

To place an inline graphic into Word, choose Insert | Picture | From File. Keep the following points in mind when placing graphics in Word:

- Don't add callouts or captions in Word floating boxes. Text in floating boxes is read after other elements on a page, or it may be skipped altogether. Add callouts in a graphics application, where they will be converted to a graphic and skipped. Then be sure to add alternate text for the graphic.
- Insert graphics into the main flow text, not into floating boxes.
- Avoid placing watermarks on pages. Watermarks also go into floating boxes.

After a graphic is inserted, you must add alternative text that can be read to the visually impaired user. To add alternative text, select the graphic, right-click and choose Format Picture. Next, click the Web tab, and then add alternative text, as shown in Figure 5-5.

Choose Adobe PDF | Change Conversion Settings | Settings. As shown in Figure 5-6, turn on the Enable accessibility and reflow with Tagged PDF option before creating the PDF.

Once the Word document is prepared, use PDFMaker to create the Word file. Be sure to test before deploying the document.

Adobe Applications

Because of Adobe's focus on creating PDFs that are accessible, several of its tools are well-suited for creating Tagged PDF. As in the case of Microsoft Word,

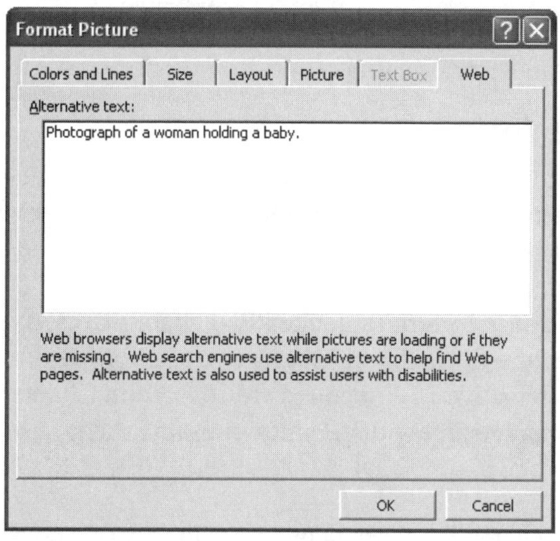

FIGURE 5-5 Alternative text for graphics in Word is placed into the Web tab of the Format Picture dialog box.

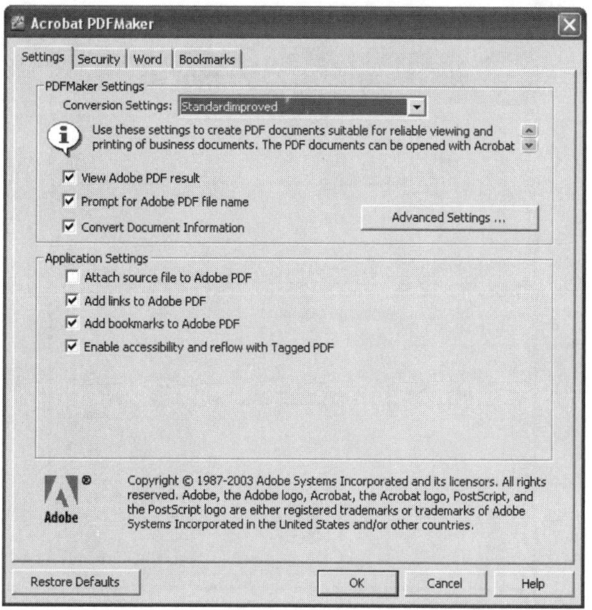

FIGURE 5-6 An accessible PDF is created in Word by using the Adobe PDF menu.

creating good online PDFs by using styles, bookmarks, and hyperlinks—helpful for all kinds of users—will go a long way toward making your PDFs accessible. See Chapter 15 for more information.

Adobe FrameMaker

Adobe FrameMaker is a tool designed for long document production, such as books, technical manuals, and reference materials. For more on FrameMaker, see *FrameMaker 7: The Complete Reference* by Sarah O'Keefe and Sheila Loring at **www.osborne.com**.

FrameMaker 7 and 7.1 produce Tagged PDF, bookmarks, hyperlinks, web links, and a new feature for including alternative text for graphics. Producing Tagged PDF and interactive PDF features are covered in Chapter 15.

To include alternative text with graphics in FrameMaker, use the following procedure:

1. Select the anchored frame containing the graphic. (Do not select the graphic!)
2. Choose Graphics | Object Properties | Object Attributes.
3. Enter the text to be read by the screen reader in the Text Attributes: Alternate dialog box, as shown in Figure 5-7.

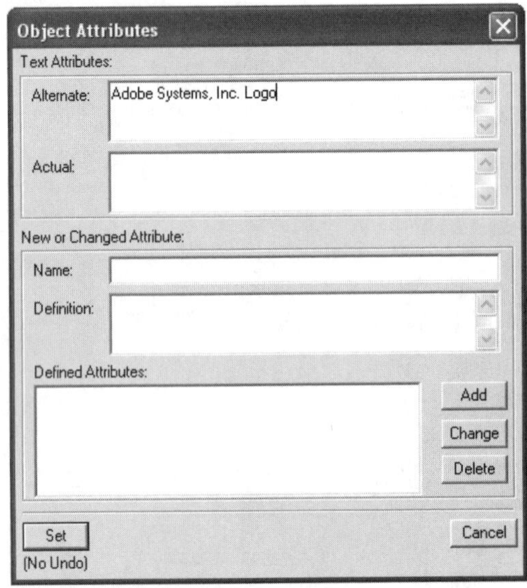

FIGURE 5-7 Object Attributes in Adobe FrameMaker 7 contains a dialog box for alternative text.

4. Click Set and Set again.
5. Choose Format | Document | PDF Setup.
6. In PDF Setup, click the Tags tab.
7. Enable Generate Tagged PDF and set up a logical structure level of the paragraph tags, as shown in Figure 5-8. Click Set and finish the PDF creation by printing to the Adobe PDF printer, or by choosing File | Save As | PDF.

Adobe InDesign

Adobe InDesign CS also contains features for creating interactive PDFs, many of which can benefit sighted and unsighted users. Like Adobe FrameMaker, InDesign CS has the capability to map styles to PDF tags. To add tags, choose View | Structure | Show Structure. Then choose Window | Tags to display the Tags palette.

If your document doesn't include any structure, choose Structure | Add Untagged Items from the Structure window. If your document consistently uses InDesign styles for formatting paragraphs, most of your styles will be mapped in logical order. An example is shown in Figure 5-9.

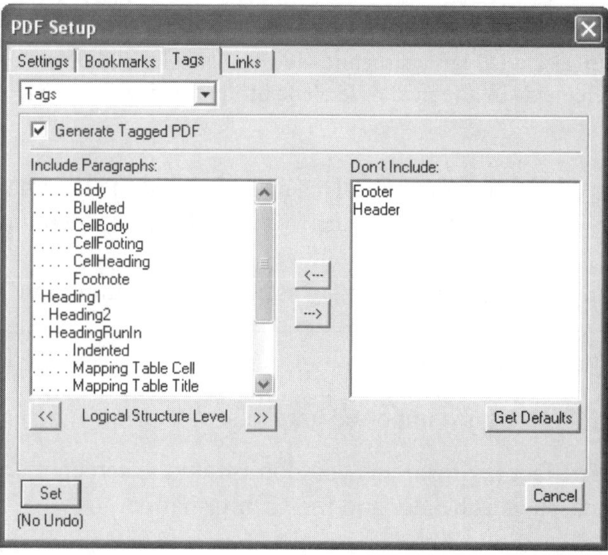

FIGURE 5-8 Adobe FrameMaker can create Tagged PDF based on the paragraph tags used in the publication.

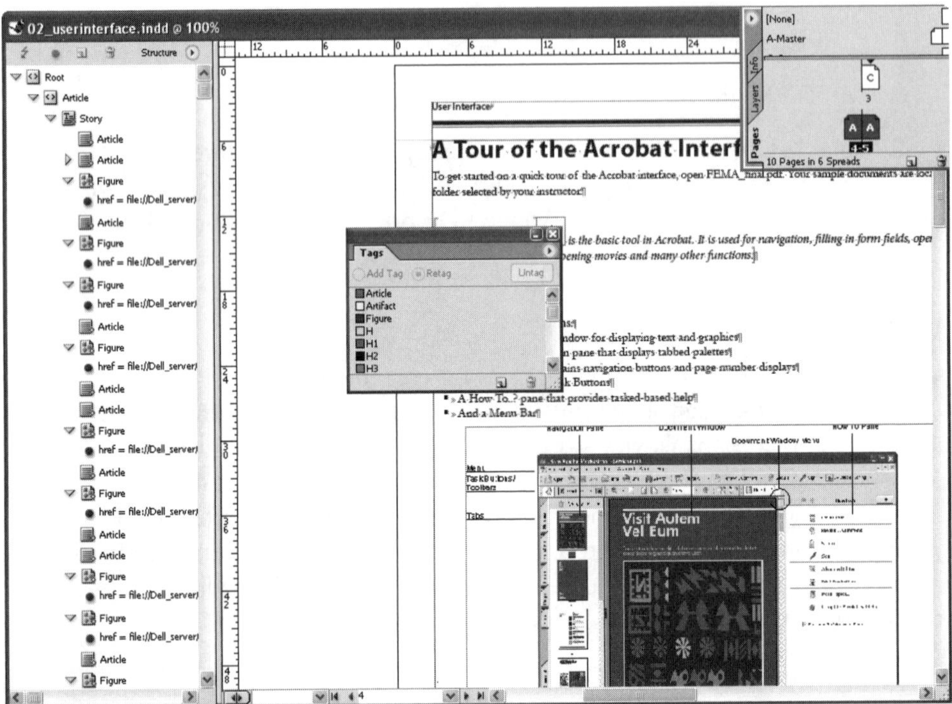

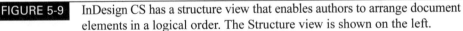

FIGURE 5-9 InDesign CS has a structure view that enables authors to arrange document elements in a logical order. The Structure view is shown on the left.

Use the Tags palette to map any InDesign styles that the automatic assignment missed. You can change tag assignments from the Structure menu in the Structure window.

Adobe recommends the following tag assignments in InDesign:

1. Use the Story tag for text in frames.
2. Use the Figure tag for imported graphics.
3. Use the Artifact tag for items you don't want the screen reader to pronounce, such as header and footer information.

You will also need to add alternative text to graphics. Use the following steps in Structure View to add alternative text:

1. Select the image.
2. Make sure it is tagged as a figure. If not, apply the Figure tag.
3. Choose New Attribute from the Structure View menu.
4. In the New Attribute dialog box, enter **Alt** for the name, and then enter the description in the Value field.

When the process is complete, export the document as a PDF. Be sure to enable eBook Tags in the PDF export options to generate tagged PDF.

Editing Tags

You may have existing PDFs that are not accessible. You can add tags to those documents, but it is a tedious process. You should set aside adequate time for this process, which can take hours or days, depending on the length and complexity of the document.

To begin, run the Accessibility checker in Acrobat 6 Professional. Choose Advanced | Accessibility | Full Check. If the report shows the document lacks tags, add them with Advanced | Accessibility | Add Tags to Document.

This process may make the text available to screen readers and enable text reflow, but you still must add alternative text to graphics. Use the following procedure to add alternative text:

1. Choose View | Navigation Tabs | Tags to display the Tags palette.
2. Expand the structure tree and select a Figure element.
3. In the Tags palette, choose Options | Highlight Content to show the relationship between the tags and the elements in the document.
4. Choose Options | Properties and select the Tag tab in the TouchUp Properties dialog box.
5. Enter a description of the graphic in the Alternate Text field.
6. Choose English from the Language pull-down menu. Click Close.

Testing

After you have created, or fixed, a PDF, you should test for accessibility. Use the following items as a check list to test for accessibility.

- Use the Tags palette to check the order of items in the document. Use the Highlight Content option to help you understand the order of documents.
- Run the Accessibility checker to look for problems.
- Use the Read Out Loud feature to listen for any errors.
- Reflow the document to see how the elements in the document are ordered.
- Save the document as accessible text. Choose File | Save As | Save As Type | Accessible Text. Open the text file and look at the order of information in the document.
- If possible, test the PDF with accessibility software.

Summary

Making PDFs (and other online information sources) accessible to the visually impaired is a new, and growing, requirement for many organizations. The U.S. government, through Section 508 of the Rehabilitation Act, mandates that, among other things, content distributed on government web sites be accessible to as many citizens as possible, including the visually impaired.

Adobe Acrobat 6 Standard and Professional, and Adobe Reader provide new tools for the visually impaired. The Read Out Loud, Text Reflow, and Automatically Scroll features make hearing and viewing PDFs easier.

Document authors have a large role to play in creating accessible PDFs. By including interactive features, such as bookmarks and hypertext links, authors can make PDFs easier to use. In addition, authoring applications can create Tagged PDF that includes structure information that guides assistive technology through a PDF.

Creating accessible PDFs is at a relatively early stage. As tools and techniques mature, it will become easier to create PDFs that are accessible.

Part II

In Business with Acrobat

Chapter 6

Putting Acrobat to Work

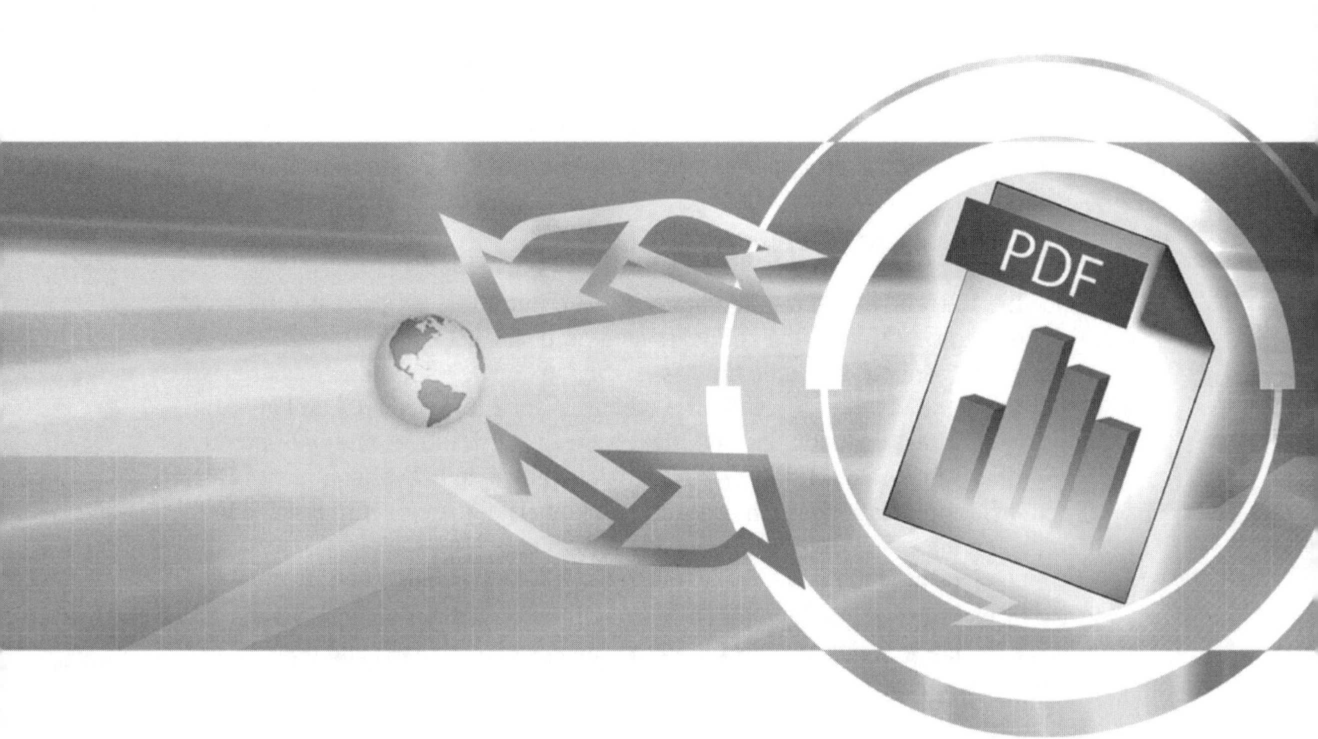

Because Adobe is known for its high-end publishing applications, there is some perception that Acrobat is only for creative people, such as graphic artists. This is simply not the case. Most users, according to Adobe, are the wide spectrum of office workers who use Acrobat for publishing electronic documents. These end users work almost exclusively on Windows-based computers.

These workers are not trained in font selection, design, or the nuances of high-end color printing. They just want to press a button to produce a PDF that looks exactly like the Microsoft Word, Excel, or PowerPoint file they are working in.

Adobe has done much to accommodate these workers. There are PDFMaker buttons in applications that cover nearly the entire working world in business and government: Word, Excel, PowerPoint, Outlook, Internet Explorer, Visio, and Project.

Adobe also has begun to branch out from integrating only with Microsoft products to including PDFMaker functionality in CAD (Computer Aided Design) applications. Acrobat 6 includes a PDFMaker for several AutoDesk AutoCAD products. Plans are underway for Bentley Software to integrate Adobe PDF technology into Bentley MicroStation desktop and ProjectWise server products.

All you have to do is click the button and out pops a PDF. But is it a good PDF? Does it look like the original document or has the text reflowed in Word? Do the graphics in PowerPoint look ugly? How do you create layers in Visio? Will my web browser allow me to view PDFs online?

Most of the time everything works fine. But regular problems often come up that can easily be solved with a little attention to certain details, which we cover in this chapter. First, let's take a look at which version of Acrobat is compatible with what application.

Matching Acrobat to Office

Adobe has diligently tried to integrate Acrobat 6 into the most current versions of Microsoft Office. Office 2003 and its related products, such as Visio and Project, were shipped at about the same time as Acrobat 6.0. The 6.0 product releases were not fully integrated with Office 2003 products. Adobe released an Acrobat 6.01 update late in 2003 that includes PDFMakers for the Office 2003 family of products.

Acrobat 6 integrates with Office in two general ways. PDFMaker buttons are placed inside applications, such as Word and PowerPoint. As is discussed later in this chapter, these buttons provide one-click PDF creation.

To enhance the online viewing experience, Adobe has integrated Acrobat with various web browsers, including non-Microsoft ones. The following sections detail Adobe's integration with various Office versions, web browsers, and non-Microsoft products.

Acrobat Integration with Other Applications

Adobe supports PDF creation in the following Windows applications:

Acrobat 6 Version	Application
Standard, Professional, Elements	Microsoft Word, Excel, PowerPoint 97, 2000, XP, and 2003
Standard, Professional	Internet Explorer (Web Capture)
Standard, Professional	Microsoft Outlook e-mail attachments 97, 2000, XP, and 2003
Professional	Layers from Microsoft Visio and Project 2000, XP, and 2003; Autodesk AutoCAD 2000–2004

Viewing PDFs Inside Web Browsers

The online experience is better for the end user if a PDF is displayed inside a web browser. End users can fill out forms online, read, and navigate through long documents, and save a PDF locally or print the file.

NOTE *PDF viewing inside web browsers is supported only in Windows. Adobe promises to support Safari for Mac users when Apple releases a shipping version.*

The following list shows which browsers support viewing PDFs from within the browser.

- Internet Explorer 5.01, 5.5, 6.0, or 6.1
- Netscape Navigator 7.0
- America On Line 6.0, 7.0, or 8.0

Web Capture from Microsoft Internet Explorer

New in version 6 of Acrobat is a PDFMaker button in the Microsoft Internet Explorer 6 toolbar. This Web capture feature also is available from the File | Create PDF | From Web Page, or from the Create PDF button in the toolbar.

Web capture includes web links, form fields, Flash animations, and text and graphics. When you use Web capture, Acrobat reformats web pages to 8.5-inch by 11-inch pages (or other page sizes, if you prefer), so they are easily printable.

Animated GIF files and rotating banners are not supported, however. These elements are displayed as they appeared at the moment the Web capture was performed.

Acrobat 6 Professional also inserts a PDFMaker button into Internet Explorer (Windows only) for one-click Web capture, as shown in Figure 6-1.

The newly created PDF takes its name from the <Title> tag from each web page. You can use the Edit | Preferences Web Capture settings to specify whether linked pages are converted to PDFs or open in a web browser.

TIP *Have you ever been frustrated by trying to give directions to a web designer? Because browsers reformat pages based on individual preferences, trying to explain where you would like changes to be made can be confusing. Acrobat can simplify and clarify the process of updating web pages. Use Web capture to convert the web pages in question to PDF. Then use Acrobat's markup tools to specify the requested changes. Web capture is a great way to archive web sites. Web capture packages text and graphics into a single file, simplifying the often complex job of maintaining multiple web pages and folders stuffed full of graphics.*

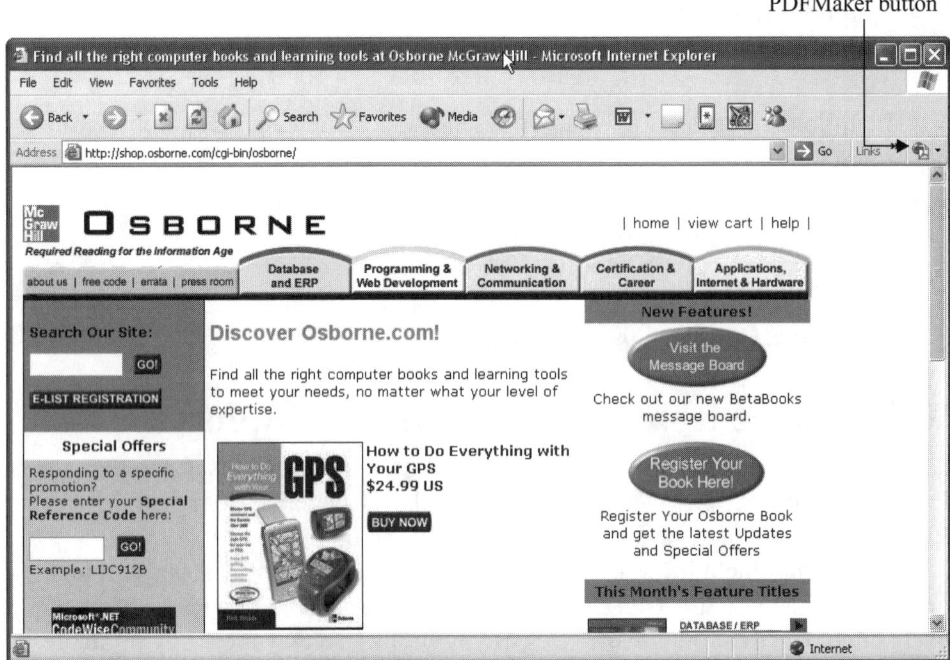

FIGURE 6-1 Acrobat 6 Professional make one-click creation of PDF web pages easy from Windows Internet Explorer.

The Adobe PDF Explorer Bar displays PDFs on local and network drives. You can move, delete, or rename PDFs from the Explorer Bar.

Microsoft Outlook Integration

Although I don't recommend this method, you can convert a document to a PDF and e-mail it in one step from Microsoft Outlook, as shown in Figure 6-2. My recommendation is that you convert the file to a PDF, and look it over before sending it.

This feature only appears when you choose New | Mail Message. Click the Attach as Adobe PDF button. You can then select an existing PDF, or convert a graphic or Office document into a PDF.

What About Microsoft Publisher?

You may notice that Microsoft Publisher is not on the list of applications with PDFMakers. Let's see—Adobe makes competing page layout programs called InDesign and FrameMaker, which are fully integrated with Acrobat. Is there any connection? Mum's the word from Adobe on this issue, but I wouldn't expect a PDFMaker in Publisher any time soon.

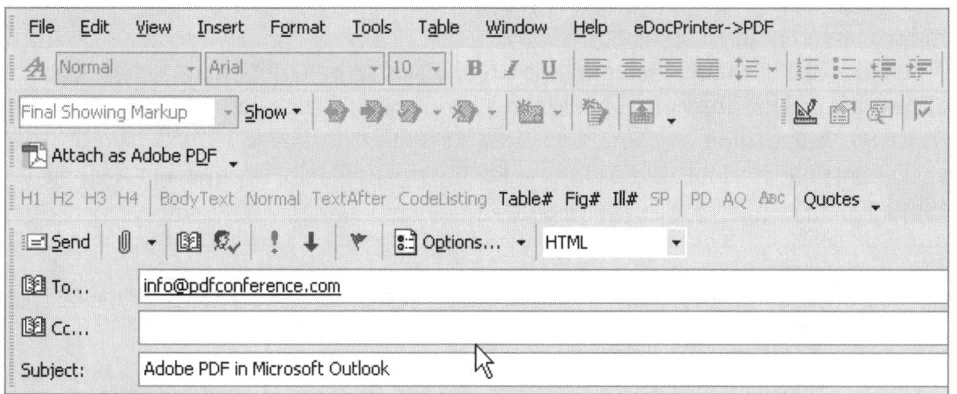

FIGURE 6-2 You can use the Attach as Adobe PDF button in Microsoft Outlook (middle left of screen) to convert Word and other files to PDF for e-mailing.

If you are a Publisher user, you can create a PDF by choosing File | Print | Adobe PDF. Be sure to use one of the PDF/X output options if you are sending a job out for printing. I've seen printers reject PDFs from Publisher just because they have an anti-Microsoft prejudice. If you send them a PDF/X1-a compliant file, they have little reason to turn your file (and your business) away. See Chapter 18 for more information on PDF/X and color printing.

If your Publisher PDF is headed for the Web, and you would like bookmarks and hyperlinks, you have to add those by hand or turn to a non-Adobe solution. Compose, FinePrint, or other applications that create bookmarks from formatting styles can automate your PDF production from Publisher. See Chapter 4 for more information on making usable online PDFs.

Microsoft Office Applications

In today's business world, the Microsoft Office suite of applications and, particularly, Microsoft Word, are the most frequently seen applications on the desktop. Adobe has tried to tightly integrate Acrobat into Office applications, especially Word, Excel, and PowerPoint. For the most part, this integration works well. However, many substandard PDFs are created from Word—primarily because the Word authors are not taking advantage of the automation available to them.

Acrobat 6 is most highly integrated with Word XP and 2003. In those applications, workgroups can import and export Acrobat comments during the review and markup phase of a document's life. (For more information on review and commenting in Acrobat, see Chapter 7.)

Online PDF creation, including the automatic insertion of hyperlinks into tables of contents and the creation of bookmarks, works with Office versions going back to Office 97. Automation is accomplished via a set of macros called *PDFMaker.* A new menu item called Adobe PDF is inserted to the right of Help, as shown in Figure 6-3.

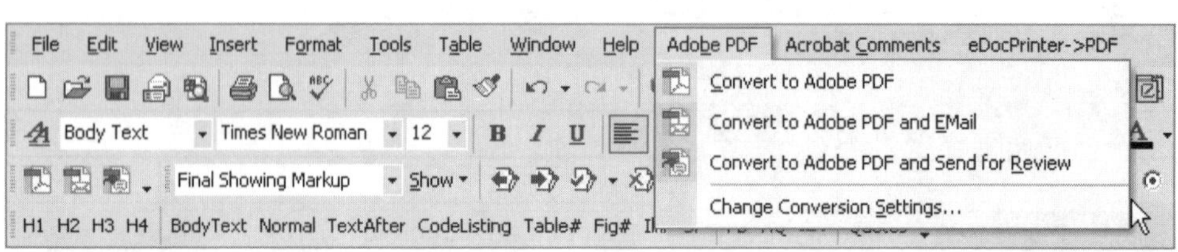

FIGURE 6-3 Acrobat 6 Standard and Professional insert an Adobe PDF menu item into Microsoft Word.

When PDFMaker is installed, you will see an Acrobat menu to the right of the Help menu. In addition, three small Acrobat buttons will be added to the toolbar. (Word XP and 2003 users get an additional menu called Acrobat Comments.)

Enable Tagged PDF for Accessibility in Word

In Microsoft Word, PDFMaker automatically creates bookmarks and links based on the styles used by the Word author. PDFMaker also must be used to create PDF documents from Word that are accessible and Section 508-compliant, as shown in Figure 6-4. (For more on accessibility and Section 508 compliance, see Chapter 5.)

In addition to making an online PDF accessible to the visually impaired, a tagged PDF can be more easily repurposed than one that is not tagged. However, tagged PDF will make your PDFs larger, and it isn't necessary if you do not need to make your documents accessible. Choose Adobe PDF | Change Conversion Settings | Enable accessibility and text reflow with Tagged PDF to automatically create tagged PDFs.

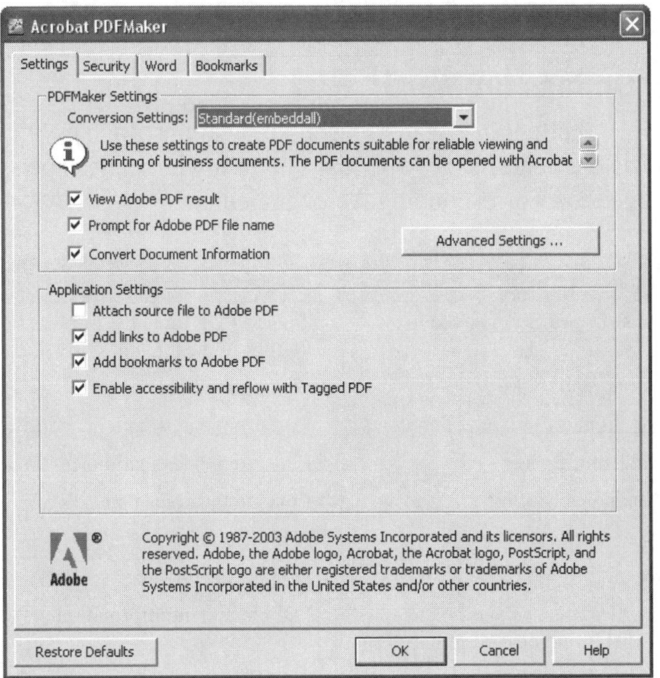

FIGURE 6-4 The *Enable accessibility and reflow with Tagged PDF* option should be checked to make PDFs accessible to visually impaired individuals.

Setting Up PDFMaker for Microsoft Word

Adobe has made it simple to create PDFs from Microsoft Word. In general, the process is quick:

1. Choose Adobe PDF | Change Conversion Settings.
2. In the Settings tab, select your preferred settings.
3. Specify any security or other options.
4. Click OK.

What could be simpler? What can go wrong with such an easy-to-use process? A lot. Although many users blame Acrobat, in my experience most of the problems occur in Word, and they occur because the Word author fails to take some basic word processing steps.

Before we go into the details of preventing problems, let's take a look at the basics. The following table shows options available in PDFMaker and the resulting output in PDF.

PDFMaker Options for Word

Although Acrobat buttons are inside several applications, such as Outlook and Excel, Word has the richest set of options. The following table shows which Word feature is mapped to a corresponding Acrobat element:

Word Feature	Equivalent in PDF
Word document structure as displayed in Outline View	Tagged PDF turns the implied structure in Outline View into an XML-like tagged format.
Headings and paragraph styles	PDF bookmarks.
Entries and page numbers in table of contents	Links to the destinations in the document.
Page numbers in list of figures	Links to the destinations in the document.
Footnotes and endnote citations	Links to the notes themselves.
Comments	PDF comments.
Linked text boxes	PDF article threads.
Document properties, such as author and creation date (File | Properties | Summary)	PDF document information.
Cross-references within a document	PDF links.
Links to other documents	PDF links.
Web Uniform Resource Locators (URLs)	PDF web links.

Prepping Microsoft Word for Conversion to PDF

You will get a better PDF if the Word document has been created using good word-processing techniques. This means you should use the features available in Word to create basic document elements, such as a table of contents. I've seen many authors who manually type in the entry and page information into their tables of contents. Don't do that! Save yourself some time, and use the automated features in Word to make your job easier, and to create a better PDF.

In general, the Word file should contain the following:

- Paragraphs formatted with Word Styles
- Updated Word fields
- An automatically generated table of contents
- All Word comments accepted or rejected
- Metadata about the file and author

NOTE *It's important to set your Default Printer to Adobe PDF before creating your PDF. This will prevent Word from repaginating as the PDF is created. This repagination effect is one of the biggest sources of complaints from Word users.*

Styles and Fields

Styles are formats applied to paragraphs. Styles give documents a consistent, professional look, and are required for automation. The all-too-common practice of highlighting text and formatting with the buttons in the Word toolbar is not recommended. This kind of ad hoc formatting is hard to apply consistently and doesn't give Word or PDFMaker anything to work with. Not only are styles required by Word's Table of Contents feature, but styles also create bookmarks in the PDF.

Instead of manually formatting every paragraph, use the styles available in the list available in the Word toolbar or in the Styles and Formatting Task Pane. Or, if you don't like those, create a template and use it.

Apply styles from the Style box on the Formatting toolbar, or by opening the Styles and Formatting task pane, shown here.

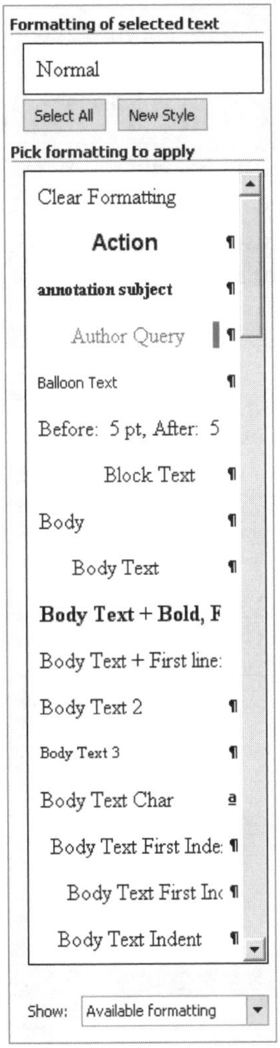

Word fields are used to create tables of contents. Fields commonly contain variable data, such as date or time. Or, they can be used for the creation of calculations or the insertion of AutoText. Dozens of fields can appear in a Word document. Choose Insert | Fields to see a list of available codes, as shown in Figure 6-5.

NOTE *To see if your document contains field codes, choose* ALT-F9. ALT-F9 *toggles field codes on and off.*

Always update Word fields to make sure that your PDF contains the most up-to-date information. Update a field by highlighting it and pressing F9.

TIP *Fields that don't update with the* F9 *command are probably locked. Unlock the field by pressing* CTRL-SHIFT-F11, *and then press* F9 *again.*

Create a Table of Contents

Acrobat creates hypertext links from Word Tables of Contents (TOCs) to the corresponding information inside the document. This process only works if you use Word's built-in TOC feature. You cannot just type in TOC entries and hope they will be magically transformed into PDF hyperlinks.

Contents¶

{TOC·\o·"1-5"}¶

Section Break (Next Page)

Introduction¶

So·you've·learned·Active·Server·Pages·and·want·to·build·a·dynamic·Web·site·or·application.· You've·gone·beyond·that·to·master·Microsoft®·ActiveX®·Data·Objects·and·drive·your·Web· content·from·Microsoft·SQL·Server™·or·another·database·server.·After·you've·made·your·Web· site·database-driven,·you'll·probably·want·to·add·a·way·for·users·to·search·and·report·on·your· database·content.··Of·course,·it's·easy·enough·to·add·a·query·form·that·lets·users·search·based· on·one·or·two·fields.·It's·much·harder·to·build·form-based·Web·pages·to·allow·searches·across· multiple·tables·and·multiple·fields.·Not·only·is·this·more·flexible·search·difficult·to·implement· (there·are·many·problems·beyond·the·mundane·user·interface·and·Web·coding·aspects,· including·defining·how·the·various·tables·and·fields·are·related·to·each·other),·but·even·the·best· interface·will·be·difficult·for·your·casual·Web·visitors·to·use·and·understand.·There's·an· inevitable·learning·curve·for·any·complex·search·of·structured·data·that·you·want·to·make· available.·This·obstacle·is·unacceptable·for·the·spontaneous·usage·of·your·Web·site·or·

FIGURE 6-5 A Word Table of Contents displays as a field code when **ALT-F9** is activated.

The consistent application of paragraph styles is required for the Table of Contents feature to work correctly. Check your document for the correct application of styles before creating a TOC.

Use the following procedure to create a Word TOC:

1. Click where you want to insert the TOC.
2. Choose Insert | Reference | Index and Tables.
3. Click the Table of Contents tab.
4. To use one of the available designs, click a design in the Formats box.
5. Select any other table of contents options you want, such as dot leaders, right alignment for page numbers and the number of heading levels to show.
6. Click OK.

Document Properties

Acrobat files contain metadata in an area called Document Properties. Choose File | Document Properties | Description to see the basic data about an Acrobat file, as shown in Figure 6-6. This data is searchable, and provides the user with information about the PDF creator.

TIP *The text in the Title field can be shown in Acrobat's title bar instead of the file name. Choose File | Document Properties | Initial View. In the Window Options panel, choose Show: Document Title.*

Pass information in Word's Summary to Acrobat by enabling Convert Document Information from the Adobe PDF menu. Of course, if you don't want the author's name and other information to appear, disable this option.

To see what information is in the Summary in Word, choose File | Properties | Summary.

Setting Up Bookmarks

Choose Adobe PDF | Change Conversion Settings | Bookmarks to specify how bookmarks will look in the finished PDF (see Figure 6-7). Select each heading or style you want to use as the basis of a bookmark, and then establish a nesting hierarchy. I would recommend no more than three levels of headings, although these can be a mixture of headings and styles. More than three levels of headings looks crowded in the Acrobat Bookmark tab window.

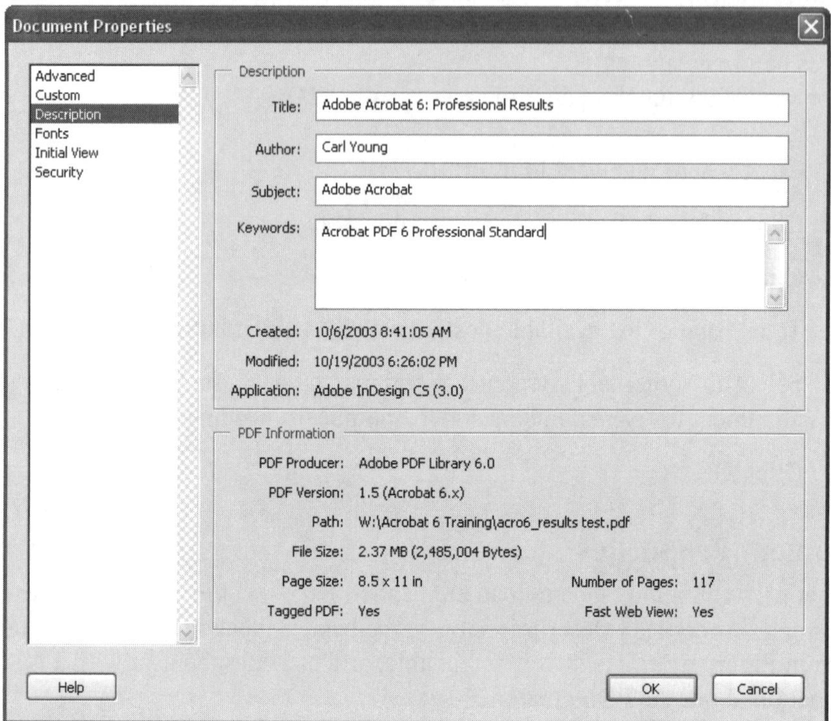

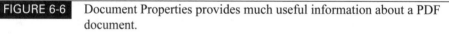

FIGURE 6-6 Document Properties provides much useful information about a PDF document.

NOTE *Be careful about the Word styles you choose to convert to bookmarks. Don't blindly select Convert Word Styles to Bookmarks—you may create bookmarks for every paragraph in your document, including each paragraph.*

Again, this is a plea for consistent use of styles and headings throughout the Word document. Random use of styles and headings will produce an erratic set of PDF bookmarks.

Settings

The *Settings* tab is where you specify the kind of PDF output you want, as well as several useful preferences. In general, I would recommend that you select View Adobe PDF result, Prompt for Adobe PDF file name, and Convert Document Information.

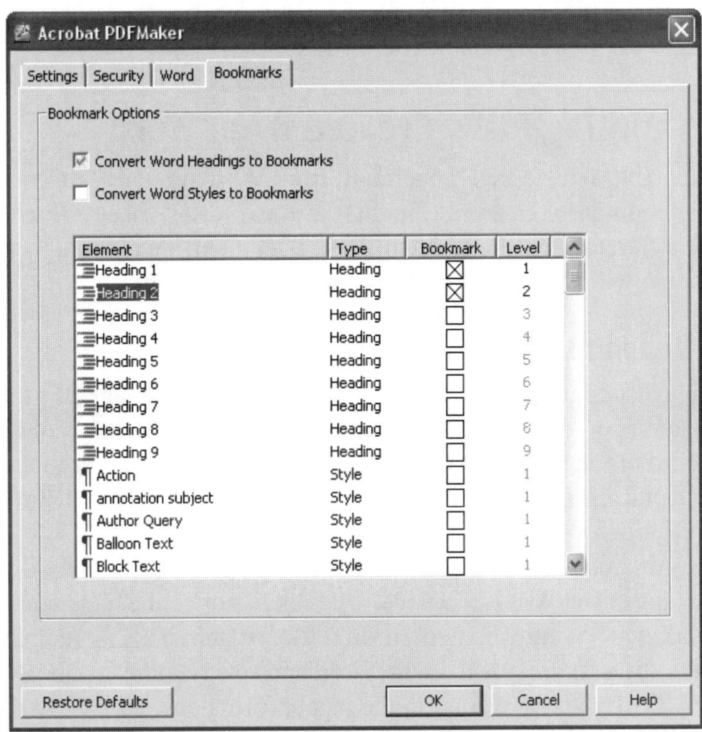

FIGURE 6-7 PDFMaker maps Word Styles and Headings to Acrobat bookmarks.

Under application settings, choose Add links to Adobe PDF, Add bookmarks to Adobe PDF, and Enable accessibility and reflow with Tagged PDF. Adding links and bookmarks will make an interactive PDF much more useful for online readers, and tagged PDF makes the PDF more accessible to visually impaired end users who are using assistive technology, such as screen readers.

The Advanced Settings button takes you to Distiller Job Options.

Running PDFMaker

Once the Word file is prepared and the correct conversion settings are selected, you are ready to make a PDF. This is the easy part!

1. Choose Acrobat | Convert to PDF or click the left Acrobat button in the toolbar.

2. Click Yes if prompted to save the document.
3. If asked for a PDF filename, type one.

Troubleshooting PDFs Created from Word

Although Adobe has made PDF generation from Word quite easy, there are a couple of common problem areas. The first is a text reflow issue, which causes the PDF to look different from the original Word document. The second is mysterious blank pages that will show up in a PDF created from Word.

The PDF Doesn't Look Like the Word Document

The single biggest complaint I hear from Word users is that the PDFs they create don't look like the original Word file. Because you are using the Adobe PDF printer driver to produce PDFs, switching from your default driver to the Adobe PDF printer can cause Word to reflow text, causing bad breaks and moving headings and graphics onto new pages.

Why doesn't Adobe fix this? They cannot. The reflow issue is hard-wired into Word. If you have used Word extensively, you may notice the page counter in the lower-left corner changing when you open a file, switch to a new template, or change printer drivers. It's just the way Word and several other applications work.

This is particularly aggravating in the legal professions, which often have documents with line numbers. Text reflow can produce PDFs that don't match the Word document line-for-line. If this happens to you, the following is Adobe's recommended procedure. You essentially reformat the document after setting Adobe PDF as the default (or target) printer.

1. Choose File | Close in Word.
2. Choose Start | Settings | Printers in Windows 2000, Me, or NT. Choose Start | Printers and Faxes in Windows XP/2003.
3. Right-click Acrobat PDF and choose Set As Default from the pop-up menu.
4. Open the document and adjust the layout so that it appears as desired. This means fixing bad line or page breaks, making sure graphics and captions appear on the same page, and so on.
5. Re-create the PDF file.

The next question that comes up is "How do I print the Word document?" The answer: You don't. Print the PDF instead. This can be an especially difficult procedure to implement, particularly if the Word file is being opened and revised by many users who are accustomed to printing the Word file, and then comparing the print job with what appears onscreen.

Keep in mind that the Word document may reflow once again if you set your default printer to something other than Adobe PDF. The best solution is a procedural one. The process is to designate the Word document formatted with the Adobe PDF printer as the "official" Word file.

Although this may seem like a trivial issue to some, it is a big headache in many offices where a Subject Matter Expert (SME) or attorney prepares a Word file, and then passes it off to an administrator or paralegal for PDF creation.

The SME or attorney prints the Word document to their local printer, and then compares their printout with the PDF. There may be slight variations between the printed document and the PDF caused by the reflow of the Word document. It usually takes some education to get the document creator to accept the idea that the Word document composed to the Adobe PDF printer is the "official" version.

Blank Pages in the PDF

Blank pages in the PDF also can be caused by a text reflow issue. The solution is to go back into Word and choose File | Print Preview | Shrink to Fit. Then run PDFMaker to produce a new PDF.

Repurposing PDFs

The concept of repurposing PDF documents is an interesting one. *Repurposing* means ripping all or part of the content out of a PDF and using it elsewhere, such as in a new document. An example is shown in Figure 6-8.

When Acrobat was first introduced, Adobe didn't give much thought to the idea of repurposing the data in a PDF. After all, the plan was for a PDF to be the final stop in the delivery of information, much as a printed, bound book is the final output of the book publishing industry. Who expects a book or magazine publisher to make the text and graphics in their publications reusable?

In the beginning, Adobe assumed PDF users and creators would always have access to the source files from which the PDF was created. That has turned out not to be the case. An end user may be far removed from the original creator and have no way to access the source files. It's not much better even within organizations where the PDF was produced. The original creator may have left the company, transferred to a new unit, or simply forgotten to archive the source files along with the PDF.

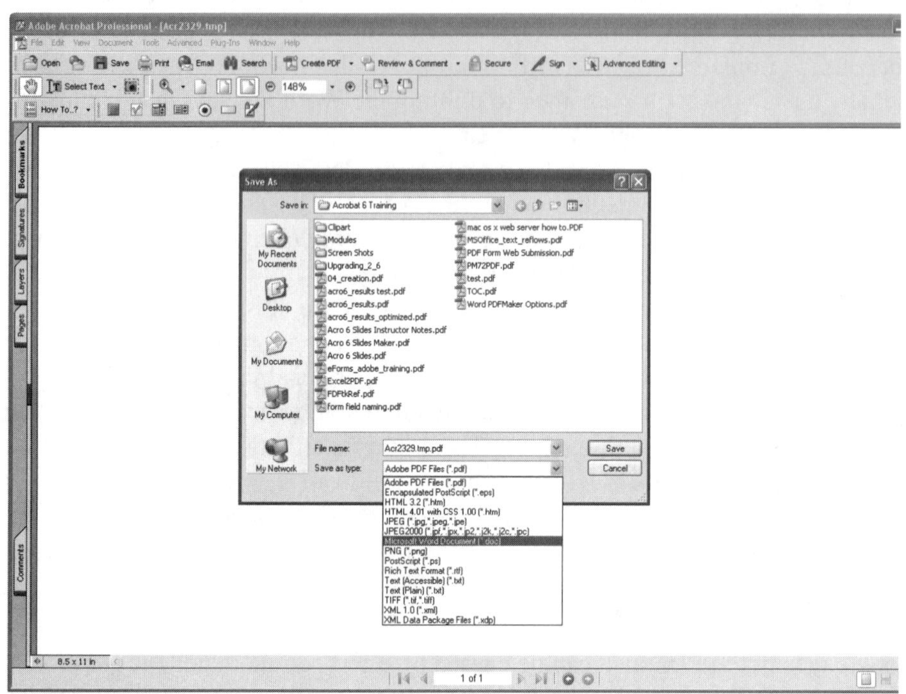

FIGURE 6-8 Acrobat 6 Standard and Professional allow end users to repurpose PDFs into other formats, such as Microsoft Word *.doc files.

For a variety of reasons, a small industry has sprung up around repurposing PDFs. Two of the best-known products for extracting data from PDFs are BCL Technology's Drake and Jade. *Drake* converts PDFs into RTF documents, including text and images. *Jade* is for extracting tabular data into Microsoft Excel. For more information, see **www.bcltechnologies.com**.

Other products in this category include Gemini from Iceni Technology (**www.iceni.com**), PDF2Word from CambridgeDocs (**www.cambridgedocs.com**), and CZ-Pdf2Txt from ConvertZone (**www.convertzone.com**). The PDF Store (**www.pdfstore.com**) carries some of these products and others. Helpful guides to similar products can be found at PDFZone (**www.pdfzone.com**).

To copy a small section of text from a PDF, use the Select Text tool, and copy-and-paste from the PDF into a word processing application. For a single image, use the Select Image tool. Click and drag to select an image, and then right-click (Windows) or OPTION-click (MacOS) and choose Copy to Clipboard or Save Image As.

Acrobat Export Options

Acrobat includes a number of export options. These are best for occasional use, and the quality of the export will depend on the circumstances under which the PDF was created.

Adobe includes some basic repurposing tools within Acrobat Standard and Professional. Outputs from File | Save as are

- **Encapsulated PostScript (EPS) or PostScript** Options are to include fonts, PostScript Language Level, whether to include all pages, and whether to include a bitmap preview image in EPS files.
- **HTML 3.2, HTML 4.01 with CSS 1.00, XML, or plain text (*.txt)** You can create links to content from XML or HTML documents. Encoding specifies which character set to use for displaying the text. Images can be exported as JPG or PNG for HTML and XML documents, or TIFF for text. Unless you make a change, images will be stored in a subfolder called images.

NOTE *Generate tags for untagged files will often improve output. However, you cannot use this command to make untagged PDFs accessible.*

- **JPEG or JPEG2000** You have options for compression levels for grayscale and color images, including a lossless compression format for JPEG2000. For JPEG files, choose Baseline Standard for the highest compatibility with web browsers. You also can include a color management profile.

NOTE *If the Picture Tasks button appears in your toolbar, you can export JPEG images with Picture Tasks | Export Pictures. The Picture Tasks button appears only when certain files are opened, such as PDFs created from JPEGs via the Create PDF | From File command.*

- **Rich Text Format (*.rtf) or Microsoft Word (*.doc)** This option converts text in a PDF into RTF or Microsoft Word format for reuse in a word processing or page layout application. Any graphics in the PDF will be converted to JPG or PNG format. The Settings options give you a choice of JPG or PNG graphics output. Older PDFs that do not have tagged PDF can be temporarily tagged for output.

- **PNG** The Portable Network Graphic (PNG) file type is a graphics format that is an alternative to GIF. Options include Interlace | None, which creates an image that displays in a web browser only after the entire file is downloaded to the end user's computer. The *Adam7 option* creates a low-resolution preview that displays while the high-resolution image downloads in the background. Compression options are varied. Check with your webmaster to obtain a recommended compression option, or whether you should choose the JPEG format instead.
- **Text**, including an accessible text format that includes alternative text included for accessibility.
- **TIFF** This option exports every page as a TIFF image, including pages that are 100 percent text. TIFF images can be edited in bitmap editors, such as Photoshop or PaintShop Pro. Note that some image editors cannot open TIFF files that use JPEG or ZIP compression. LZW or None will create files that are most compatible.
- **XML Data Package Files** Used by the XML Forms Architecture (XFA) plug-in. XFA is Adobe's XML implementation for XML-based forms.

The results of any of these export options will vary, depending on the quality of the PDF. For example, a PDF created with low-resolution graphics will export low resolution graphics back out—you probably would not want to print those. However, a PDF with high-quality graphics can export graphics that will print well.

While text will generally export completely, you may see formatting problems when exporting to Word or RTF. In some cases, you may see soft returns at the end of every line. Text in tables may not be formatted properly, either. Although I've called attention to the problems you may encounter, I generally prefer to fix formatting issues instead of retyping a document.

You will obtain the best RTF or Word output from documents that were created with tagged PDF, which applies logical structure to graphics, headings, and text. InDesign CS, FrameMaker 7, and PDFMaker in Word 2000/XP/2003 create tagged PDFs. Choosing File | Print | Adobe PDF from Microsoft Word does not create tagged PDF.

What happens if you do not want someone to repurpose your PDF? In that case, you will want to apply security to your PDF. See Chapter 9 for more information.

Tabular Data

The Select Table tool has been downsized from Acrobat 5. In Acrobat 5, you could use the *Select Table* tool to copy tabular data, or to copy a block of text. When you copied text and pasted it with the old tool, the pasted text would not have soft returns at the end of every line. In Acrobat 6, this tool only works on tables.

To use it, choose the Select Table tool, and click and drag over a table. Then right-click (Windows) or OPTION-click (MacOS) and choose Copy Selected Table (to the Clipboard), Save Selected Table As, or Open Table in Spreadsheet.

Creating from Microsoft Excel

Converting from Excel is similar to Word. By default, only the active worksheet will be converted. Choose Adobe PDF | Convert Entire Workbook to convert all worksheets.

Bookmarks are generated from Worksheet names, not from the formatting from within a spreadsheet. For complicated spreadsheets, create bookmarks manually to important sections of the document.

Troubleshooting Excel Spreadsheets

Some users report getting separate Worksheets when they would like the entire Workbook to be a single PDF. This is usually the result of different printer settings being set for each worksheet. The solution is to select all worksheets and choose File | Page Setup | Page | Print Quality and select 600 dpi, which is the recommended setting for the Adobe PDF printer. Select all worksheets by holding down the CTRL key (Windows) or the SHIFT key (Mac OS).

Creating PDFs from Microsoft PowerPoint

I always encourage presenters at the PDF Conference to use Acrobat as their presentation tool. Some presenters resist because they like the flashy transitions that PowerPoint includes, and older versions of Acrobat had limited transition functionality. Now, though, Adobe has added new capabilities in Acrobat 6 to add more transitions, including the popular bullet fly-in effect.

Overall, the PowerPoint options are similar to those in Word and Excel, but the most exciting feature is the capability to map PowerPoint page transitions and bullet fly-ins to PDF. Enabling this option passes PowerPoint transitions to PDF.

Options available in the PDFMaker for PowerPoint:

- Convert Multimedia to PDF Multimedia embeds multimedia objects into the PDF.
- PDF layout based on PowerPoint printer settings transfers print settings to the Adobe PDF printer (orientation, and so on.).
- You can manually set page transitions in Acrobat from the Document | Pages | Set Page Transitions menu.

To view these transitions, set Acrobat to run in Full Screen, or Presentation, mode, by choosing Window | Full Screen View, or CTRL-l. Click once with the mouse or press the PAGE DOWN key to advance to the next slide.

Preferences for Full Screen mode are in Edit | Preferences | Full Screen. You can set Acrobat to run presentations automatically or manually. You can also add a default transition and a background color.

Why Use a PDF Presentation?

Because PowerPoint is a pretty common application, some students wonder why they should bother with converting a PowerPoint file to a PDF. There are three main reasons: file size, security, and usability.

Acrobat has the capability to compress graphics and can make PowerPoint presentations much smaller. One presentation that I was recently required to do in PowerPoint was 17MB. When converted to PDF, it was a mere 5MB. Second, you can use Acrobat's security features to protect the file. See Chapter 9 for more information. The third reason is the ubiquity of the Adobe Reader. By making a presentation available in Acrobat, you can be reasonably assured that your audience can view an online version of the presentation. And this presentation will look like the one in PowerPoint, not like a PowerPoint presentation converted to HTML.

If you use PDF as your presentation medium, you are not limited to PowerPoint as your authoring tool. You can use InDesign, Illustrator, QuarkXpress, PageMaker, CorelDRAW, or any other high-end page layout or design program to produce your presentation, and then export the file as a PDF. You can use Acrobat or Adobe Reader to display the presentation and to make full use of Acrobat's linking capabilities.

If you create a unique look with a page layout or illustration program, you can be assured that your presentation will be different from the PowerPoint formats that everyone has seen hundreds of times.

Create from Multiples (eBinder)

You can combine several Office documents into a single PDF with the Create from Multiples command, which is also known as *eBinder.* In addition to Office documents, this technique can work with TIFF, JPEG, GIF, BMP, PCX, EPS, and PNG images. You also can convert Project, Visio, and AutoCAD files if those applications are installed on your computer.

The easiest way to use this technique is to choose File | Create PDF | From Multiple Files. You can also CTRL-click multiple files in Windows Explorer, and then right-click and choose Combine in Adobe Acrobat. Click Browse in the Create PDF from Multiple Documents dialog box and navigate to the location where the files are located. Use the CTRL key to add multiple files at one time.

The files will be combined in the order in which they appear in the Files to Combine window. To rearrange the order, select file and use the Move Up/Move Down buttons to reposition it.

The Create from Multiples command creates PDFs by using the applications installed on your computer, and you will see your applications opening, running the Acrobat conversion utility, and closing. The conversion process can be quite dramatic, especially for some Word files. You will see lots of flashing, color shifts, and zooming in and out. This is normal and is to be expected.

The result of Create from Multiples is a file called Binder1.pdf. You can use the File | Save as command to save the PDF with a different name.

Creating from Microsoft Visio and Autodesk AutoCAD

One of the great new features in Acrobat 6 is the capability to display layers. Word, Excel, and PowerPoint don't have layers. Microsoft Visio and Autodesk AutoCAD do have layers, and these can be transferred to Acrobat.

Visio and AutoCAD files can be complex, and using layers can make understanding those drawings much easier. For example, you can use layers to put plumbing, electrical, and structural elements of a building on separate layers. Because the wiring and structure can obscure the plumbing, you can hide the electrical and structural layers to reveal just the plumbing.

1. Open the file to be converted in AutoCAD or Visio.
2. Choose Adobe PDF | Convert to Adobe PDF.

3. Specify whether to flatten or retain some or all layers.
4. Use the Layer Mapping dialog box to group, lock, remove, or layers.
5. Click Convert to PDF.
6. Save the file.

NOTE *Layers must be present in Visio or AutoCAD for this process to work. Acrobat 6 cannot create layers itself.*

Open Office 1.1

If you are looking for a non-Microsoft solution for budgetary or other reasons, you should consider *OpenOffice 1.1,* the open source office suite from Sun Microsystems and **OpenOffice.org**. Unlike Microsoft Office, OpenOffice runs on Windows, Mac OS, Linux, and UNIX.

The applications in OpenOffice include a word processor, a spreadsheet, a presentation package, and drawing software. OpenOffice 1.1 includes its own PDF generator, which works similarly to the Publish to PDF functionality in Corel WordPerfect.

From any of the applications, choose File | Export as PDF. Your only options are to select a page range and compression type: Screen Optimized, Press Optimized, and Press Optimized. No bookmarks or hyperlinks can be created. The PDFs created are Acrobat 5-compatible.

Summary

Adobe has worked hard to integrate Acrobat into Microsoft Office workflows. Acrobat Professional 6 inserts PDFMaker buttons into Microsoft Word, Excel, PowerPoint, Explorer, and Outlook. Adobe has released updates to integrate Acrobat into new versions of the products it supports, such as Microsoft Office 2003.

Chapter 7

Working Together: Acrobat Collaboration

I've often had to manage the review process for technical documents, such as marketing collateral, user guides, and reference manuals. And, I've been the customer for advertising and marketing firms.

When you work with a number of authors, graphic artists, subject matter experts, and page layout experts a lot of information has to be passed around. Technical experts often review documents for accuracy. Marketing experts make sure "the message" is delivered accurately. And someone in authority must say, "Approved."

If the document is lengthy, it is often printed and passed around via FedEx or interoffice mail. Some advertising agencies are still faxing (in awful black and white) proofs for client approval, or sending color printouts via a courier service. It doesn't have to be this way—PDF is a great tool for marking up and approving documents of all sizes and lengths.

Onscreen Reviewing with Acrobat

Here's the way long documents get approved in many offices: paper copies are made, and the chief reviewer runs around the office dropping off copies at the desks of the appropriate people. Those not in the local office are sent a copy via courier.

All the reviewers make their comments, and send the paper back to the review chief's desk. The review chief then goes through every copy page-by-page and line-by-line. When disputes among reviewers occur, everyone gathers for a meeting and hashes out a solution. A new copy of the document is created incorporating all the reviews, and the process starts over.

Some companies use Microsoft Word as the main tool for the review process. Word has a comment tracking features that permits reviewers to add comments to documents electronically—documents can be distributed via e-mail or posted to a network drive.

There is one problem with using Word, however. The comments become part of the publication. If the comments are not stripped out prior to making the Word document public, the thoughts and opinions of the reviewers may be published. Few organizations want their internal battles made public, so good control over the Word comment features are essential.

Other issues exist as well. While Word is popular, it doesn't serve all purposes. There are better tools for creating graphics-heavy publications, such as magazines, newsletters, and direct mail pieces. And many organizations need management and other approvals on documents created with specialized applications, such as CAD drawings or database reports.

Adobe includes effective review and markup tools in Acrobat 6 Standard and Professional. While users must have a copy of Acrobat to mark up documents, comments can be viewed in the free Adobe Reader.

Types of Onscreen Reviews

With Acrobat, you have a choice of three basic review types:

- Passing PDFs around just like paper. Unlike paper, the chief reviewer can easily consolidate all comments into a single PDF.
- Using an e-mail–based review.
- Posting the PDF to a web or network drive "repository" that all reviewers can access.

In addition, you can incorporate Acrobat 6 review comments into Microsoft Word XP, 2002, and 2003 (Windows only). This means review comments can be kept out of the Word source file, helping to avoid the potential embarrassment of making internal comments public. You will learn how to establish these kinds of reviews in following sections of this chapter.

First, let's take a look at the tools available to all kinds of reviewers.

Review and Markup Tools

Adobe has beefed up and reorganized the review and comment features in version 6. The starting point for most review activities is the Review & Comment task button.

The Review & Comment button accesses:

- The Commenting toolbar
- The Advanced Commenting toolbar
- The Comments List (which opens the comments palette)
- Options for starting web-based and e-mail–based reviews
- Help for inserting comments and managing reviews
- Commands for exporting comments from a PDF for incorporation into a Word XP, 2002, and 2003 document

Commenting Tools

The toolset for making comments in a PDF are divided into two categories: the Commenting toolbar and the Advanced Commenting toolbar. Both toolbars can be accessed from the Review & Commenting Task button, or from the Tools menu.

The Commenting toolbar includes tools for adding sticky notes, indicating text edits with traditional editor's marks, a stamp tool, and a highlighter. Each has options for controlling the appearance of the comment, and indicating who is the author of the comment.

The Advanced Commenting toolbar includes graphic tools, including lines and circles. Acrobat 6 Professional users get a Cloud tool, often used in engineering documents. Other tools include the Text Box tool, a Pencil tool, and attachment tools for attaching supporting documents and sound comments, and for pasting from the clipboard.

Commenting Preferences

Commenting preferences affect all comments the Acrobat user makes on a document. Choose Edit | Preferences | General | Commenting to accessing these preferences. Example settings are shown in Figure 7-1.

In preferences, the Acrobat user sets the behavior and appearance of comments. There are many options, but some common settings follow:

- Reduce note size when zoom level is below 100 percent
- Show indicator arrows pointing to offscreen comments
- Show lines connecting comment markups to their pop-ups on mouse rollover

For many businesses, authors will want to be identified with names coworkers will recognize. The identity of the author is set in the Making Comments section. Enable Always Use Login Name for Author Name, and then set the Login name in Acrobat's Preferences | General | Identity section.

You can change the appearance of most comments by selecting the comment, and then right-clicking (Option-click in Mac OS X) and choosing Properties. New shapes, colors, and options are available on many tools. You can also change the Author's Name and the Subject of the comment in Properties.

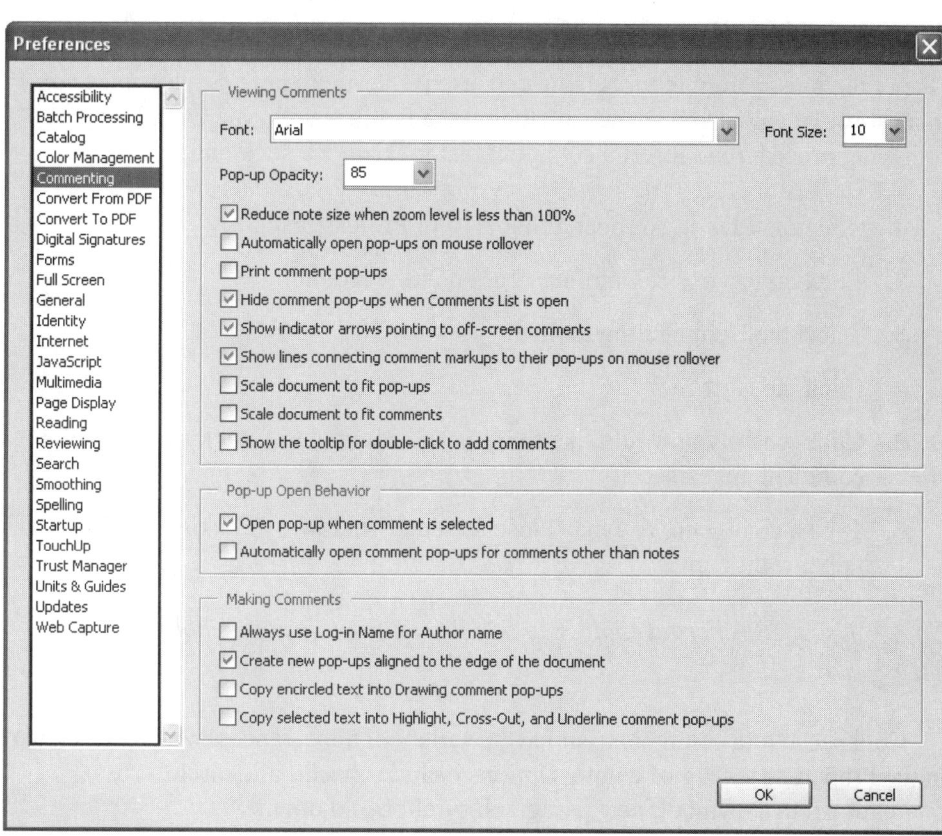

FIGURE 7-1 Commenting Preferences available in Acrobat 6

Commenting Toolbar

The tools in the Commenting toolbar are among the most frequently used. The *Note* tool is the onscreen equivalent of a sticky note. The *Text Edits* tools insert editorial changes in a manner traditionally used in the printing industry. The *Stamp* tool has a variety of stamps, including many often used in business, such as Approved, Confidential, and Received.

In the following sections, you will learn how to insert a Note or a Text Edit comment.

Insert a New Acrobat Note Comment

One of the most common tools reviewers use is the sticky note. Sticky notes come in a variety of colors and shapes, including the familiar yellow square. Use the following procedure to insert a comment that looks like a sticky note:

1. Open the PDF in Acrobat 6 Standard or Professional.
2. Click on Review & Comment button in the toolbar.
3. Select the Commenting toolbar.
4. Click the Note tool.
5. Click where you would like to insert the comment. A sticky-note type of comment appears.
6. Type a comment. You may close the note window by clicking the *X* in the upper-right corner.

TIP *Use the Properties toolbar to add formatting to text in a note.*

Collapsed Note comments can have a variety of appearances, which are shown in the Properties setting of a note. Options include checkmark, circle, cross, international help symbol, new paragraph symbol, and others.

TIP *Right-click (Option-click Mac OS X) and choose Make Current Properties Default to keep using the same opacity, color, and symbol type for additional comments.*

Use similar techniques to insert other comment types. Double-clicking on many drawing types will open a note for additional text.

Using Editor's Marks

The publishing industry traditionally used a specific set of symbols for proofing and editing paper documents. Adobe has included a few of the most common in Acrobat 6, and calls these Editor's Marks. The Text Edits button is used to indicate text insertions, deletions, and replacements, as shown in Figure 7-2.

Use the following procedure to indicate a text replacement:

1. Click the Text Edits button.
2. Highlight the text to be replaced.
3. To indicate the strikeout, use one of the following:
   - Press the DELETE or BACKSPACE key.
   - Right-click (Option-click Mac OS X) and choose Replace Text.
4. A red strikeout line will appear in the text you highlighted, and a caret symbol will appear at the end of the word. A line will connect to a Comment window, where you can enter the replacement text.
5. Enter the replacement text.

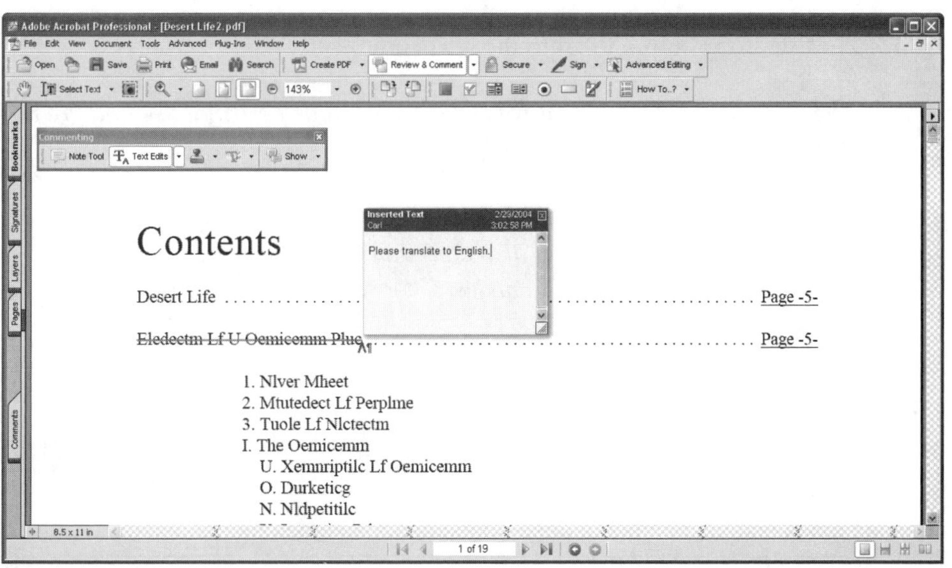

FIGURE 7-2 A Text Edit indicated with Editor's Marks available in Acrobat 6

Working with Comments

Once a document is loaded with comments, reviewers will begin to comment on other reviewer's comments, and the appropriate person will make the final decision whether to accept or reject a comment.

You manage comments from the Comments List, which appears in a separate window at the bottom of the Acrobat 6 interface.

Use the following procedure to work with comments in a PDF document. For an example of how comments appear in the Comments List, see Figure 7-3.

1. Click the Comments tab to open the Comments List.
2. Accept a comment by highlighting the comment and choosing Set Status button | Accepted.
3. Reject a comment by highlighting the comment and choosing Set Status button | Rejected.
4. Reply to a comment by highlighting a comment and clicking the curved arrow button.
5. Click the Next button to go to the next comment.

NOTE *The status indicators or status marks are for your personal use and are not displayed to other users.*

TIP *You can spell check comments and form fields. Misspellings will have red squiggly underlines. You also can run the spell checker to check all comments and form field entries. Choose Edit | Check Spelling | In Comments and Form Fields.*

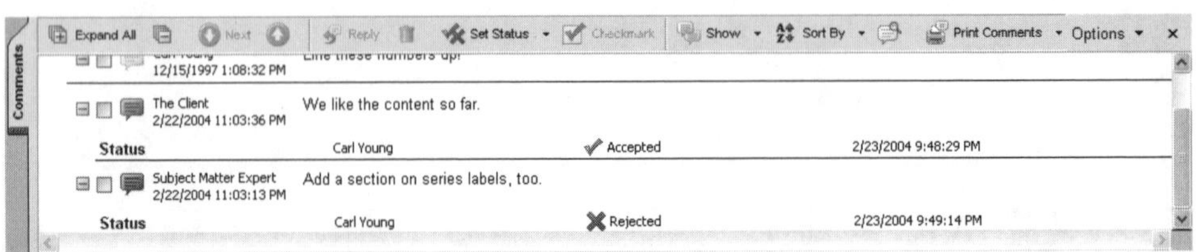

FIGURE 7-3 Reviewers' observations are shown in the Comments List window in Acrobat 6.

Sorting and Filtering Comments

Documents can become cluttered with comments if you have lots of active reviewers. Acrobat 6 includes several methods of sorting and filtering comments, so a clear picture of what needs to be done will emerge.

To manage a number of comments, you can sort comments by:

- Date
- Author
- Page Number
- Type
- Color
- Checkmark Status
- Status by person

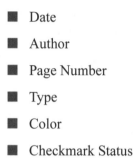

NOTE *The first comment in a thread of replies is sorted. The others fall underneath the first comment in the thread.*

You also can filter comments to see which comments have not been approved or rejected, or which ones are written by certain individuals. Filtering is called showing and hiding comments in Acrobat.

You can filter comments from the Comments List, or from the Show menu in the Commenting toolbar. Your options are

- Choose Show | Hide All Comments\Show All Comments to hide or show all comments.
- Choose Show | Show by Type to display only certain kinds of comments, such as Text Editing Markups.
- Choose Show | Show by Reviewer to choose from the list of users who have made comments in the document.
- Choose Show | Show by Status, and then select one or more status types.
- Choose Show | Show by Checked State and select whether to display comments you have checked off.

Reporting on Comments

Acrobat 6 includes enhanced tools for producing reports of comments. These reports can be stored electronically, printed, or used to analyze the construction of the document. Reports can be organized in a variety of ways, as shown in Figure 7-4. You can produce a report with comments and details on the same page, or side-by-side on separate pages.

To create a summary, hide the comments you do not want to appear, or filter the comments in an appropriate manner. Then choose Options | Summarize Comments.

As shown in Figure 7-5, one formatting option is to show connector lines between comment details and the items the comments refer to.

Reviewing with Acrobat

Although Acrobat 6 has new ways to conduct reviews, you can easily use Acrobat to duplicate an older, paper-based review cycle. Instead of sending out documents for review and approval via courier or interoffice mail, you can simply e-mail PDFs to reviewers for comment.

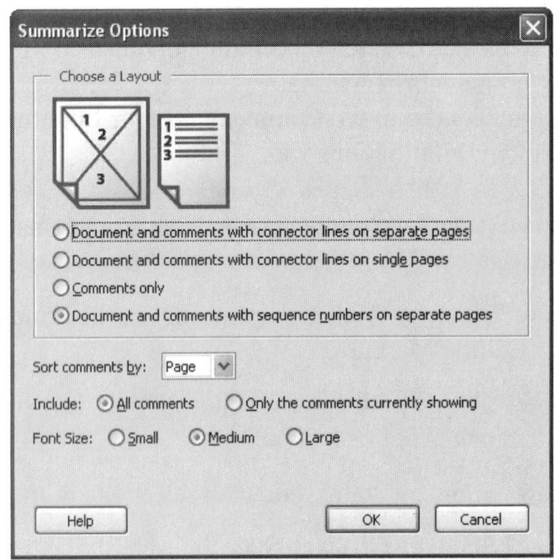

FIGURE 7-4 Options for creating a summary of comments in Acrobat 6

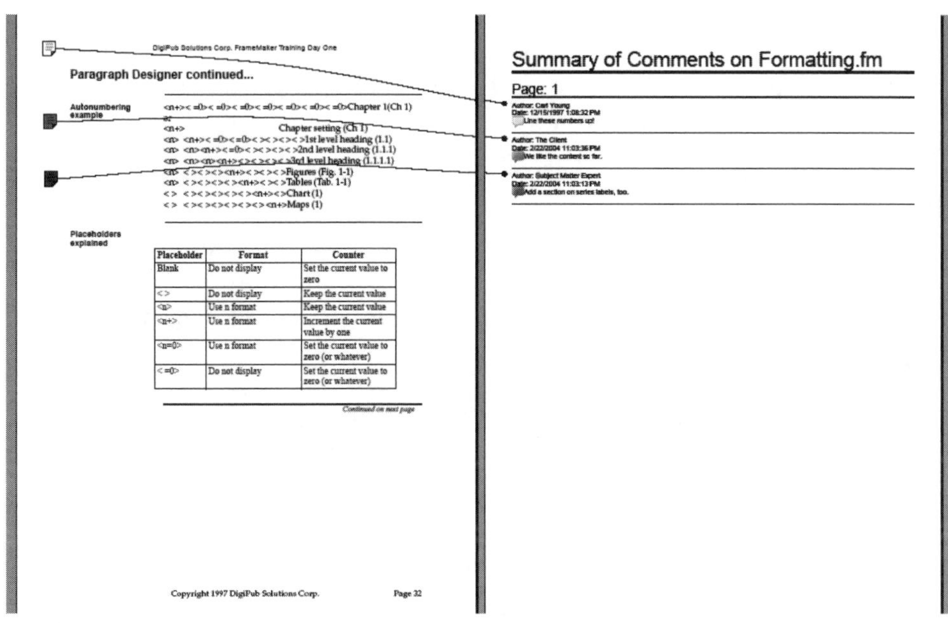

Placeholder	Format	Counter
Blank	Do not display	Set the current value to zero
< >	Do not display	Keep the current value
<n>	Use n format	Keep the current value
<n+>	Use n format	Increment the current value by one
<n=0>	Use n format	Set the current value to zero (or whatever)
< =0>	Do not display	Set the current value to zero (or whatever)

FIGURE 7-5 A summary of comments printed side-by-side with lines connecting notes with comment details

The person who manages the review process does not have to be the author of the PDF. The person in charge of the review process is called the *Review Initiator*.

Using Acrobat to Duplicate a Paper-Based Review Cycle

Unlike paper-based reviews, consolidating comments in Acrobat is simple. Reviewers can e-mail you their comments or the entire PDF with comments attached. The person in charge of the review can import all the reviewer's comments into a single PDF for analysis and approval. You can consolidate files of saved comments, or take comments from a PDF. Imported comments appear in the same location as they appeared in the source document.

The original file format for comments was Forms Data Format (FDF). Adobe has introduced a newer format called XML-based FDF (XFDF). In most cases, you can use either format.

While most Commenting operations are concentrated in the Comments window, exporting all comments is done from the Document menu. Use the following procedure to export all comments from a PDF.

1. Choose Document | Export comments.
2. Navigate to a folder where you want to store the comments. Enter a filename, and keep the file extension of FDF or XFDF. Be sure to use unique filenames for each reviewer's comments.
3. Save the file.

To consolidate comments into a single, master file, use the following procedure:

1. Open the PDF you have designated as the master review document.
2. Choose Document | Import Comments.
3. Select Files of Type Acrobat FDF Files (*.fdf), Adobe PDF (*.pdf), or Acrobat XFDF (*.xfdf).

NOTE *You will receive a warning message if the comments you are importing do not come from a PDF that is identical to the PDF you are importing into.*

Once you have consolidated comments into the master PDF, you then accept or reject comments. Accepted comments would then be manually entered into the source document that the PDF was created from. The exception is Word XP/2002/2003, which can import Acrobat comments directly into the source Word file. See the following section for integrating Acrobat comments into Word.

If shuffling PDFs and files of FDF (or XFDF) around seems awkward, you can use the more automated features available in either the e-mail or browser-based review.

NOTE *You can export a single comment, or a group of selected comments, from the Options menu in the Comments window.*

Using E-mail–Based Reviews

The assumption behind the e-mail–based review is that you have a document that groups of people need to review. E-mail–based reviews are designed for one-time reviews, but may be used for multiple review cycles.

You can create a new document based on the comments and send it out for review again. Or, you can use browser-based reviews that permit more interaction among reviewers.

How It Works

The software wizards at Adobe have automated the review process if you choose the e-mail–based review. The Review Initiator sends to each reviewer a package containing the PDF enclosed in an FDF wrapper, which provides information about the Review Initiator, the location of the PDF on the review initiator's computer, and a list of all the reviewers.

The reviewers make their comments, and then click the Send Comments button in the Comment window. Only the comments are sent back to the Review Initiator. By transferring only the comments, the load on a network will be much less than if the comments and PDF were being mailed back and forth.

Starting an E-mail–Based Review

It is not difficult to use the special e-mail review process, but you should use the following steps:

1. Make sure your e-mail address is listed in the Identity section of Preferences, as shown in Figure 7-6. Choose Edit | Preferences | General | Identity to enter your address.
2. Open the PDF document.
3. Choose File | Send by E-mail for Review.

NOTE *You can also start an e-mail–based review directly from other applications, such as Microsoft Word, that use PDFMaker. Choose Adobe PDF | Convert to Adobe PDF and Send for Review.*

4. If you have not specified an e-mail address in the Identity panel of the Preferences dialog box, you are prompted to enter your e-mail address, and then click OK. The e-mail address you enter is saved in your preferences. An example is shown in Figure 7-7.
5. In the e-mail dialog box that appears, specify the reviewers' e-mail addresses in any of the To:, Cc:, and Bcc: fields; edit the message to reviewers as necessary; and then click OK or Send. (You cannot include all reviewer names in the Cc: and Bcc: fields; at least one name must be in the To: field.)

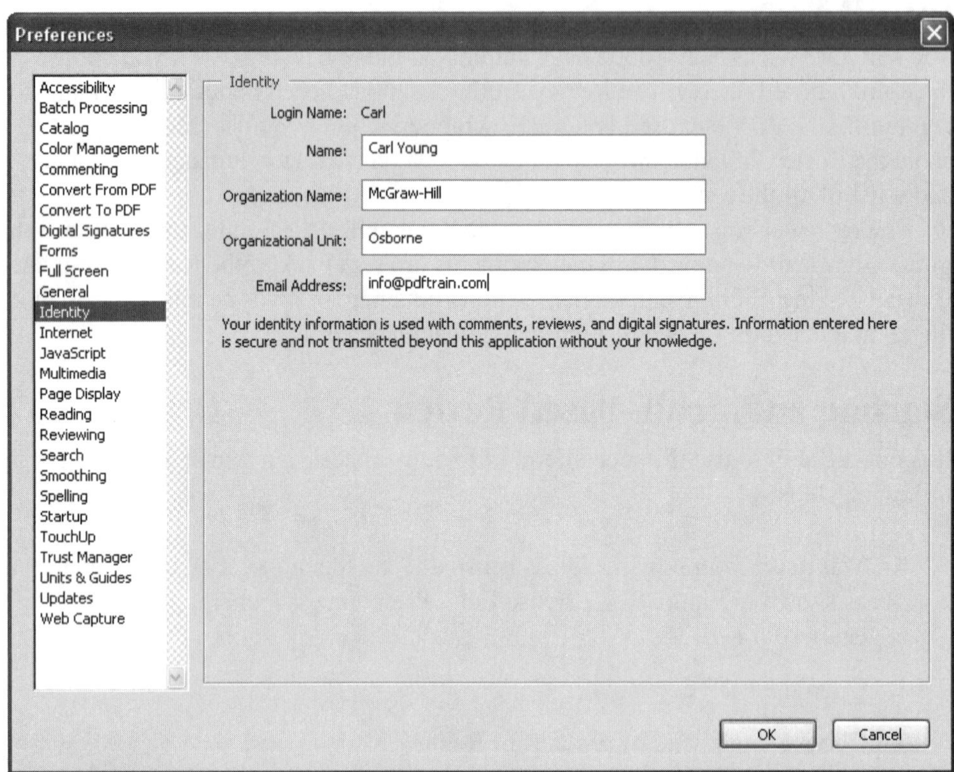

FIGURE 7-6 Your name and e-mail address should appear in the Identity section of Acrobat preferences.

NOTE *If your e-mail application does not allow you to send e-mail automatically for security reasons, make the e-mail application active, answer any alert messages that may appear, and then click the Send for Review button in Acrobat.*

Participating in an E-mail–Based Review

While it may take reviewers a brief time to become familiar with Acrobat's commenting tools, taking part in an e-mail–based review will seem familiar to most end users who are comfortable using e-mail.

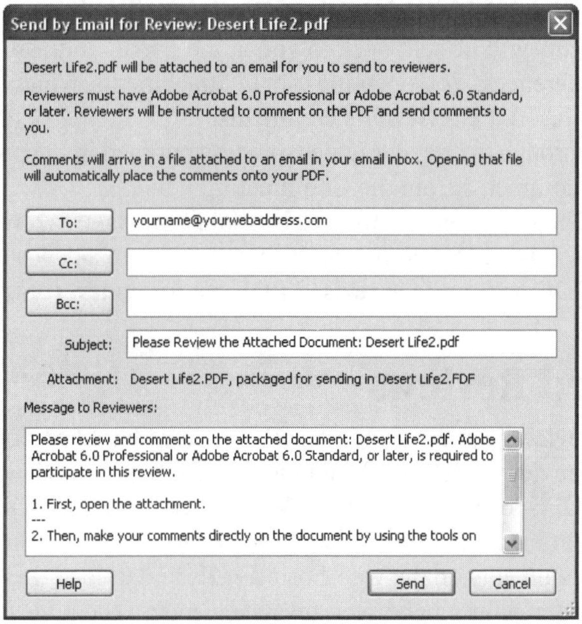

Send by Email for Review: Desert Life2.pdf

Desert Life2.pdf will be attached to an email for you to send to reviewers.

Reviewers must have Adobe Acrobat 6.0 Professional or Adobe Acrobat 6.0 Standard, or later. Reviewers will be instructed to comment on the PDF and send comments to you.

Comments will arrive in a file attached to an email in your email inbox. Opening that file will automatically place the comments onto your PDF.

To: yourname@yourwebaddress.com

Cc:

Bcc:

Subject: Please Review the Attached Document: Desert Life2.pdf

Attachment: Desert Life2.PDF, packaged for sending in Desert Life2.FDF

Message to Reviewers:

Please review and comment on the attached document: Desert Life2.pdf. Adobe Acrobat 6.0 Professional or Adobe Acrobat 6.0 Standard, or later, is required to participate in this review.

1. First, open the attachment.
---
2. Then, make your comments directly on the document by using the tools on

Help Send Cancel

FIGURE 7-7 The e-mail screen for sending a PDF for an e-mail–based review

TIP *Do not add, delete, or rearrange pages in PDFs you are reviewing. Moving pages around will put your comments out of sequence with those of other reviewers and the original document.*

To participate in the review process, use the following procedure:

1. Open the PDF document by double-clicking the FDF e-mail attachment. Acrobat launches. You are told that the document is to be reviewed. The Commenting toolbar automatically pops up and the How To window is presented and explains what to do next.
2. You add comments using whatever commenting tools you think are most appropriate.
3. Click the Send Comments button on the Commenting toolbar. Your comments are sent to the Review Initiator as an FDF e-mail attachment.

Receiving and Reconciling Comments from Reviewers

Reviewer comments will be sent back to you at the e-mail address specified in your Identity preferences. You open the e-mail attachments, which look for the master PDF, and insert the reviewer's comments.

You then go through the regular review process outlined in the preceding section. Accept or reject comments from the Commenting window.

You can use the Reply feature to send an e-mail message to a reviewer but, in most cases, you will want to incorporate the comments into a new source document, generate a new PDF, and send the revised PDF out for review (or approval).

Browser-Based Reviews

Browser-based reviews can be used in an all Windows-based environment. In a browser-based review, a PDF is placed on a web site or a network. Users are notified of the PDF's location via e-mail. When users open the PDF inside Internet Explorer (IE), Acrobat launches as a helper application and runs inside IE.

Users make comments on the web-hosted PDF, and upload their comments to the web server. Comments can be seen by all reviewers, and reviewers can reply to each other's comments. An example is shown in Figure 7-8.

TIP *Don't make comments on a PDF before uploading it. Comments added before the PDF is uploaded cannot be deleted, as can comments added after the file is at the web site.*

While browser-based reviews can work on files placed on network drives, Adobe recommends placing PDFs on web servers for the best results. You likely will need the assistance of a web administrator to set up this process, which can use certain databases to manage comments, or the Web Discussions or WebDAV (Distributed Authoring and Versioning) standards.

Your web and information technology administrators likely will have strong opinions on which method they prefer you use. If they do not, you can suggest WebDAV, which is incorporated into recent versions of Microsoft Internet Information Services and Windows servers.

First, enable Microsoft Internet Information Server (IIS). Use the Windows control panel and choose Add or Remove Programs. Follow the wizard to set up IIS.

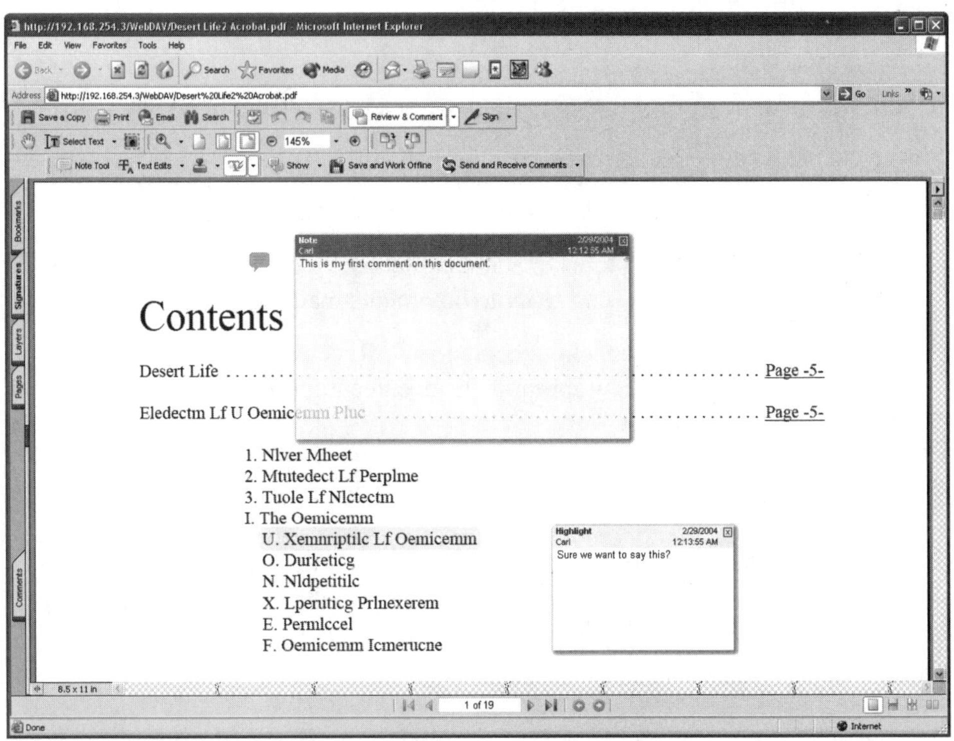

FIGURE 7-8 Acrobat is running inside Internet Explorer. Notice the Send and Receive Comments, and the Save and Work Offline buttons in the toolbar.

To learn more, enter **http://localhost** in IE after installing IIS and review the documentation there on setting up WebDAV. An example for using WebDAV in Windows XP is used in a following section.

Using Browser-Based Reviews

The browser-based review is similar to the e-mail review process, except that reviewers have real-time access to the comments of other reviewers. Reviewers can reply to the comments of other reviewers. These threaded discussions are useful for settling disagreements among reviewers.

When the Review Initiator invites you to participate in a review, you receive an e-mail message with instructions and an attachment. The attachment is an FDF file that automatically configures your Commenting Preferences, enabling you to upload and download comments from the review document.

NOTE *Acrobat will upload your comments to the server automatically if you close the browser window before uploading comments.*

Use the following procedure to participate in a browser-based review:

1. Double-click the FDF message attachment. A new browser window will launch, and the review document will appear inside.
2. Use the Commenting tools to add comments to a document, or open the Commenting window and reply to comments made by other reviewers.
3. When you are finished, click the Send and Receive Comments buttons. Your comments will now appear in the document for other reviewers to see.

TIP *You can delete your comments later, but you cannot delete the comments of other users.*

You can use the Save and Work Offline button to save a copy of the review document and comments on your local computer. Use the Go Back Online option to upload your comments when you are ready to upload your comments to the server.

Setting Up WebDAV for Browser-Based Reviews

To use WebDAV, a system administrator must set up a WebDAV server. WebDAV is designed specifically for organizations to publish, manage, and lock documents. It is an extension of the HTTP protocol that permits users to move and copy files, lock and unlock files for various users, and to search WebDAV directories.

While WebDAV can be used in any operating system environment, the Acrobat browser-based review works only with Windows.

An Example of Using WebDAV

The specific instructions for creating a WebDAV publishing directory will vary by which version of Windows and IIS you are using and what you would like to accomplish. The following procedure provides an example of setting up WebDAV for review if the Review Initiator is running Windows XP:

1. Create a folder on the web server in any location except WWWRoot.

2. Use Internet Services Manager to create a virtual directory. (Enter **http://localhost** in IE to bring up documentation on how to create a virtual directory and how to enable WebDAV.)
3. Use WebDAV as the alias for the virtual directory that points to the folder you created in the first step.
4. Modify the permissions of the publishing directory to give users the capability to Read, Write, and Browse files.

Once the web server is prepared for WebDAV, you, as the Review Initiator, must take a few steps. An example is shown in the following procedure:

1. Choose Start | My Network Places | Add a Network Place. Enter the address of the WebDAV publishing directory, such as **http:\\192.168.254.3\WebDAV**.
2. Start Acrobat and choose Edit | Preferences | General | Reviewing and set the Server type to WebDAV and the address of the publishing directory, such as **http:\\192.168.254.3\WebDAV**. The comments of reviewers will be stored at this location.

NOTE *Be sure to add the closing backslash (\) in your preferences setting. You may not be able to upload comments if the backslash is missing.*

3. Open the PDF to be reviewed and choose File | Upload for Browser-Based Review. Enter the Network Place created in the first step as the location.
4. Once the file is uploaded, you will be presented with an e-mail message (shown in Figure 7-9) to notify reviewers that the review is about to begin. Adobe includes a standard list of instructions to reviewers in the body of the message. You can keep this message, or modify it as you want.
5. Additional reviewers can be added later by using the Invite Others to Comment option from the Review & Comment button. The document to be reviewed must be open in Acrobat running inside IE for this option to appear.

TIP *Be sure to enter backslashes (\\) instead of slashes (//) in your settings and review invitations.*

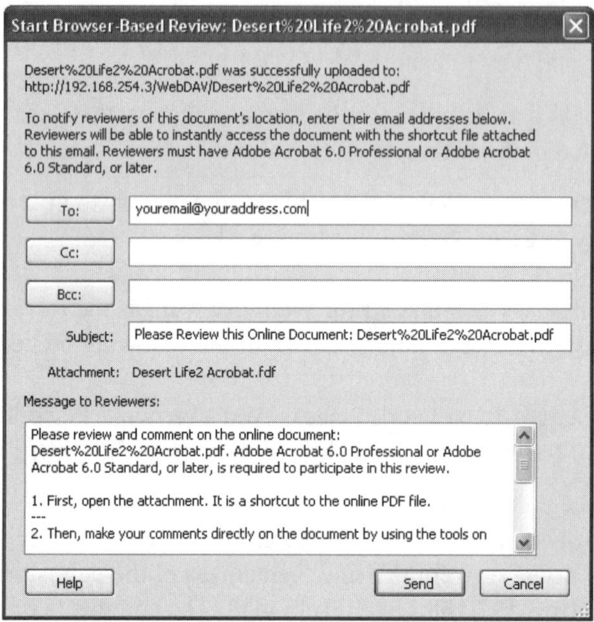

FIGURE 7-9 An invitation for reviewers to take part in a browser-based review

Comments are stored as FDF files in the WebDAV publishing directory. Users must use the Send and Receive Comments button to upload their comments to the server, and to see recently added comments from other reviewers.

Importing Comments into Word XP/2002/2003

Acrobat comments can be imported directly into Word XP/2002/2003. No re-keying of comments is necessary. The comments can come from a single reviewer, or a group of e-mail or browser-based reviewers.

You don't need to be running the Windows XP or 2003 operating system to have Word XP/2002/2003 on your computer.

Use the following procedure to incorporate Acrobat comments directly into Word:

1. Consolidate all comments in a master PDF. Be sure to save the PDF before continuing.

2. Open the source document in Microsoft Word XP/2002/2003.
3. Choose Acrobat Comments | Import Comments from Acrobat from Word's main menu.
4. Click Yes in the warning screen.
5. Click Browse.
6. Navigate to and select the PDF file you want to import comments from.
7. Select which kinds of comments you want to import.

If you use Editor's Marks to indicate text edits, there is an interactive process to integrate those edits into the Word document. To integrate text edits:

1. Click Apply or Discard to integrate the edits into Word, or to discard them.
2. Click Next to go to the next change.
3. You can always Undo if you don't like the result after you click Apply.

TIP *Uncheck Show Comment Bubbles to hide comment bubbles to reduce screen clutter. Use Delete All Comments in Document if you want to delete all comment bubbles.*

Checklist for Integrating Acrobat and Word Comments

Adobe has worked diligently to integrate Acrobat into the Word review process. However, you still must take certain steps to make the process work smoothly. For best results, keep the following list of tips in mind:

- The Word document should be the source document of the PDF. If pages are added or deleted from the Word document after PDF creation, then comments may not be integrated at the proper locations.
- You can only copy comments into a Word document once. Use copies of the Word document if you must import comments again.
- Use Word Styles to format the document, and enable Logical PDF in the Adobe PDF | Change Conversion Settings | Settings | Enable text reflow and accessibility with Logical PDF.

- The PDF with comments must be created with PDFMaker button or menu command (Adobe PDF | Convert to Adobe PDF).
- Filter, sort, and approve comments in the PDF before bringing them into Word.
- Watch for extra words when reviewers have used Editor's Marks. Reviewers unfamiliar with the procedure of using Editor's Marks may enter text marked for replacement with the phrase "Replace with (replacement word)," instead of simply (replacement word). Extra words can be deleted manually.
- Comments formatted with the Properties toolbar in Acrobat will appear as regular text in Word.

Review Tracker

The person in charge of reviews has a new management tool in Acrobat 6. The Review Tracker lets you initiate and manage the Acrobat review process. With Review Tracker, you can send reminders, keep a record of when documents were sent out, end a review, and invite more reviewers to participate.

Review Tracker is not used to begin the review process. You must begin a review by using the e-mail or browser-based review process. Once you've begun a review, it will appear in the Review Tracker window, as shown in Figure 7-10.

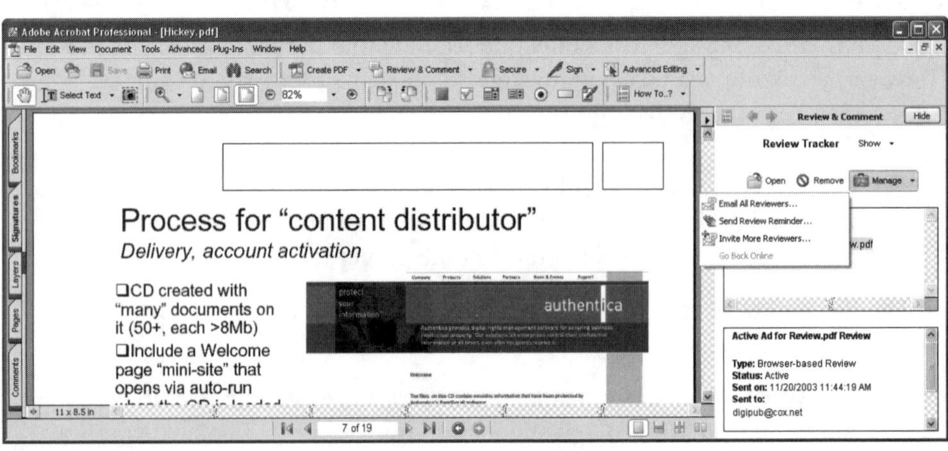

FIGURE 7-10 The Review Tracker in Acrobat 6 helps to track reviews, to invite more reviewers, and to remind reviewers to send comments.

To start Review Tracker, click the Review & Comment button and choose Track Reviews. The Review Tracker opens on the right side of the screen, in the same area where the How To…? and Search results appear.

Documents you have initiated appear in the top window. Highlight a document and information about it appears in the bottom window. Click the Show button to filter which kinds of documents will appear. You can show all documents, active and completed documents, and PDFs sent and received.

Double-click the PDF filename to launch a browser-based review, or choose the Go Back Online option from the Manage button.

To manage a review, select a document in the Review & Comment window and click the Manage button. You can choose from the following options:

- E-mail All Reviewers sends an e-mail with the subject line Follow-up to (Name of Your Review Document) to those you have invited to a review. You can change the subject line in your e-mail tool, and expand on the subject line by typing in the body of the e-mail message.
- Send Review Reminder also could be called "auto-nag." The subject line again is Follow-up to (Name of Your Review Document) and message body text of If you have not already, please contribute to the document review. You can change the subject line and add your own body text, or use the defaults.
- Invite More Reviewers starts either the e-mail or the browser-based review again. You can add more reviewers to the process and cc: and bcc: others. The standard Message to Reviewers with instructions on how to participate is included.

Comparing Documents

Another review option is Acrobat's Compare Documents feature. With *Compare Documents,* you can view versioning differences. Use the following procedure to compare two PDFs:

1. Open the two documents to be compared.
2. Choose Document | Compare Documents. Select the documents from the pull-down list.

3. For text-based documents, choose the Textual Differences option. Use Page by Page Visual differences for graphics intensive documents, such as advertisements or engineering drawings.

4. Use the Side by Side report type for text documents. Choose the Consolidated report for graphics-intensive documents.

Side by Side reports creates a new PDF showing each page and the differences between the pages. A Consolidated report inserts comments in the current document where changes are detected. Move the Hand tool over a comment to see more detail about the differences.

Summary

You can save time and money during the review process by using the built-in commenting tools in Acrobat 6. No longer do you have to print documents and send them by courier or interoffice mail for review. You can move around PDFs and comments much as you would paper, or you can set up e-mail or browser-based reviews.

You can add comments with a variety of tools in Acrobat, reply to the comments of other reviewers, and generate reports of comments. If you are using a recent version of Microsoft Word, you can import Acrobat comments into Word for integration.

Chapter 8

PDF from Corel WordPerfect

Adobe has worked hard to integrate Acrobat with Microsoft Word, as discussed in Chapter 6. Unfortunately, Adobe hasn't provided any integration features for users of WordPerfect.

Although it has largely disappeared from the corporate desktop, WordPerfect thrives in government offices and in the courts. Check any court web site that requires electronic submissions—most require a PDF—and you'll find many postings originated in WordPerfect. For example, the United States Bankruptcy Court in Arizona (see **http://www.azb.uscourts.gov/**) requires electronic filing. The document explaining why attorneys must file briefs and motions electronically is a PDF created from WordPerfect 9.

Many of my students come from state and federal agencies from across the country, and they report WordPerfect is alive and being used in their offices. Zoning reports, grant applications, meeting notices, and other public documents are being written every day in WordPerfect. To make these documents available to the public, the authors create PDFs that are posted to a web site.

Searching for a Perfect PDF from WordPerfect

Unfortunately, just like many Microsoft Word users, WordPerfect authors tend to produce PDFs that are difficult to navigate and confusing for readers. WordPerfect's built-in PDF generator doesn't create accurate PDF bookmarks and links, so few PDFs coming from WordPerfect are created with the online reader in mind. A review of WordPerfect user web sites shows WordPerfect users are as confused as to how to create a good PDF as Word users are.

In this chapter, you learn how to create a user-friendly PDF from WordPerfect. I recommend that you use the built-in Publish to PDF feature to create links from a table of contents, and then add bookmarks manually.

NOTE *Acrobat itself doesn't automatically create bookmarks and links from any application. Acrobat installs a macro inside of Microsoft Word that creates links and bookmarks, and other Adobe products have special features to create bookmarks and links.*

Terminology

In my online discussions with WordPerfect users and during telephone conversations with WordPerfect technical support, it became clear that WordPerfect and Acrobat users use the same terms to mean different things. To clarify what I mean, let's talk about the term that causes the most confusion.

In the Acrobat world, a *bookmark* is a navigational aid that appears in the Bookmarks Tab. See Figure 8-1 for an example. In the WordPerfect world, a *bookmark* is the destination of a hyperlink. In this book, I use the term "bookmark" as it's commonly used in the Acrobat community.

Publish to PDF

Beginning with version 9, WordPerfect has included a *Publish to PDF* feature that creates PDFs without Acrobat. This is a non-Adobe solution based on the PDF specification. Unfortunately, in my experience and in the experience of many others, the Publish to PDF feature doesn't produce usable Acrobat bookmarks.

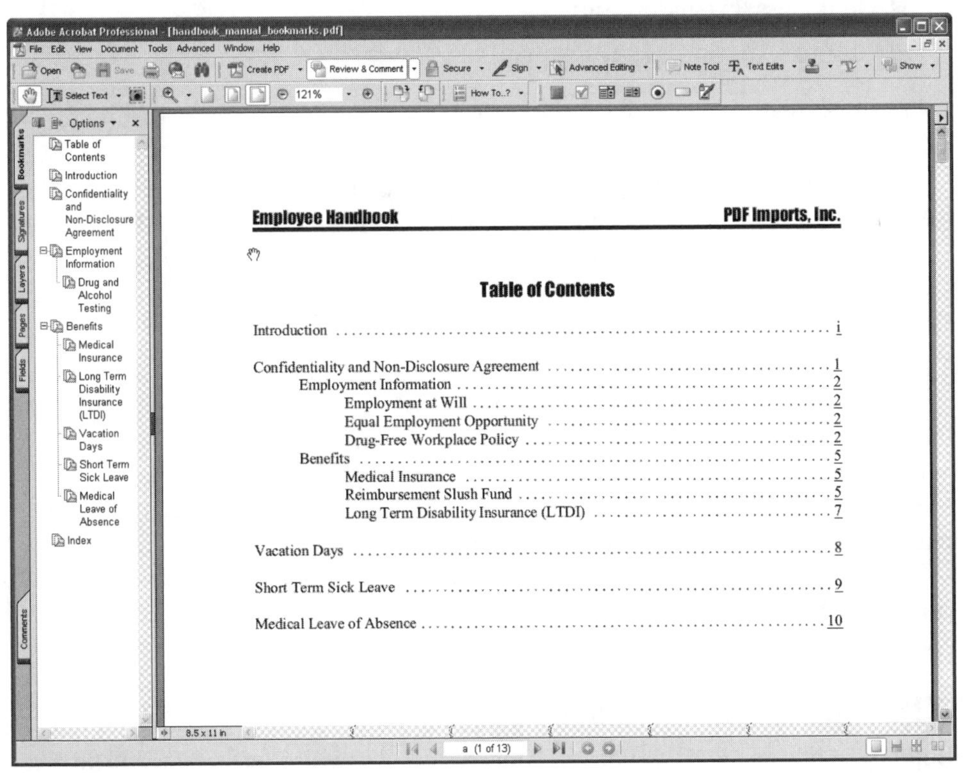

FIGURE 8-1 Bookmarks in Adobe Acrobat. These bookmarks are wrapped to fit inside the Bookmark Tab, a new feature in Acrobat 6.

It does create links from a table of contents, but only from the page numbers. WordPerfect technical support says the issue has been logged for a bug fix.

Why am I so lukewarm about Publish to PDF? Because it creates unusable bookmarks. In all my tests, Publish to PDF listed page numbers, not text, as Acrobat bookmarks. WordPerfect technical support verifies my results. However, the Publish to PDF feature does have some uses. With Publish to PDF, WordPerfect users can do the following:

- Make a PDF compatible with legacy versions of Acrobat
- Fill in document information fields
- Embed and subset fonts
- Compress graphics
- Compress text and line art
- Set the opening view of the PDF
- Specify the color model (RGB or CMYK)

Missing from Publish to PDF are security settings, tagged PDF for Section 508 compliance, and many of the other features found in the Acrobat PDFMaker utility installed in Microsoft Word and also available from other non-Adobe PDF generators.

Results from Publish to PDF

To test the capabilities of Publish to PDF, I imported a sample text file and placed a standard set of JPEG and TIF files into a WordPerfect 11 document. I added an interactive table of contents and formatted some text as headings 1 and 2. The completed WordPerfect document was 18MB. When processed with Publish to PDF with graphics compression quality set to maximum, the resulting PDF was only 4MB. That is less than one-fourth the size of the original WordPerfect file.

Using a similar setup with the Adobe PDF printer driver, the PDF was even smaller—3MB.

Setting Up Your Document

Before you create a PDF, you need to make sure your WordPerfect document is set up correctly. As with Word, you should apply styles to all text in the document, and use the software's built-in table of contents generation feature.

WordPerfect is a powerful word processing document with lots of page layout features. Because so many people are occasional users or only write short documents, they often overlook WordPerfect's hyperlinking and table of contents' creation features. If you plan to produce PDFs of more than two or three pages, you should learn to use these tools. Not only will you be able to add one-click hyperlinks to your WordPerfect file, but those links, as well as links from a table of contents generated by WordPerfect, will be passed on to the PDF.

NOTE *In most cases, you can't fake an autogenerated table of contents and get a PDF with hyperlinks and bookmarks. By faking, I mean manually creating a table of contents, instead of letting WordPerfect do the work for you.*

If you type in a table of contents, and manually update the page numbers every time you have a change, you lose the hyper linking features. You have to insert an autogenerated table of contents to have links magically passed over to the PDF.

If you don't know how to create a table of contents in WordPerfect, the next section shows you how.

Create a Table of Contents

A table of contents lists major headings in the order in which they appear. Unlike an index, which lists subjects in alphabetical order, a table of contents displays how the information in your document is organized. Traditionally, table of contents' headings are left aligned and the page numbers are flush with the right margin. The chapter name usually is flush with the left margin, and subheadings are slightly right indented stair-step fashion.

As discussed in Chapter 3, your online PDF readers should be able to click an entry in the table of contents and have that page appear.

NOTE *If you're using WordPerfect's built-in styles, you needn't mark the text as the following shows. The prebuilt styles are marked for the Table of Contents as soon as they're applied. WordPerfect's styles are called Heading 1, Heading 2, Heading 3, Heading 4, and Heading 5.*

Mark Entries for the Table of Contents

WordPerfect will create a table of contents for you, but you need to let the software know what you would like to include.

To start, choose Tools | Reference | Table of Contents.

The Reference Tools screen, shown in Figure 8-2, has a row of five buttons across its middle. Mark 1 is for the top level heading of each unit of your document, Mark 2 is for subheadings, Mark 3 is for sub-subheadings, and so on. In many templates, they equate with H1, H2, H3, and so on.

To mark text:

1. Highlight the uppermost heading of your document. A triple click will do it.
2. Click the Mark 1 button.
3. Go to your next heading. This likely will be a subheading to the first one you marked, so highlight the text in that heading and click Mark 2.
4. Continue marking the text in your document until you finish.

You should be consistent in marking text. When you're done, the completed table of contents will show the logical structure of your document.

NOTE *Few documents will require that you use all five levels of headings.*

Set Up a Table of Contents

Once the text is marked, or the built-in styles are applied to text, you're ready to tell WordPerfect how you want your table of contents to be organized.

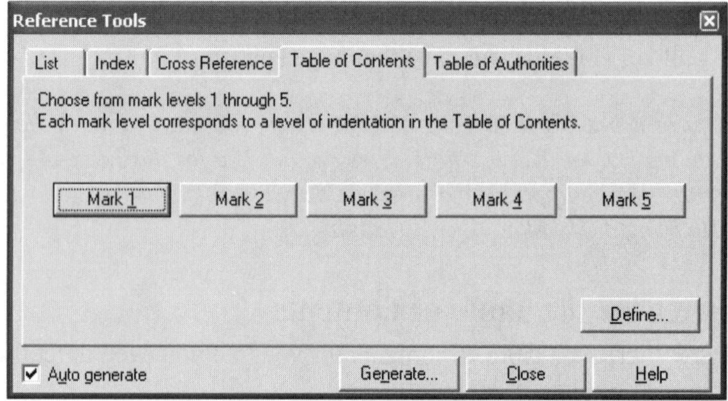

FIGURE 8-2 The Reference Tools screen lets you mark headings for inclusion into an automatically generated table of contents.

Most authors create a new page to hold the table of contents. In any event, place the insertion point in the position where you want the table of contents to be created.

To proceed, use the Define Table of Contents screen shown in Figure 8-3.

To set up a table of contents:

1. Click the Define button in the Reference Tools screen.
2. Select a number of levels equal to the number of levels you marked earlier.
3. Make sure the TOC will be placed in the correct position.
4. Check the preview area at the bottom of the screen to get an idea of what your table of contents will look like.
5. Click OK.
6. Click Generate.
7. Make sure the Build Hyperlinks checkbox is turned on.
8. Click OK.

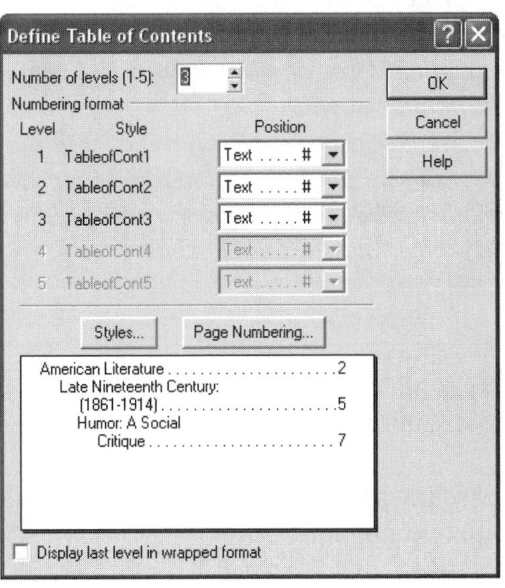

FIGURE 8-3 You can specify that entries in a Table of Contents include heading text, a dot leader, and the page number where the heading is found.

If set up properly, you now have a table of contents. WordPerfect scanned your document for marked text, found it, noted the page number, and built the table of contents automatically.

If you make changes to the document, generate the table of contents again to update the page numbers.

Take a look at your new table of contents. The page numbers are probably blue. Float your mouse over one of the blue page numbers. See how the mouse pointer changes to a hand? Click one of the blue page numbers. Presto! You see that page onscreen. These are hyperlinks, and Publish to PDF will transfer these links to your PDF.

Create WordPerfect PDF

If you only need a PDF for print production, you don't need an interactive table of contents, bookmarks, or other links. However, most of my students are trying to cut printing costs by publishing online PDFs, and my assumption is that you are, too. This next section details how to create a WordPerfect PDF that contains user-friendly links and bookmarks.

NOTE

PDF Tweaker is a WordPerfect macro developed by Dave Braze that's supposed to fix hyperlinking issues in WordPerfect 8, 9, and 10. I was unable to get it to work with WordPerfect 11, even after recompiling. The macro is available free at ***www.wpuniverse.com****. Look in the Tips, Tricks, and Techniques section.*

Because PDF Tweaker is a volunteer project, don't expect any support for its use. This isn't a PDF generation tool—you must use it with Adobe Acrobat or another product that turns postscript files into PDF, such as Jaws PDF Creator or activePDF Composer.

Publish to PDF

Until Corel fixes the bugs in Publish to PDF, I half-heartedly recommend this feature. It creates links from the table of contents, and you need to add bookmarks manually.

The following procedure is based on WordPerfect 11. Earlier versions have similar procedures with fewer options.

1. Choose File | Publish to | PDF.
2. Select the General tab.

3. Choose Browse in the File name box.
4. Select a location to save the PDF.
5. Type in the filename.
6. Click Save.
7. In the General tab, choose Acrobat compatibility level and output type.
8. In the Objects tab, select Embed fonts in document, Convert TrueType fonts to Type 1, Subset fonts, and Compress text and line art.
9. In the Document tab, turn on Include hyperlinks and turn off Generate bookmarks. Turn on Page Only.
10. Click OK.

You now should have a PDF that has links from its table of contents to the relevant headings inside the document. Unlike the Create PDF macro in Word, Publish to PDF only creates a link from the page number to the heading inside the document. The linked page number is blue and underlined. The text of the TOC entries isn't linked.

NOTE *Many reports of Publish to PDF are producing incorrect links. Use a tool such as ARTS Link Checker (**www.artspdf.com**) to verify that your document includes proper links, or test all of them manually.*

Finish the Job

To make a usable online PDF from WordPerfect, you need to add bookmarks and set page numbers manually. See Chapter 4 for postcreation techniques and some products that can speed the process.

Making a WordPerfect PDF Accessible

It takes a bit of work, but you can add the structure to a WordPerfect file that will make it accessible to the visually impaired. Unfortunately, WordPerfect out of the box doesn't produce *Tagged PDF,* which includes an XML-like structure that helps assistive technology decipher a PDF. Accessibility is becoming a more and more important issue for all federal agencies and federal contractors. For details on accessibility, see Chapter 5.

As with bookmarks and page numbers, this operation takes place after the PDF has been created. Acrobat 6 Professional is required.

First, run a Quick Check on the document. A *Quick Check* examines a document's structure and reports any problems. It likely will report that the document has no structure.

To run a Quick Check, choose Advanced | Accessibility | Quick Check.

To add structure to a PDF from WordPerfect and make it accessible, use the following procedure.

1. Choose Advanced | Accessibility | Add Tags to Document.
2. Run Quick Check again. If your document doesn't contain any graphics, Quick Check might give you a passing score.
3. Test the document with Acrobat's Read Aloud feature. Navigate to a page of text and choose View | Read Out Loud | This Page Only.
4. Listen to the voice. Does it read the words properly? If so, you have a document that is accessible.

Graphics are more of a challenge. A graphics-heavy document of any kind is more work to make accessible. This is because someone must describe in words what meaning the graphic conveys. In general, the more complex the graphic, the more description required.

1. Choose View | Navigation Tabs | Content.
2. Expand the tree structure until you see a <Figure> container.
3. Select the <Figure> container.
4. Right-click and choose Properties.
5. Click the Tag tab.
6. Type a description in the Alternate Text field. This is the text that will be read to the user.
7. Set the Language required for your audience.
8. Click Close.

9. Close the Content Tab.
10. Test the document with Acrobat's Read Aloud feature. Navigate to a page of text and choose View | Read Out Loud | This Page Only.

If the built-in Read Out Loud feature works, your document should be accessible. You can also use the Advanced | Accessibility | Quick Check feature to look for possible problems.

Summary

Adobe has gone to great lengths to tightly integrate Microsoft Word with Acrobat. WordPerfect lacks that integration, but has its own built-in PDF generator. The Publish to PDF feature in WordPerfect isn't perfect, but it can produce a table of contents that's linked to the information inside the document.

WordPerfect users must manually add bookmarks, fix page numbers, and add structure to their documents—tasks that we hope Corel will fix in a future release of WordPerfect. Also needed is a way to make PDFs from WordPerfect compliant with Section 508 requirements.

Even with these limitations, WordPerfect can be a useful tool for creating high-quality PDFs.

Chapter 9

Working with Acrobat Security and Digital Signatures

Security is a constant high-priority item on any Information Technology (IT) Manager's to-do list. Terror attacks, spyware, hackers, worms, e-mail viruses, and all kinds of threats make security an important issue.

I consult with many government agencies that have high-security levels—I can't even bring a cell phone into some job sites. You've undoubtedly seen heightened security at your work environment, too.

Adobe has responded to the need for more security by adding new features to Acrobat 6, building on a foundation that started in earlier versions. Acrobat has lots of flexibility to meet your security requirements. You can have no security at all—a requirement of many government agencies who try to make as much information available to the public as possible. Or, you can have lots of security with your PDF files. Acrobat has an open security architecture that integrates with many security devices. Eye scanners, fingerprint readers, written signature detection, electronic certificates, and encoded swipe cards can all be configured to work with Acrobat.

Unlike other electronic document formats, Acrobat security is *persistent.* This means user permissions and access controls travel with the PDF.

Why Secure a PDF?

The first question you might ask is, "Why bother?" For many organizations, the answer is you don't have to. For others, it is important to keep confidential information private, or to prevent someone from tampering with documents.

Let's take court opinions from the United States Supreme Court, for example. The court publishes its opinions at its web site (**http://www.supremecourtus.gov/**) as soon as it can, and the files are unsecured. You can change the PDF of a court opinion, but the change won't have any legal impact. In fact, many schools and courts will copy-and-paste sections from Supreme Court opinions into new documents.

Because everyone has access to U.S. Supreme Court opinions via the Web, and changing them won't have any legal impart, let's use a court opinion to see what can happen to an unsecured file.

1. Go to **http://www.supremecourtus.gov/** and download one of the court's recent opinions in PDF to your local hard drive by choosing Save a Copy in Acrobat.
2. Close the web browser and open the file in Acrobat. Navigate to the last page and look for the line that says either *It is so ordered* or *It is so denied* in italic type.

3. Go to Tools | Advanced Editing and select the Touchup Text tool. Now, reverse the court opinion. In the sample I am using, I will change *ordered* to *denied.* Notice the slight variation in the font from the original as Acrobat does its best to reproduce the original font, as shown in Figure 9-1.

You can also copy-and-paste any text from the opinion, or choose File | Save As… and save the text as a Word document.

You can make these changes because the file is unsecured. As the top court in the land, the Supreme Court doesn't have to worry about the security of its published documents or the legality of what might happen if someone tampers with an opinion or extracts the text. Lower courts often use the Supreme Court's opinions as part of their own rulings.

Other government agencies and private businesses do care about the security of their documents. Authors and artists want to protect their works from unauthorized duplication, companies want to preserve trade secrets, and government agencies need to protect the public from terrorists.

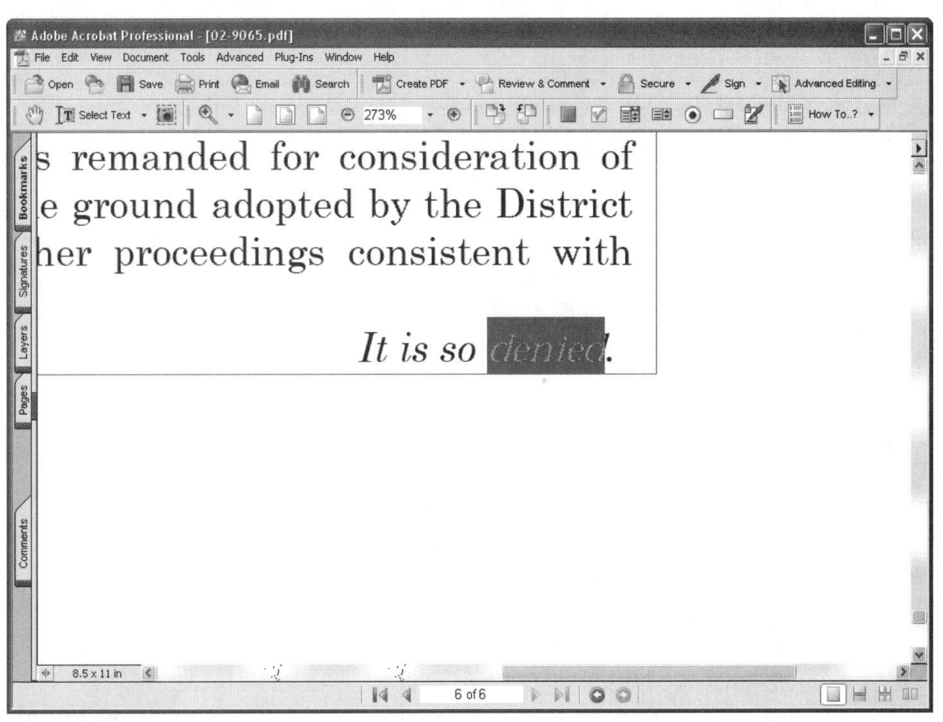

FIGURE 9-1 Acrobat's Text Touch-Up tool can be used to make textual changes in unsecured PDFs.

Acrobat Security Types

There are three basic types of Acrobat security: password protection, device protection, and digital signatures.

Password protection is the easiest to implement. Passwords can be applied to keep unauthorized users from opening files, or from extracting or modifying documents that the public can open and view.

Device protection and *digital signatures* rely on Acrobat's integration with a public key infrastructure (PKI) system or through custom programming. For example, a fingerprint reader can be integrated with Acrobat, so only the user whose thumbprint is on file can make changes to a document's security level. Digital signatures can be used to encrypt PDFs, so the documents can be read only by a group of authorized users.

Displaying Security Settings

You have several ways to see whether a PDF has security applied. A gold key will appear in the left-hand corner of the Acrobat status bar if a PDF is restricted. Use one of the following to display details of how a PDF is secured:

- Click the Secure task button and choose Display Restrictions and Security.
- Choose Document | Security | Display Restrictions and Security.
- Choose File | Document Properties (CTRL-D) | Security.

The Document Security Screen, as shown in Figure 9-2, shows the backward compatibility of the security applied, which editing functions are permitted, and the type of security applied to the document.

What About eBooks?

eBooks are in a category by themselves. Adobe uses special Digital Rights Management (DRM) technology that controls whether an eBook can be printed or loaned to other users. This electronic enforcement of copyright is embedded into the PDF by Adobe Content Server. You can't create this kind of security from within Acrobat.

If you don't want to go into the eBook publishing business, you can turn to an authorized application service provider who can create an eBook for you. These vendors are listed at **http://www.adobe.com/products/contentserver/partners.html**.

Adobe has consolidated its Acrobat eBook Reader product into Acrobat 6 and Adobe Reader, so you no longer need to install two products—one for eBooks

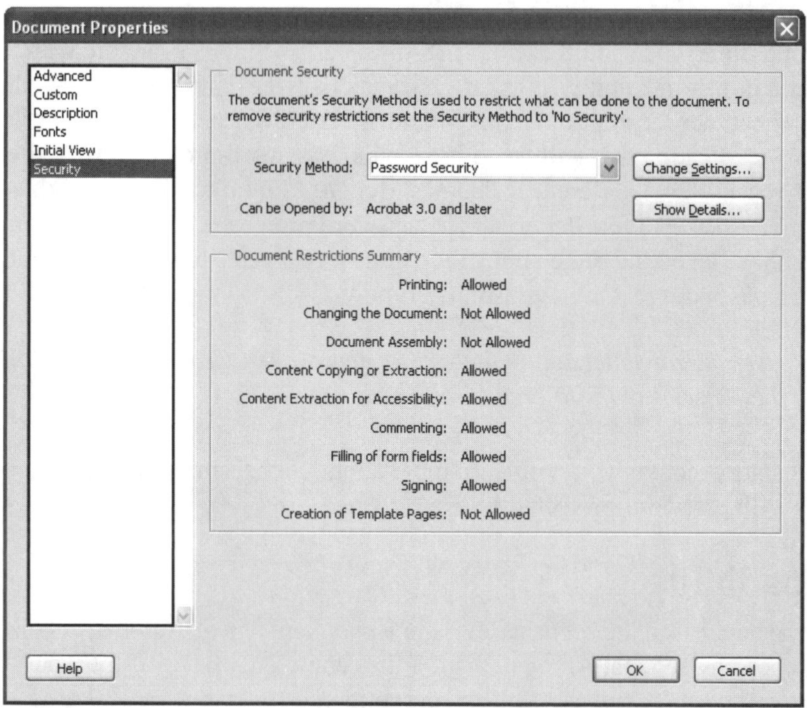

FIGURE 9-2 Document Security shows whether a PDF can be edited or printed, and whether the security is backward-compatible with early versions of Acrobat.

and another for regular PDFs. Either Acrobat 6 or Adobe Reader will read an eBook with DRM restrictions.

Password-Protected PDFs

You can use passwords to restrict access to PDFs, or to control whether users can print or edit PDFs. Adobe calls password-protected PDFs *restricted documents*.

Passwords can be applied to PDFs at two levels: to restrict opening, or to restrict editing, printing, or copying a PDF. Security can be applied at creation via the Security settings in Acrobat Distiller, or from within an already created PDF. Add your password-applied security by choosing Document | Security | Restrict Opening and Editing from within Acrobat 6. In Distiller, choose Settings | Security.

NOTE *To remove security, choose File | Document Properties | Security and change the security method to No Security.*

Which Security Level Is Best?

If at all possible, you should use the 128-bit security options available with Acrobat 5 or 6 compatibility. It is far easier to crack the 40-bit security available with Acrobat 3 or 4 compatibility. How much easier? There is a $60 "password retrieval" application that will try to break your password-protected PDF files.

At a recent PDF Conference, Thomas Merz of PDFlib demonstrated this program. It cracked a four-letter, 40-bit password protected PDF in 20 seconds. It would have taken the same application almost two years to retrieve an eight-character password that used 128-bit encryption.

TIP *Use random letters and numbers for passwords. Cracker applications use dictionaries to try to break passwords.*

In the next section, you will learn more about your security and compatibility options with password-protected PDFs.

Compatibility

Adobe has increased the security levels in newer versions of Acrobat. As discussed in the preceding section, Acrobat 3 and 4 files could only have 40-bit security. Acrobat 5 and 6 files can use 128-bit encryption.

In Acrobat 6, you can keep document metadata unencrypted. Metadata can include author name, document name, subjects, and other useful search information. This option permits web search engines and document management systems to index the metadata, making the PDFs easy to find. Use the Acrobat 6.0 and Later option if you want to expose your document's metadata. Remember, if you choose a high level of encryption for Acrobat 5 and later, users of Acrobat 3 and 4 cannot open the files. The security settings available to you will depend on the compatibility level you select.

Document Open Password

If you don't want unauthorized persons to even open your PDF, set a Document Open Password. Choose the Require a Password to Open the Document option, and enter a password of at least one character. Keep in mind that the password is case- and space-sensitive. Remember to store your PDF passwords in a safe place.

When someone tries to access a PDF with a Document Open Password, they will receive a security dialog box. They will have to correctly enter the password to open the PDF.

Permissions Password

Choose the Require a Password to Restrict Printing and Editing of the Document and Its Security Settings if you want to add security to your PDF. You cannot leave the password field blank, but it will accept one-character passwords. Passwords of at least eight random letters and numbers are much more secure than simple ones, as noted in the preceding section.

TIP *Document Open, and Restrict Printing and Editing passwords must be different.*

Printing Allowed

You have three options with this setting:

- **Not Allowed** grays out the printer icon and the File | Print menu settings. Users cannot print the document.
- **Low Resolution** (available with Acrobat 5 and Later) prints at a maximum level of 150 dpi. The purpose of this setting is to protect high-quality images from being printed at a high resolution, and then resold without the artist's permission.
- **High Resolution** permits users to print to high-resolution printers, such as imagesetters.

NOTE *You cannot void the security of a document by printing an encrypted PDF to the Adobe PDF printer. The Adobe PDF printer will refuse to process an encrypted PDF.*

Changes Allowed

The *Changes Allowed* options give you flexibility. For example, you may want your end users to be able to fill out a PDF form, but you don't want them to be able to add comments. The Changes Allowed options give you choices in how much security you want to apply to a document.

Your options are

- **None**, which applies the maximum amount of security to a document. Users cannot make comments, fill in form fields, digitally sign documents, or add or remove pages. They can read the PDF and print it (with your permission), but they cannot modify the PDF.

- **Inserting, Deleting, and Rotating Pages** lets your end users manipulate the pages of your PDF, and enables them to add bookmarks and embed thumbnail images of pages. Previous versions of Acrobat called page manipulation *Document Assembly*.
- **Fill-in Form Fields and Signing** is used in PDF forms. End users can then fill in a form and sign it, but they cannot create form fields or add comments.
- **Commenting, Filling in Form Fields, and Signing** is the same as Fill-in Form Fields and Signing, except that users can also add comments.
- **Any Except Extracting Pages**, which means anything goes except pulling pages out of the PDF.

Enable Copying of Text, Images, and Other Content

Use this option (available only with Acrobat 5 or higher compatibility) if you want to use Acrobat Catalog to index your PDFs. Enabling this option also permits users to copy-and-paste information, including text and graphics, from your PDF. Disable this option if you are seeking to protect intellectual property in a PDF.

Enable Copying of Text, Images, and Other Content and Access for the Visually Impaired

This option is only available at Acrobat 3- or 4-level compatibility. It permits the screen readers of the visually impaired to read the contents of a PDF. Use the following option if you are using a higher security level.

Enable Text Access of Screen Reader Devices for the Visually Impaired

Used with the higher level of encryption available with Acrobat 5 or later compatibility, this option enables the screen readers of the visually impaired to read the PDF.

Enable Plaintext Metadata

This option exposes the metadata in the PDF, so it can be indexed by web search engines and document management systems. It is available only with Acrobat 6 or later security.

Adobe Policy Server

Adobe was piloting a new product, Adobe Policy Server, at press time. This new product makes security dynamic, and moves beyond securing one PDF at a time.

Adobe Policy Server provides authors and IT administrators with the capability to dynamically control who can view a PDF document, and whether the recipient can modify, copy, print, or forward the document.

The product is meant to be dynamic, so permissions can be changed after the document has been distributed. Documents can expire on a specific date or be revoked immediately, regardless of how many copies were distributed. Because Adobe Policy Server controls usage policies, documents do not need to be redistributed if a policy is changed.

How would this work in the business world? If a PDF is sent for review to a certain group of users, then no one outside of that group can view the document. For example, a confidential marketing plan could be sent to vendors for bids. If a vendor forwards the plan to an unauthorized person, that recipient will be unable to open the document.

Policy Server also can help keep customer communications secure. For example, a bank can send monthly customer statements as protected PDF e-mail attachments. Policy Server would ensure that only the customer can open the statement, and not someone else.

Digital Identities

With Acrobat, you can use digital identities to sign documents, or to encrypt PDFs for a certain group of people.

When you encrypt PDF files for a list of recipients, you are using Acrobat's certificate authority features. With this kind of security, only certain *trusted identities* can access a PDF, or add comments to it. You use these same digital identities to sign documents and to verify the digital signatures.

These relationships are managed with security certificates. You can create your own from within Acrobat, use the Windows certificate manager, or use the certificates issued by third parties, such as VeriSign, Entrust, and RSA Security.

The basic process involves selecting a security method, creating your own digital identity, and creating a list of recipients (or signers) from their digital identities. You then apply various permissions based on the list of digital identities to encrypt a PDF for a group.

These digital identities can arrive on a disk, USB drive, a Lightweight Directory Access Protocol (LDAP) server, or the Windows Certificate Store. Consult your IT department for its preferred method.

About Digital IDs

Digital IDs usually contain a public key, which you share with others. Think of the public key as your passport—it vouches that you are who you say you are. Others share their public keys with you, and you assemble these into a list of trusted identities.

Acrobat has a built-in digital ID creation system. You log in, create your identity, and share it with others. IDs created from this system are not verified by a third party. It is kind of like creating your own passport. You can do it, but it won't be widely accepted because it isn't issued by a trusted source (like your country's passport authority).

You also can use the Windows Certificate Security system built into your Windows operating system (OS). See your IT manager about using the Windows Certificate Store for managing your digital IDs.

In the following section, you will learn how to create and share your own digital ID, and then how to manage the certificates of others.

Creating Your Digital ID

The easiest way to create a digital identity is to use Acrobat's built-in, self-signed security. However, this ID may not be widely accepted because you are the certifying authority, not a well-known third party such as VeriSign, Entrust, or other Adobe partner.

Your self-created digital ID file will have a .pfx extension in Windows or a .p12 extension in Mac OS X.

Use the following procedure to create a self-signed digital ID:

1. Choose Advanced | Manage Digital IDs | My Digital ID Files | Select My Digital ID File.
2. Click New Digital ID File, and then click Continue.
3. In the Create Self-Signed Digital ID dialog box, enter a name for your digital ID. This is the name that will appear to other users.
4. Select either 2,048-bit or 1,024 RSA security. A higher level of security is offered by 2,048-bit, but 1,024-bit RSA is more commonly used.
5. Choose whether you want to use the digital ID for digital signatures, data encryption, or both.

6. Enter a password of at least six characters in the Choose a Password and Confirm Password text boxes. Passwords are case-sensitive and should not contain spaces.
7. Click Create, enter a filename, and Save the ID.

You can now export your digital ID. See the following section for more information.

NOTE *You cannot use your digital ID if you lose it, or if it becomes corrupted. Be sure to make a backup copy of your digital ID file.*

Sharing Your Digital ID

You can export your digital ID as an FDF file, or you can e-mail your certificate to others. If you are using a third-party certificate, see whether you need to share it. The third party may provide a mechanism for sharing IDs.

Use the following procedure to share your self-signed digital ID:

1. Choose Advanced | Manage Digital IDs | My Digital ID Files | My Digital ID File Settings.
2. Click the Find Your Digital ID File button.
3. Select your digital ID and select Open.
4. Enter your password and click OK.
5. Click Export, and either e-mail the file or save the data.

Requesting Digital Certificates

You can use a list of trusted identities to validate the digital signatures of others, or to encrypt a file for a group of users.

Adobe recommends importing a certificate sent by the user, but it notes you can add a certificate that has been digitally signed with a self-signed digital ID. You can request that users e-mail their certificates to you by using the following procedure:

1. Select Advanced | Manage Digital IDs | Trusted Identities.
2. Click Request Contact.

FIGURE 9-3 You can request that others e-mail you their digital IDs so you can build a list of trusted identities.

3. Enter your name and e-mail address, as shown in Figure 9-3. Choose Include my Certificates to e-mail your certificate.
4. Choose whether to e-mail the request, or to save it as a file. Click Next.
5. Select your digital ID file, enter your password, and click OK. Select the digital ID file to use, and then click Select.
6. Enter the e-mail address and click e-mail, as shown in Figure 9-4. If necessary, click Send in your e-mail application.

Your request arrives via e-mail, and the recipient can send their certificate to you.

Assembling a List of Trusted Identities

When your associates begin responding to your requests for certificates, you will begin to build your list of trusted identities. To add an e-mailed certificate to your list of trusted identities, open the attachment and choose Set Contact Trust. Specify trust options, and then click Import. You can also import certificates from a network directory or other centralized location.

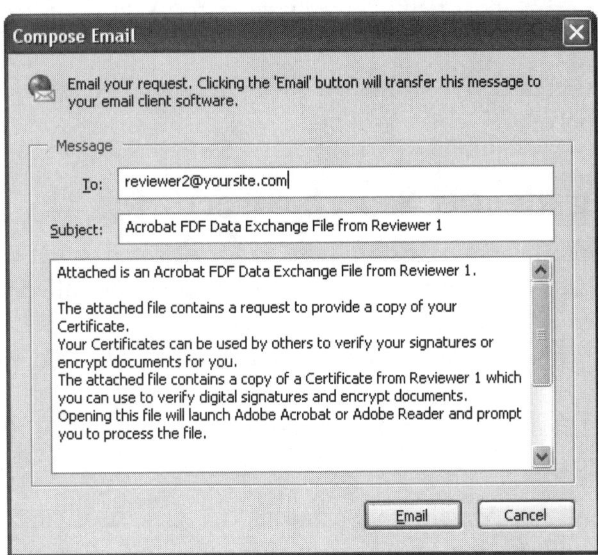

FIGURE 9-4 Acrobat 6 automates the process of requesting digital certificates.

Use the following procedure to add a certificate from a file:

1. Specify a default signing method by choosing Edit | Preferences | Digital Signatures.
2. Choose Advanced | Manage Digital IDs | Trusted Identities.
3. Click Add Contacts and browse for the digital ID, or choose Browse for Certificates and Open it.
4. Click Add to Contacts List and click OK.
5. Click Close.

You also can pull a certificate from a digital signature in a PDF. To do so, use the following procedure:

1. Open the PDF document containing the user's self-signed signature.
2. Click the signature in the document to check whether it is valid.

3. Click Signature Properties, and then click Show Certificate. Call the certificate originator or otherwise confirm that the certificate is valid.
4. Click Close, click Trust Identity, click OK, specify trust options, and then click Import.

Configuring Identity Search Directories

Many organizations maintain lists of digital ID certificates on network servers, including LDAP servers. These lists of digital IDs are often called *identity search directories.*

Use the following procedure to configure an identity search directories:

1. Choose Advanced | Manage Digital IDs | Configure Identity Search Directories.
2. Click New, specify a directory name and server settings, and then click OK. For more information on server settings, contact your system administrator.

Encrypting a Document for a Group of Users

Once your list of trusted identities is established, you can use either Acrobat's self-signed signatures, the Windows Security Store, or a third party to encrypt a document for a group of users.

You can give everyone in the group the same level of access, or you can give different levels of access to members of the group. You can specify whether users can edit, print, or extract information from a PDF.

Use the following procedure to use Acrobat self-signed security certificates to encrypt a document for a group:

1. Open the PDF you want to encrypt and choose Document | Security | Encrypt for Certain Identities Using Certificates.
2. Select which digital ID you want to use, enter a password, and then click OK.
3. In the Restrict Opening and Editing to Certain Identities dialog box, select a name and click Add to Recipients List, as shown in Figure 9-5.
4. To manage the users, highlight the recipient or recipients, and click Set Recipient Permissions, as shown in Figure 9-6. If you do not set specific permissions, recipients will have full access. Acrobat will warn you that

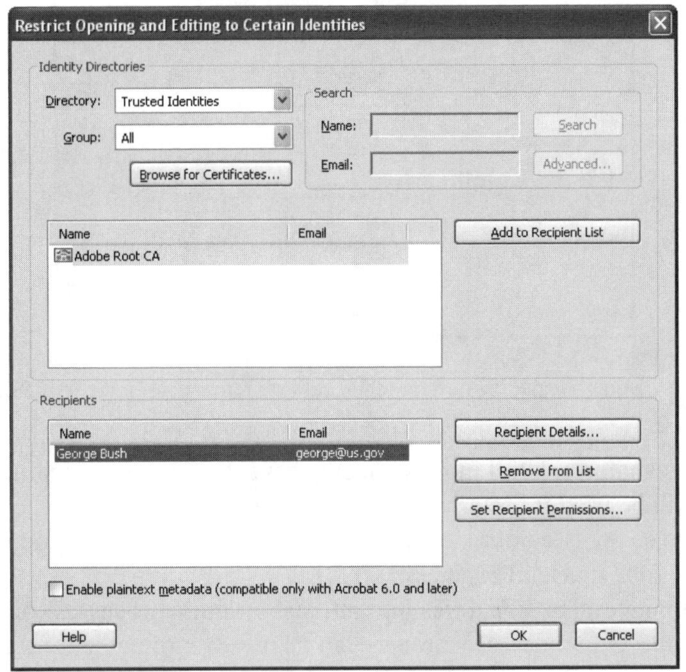

FIGURE 9-5 You can use Acrobat security certificates to manage who can edit, print, and comment on PDFs.

some third-party products may not honor the security settings. These are the same options discussed in the preceding section.

5. Click OK, and then click OK again.
6. Continue the process until you have added all the recipients and set their permissions.
7. Save, close the file, and send it to your group.

When someone from your recipient list opens the PDF document, the security settings you specified for that person are used.

Using Digital Signatures

Digital Signatures are a new way of doing business. While technically legal in most states, digital signatures lack the large body of case law that stands behind

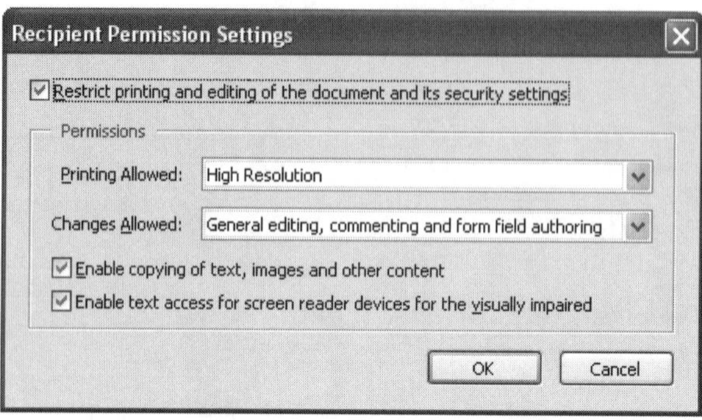

FIGURE 9-6 You can specify how much access recipients can have to a PDF.

handwritten signatures. Until more standards develop, I expect most digital signatures will be used for internal approvals—vacation requests, benefits selection, and so on. See your attorney for advice on the legality of digital signatures in your state and business.

Incorporating digital signatures into internal business processes can save substantial time and money. Documents can be routed more quickly and have a built-in audit trail.

Acrobat has an open architecture that supports nearly every kind of digital signature device—signing pads, eye scans, fingerprint readers, cards, and so on. In this section, you will use Acrobat's Certificate Authority.

About Acrobat Digital Signatures

Acrobat has two basic methods for signing documents. One is called *invisible signing*—the signature only appears in the Signatures window. The second is called a *visible signature*, which appears both on the document and in the Signature window. You can either sign with the Signature tool, or activate a special kind of form field that signs the document.

You can configure your signature to look like a handwritten signature, or it can look like a digital watermark. See the following sections on how to change the appearance of your signature.

Using Your Signature

You will need a digital ID before you can sign a PDF. See the preceding sections on methods to create a digital ID. Use the following procedure to log in and select a digital identity.

1. Choose Advanced | Manage Digital IDs | My Digital ID Files | Select My Digital ID.
2. Choose a digital ID file, or click Find Your Digital ID File and browse to find a digital ID.
3. Type your password and click OK.

Now you are ready to sign a PDF.

Applying an Invisible Digital Signature

You can sign a document in a specific area, such as a signature field on a form. Or, you can invisibly sign a document, and your signature will only appear in the Signatures tab. Use the following procedure to invisibly sign a document.

1. Choose Document | Digital Signatures | Sign This Document.
2. Acrobat will generate a warning that the document is not certified. Click Continue Signing.
3. If the document does not contain digital signature fields, Acrobat will ask if you want to create a new signature field or to invisibly sign the document. Choose Create New Invisible Signature and click Next.
4. Select your Digital Signature and click OK.
5. Enter your password. You have the option to enter a reason for signing the document.
6. Choose either Sign or Sign and Save As. Specify a filename, and click Save if you choose Sign and Save As.
7. Acrobat displays a confirmation message indicating you have signed the file. A pen and paper icon appears in the lower-left corner of the Acrobat window indicating you are viewing a digitally signed document.

Displaying an Invisible Signature

By invisible signature, Adobe means that no signature appears on the document. You can see it in the Signatures window. Choose View | Navigation Tabs | Signatures if the Signatures window isn't showing. An example is shown in Figure 9-7.

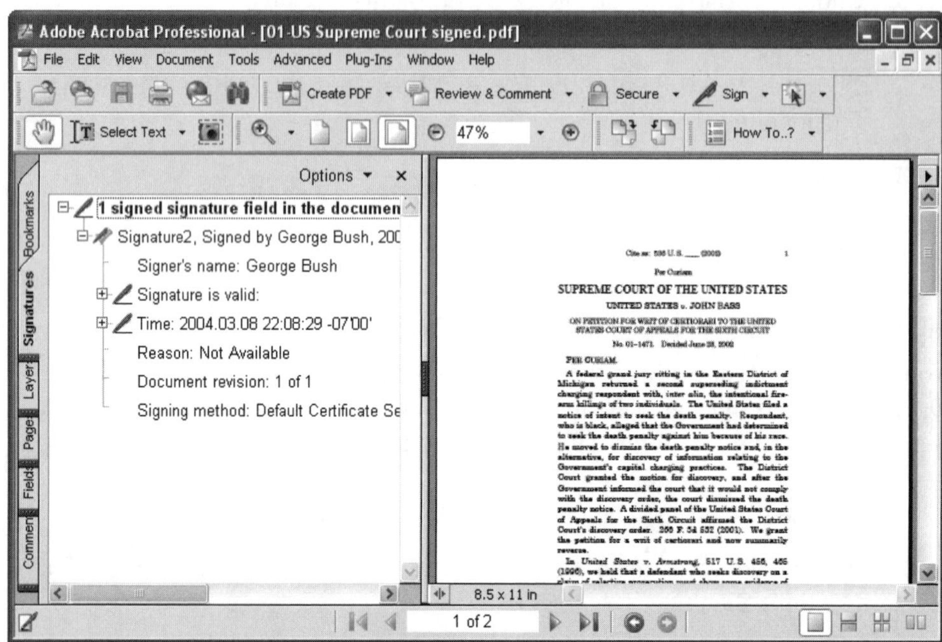

FIGURE 9-7 An example of an invisible digital signature. The signature shows in the Signatures window, not on the document.

Creating a Digital Signature Form Field

You can add a digital signature form field to a document by using the Digital Signature Form tool (Tools | Advanced Editing | Forms | Digital Signature Form Tool). Click and drag to create a signature field. This field is similar to other form fields, except for the unique properties in the Signed tab in the field properties window.

It is recommended that you select the Mark as Read-Only All Fields option. Once a form is signed, no one can change the entries in the fields.

Signing a Digital Form Field

Use the Hand tool to activate a signature field. Acrobat will issue a warning about the document being uncertified, and then you will go through the process of

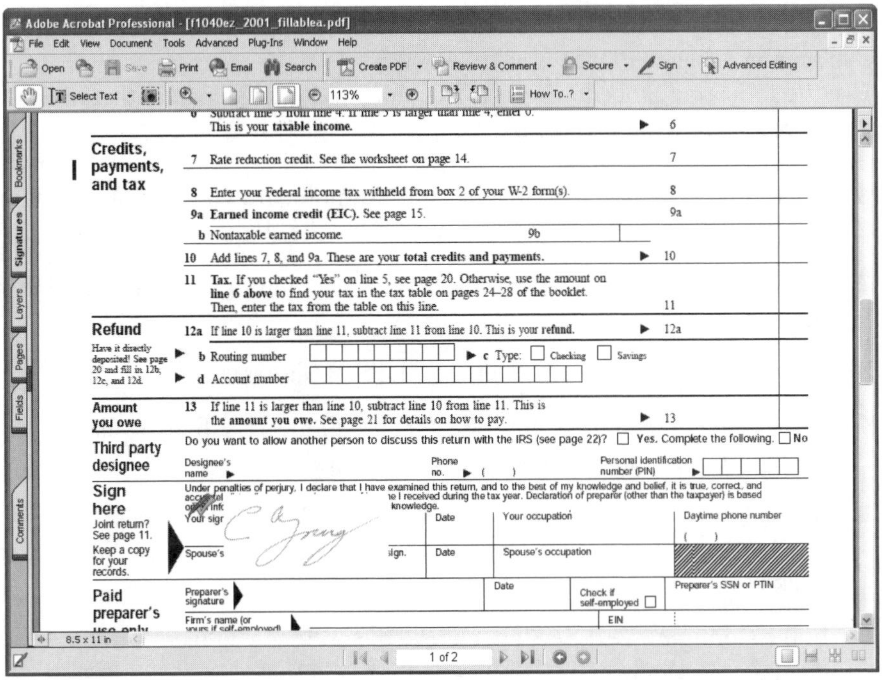

FIGURE 9-8 Digital signatures can be configured to display images that look like handwritten signatures.

selecting a digital ID, as described in the preceding section. See Figure 9-8 for an example of a signed signature field.

Configuring the Appearance of Your Digital Signature

The default appearance of Acrobat's digital signatures looks like a text block—it doesn't look like anything like a handwritten signature. You can modify the appearance of your signature so it looks more familiar, as shown in Figure 9-8.

While you can scan an image of your complete signature and incorporate it into your PDF digital signature, most security experts recommend that you do not. Keep your handwritten signature for your personal use.

Instead, create a new version of your signature for use with digital signatures. That way, you can tell if someone tries to forge your signature based on what they've seen in a signed PDF.

Use the following procedure to create a custom digital signature that looks more like your handwritten version:

1. Write a version of your signature. For example, use your initials and family name instead of your complete name. Place the signature on a scanner.
2. Choose Create PDF | From Scanner | and scan the signature into a PDF. Save the file.
3. Choose Edit | Preferences | General | Digital Signatures.
4. Click New. Enter a name for the signature in the Title field of the Configure Signature Appearance dialog box.
5. In Configure Graphic section, select Imported Graphic and click the PDF File button. Browse to the location of your scanned signature. Select it and click OK.
6. In the Configure Text Section, choose the options you like. Acrobat displays a preview of how your signature will look.
7. Click OK and click OK again to close the Preferences window.

Certifying a Document

As organizations become more concerned with security, an interesting question comes up. How do you trust that a document is authentic? Adobe's answer is the certified document. When you certify a PDF document, you are attesting to its genuineness.

For example, a government agency could issue certified PDFs so citizens would know the PDFs are authentic and not forgeries. A company could file a financial report and certify the PDF, attesting to its validity. Any modifications to the PDF invalidate the certification.

A blue ribbon appears in the lower-left corner of certified documents, and optionally on the document. An example is shown in Figure 9-9.

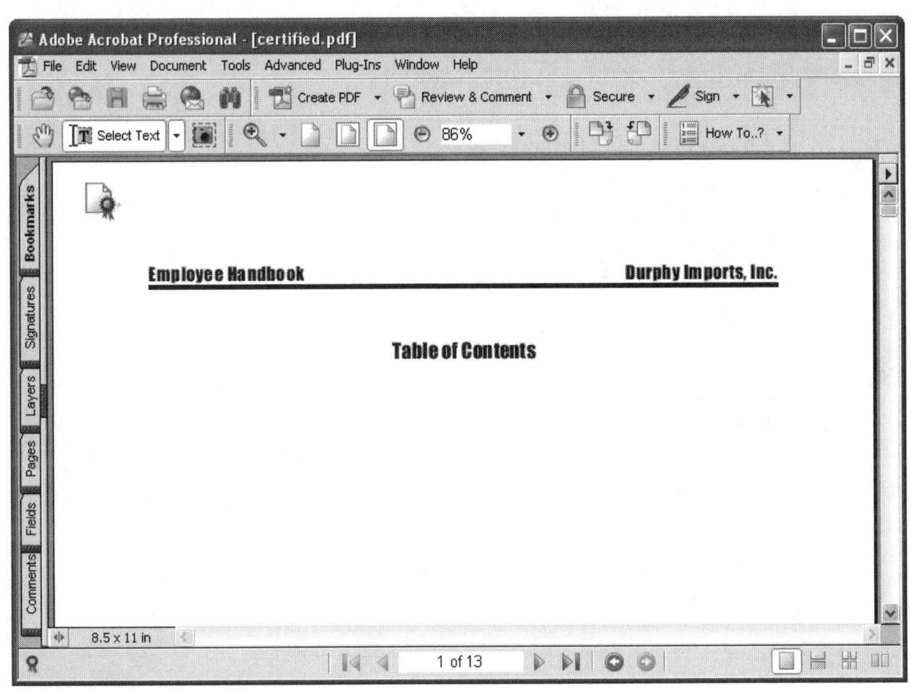

FIGURE 9-9 An icon of a blue ribbon appears in a certified document.

(The phrase "certified document" has caused some confusion among users. *Enfocus,* a maker of PDF pre-press tools, uses the phrase "Certified PDF" to mean that a PDF meets certain production standards and is ready for high-quality printing. Adobe's certified document is all about security and is in no way connected with the Enfocus Certified PDF Workflow.)

Steps to Certify a PDF

When you certify a PDF, you are establishing a higher level of trust for your document. For example, you could distribute a certified form to customers for signing. If the signed form comes back and it is still certified by you, you can be assured that the terms and conditions of the signed form have not been changed.

Use the following procedure to certify a PDF:

1. Open the document to be certified.
2. Choose File | Save as Certified Document. You can use your existing Digital Signatures preferences or go to a page at the Adobe web site where you can obtain a third-party digital ID.
3. Click OK.
4. In the Allowable Actions menu, choose Disallow Any Changes To Document to completely protect the document. Choose Only Allow Form Fill-In On This Document if you want end users to fill in the form, or Only Allow Form Commenting and Form Fill-In Actions On This Document if you want to permit form fill-in and commenting.

   You can select Lock the Certifying Signature So It Can't Be Cleared or Deleted by Anyone if you permit end users to modify the document.
5. Click Next.
6. Choose Show Certification on Document or Do Not Show Certification on Document. Even if you select Do Not Show Certification on Document, Acrobat will display a blue ribbon in the lower-left corner of the Acrobat screen. Click Next.
7. Click OK. If you selected Show Certification on Document, draw a box in the upper-right corner of the first page to display your signature and the certification blue ribbon.
8. Select the Digital ID you created earlier (or create a new one) and click OK.
9. Select I Attest To The Accuracy And Integrity Of This Document, or some other reason for certifying the document. See Figure 9-10 for an example.
10. Enter your password and click Sign and Save As….
11. Save the file.

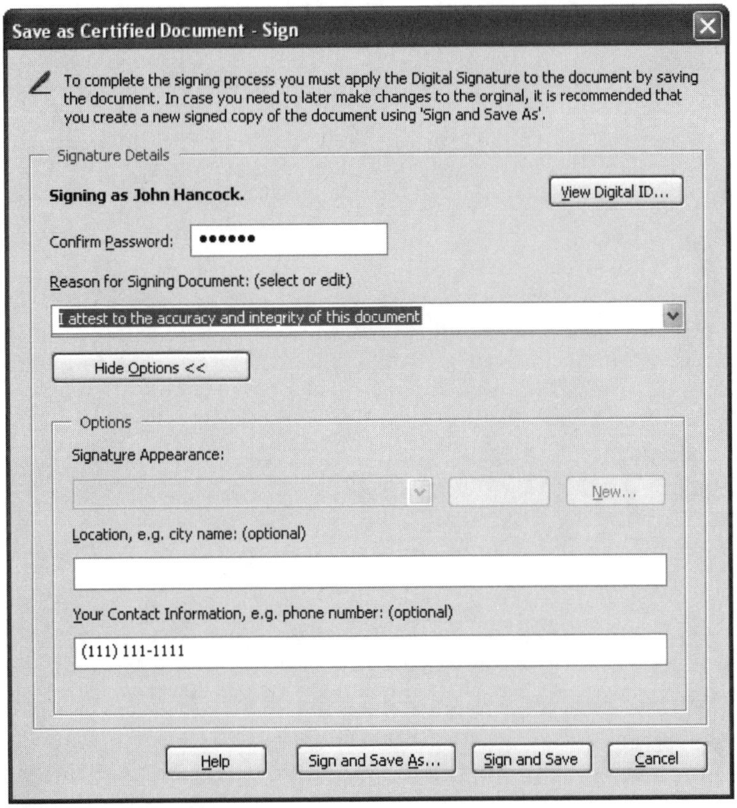

FIGURE 9-10 Your digital ID is required to certify a document.

Summary

Acrobat 6 improves on the security features found in earlier versions. With Acrobat 6, you can digitally sign documents and forms, certify the authenticity of a document, or encrypt a document, so that only a certain group of users can view it. You can customize the look of your digital signature and set up a hierarchy of trusted users whose digital identities you keep on file.

Chapter 10

The Wide World of Acrobat

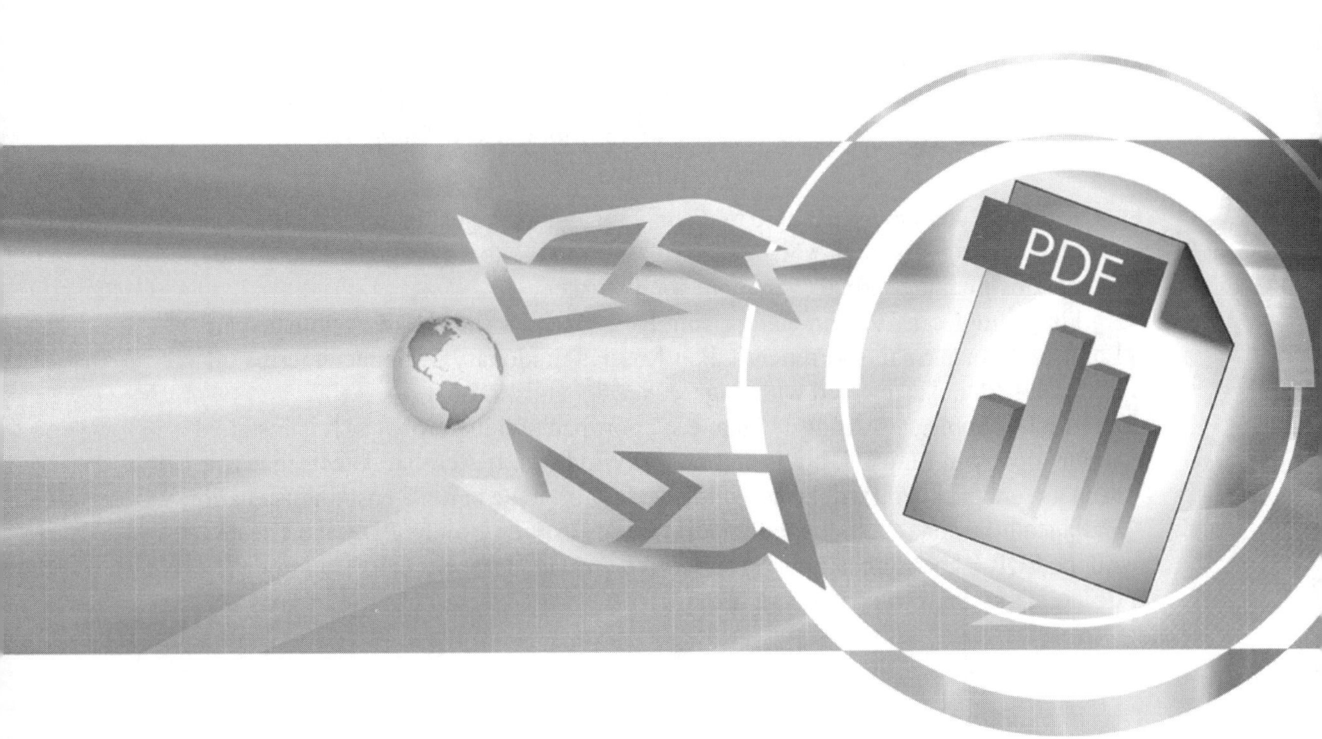

No matter where you travel in the world, PDF is spoken—or at least available for reading. Not only are PDF tax forms available in all 50 of the United States (and the District of Columbia) in English, but you can find interactive claim forms in French and English in Canada, PDF reports on the textile trade in Chinese, and PDF newspapers in Arabic. Because the Adobe Reader is free and available in many languages, PDF has been widely adopted by governments and businesses worldwide, as the following list of supported languages shows:

Arabic	Brazilian Portuguese	Czech	Chinese
Danish	Dutch	English	Finnish
French	German	Greek	Hebrew
Hungarian	Italian	Japanese	Norwegian
Korean	Polish	Russian	Spanish
Swedish	Turkish		

PDF Covers the Map

PDF is the Rosetta Stone of electronic publishing. It works in nearly every language, it can display different languages on the same page, and, now, it can even have layers with different languages for truly multilingual documents, as shown in Figure 10-1.

NOTE *Although Acrobat can display almost any language onscreen, the preceding table shows the languages Adobe Reader supports.*

Although you have been able to display many languages for several years, Acrobat keeps getting better with each release and the tools for generating multilingual documents become even more sophisticated.

For example, in 1998 an enterprising Russian, Igor Sharshakov, published an English/German/Spanish/French/Italian/Russian dictionary of financial terms in PDF. This PDF was created with PageMaker 6.5 and Acrobat 3.

Adobe supplies an Asian-language support pack with Acrobat 6. It is installed automatically in Mac OS, but is optional in Windows. If Acrobat detects that you need its font pack, you will be asked to install it, or you can run a custom installation and install the Asian Language Support options in View Adobe PDF and Create Adobe PDF. The Asian languages supported are Japanese, Korean, Traditional Chinese, and Simplified Chinese text.

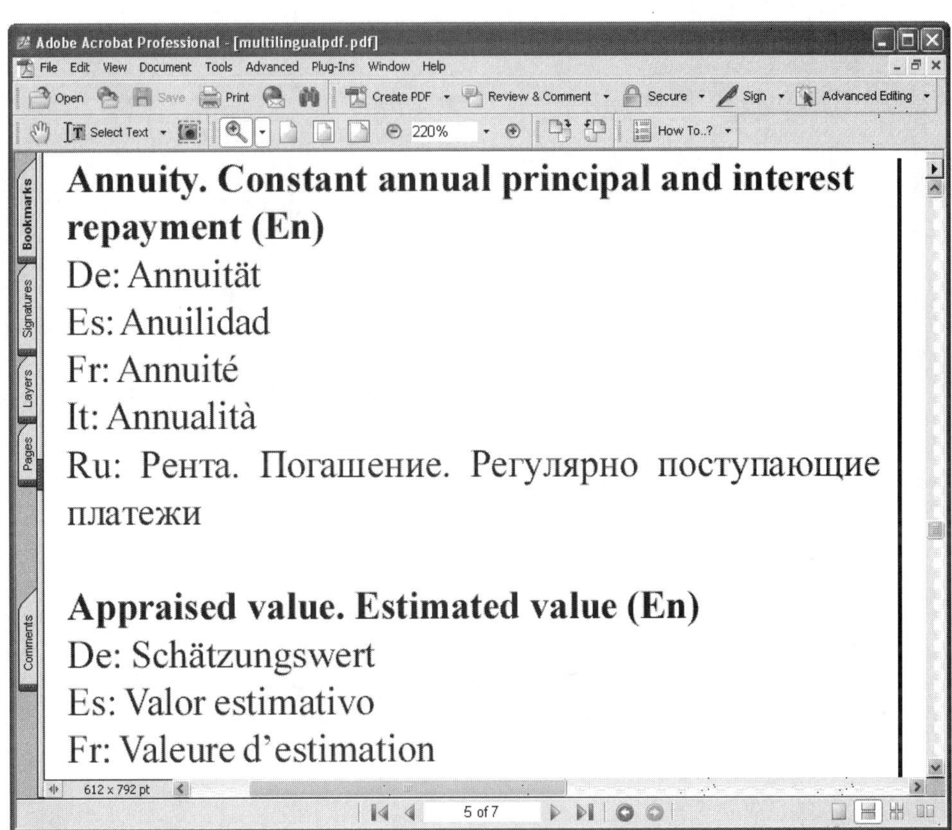

FIGURE 10-1 Acrobat speaks many languages. Here it is displaying six languages in a multilingual dictionary.

Windows users must also have Asian language support installed on their computers. In Windows, open Control Panel and choose Regional and Language Options. Move to the Languages tab and choose Install Files for East Asian languages and click OK. You will need to supply your installation disk. Use the same procedure to enable support for complex script and right-to-left languages, such as Thai and Hebrew.

Once these steps are taken, you don't have to do much to display a foreign language text in PDF. Simply open the file, and there is the PDF in a different language. At Adobe's web site, for example, PDF news releases are in English, Korean, and Japanese. An example of a Japanese news release from Adobe is shown in Figure 10-2.

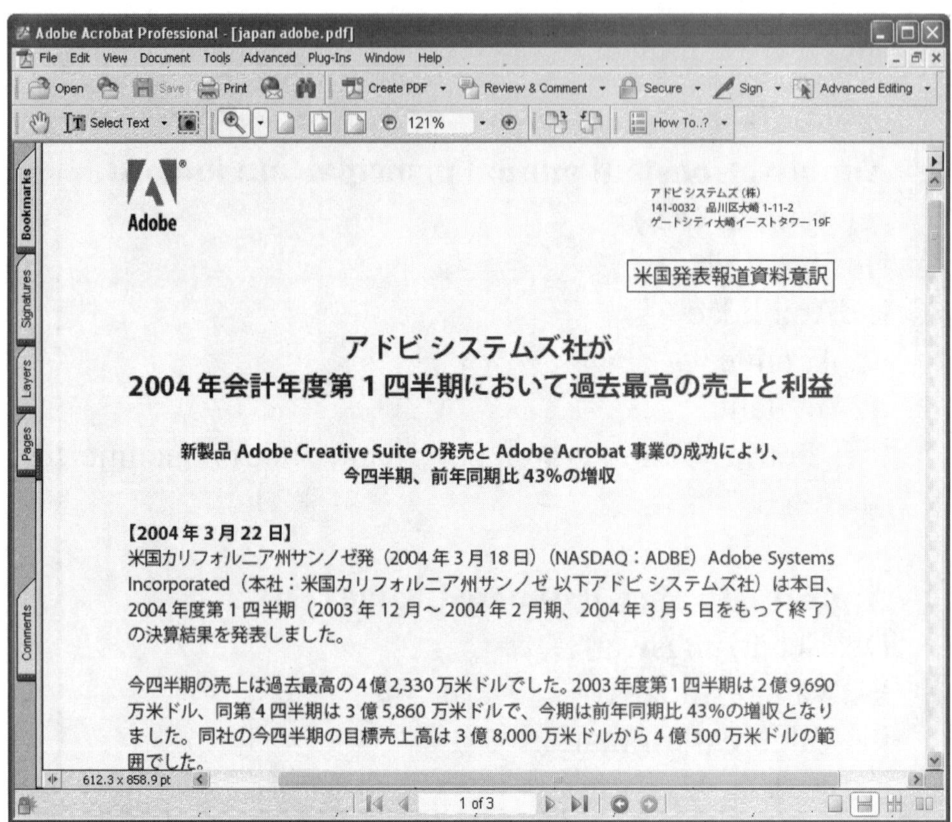

FIGURE 10-2 News release from Adobe Japan about the availability of the Adobe Creative Suite

New Features in Acrobat 6

You will be able to display Asian-language and other non-English language text when fonts are embedded and subset. However, some font foundries forbid font embedding, especially for Asian-language fonts. Acrobat's built-in font technology will help to display Asian language text, even if the fonts are not embedded. In addition to simply displaying languages, you can now more actively interact with PDFs in multiple languages.

Multilingual PDFs

For example, you can now easily conduct reviews in multiple languages, as shown in Figure 10-3.

Even if you don't have an Asian language keyboard, you can cut-and-paste comments from other applications into Acrobat comments. The example in Figure 10-3 was assembled from three randomly selected Adobe news releases.

The base document is an English-language news release that was edited on a western Microsoft Windows XP computer. I simply opened three other PDF news releases, and cut-and-pasted contents from those three as comments into the base document.

For organizations with worldwide operations, the capability to add comments in multiple languages can be a big help in enabling faster business response times. Multilingual documents can be reviewed and marked up in one cycle, rather than in one cycle for each language.

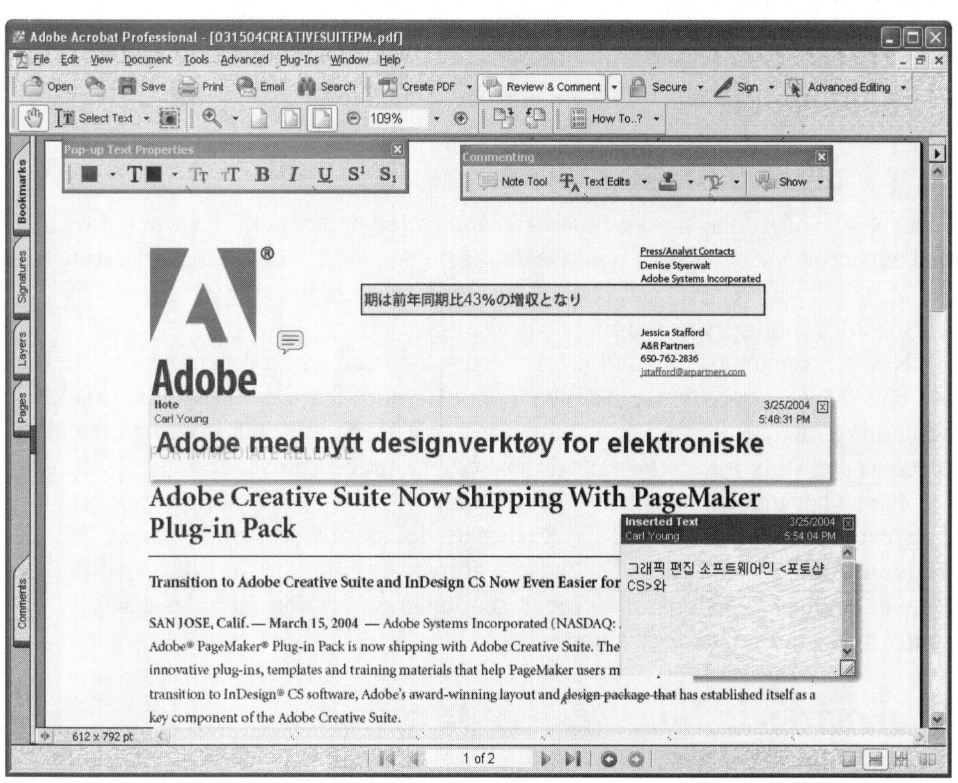

FIGURE 10-3 A news release from Adobe with comments in Norwegian, Korean, and Japanese

You also can create an Acrobat index of documents using Roman, Chinese, Japanese, or Korean fonts. Use Acrobat Catalog, available at Advanced | Catalog, to create the index. As with indexing, you can search Chinese, Japanese, and Korean text.

Different Languages on Separate Layers

Some of Adobe's first sample files demonstrating the use of layers were for multilingual ads. One ad design could hold copy in separate layers for each language. For example, consider an ad designed for the European Union. When the ad is published in the United Kingdom, all languages but English would be hidden. When published in France, the French layer would be shown, and so on.

While layers are tantalizing for multilingual uses, they are limited. For example, you probably could create a quick reference guide with several languages on separate layers. However, you couldn't create an entire user manual or book that way. The text reflows caused by translation and character differences would make keeping the matching text on identical pages difficult, if not impossible.

New Features for Japanese

Japan is one of Adobe's largest markets, and the company has long worked to make its products work well with the Japanese language. For example, starting in Acrobat 5, Japanese text could be reflowed if it was produced by a tagged PDF. This feature continues in Acrobat 6.

New for version 6 is that all users, even ones using western language operating systems (OSs), now can use Adobe's Paper Capture feature on scanned image containing Japanese text. The installation is off by default, but it will be installed if run as a custom installation, as described in a preceding section.

Adobe has made it possible to make Japanese language documents accessible. The text can be reflowed, and the Read Aloud feature works on Japanese text. The free Adobe Reader also has these features. Although it isn't included in the Roman language versions of Acrobat, the Japanese version includes a set of standard Japanese business stamps.

Bookmarks in Non-Western Languages

One of Acrobat's strengths is its bookmarking capability. Acrobat 6 makes it easier than ever to create bookmarks in multiple languages, as shown in Figure 10-4.

You can create bookmarks automatically from Microsoft Word using PDFMaker, or you can manually create bookmarks. The sample in Figure 10-4 was put together by manually assembling bookmarks from a variety of sources.

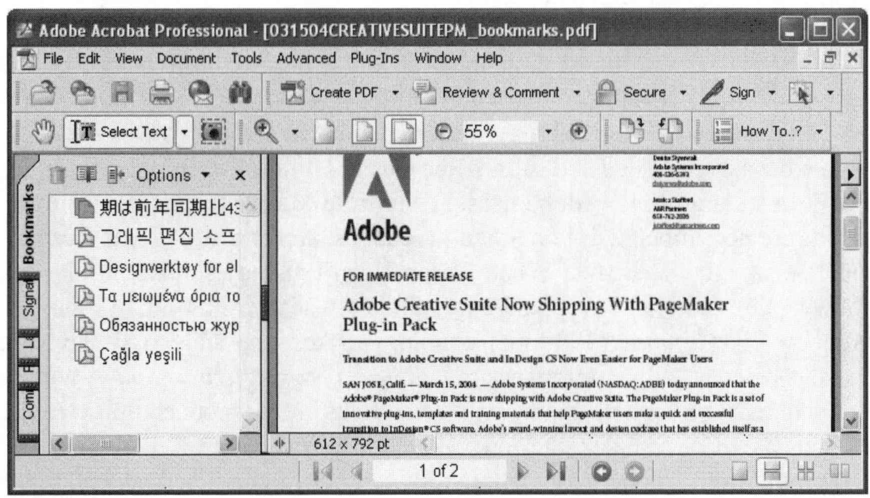

FIGURE 10-4 Bookmarks in Japanese, Korean, Norwegian, Greek, Russian, and Turkish

While bookmarks work well with western and Asian languages, there are difficulties with Middle Eastern languages. For example, I was able to easily copy-and-paste Hebrew into Microsoft Word, but I could not paste the Hebrew text into a bookmark. You would likely see better support if you use the Middle Eastern version of Acrobat.

Creation Is the Key

As with most things regarding Acrobat, how you create the file is key to producing a multilingual PDF. For example, if you want readers in foreign lands to be able to display your PDFs, you should embed and subset your fonts. If you do not, then end users may not be able to display the PDFs correctly—they may see white square boxes instead of your text.

NOTE *When working with Asian language documents, PDFMaker and the Adobe PDF printer automatically embeds and subsets most Asian fonts.*

Font Terminology

In almost any discussion of PDFs in multiple languages, the subject of fonts starts and ends the discussion. Fonts are required to display a language, and are critical to Acrobat's goal of producing an electronic carbon copy of the document as displayed in the authoring application.

As noted in the preceding section, the best course of action is to embed and subset fonts, especially for documents that will be read on machines that may not have a font particular to your language installed. For this reason, you should choose a font that can be embedded and subset. See Chapter 3 for more information.

For Roman languages, Adobe uses its Multiple Master technology to mimic fonts that are not embedded. For Asian languages, Acrobat uses fonts from the optional Asian language pack. When Acrobat can't display a character, it inserts a hollow square bullet, although other symbols are seen from time to time.

Adobe's CID (Character ID) font technology makes it possible to display Asian language characters. While most western languages are *single-byte fonts*—with one byte of data representing one character—Asian fonts are far more complex. Because Asian fonts are more complex, they are called *double-byte fonts*.

CID fonts from Adobe may contain any number of characters, a technique that is helpful in displaying the complex symbols used in Asian languages. When document authors enter the symbols from the keyboard, the keystrokes are mapped through a CMap Resource, producing what Adobe calls CID-Keyed Fonts. (For more information, see Adobe support document 323835 and the related technical notes mentioned in the document.)

Acrobat also supports Unicode, the worldwide standard for encoding characters. Unicode was developed by the Unicode Consortium. Information is available at **www.unicode.org**.

Unicode supports the display of the written languages and technical disciplines of the modern world. Many classical and historical written languages also are supported. Each character is given a unique two-byte code. Non-Unicode fonts have their own coding system, and often are limited to 256 characters.

The OpenType font technology used by Adobe, Apple, and Microsoft supports Unicode. Windows 2000/XP/2003 and Mac OS X support Unicode.

Adobe's OpenType fonts include Roman characters and common international characters, such as the liter and euro currency symbols. Adobe's OpenType Pro fonts add many accented characters to support central and eastern European languages, such as Polish and Greek. Some Pro OpenType sets also include Cyrillic and Greek character extensions. All Adobe OpenType fonts can be embedded in Acrobat.

Microsoft supports a variety of fonts, including OpenType and TrueType. A font to consider is a special OpenType font called *Arial Unicode MS,* which includes characters for Roman, Arabic, Hebrew, Chinese, Japanese, Korean, Greek, Tibetan, Thai, Malaysian, Cyrillic, and other languages. This font can be embedded in Acrobat.

Application Support for Unicode

While the technology exists to display many languages and characters, whether your authoring application supports Unicode is another question. When a software company says it supports Unicode, it may mean it does not support it completely.

Check with your software vendor to see just what is meant by Unicode support before you try to produce a document in Cherokee or ancient Goth.

Non-Adobe applications that support Unicode:

- Word 2000/XP/2003
- QuarkXPress 4, 5, and 6
- Macromedia Freehand 10 and MX
- CorelDRAW 10 and 11

Adobe applications that support Unicode:

- InDesign 1, 2, and CS
- Illustrator 10 and CS
- Acrobat 5 and 6

NOTE *Unicode support in Acrobat and Reader may not be universal. For example, a bookmark with Unicode characters may not display in all versions of the product.*

Summary

Acrobat is truly a worldwide publishing medium. PDFs can contain multiple languages using multiple fonts. You can add comments to PDFs in more than one language, including Asian languages.

New features in Acrobat 6 include *Paper Capture for Japanese,* which can be optionally installed in the English version of Acrobat. Acrobat 6 can reflow Japanese text, and the Read Aloud functionality works with Japanese on computers running the Japanese version of Windows.

Languages can be placed on separate layers for the creation of international ads or quick reference guides, and Acrobat bookmarks can contain non-Roman characters, such as Asian languages or Russian.

Chapter 11

Moving Beyond One-Document-at-a-Time Creation

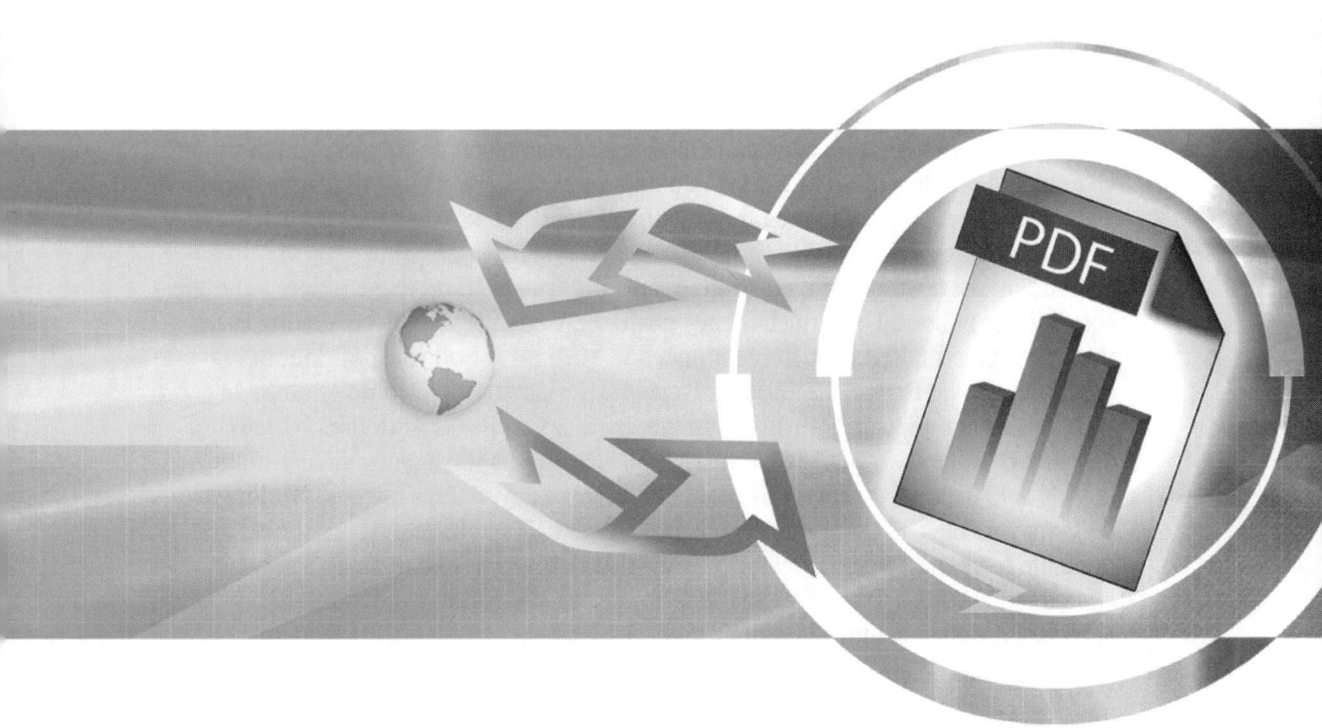

Throughout the book, we have been looking at Portable Document Format (PDF) creation from a lone author's point of view—even if that lone author is working in a group with others. In this chapter, we begin by looking at how the lone author can manipulate more than one file at a time. The next section moves beyond the single PDF creator to look at how server-based products can create many hundreds or thousands of PDFs at once. The chapter ends with a specialized type of batch processing: scanning paper documents into PDF.

Introduction

Acrobat is designed as a desktop product—the typical use is one person creating one PDF at a time. That workflow is fine for many uses, such as a technical writer producing an online manual or a designer producing an ad.

But what about other business processes? For example, the person in charge of producing a CD, who needs to add security settings to hundreds of PDFs. Opening one file at a time and manually specifying security options is a great way to waste time doing a repetitive procedure. Wouldn't it be great if that process could be automated? Well, it can, because Acrobat includes a feature called *batch processing,* which gives you the power to process dozens, or hundreds, of files at a time.

Let's step back a bit and look at the use of PDF in a large organization, such as a financial institution, a human resources department, or a government agency. Suppose that, each month, one of these entities has to produce thousands, or millions, of reports that are mailed to customers each month. For the financial institution, it might be a customer financial statement. For a human resources department, it might be a summary of health benefits used or a retirement benefits statement. A government agency might need to produce monthly business sales tax reports for thousands of small businesses.

Add up the cost of printing, folding, stuffing, and mailing these reports, and the cost is in the billions. How much money could these entities save by generating PDFs that could be e-mailed to customers instead? Millions, or billions, of dollars.

In the United States, the Internal Revenue Service has been able to close warehouses and reduce its printing budget by many millions of dollars by making tax forms available in PDF at **www.irs.gov**. Not only is the agency saving money, but it's also making the forms available 24 hours a day, 7 days a week. No longer do taxpayers have to go to the library or the post office during business hours and hope the form they need is in stock. They also don't have to call an IRS service center and ask for a form to be mailed. Forms are always on hand at the IRS web site, ready to be downloaded day or night.

But how do you create 100,000 retirement reports overnight? You do it by not using the desktop version of Acrobat. You would have to have an army of workers equipped with the desktop version of Acrobat to turn out that many reports. Instead, you use a server-based solution from Adobe or another company.

In this chapter, you first learn how to power Acrobat to manipulate hundreds of files at once, and then you look at some of the many Adobe and non-Adobe server-based solutions.

NOTE *Why produce reports in PDF instead of HTML? Because a PDF looks like a paper document, it's an easier transition for users to make than shifting to an HTML document that probably won't look a thing like the statement customers are used to seeing—especially in print. Greater customer acceptance means fewer people will be asking for paper-based statements, which results in more cost savings. In addition, a PDF can be highly formatted, which is great for documents with lots of numbers in tables, as is the case with nearly all financial reports. And, for many businesses, legal requirements exist for keeping form data with the actual form that customers saw. And, unlike HTML, a PDF can be easily secured to prevent tampering, and then can be filled out offline.*

Acrobat Batch Processing

Before moving on to the world of server-side PDF, let's take a look at what you can do with Acrobat.

Beginning with version 5, Adobe added a macro-like capability to Acrobat called batch sequences. Acrobat *batch sequences* only work inside of Acrobat. In other words, you can't use an Acrobat batch sequence to control PDF creation from Microsoft Word.

NOTE *If you want to connect an Acrobat batch sequence to another program, you have to use platform-specific scripting languages. In Windows, you can use Visual Basic to control Acrobat, and use batch sequences to run operations inside of Acrobat. In MacOS, you would use AppleScript instead of Visual Basic.*

What Is Batch Processing?

Acrobat's *batch sequences* are a lot like macros in Word and WordPerfect. You are essentially replacing manual keystrokes with automation. Each sequence is a specific set of commands carried out in a specific order. You fire off the batch sequence, and then sit back and watch Acrobat do the work. Or, you can leave for a cup of coffee. Batch sequences can be run on one file or hundreds or thousands. Sequences can run without your intervention, or you can interact with the sequence to make a choice at a predefined step.

Acrobat comes with some sequences already written, or you can roll your own custom batch. You can share your sequences and use batches written by others. Sequences are saved for reuse, and your custom sequences appear alongside the sequences that come with Acrobat. Let's start by looking at the sequences that come with Acrobat.

Running a Sequence

Tucked away in the Advanced menu are several simple sequences that Adobe has provided for you. Looking at these sequences is a great way to learn how to create your own. While Acrobat 5 shipped with 8 batches already installed and 19 optional batches on the installation CD, Acrobat 6 comes with only the 8 preinstalled sequences. No additional batch sequences are on the installation CD.

NOTE *Start Acrobat, but don't open any files to run these sequences.*

Using Prebuilt Sequences

Sequences are stored in the Acrobat 6/Acrobat/Sequences/ENU folder. The file extension for Acrobat batch sequences is *.sequ. The prebuilt sequences in Acrobat 6 include the following:

Create Page Thumbnails Permanently embeds miniature pictures of each page for display on the Pages tab.

Fast Web View This speeds the user viewing experience for PDFs posted on the Web. PDFs that aren't set up with Fast Web View (also known as *linearization*) must completely download to the user's machine before they can be viewed. Fast Web View lets users see each individual page as soon as it's transferred.

Open All This opens all the selected files. It will even automatically create PDFs if you select a file type that Acrobat can convert, such as Microsoft Office files and TIFF images.

Print 1st Page of All This prints only the first page of each selected file using your current print settings.

Print All This prints all selected files using your current print settings.

Remove File Attachments This strips files that are attached to the selected PDFs.

Save All as RTF This converts the selected files to Rich Text Format (RTF).

Set Security to No Changes This restricts access to a PDF by setting up passwords and disabling certain features, such as printing and editing.

Sequences on the Acrobat 5 CD

Instead of building a sequence from scratch, you might find what you need on the Acrobat 5 CD. If you don't have one, ask a friend for a copy of the sequences.

One sequence from the Acrobat 5 CD that I find useful is Spell Check a Document. While Acrobat 6 will spell check form fields and comments, this sequence checks the spelling of the entire PDF. Red squiggly underlines appear beneath suspect words.

Batch-Process Documents

The following procedure can be used to run any batch process. If a step calls for a manual process, you would stop at that point, and then continue. Figure 11-1 shows the Batch Sequences dialog box.

1. Choose Advanced | Batch Processing.
2. Select a process from the list on the right side of the Batch Process dialog box.
3. Click on the Run Sequence button.

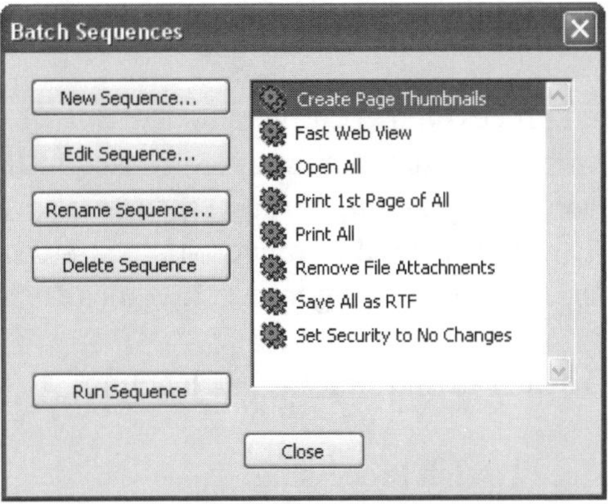

FIGURE 11-1 Acrobat's batch processes (prebuilt and any custom) appear in the Batch Processes Screen.

4. Make sure the sequence you selected is the one you want.
5. Click OK.
6. Choose the files you want to process.
7. Click Select.
8. Some sequences have options at this point. Specify your options if applicable and click OK.
9. Repeat the process on another file, or click Close in the Batch Sequences dialog box to end.

A Comparison of Batch Processing and Manual Input

Let's look at a manual process and see how a batch sequence automates it. In this example, we manually convert a file to RTF, and then run a batch sequence to do the same thing.

1. Choose File | Save As….
2. Save as Type (Windows) or Format (MacOS) | RTF Rich Text Format (*.rtf).
3. Click the Settings button.
4. Make sure the Generate Tags for Untagged Files is selected.
5. Click OK.
6. Enter a filename and location where you want the file to be located.
7. Click Save.

This isn't a difficult process to perform manually. But what if someone sends you a DVD full of Acrobat files that they want converted to RTF? Is spending a morning, a day, or several days running through the same seven steps a good use of your time? Probably not. This kind of repetitive, lock-step process is what batch sequences are good for. As shown in Figure 11-2, you can select multiple files to run the batch on.

Here's the process again, configured for batch action.

1. Choose Advanced | Batch Processing.

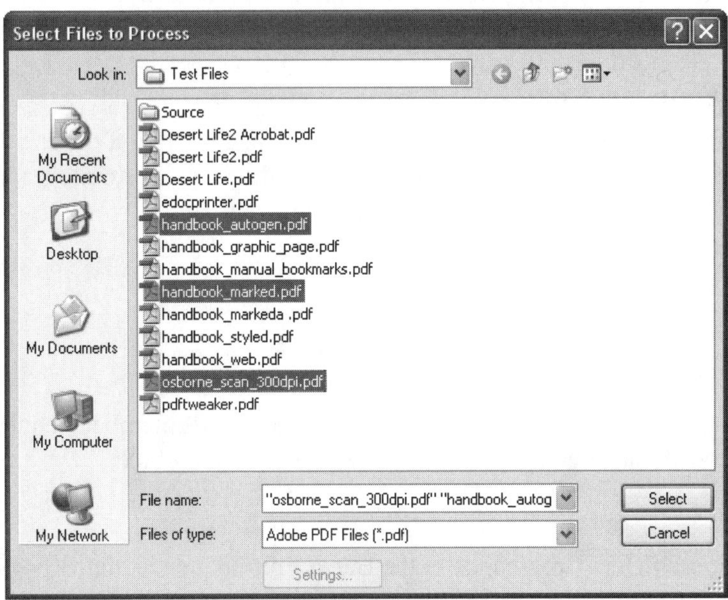

FIGURE 11-2 Multiple files selected for batch processing

2. Select Save All as RTF from the list on the right side of the Batch Process dialog box.
3. Click the Run Sequence button.
4. Make sure the sequence you select is the one you want.
5. Click OK.
6. Highlight the files you want to process. See Figure 11-2 for an example.
7. Click Select.
8. No options are available at this point. Click OK.
9. Click Close in the Batch Sequences dialog box to end.

Running the Convert to RTF batch sequence takes nine steps, instead of the seven steps needed for a manual conversion, but you can process many files at once with the batch sequence. Just remember, processing can take time, so don't plan on using your computer for any heavy work while the batch is running.

Rolling Your Own Batch

You can create custom batch sequences to speed the completion of repetitive tasks. As shown in Figure 11-3, Acrobat includes an Edit Sequence dialog box from which you can pick commands to be included in your batch.

To create a new batch sequence:

1. Select Advanced | Batch Processing.
2. Choose New Sequence.
3. Enter a descriptive name for the new sequence. Remember, sequences are listed alphabetically in the Batch Sequences dialog box.
4. Click OK.
5. Choose Select Commands in the Batch Edit Sequence dialog box.
6. Choose a command on the left side of the Edit Sequence dialog box.
7. Click Add to place the command in the list on the right.
8. Continue selecting as many commands as required.

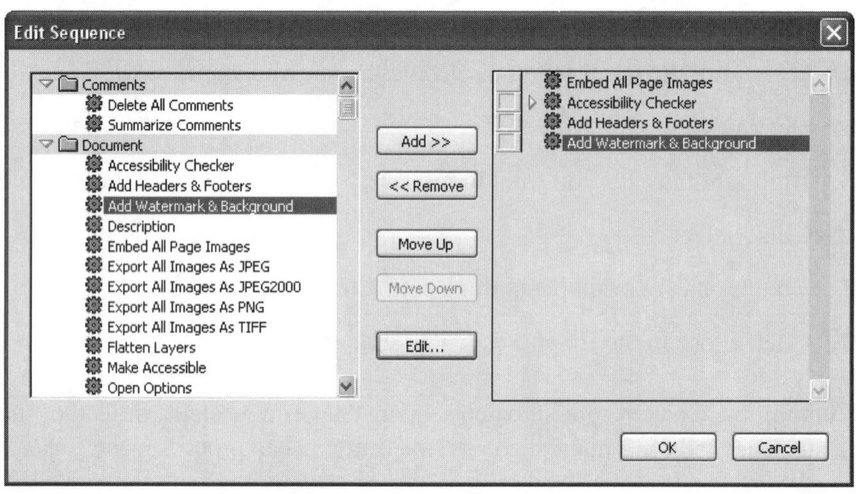

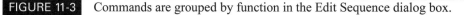

FIGURE 11-3 Commands are grouped by function in the Edit Sequence dialog box.

9. Set the order of the commands by selecting commands on the right side of the dialog box, and then using the Move Up and Move Down buttons to place the commands in the order the commands should be executed.

NOTE *Batch Edit Sequence can specify options, as well as when and where the sequences run.*

10. Click OK.
11. Choose the options you need for the Run Commands On and Select Output Location choices.
12. Specify Output Options.
13. Click OK.

Preferences for Batch Processing

If you work a lot with batch processing, you might want to set preferences that will be used every time you run a batch. Preferences are available in Edit | Preferences on Windows or Acrobat | Preferences in MacOS. Select Batch Processing to see the options available. See Figure 11-4 for the preferences options.

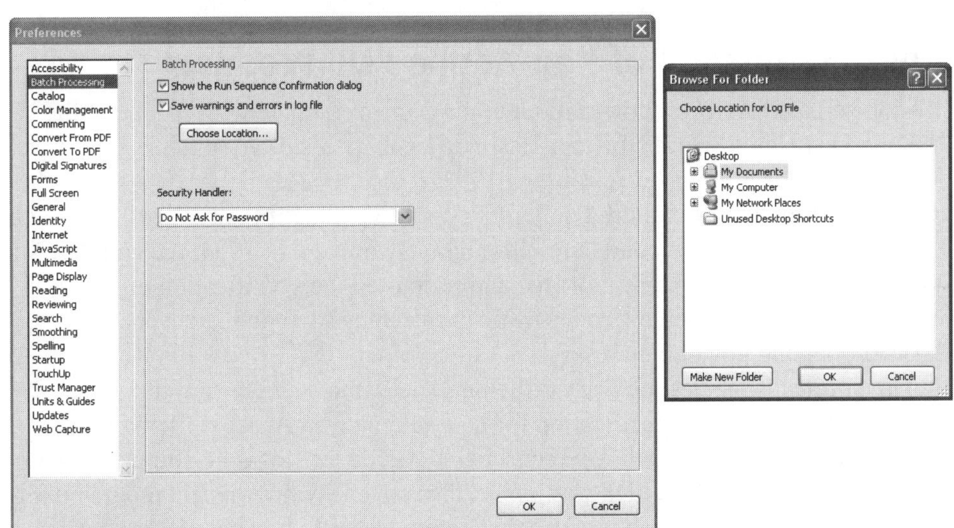

FIGURE 11-4 Batch Processing Preferences in Acrobat 6.

A useful preference is to create a log file that saves error messages. Choose Save warnings and errors in log file to create log files. Choose location and navigate to the folder where you want to store the logs.

Adobe and Non-Adobe Server Solutions

In the batch-processing section, we went deep into Acrobat and worked with individual commands. In this section, we zoom out to the big picture view of business processes. We'll look at Adobe and non-Adobe solutions, and I'll explain why the non-Adobe solutions came into existence.

As discussed in the introduction to this chapter, many complex business processes aren't solved by a desktop application like Acrobat. To produce thousands of PDF files or generate tens of thousands of individual financial statements just isn't the role of a desktop product. Adobe realizes the issue, and is continually rolling out new products meant to be deployed department- or enterprisewide. See Chapter 1 for descriptions of many of these products. (Check **www.adobe.com/enterprise/main.html** for the latest news.)

While Adobe is aggressively moving into the enterprise market, it wasn't the first to do so. Because Adobe historically focused on desktop applications, such as Photoshop and Illustrator, it basically ignored the server market when it began marketing Acrobat. Other, generally smaller, companies realized the opportunity, and jumped in with their own solutions.

The Development of Non-Adobe PDF Products

If Adobe created Acrobat, how can other companies compete with Adobe in the PDF market? Here's a quick history lesson to explain this development.

When Adobe introduced Acrobat in 1993, it sold the Reader for $50 and the creation tool for several hundred dollars. Few people bought the product, so Adobe went back to the drawing board and rethought its strategy. In 1994, the company started to give away the reader for free and promoted the specification on what makes up a PDF. Why would a company do such a thing? To win market acceptance, especially among government users.

Government agencies are wary of being locked into a single supplier for a product. By making the specification for how to create an Acrobat file public, Adobe could assure buyers they weren't being forced into a single-source decision. If the roadmap to creating a PDF was public, then anyone with sufficient programming skills and time could create a product that competes with Acrobat. Adobe earlier had used a similar tactic to win acceptance of its PostScript printer technology.

This plan was a big success. Government buyers began flocking to Adobe to buy Acrobat licenses, and private and public companies began to realize they could save tons of money by turning paper documents into electronic ones. All the end user had to do was install a copy of the free Reader. Also, in 1993, the World Wide Web (WWW) was becoming popular. Any user could easily download and install a copy of the free Reader, making it nearly as ubiquitous as web browsers. The Web also became the leading way to distribute PDF content.

Entrepreneurs noticed the wide acceptance of Acrobat. They looked at the PDF specification and saw how PDF files were created. They looked at what Adobe was doing, and at what it wasn't doing.

The biggest market void was in the server market. For many years, Adobe didn't have a real server-based product. Adobe did make some progress in the server market by licensing its PDF creation technology—the Adobe PDF Library—to large companies such as IBM, H-P, and Xerox for inclusion in those company's products. But it wasn't until 2002 that Adobe began to focus on the PDF server market.

That meant, for several years, others had a great opportunity to jump into the PDF server market. If Adobe is the Big A, then leaping into the PDF server market were the four little As and the P: activePDF, Appligent, Amyuni, AdLib, and PDFlib. Global Graphics, which had a history of competing against Adobe in the PostScript market, would eventually enter the server market with its JawsPDF Server, as would others.

The Server-Side PDF Opportunity

What market did these small companies see and exploit ahead of Adobe: the explosive growth of server technology in the 1990s. While mainframes dominated computing in the 1960s and 1970s, and personal computers in the 1980s, the UNIX and Windows-based server markets grew explosively in the 1990s. The emergence of the Web and the economic boom of the 1990s fueled growth in server-based computing.

While one-at-a-time PDF creation is fine for an individual, the lone worker model doesn't scale up to work at the enterprise level, but the cost-savings of PDF do. One person creating a PDF and e-mailing it might save 40 cents in ink, paper, and postage. One million one-page financial statements e-mailed instead of sent via the United States Postal Service can save hundreds of thousands of dollars.

But how do you create a million PDF pages at a time? You use a server. Database reports, customer statements, grant applications, and hundreds of other reports can be sent to a server, which then turns the reports into PDFs.

The disadvantage to server-based solutions is they standardize production. If a file needs special handling, programming a server to accommodate it can be cumbersome. Not all server products create bookmarks and links, either, so be sure to specify your requirements before investing in a server-side solution.

PDFs from Web-Based Products

One of the most popular approaches to server-based PDF production is to install a web interface. Users can upload, or simply drag-and-drop files into a web page, and the server turns the files into PDFs.

With a web-based interface, the PDF creator is the machine, not the document author. Instead of choosing File | Print and selecting Adobe PDF, the user drops a document into a web folder. The server-based product sees the file and runs it through a standard conversion routine.

Web-based interfaces are well suited for organizations with intranets or that want to provide PDF conversion services to partners or customers via the public Internet. Nearly all the companies listed at the end of this section can be tied to a web interface.

PDFs from Big Iron and UNIX and Windows Servers

Most large organizations today run on mainframe computers—Big Iron—or servers running Microsoft Windows or a version of UNIX. Large businesses are especially tied to mainframe computers to house and analyze hundreds of millions of customer records.

During the 1990s, many companies shifted data from mainframes to servers, especially UNIX- and Linux-based servers. Many choices for PDF-based server solutions are in this area. Adobe, Appligent, and Amyuni support popular UNIX and Windows servers. AdLib eDocument Solutions and activePDF specialize in Windows-based servers, and PDFlib GmbH makes products for nearly all platforms, including mainframes.

PDF is, in many ways, the ideal platform for outputting data from mainframes and heavy duty servers. Nearly all that data is financial in nature and, to be readable, must be printed in tables or columns and rows. Because PDF can contain highly formatted data, it's a great delivery mechanism for documents loaded with numbers, such as monthly financial statements or quarterly reports. In the next section, you see some examples.

Examples of Server-Based PDF Creation

Let's look at a few examples. All are taken from customer testimonials from PDF server-based companies. For products that convert paper forms to PDF, see Chapter 12.

A Pharmaceutical Company

The approval of a new prescription drug for sale in the United States requires a massive amount of paperwork. Submissions to the Food and Drug Administration (FDA) from a pharmaceutical company can run into millions of pages. Not only are paper-based submissions time-consuming to prepare, but the FDA had to process all that paper by hand. The time required to approve a new drug could run into years.

By shifting to PDF, the time required for new drug approvals has been cut from years to months. FDA staff can search and sort through the submitted data faster, and the drug company can create its submission much more quickly. No longer must paper submissions be shipped by the truckload to the FDA. Instead, a pharmaceutical company can overnight a set of CDs containing the submissions in PDF.

A Court System

One of the great things about Acrobat is its flexibility. Users can control how much compression to apply to graphics, whether the fonts are embedded in the PDF, and whether bookmarks are created. If you want to standardize PDF output, giving individuals that much creativity can create problems of inconsistency. If you want every PDF to be created equally, you can't beat a server. The machine doesn't mind doing the same thing over and over again.

Many courts are moving to a PDF-based workflow. PDFs look like traditional legal documents, so attorneys and their clients find them easy to accept. (If you've ever seen a paper document move to HTML, you know how different the document looks in a web browser.) Unlike paper, a PDF costs nothing to create and it can be filed in a database for easy retrieval.

While some courts encourage the use of desktop Acrobat, other court systems are moving to server creation. The server can be programmed to create PDFs consistently, assuring court administrators that the PDFs meet certain standards. All users have to do is drag-and-drop files into monitored folders. The server does the rest. In addition to creating PDFs, some server products will route the PDFs to the appropriate judge by looking at form fields inside the document. That speeds the flow of information and cuts down on clerical mistakes.

Some courts are even implementing digital signatures. With just a few mouse clicks, a judge can sign an order and route it to the appropriate attorneys and court support staff. There are even tools to redact high security or proprietary information from PDFs. *Redaction* keeps the data from being made public through court filings or Freedom of Information Act requests.

A Government Agency

Obtaining construction and zoning permits can be a chore. Contractors often have to drive to multiple offices to file permit applications and copies of blueprints, and to complete forms. The picture wasn't pretty on the agency-side either. Imagine receiving a stack of paper and a set of oversized drawings, routing the paper to the correct person inside the organization, and then sending copies to related agencies for review. Just shuffling the paper to the right desks can take months. And, meanwhile, the builder has to wait.

As in the previous cases, it's PDF to the rescue. A server-based process can accept PDF-based form data for analysis and internal routing. Engineering drawings can be scanned into a PDF-based document management system. Documents can be signed electronically, and then automatically routed up the approval ladder.

The bottom line is this: the time required for approvals can be cut from months to weeks. Contractors can obtain permits far more quickly, and the agency saves money and becomes more efficient.

A Manufacturing Company

In this case, an aerospace company is required to file daily reports on the status of a multimillion dollar development project. The customer wants a weekly report in PDF showing whether the project is on schedule and on budget.

The manufacturing company writes a report in Microsoft Word, and then develops a project status report showing schedule milestones in Microsoft Project and a cost analysis in Microsoft Excel. While these file types can be converted to PDF individually, and then combined into a single file, the process is both time-consuming and tedious.

A server-based solution can generate the report quickly and add new features. It can convert the Word, Project, and Excel files to PDF, and then group the individual files into a single one. In addition, the server solution can create an interactive table of contents and insert the table of contents into the report. Finally, the project can stamp a new page-numbering scheme across the entire document. Once the process is set up, the server can generate those reports the same way—every day—freeing engineers and writers to do more productive tasks.

A Human Resources Department

Human resources departments typically generate stacks of paper, whether they are supporting an enterprise or a government agency. Forms are required for hiring, for calculating tax withholding, for vacation requests, and on and on. Scheduled reports are mandatory for retirement plans, health benefits, and payroll. In addition, human resources must train supervisors to meet state and federal hiring requirements. While the human resources department could be centralized, it often has to support far-flung offices across the country or even around the world.

It often takes days or weeks to implement changes requested by personnel because the paper needs time to move from one location to another. By switching to PDF from paper, human resources departments can become more efficient and reduce costs. For example, server-based solutions can generate PDF-based statements or form letters from the human resources database. The PDFs can be e-mailed or printed and sent via the United States Postal Service.

An advantage of PDF is it's accepted by most document management systems (DMS). Unlike paper, a PDF document can be stored in the DMS, and then recalled if needed. Because most large companies use DMSs to run other parts of their businesses, human resources departments can integrate personnel information in the form of PDFs into the DMS.

A Financial Institution

Financial institutions generate thousands of pages of statements on a regular schedule. Each statement has the same format, but the data in each statement changes for each customer.

The process of extracting information from databases and merging it into templates is called *variable data printing* or *personalization.* Many companies and government agencies use variable data printing to produce thousands of pages of form letters and reports.

Unlike HML, PDF produces reports that look just like the printed ones customers have traditionally received. PDF is also flexible: the statements can be sent via e-mail, or printed and sent through the postal service.

A Publishing Company

Although many graphic design and advertising agencies use Acrobat for review and markup (see Chapter 6 for more information), some publishing companies use PDF server technology for variable data printing and PDF creation.

Directory and similar publishers can use variable data publishing to produce PDFs of industry guides, business listings, and so on.

Other printers provide PDF creation services for clients. Users can drop Quark, Word, or other types of files into the company's web site, along with print job requirements. The printers then convert the source files to PDF. The PDF is sent to the client via e-mail for approval and, once approved, is sent to the press for reproduction.

What Is Not Legal

Inside Acrobat is a creation tool called *Acrobat Distiller,* which takes a PostScript print file and turns that print file into an Adobe PDF. Inside Distiller is a feature called *watched folders,* which points Distiller to specific folders that Distiller monitors. As soon as a PostScript file arrives in the watched folder, Distiller goes to work and creates a PDF.

Smart people quickly figured out they could set up a watched folder on a network drive that everyone in the organization could access. Users would create PostScript files and drop those into the watched network folder. One copy of Acrobat could serve an entire organization, they thought.

Adobe quickly banned the practice through its license agreement. Using watched folders to avoid buying copies of Acrobat is a violation of the license. The license says a watched folder cannot process files created by more than the licensed number of Acrobat users. See Section 2.2 of your Acrobat 6 license for the exact wording. Adobe has a server-based version of Distiller for use in workgroups or departments.

Converting File Cabinets of Paper to PDF

What's the most common thing you see in a cubicle or on a desk? There likely will be only one telephone and one computer, but you will see more than one piece of paper. Probably lots more.

Paper spills onto our desks and our floors and into our filing cabinets. Finding the right piece of paper can be a frustrating experience if you don't know the filing method of the person who last stored it. Acrobat has a solution for finding the right snowflake in this blizzard of paper.

One of my customers is a large nuclear generating plant. The plant was designed in the 1970s and built in the 1980s. Most of the design and operating instructions were created with typewriters. And all these paper documents were stored in filing cabinets.

To find a document, a requester had to fill out a slip and have a clerk retrieve the document. This manual process was time-consuming, and relied on the clerk having a good knowledge of the filing systems and correctly understanding the request.

The plant wanted to centralize its documents in an online library. There was one mandate: the Nuclear Regulatory Commission (NRC) requires the online documents to look exactly like the paper originals.

Adobe Acrobat Capture

The answer for this nuclear power plant (and several others) was *Adobe Acrobat Capture,* a specialized product that turns paper into a special kind of PDF. This product has had several names over the years, such as Original Image plus Hidden Text. It's currently known as *Searchable Image.* This PDF contains a scanned image of the original document, but it has a hidden layer of text behind the image. The text is created via Optical Character Recognition (OCR). The Searchable Image format pairs the hidden text layer with the words on the image. When a user selects text on the image, Acrobat retrieves the words from the hidden layer, making it appear that the text in the image is now selectable. This combined image format achieves two goals. First, the image meets the NRC requirement of looking exactly like the original. And second, the OCR text makes the document searchable. In many ways, Searchable Image is the best of both worlds.

So what's not to like? There's only one problem. OCR isn't 100 percent accurate. How accurate the OCR is depends on the quality of the original document. If you have a poor quality original, the OCR will be less accurate. A high-quality original will have a low OCR error rate. A high-quality OCR document will have an error rate of only 5 to 2 percent. In practical terms, this means an error will occur in five (or two) out of every 100 words. A low-quality OCR document will have an error rate of 10 to 20 percent.

Capture calls these errors *Suspects* and it does allow you to correct them. However, most of my clients are processing thousands of pages at a time, and they don't have the time to fix the mistakes, except those that occur in the title, document number, and other critical areas. If an OCR error creates a valid word, that word is not flagged as a problem.

This plant, and others, live with the OCR error rate. They calculate that having more than 90 percent of the document searchable is far better than the 0 percent they have if the paper is filed in a cabinet.

Capture also delivers OCR text in Microsoft Word format and has lots of other features. It runs on a Windows-based server and is designed to process hundreds or thousands of pages at a time. See the Adobe Acrobat Capture section of **www.adobe.com** for details.

Capture "Lite"

Adobe includes a scaled-down version of Capture in Professional and Standard. Unlike Acrobat 5, Adobe doesn't put a limit on the number of pages that can be processed in this "lite" version of Capture.

To use the Paper Capture plug-in, you must either scan documents into Acrobat, or convert scanned images created by others.

To scan a document into Acrobat, follow this procedure:

1. Close all open documents.
2. Click the Create PDF button and choose From Scanner, or File | Create PDF | From Scanner.
3. In the Create PDF from Scanner dialog box, select your scanner and whether you're scanning a single sided or double-sided document.
4. Choose Open New PDF Document.
5. Turn off Adapt Page Compression to Page Content. See Figure 12-5 for a recommended setup for mainly text documents.

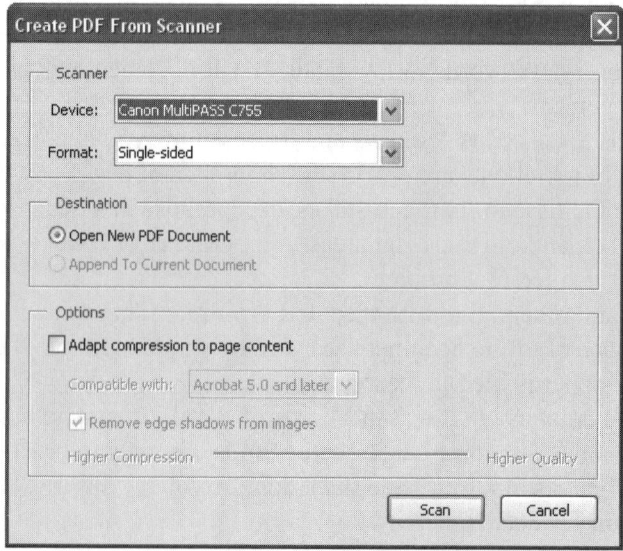

FIGURE 11-5 Recommended Capture settings for mainly text documents

6. Click Scan.
7. When your scanning software appears, make sure you set a resolution of at least 200, the minimum required by Acrobat. A resolution of 300 is a good starting point. The maximum resolution is 600 dpi, but this setting results in unacceptably large files. Scanning in black-and-white is by far the most common selection because it produces the smallest files.
8. Start your scanning software.
9. When the Acrobat Scan Plug-In appears, choose either Next to continue scanning or click Done when you finish.

NOTE *Adobe recommends using Adaptive Compression only on documents with a large number of graphics.*

What you now have is an image wrapped inside an Adobe PDF. Click the Text Select Tool and try to select some text. You won't be able to do so. Try using Search on the document. It won't work. See Figure 11-6 for an example. Now, it's time to put Capture to work.

1. Choose Document | Paper Capture | Start Capture....
2. Accept the default settings of Searchable Image (Exact) and Downsampling (none). See Figure 11-7 for an example of the recommended settings.

NOTE *Searchable Image (Exact) doesn't apply any compression to the scanned image. Searchable Image (Compact) does apply compression. Whether to use Exact or Compact depends on the number and quality of graphics of the scanned pages. You need to test each type to see which is best for you. The Compact setting will produce the smallest file size, but it could result in unacceptable image degradation.*

Now use the Text Select Tool again to select text. You can! You can copy-and-paste the text you select, or even choose File | Save As... | Save as Type | Microsoft Word Document to save the OCR text as a *.doc file. See the successful search results in Figure 11-8.

Notice the onscreen image hasn't changed. We've just added a hidden layer of text behind it.

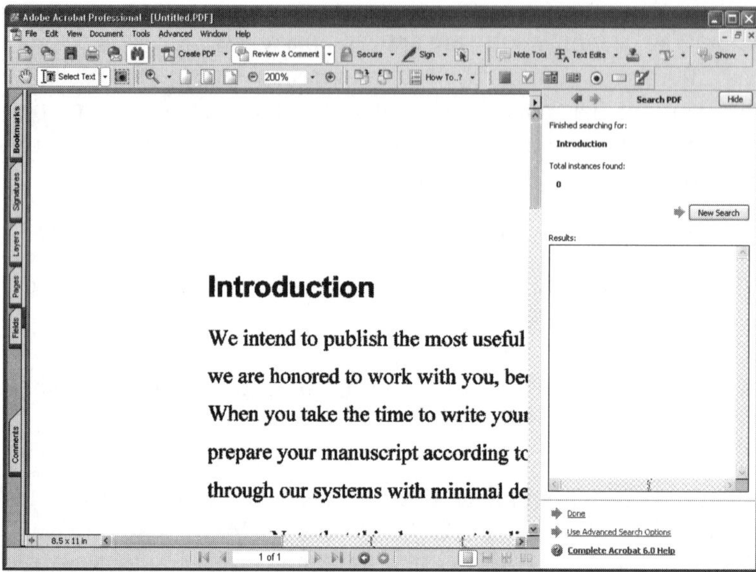

FIGURE 11-6 In this example, a search for the word "Introduction" failed because there's no text to search.

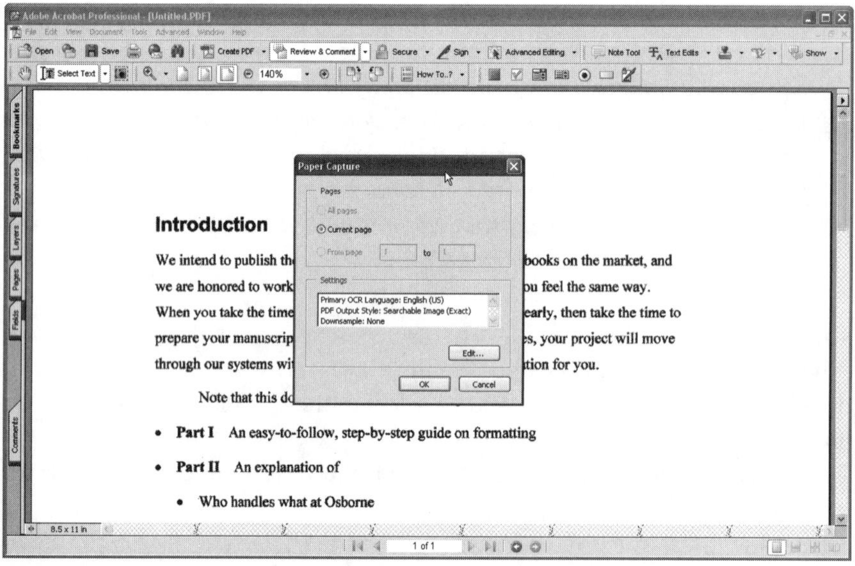

FIGURE 11-7 The default settings for the Capture plug-in are good choices for producing searchable PDFs.

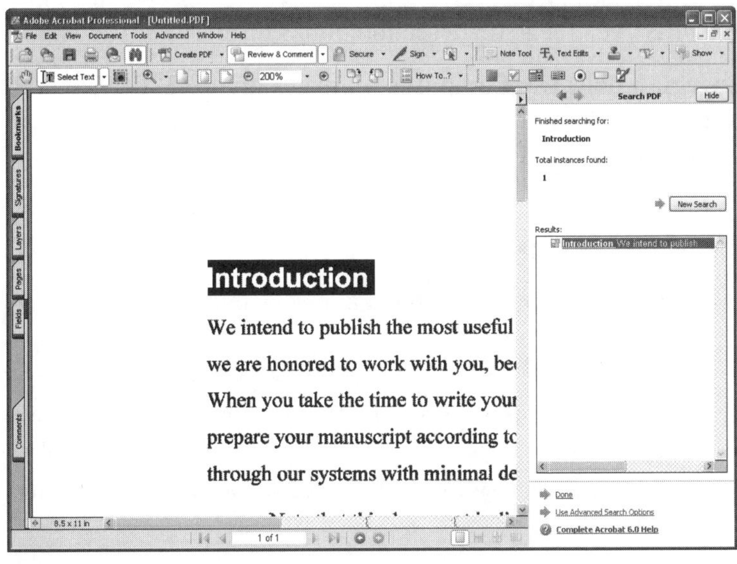

FIGURE 11-8 Once Capture has added OCR text to a hidden layer behind the image, the document is searchable.

NOTE *You can turn a scanned page into a regular PDF by changing the default Capture settings to Formatted Text & Graphics. This option almost always requires manual cleanup with Document | Paper Capture | Find First OCR Suspect, and continuing to clean up Suspect words. This file won't look identical to the original document.*
Fixing Suspect words only works in a Formatted Text & Graphics document. The feature doesn't work in a Searchable Image Format.

Whether you use the Paper Capture plug-in inside of Acrobat or the stand-alone version of Capture depends on your needs. The full Capture runs with minimal manual intervention and is optimized to run on high-powered workstations or servers. The Capture inside Acrobat requires the participation of the user to scan every page.

Alternatives to Capture

As in many cases in the PDF world, alternatives exist to Adobe Acrobat Capture:

- **AdLib eDocument Solutions eXpress & OCR** Creates Image+Hidden Text searchable PDFs from a wide variety of source files, including TIF images from scanned paper documents. See AdLib's contact information in the PDF Server Technology section of this chapter.

- **Image Solutions DocComposer** Creates Image+Hidden Text PDFs from scanned images. Adds bookmarks and page numbers, deskews pages, and can remove punch hole marks.

Company Information

The following companies were mentioned in this chapter:

activePDF, **www.activepdf.com**	Adobe Systems, Inc., **www.adobe.com**
AdLib eDocument Solutions, **www.adlibsys.com**	Amyuni Technologies, **www.amyuni.com**
Appligent, **www.appligent.com**	Global Graphics, **www.globalgraphics.com**
Image Solutions, **www.imagesolutions.com**	PDFlib GmbH, **www.pdflib.com**

Summary

Most PDF creators use Adobe Acrobat as just another desktop tool and work on one document at a time. In some circumstances, working on multiple files at once with Acrobat's Batch Sequences feature can be valuable.

For those organizations that need to produce large volumes of PDFs quickly, a server-based PDF application is a good solution. Both Adobe and non-Adobe server solutions are available.

Finally, there's Adobe Acrobat Capture for those organizations with a large amount of legacy paper documents that need to be placed in an online repository. Capture is a stand-alone product designed to convert hundreds of pages to PDF at once. Capture "Lite" is a component of Adobe Acrobat designed for low-volume conversion.

In Chapter 12, you look at creating PDF forms from scratch, as well as some solutions to convert existing paper and electronic forms to PDF.

Chapter 12

PDF Forms

I spend a lot of time in front of students from the business world who are paying me to show them how to use Adobe Acrobat Professional. Their bosses generally want these students in class, so they can help the company save money through more efficient distribution of information by moving to electronic publishing.

When we come to the Forms section in class, many students ask to skip it. I can understand that—how many of us grew up wanting a career in form design? You might be thinking the same thing when you open this chapter, but here's my pitch: moving from paper to PDF Forms can probably save your company tons of money. Isn't that a nice idea to take to management?

Why PDF Forms?

Let me explain why I think PDF Forms are so important. First, we use forms for many routine, but essential, tasks. Paying taxes? Better send in the right form with that check. Does your employer owe you money for that last business trip? You'll need to fill out an expense report. Need a building permit? You have to fill out a stack of forms. The list is endless.

Business processes that rely on paper forms are notoriously inefficient for many obvious reasons. Handwritten forms can be misread. Paper must be delivered physically—either through interoffice mail or an outside delivery service, a process that can take days or weeks. A person must process a paper form one at a time, except for some rare exceptions, such as test results.

Studies show paper forms cost organizations thousands and thousands of dollars as workers deal with missing or incorrect data, paper shuffling, blurry faxes, illegible handwriting, rekeying data, incorrect hand calculations, and other inefficiencies.

Before PDF Forms, the computer industry relied on proprietary computer software and scan imaging to process paper forms. Both approaches have limitations when compared to PDF Forms. The proprietary solutions tended to be expensive—even the end-user product for filling in these forms could cost hundreds of dollars. The creation tools tended to run well above $1,000. While imaging turns paper into a picture stored in a computer, the data on the form was still locked inside the image.

PDF Forms, introduced with Acrobat 3, opened up new possibilities. Unlike imaging, PDF Forms free the data from the form itself. While a background image of a paper form could be in the PDF form, the PDF form fields are on a separate, editable layer on top of the image.

And, unlike proprietary form solutions, Adobe published the specification on how to make a PDF form. This means any developer can use the specification to create a PDF form, not just Adobe. Plus, Adobe gave away the form filler for free, and continues to do so. Remember, many other form solutions require that users pay for a form filler.

The Internal Revenue Service (IRS) was one of the first major form players to recognize the power in PDF Forms. By making United States tax forms available in PDF at **www.irs.gov**, the agency has saved American taxpayers millions of dollars and provided better service by making tax forms available 24 hours a day. Adoption by the IRS spurred other federal, state, and local government agencies to make PDF Forms their standard.

PDF Forms are a cost-effective solution that's quite popular with users. At press time, taxpayers have downloaded more than 1.5 billion PDF Forms from **www.irs.gov**, which means the IRS has saved the costs of printing and distributing 1.5 billion documents. As even more automation is built into the process, future savings could be even greater.

How PDF Forms Can Benefit Your Organization

Your company probably won't ever deliver 1.5 billion forms, but it certainly does use lots of them. Forms are required when prospects apply for jobs. Sales orders require forms. New vendor setup requires forms. Expense reports require forms. Funding and budget requests require forms. The list goes on and on—nearly every business process ends up as a form at some point.

With PDF Forms, the same form can be printed or it can be posted to your corporate intranet. The viewer and filler are free—it's called Adobe Reader.

Creation is handled by Acrobat Professional, which includes a broad set of tools for generating forms. You can create new forms or import an image of an existing paper form and add fillable fields. Professional, Standard, and an older version of Acrobat called Approval let users fill in, save, and submit form data. (In most circumstances, Reader doesn't permit users to save data. See Adobe Document Server for more information.)

Moving Up the Food Chain

Most of my customers don't immediately stop using paper. They start with some simple PDF Forms, add some intelligence with JavaScript, and then, finally, they link their "smart" forms with a database.

The first stage for many users involves creating forms that are fillable, but still designed to be printed, and then shipped via interoffice mail. Once the organization becomes comfortable with filling out forms online instead of on paper, they make the forms more accurate by adding automatic calculations. The next step is to ship the forms, or form data, electronically via e-mail, instead of through interoffice mail. Once organizations have that system down, they take the final step and link the forms to a database and, perhaps, add digital signatures.

Each stage brings cost savings. With fill-and-print, forms can be reproduced on demand on local laser printers, instead of in batches of hundreds or thousands at a print shop, and handwriting mistakes are eliminated.

Making PDF Forms smart requires the use of JavaScript, which is covered in the next chapter. Adding JavaScript to a form means fields can perform calculations, increasing the accuracy of data in the form. Higher accuracy means fewer forms are rejected, further lowering costs.

Transmitting forms and form data reduces transaction approval time. Customers see orders fulfilled more quickly. Employees notice payroll and benefit changes occur more quickly. In today's business world, increasing the speed of business processes translates into greater productivity.

The final stage, linking PDF Forms to databases, could require some upfront programming costs, but this final stage has its own set of savings. No longer is human intervention required to rekey or import form data. Accuracy goes up, and business process time can be cut from days or weeks to seconds.

TIP *Has someone sent you a PDF Form without a Reset button? To clear a form in Acrobat, choose File | Revert.*

PDF or HTML Forms?

PDF Forms are, of course, not your only choice. As you consider electronic forms, the most common options are PDF Forms or HTML forms. Which one is best? Well, that depends. An HTML form might appear more appropriate at certain times while, at other times, PDF seems a clear winner. The following are some considerations when you're making a PDF- versus an HTML-form decision.

- *Does it need to be printed?* If so, go with a PDF form. PDF Forms print reliably. HTML is notoriously difficult to print—information is often splattered around a page and looks terrible.
- *Are users moving from a paper form?* If so, PDF is, again, a good choice. You can make the PDF form look exactly like the original paper form. This makes a PDF form easier for users to fill out and it might also meet certain regulator requirements.

- *What browser is required?* Because PDF Forms rely on the free Adobe Reader plug-in, they are less browser-dependent. PDF Forms do, however, require the free Reader be installed.
- *PDF Forms are easy to create.* Anyone with Acrobat 6 Professional has a built-in form design tool. As you learn in the section "PDF Forms from Acrobat Professional," creating forms with Acrobat is quite easy.
- *Do you need to support older Macs?* HTML forms might be best for a Macintosh audience. Only Reader 6.0, which requires Mac OSX, lets Macintosh users submit form data. Users of older Macs running an operating system (OS) below OSX can download, view, and print PDF forms, but they cannot submit form data.
- *Is handheld device support required?* HTML forms also support PocketPC and PalmOS, as well as other handheld and mobile devices. The Adobe/Acrobat Readers for those platforms don't include form submission support.
- *Will most users finish the form in one session?* HTML forms are single session—if you stop and close the form, your data is lost. Users of the free Adobe Reader are also limited to single sessions. PDF forms can be multisession if users have Acrobat Standard, Professional, or Approval. They can save data halfway through a form fill-in session, stop, and finish later.

TIP *Do you want to convert an HTML form to PDF? If so, just use the Web Capture feature. Browse to the HTML page you want to convert in Internet Explorer for Windows, and click the Acrobat icon in the toolbar. Not only does Acrobat convert the web page to PDF, but it also turns an HTML form into a PDF one. (Macintosh users should start Acrobat, click on the Create PDF icon, and then enter the URL of the form.)*

- *Do your users have low-speed Internet connections?* If so, use HTML forms. An HTML form is generally smaller than a PDF one, so users with dial-up connections can download an HTML form more quickly.

PDF Forms from Acrobat Professional

The form creation tools in Acrobat are located in the Forms Toolbar, which is tucked away at Tools | Advanced Editing | Forms | Show Forms Toolbar. Previous versions of Acrobat had a single form design tool. As shown next, Acrobat Professional 6 provides a tool for each function. To help you understand the uses of these tools, the next section explains how to create a relatively uncomplicated form with a bit of intelligence.

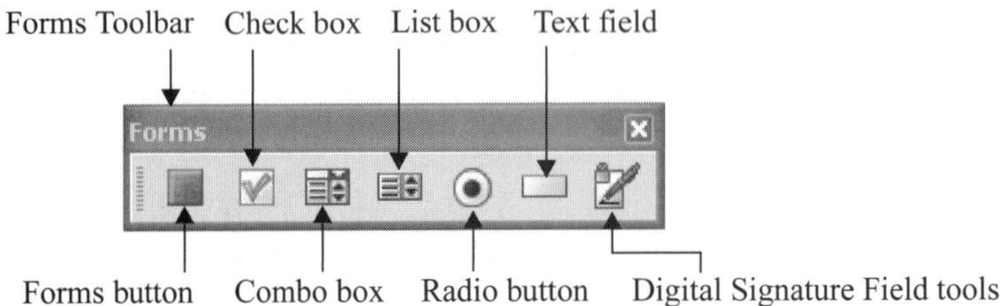

Create a Simple Form

This exercise can help you become familiar with the basics of form design. You create fields to accept text such as name, title, and address; radio buttons that permit only one option to be selected; pull-down lists; and fields that only accept properly formatted data, such as a Social Security number.

Where Do PDF Forms Come From?

Many Acrobat forms are created with two layers. A background layer contains an image that resembles a paper form. Overlaid on this background image are PDF form fields, in which users can input data.

This is a common way to begin if you don't have an existing form or if you have a paper form you want to automate. You create a background image of the form using your favorite page layout or word processing software, and then use Acrobat to lay in fields on top of the image. If you have an existing paper form, you can scan the paper form into Acrobat, and then add the form fields on top of it.

You can create PDF Forms in other ways. Several companies, including Adobe, have specialized form design tools or add-ons that produce PDF Forms. See some examples at the end of this chapter and in the company reference at the back of the book. In this book, we stick with forms created with Acrobat Professional.

Start with an Image

Let's begin with a form all United States taxpayers should be familiar with: an IRS 1040 form for reporting personal income. To keep things simple, we'll use the 1040EZ form. Go to **www.irs.gov** and download the 1040EZ form that isn't fillable. Use the Search feature at irs.gov and search for "1040EZ." We're going to create a fillable PDF, so don't cheat by starting with one that's already fillable. There's a 2002 version that doesn't have fillable fields and is a pure image. It's this pure image file that we're going to work with.

The 1040EZ form is two pages long and is a great form to practice on. We'll use text fields, radio buttons, buttons programmed with actions, and even a little JavaScript to soup it up. We don't have space in this chapter to fill out the entire form, but we can do enough to give you a taste of what the form design is like. Feel free to add all the fields on your own, if you like.

TIP *In general, each field in a PDF form should have a unique name. The exception is radio buttons, which should have identical names, but different export values. See the following section for an example.*

Add Text Fields

TIP *Field names in Acrobat 6 can be linked in a parent-child relationship, although this isn't required. A period between the names indicates the relationship, with the parent name coming first. For example, if a parent field named PersonalData has a child whose name is Address, which, in turn, has a child with the name ZipCode, then the full name of this last field would be PersonalData.Address.ZipCode.*

To begin, open f1040EZ.pdf in Acrobat Professional. Make sure you're viewing the file in Acrobat, not inside your web browser. These instructions are based on the 2002 1040EZ. Forms for later years might vary. To begin, follow these steps:

1. Choose Tools | Advanced Editing | Forms | Show Forms Toolbar.
2. We'll start with the name and address fields. Select the Text Field tool.
3. Marquee (click-and-drag) a box in the First Name area of the form.
4. In the General tab, name the field **FirstMI**.
5. Enter a Tooltip saying **Enter first name and middle initial**. The Tooltip appears when the cursor floats over a field and also is the text read by a computer to a visually impaired person.
6. Click the Appearance tab. Make sure the border and background are deselected, rendering them invisible.

7. Set the font size to **9**.
8. Click the Text Color button and change the color to a dark blue. If you look at other IRS forms, you'll notice they all use dark blue for the font color. Leave the font at Helvetica, the default font.
9. Click the Options tab. Make sure the alignment is set to Left.

NOTE *The Scroll long text option in the Text Field Properties dialog box might or might not be a good option. Scroll long text lets users input data past the right edge of the form field. If the form is to be printed, don't select this option. It's fine to use the Scroll long text option if the data from the form will only be used electronically, such as being transferred to a database or sent via e-mail.*

10. Deselect the Check Spelling Option. You don't want to spell check names.
11. Click Close.

Use the same procedure to create fields for Last Name, Home Address, City, State, and ZIP. Be sure to give each field a unique name and fill in the correct Tooltip. Leave the Social Security Number field alone for now.

TIP *Here's a quick way to create new fields based on an existing field. Select the field you want to duplicate. Click on the field and hold down the* CTRL *key (Windows) or the* OPTION *key (Macintosh), and then drag the duplicated field to its new position. A plus (+) sign will appear next to the cursor if you're in Duplication mode. Many of my students find this motion a bit awkward at first, but it's quite simple.*
Once you have the basic technique down, you can keep the duplicated field in horizontal or vertical alignment with the original by adding the SHIFT *key after you begin to drag.*

Once your fields are created, select the Hand tool and enter some data into the form. See Figure 12-1 for an example of a partially completed form.

Formatting Special Numbers

Next is the Social Security number. Our background image has three vertical double lines to separate the number into its parts, as in 111-11-1111. While you

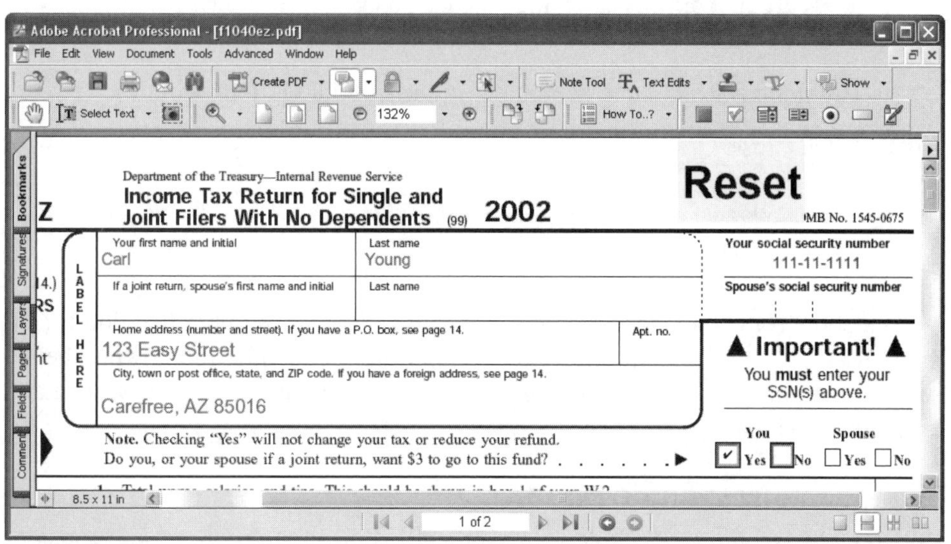

FIGURE 12-1 Top half of a completed 1040EZ form with sample user data

can write some JavaScript to make the field fit into that format, I'll show you a much simpler way. To add a special format to a form field, follow this procedure:

1. Make sure you still have the Text Field tool selected.
2. Marquee an area for the Social Security number.
3. In the Text Field Properties box, choose the General tab and name the field **SSN1**.
4. Enter a Tooltip of **Social Security Number**.
5. Notice the warning that says "Important! You must enter your SSN(s) above." This is obviously a required field. Click the Required option in the Common Properties section to make filling in this field mandatory.
6. Move to the Appearance tab. Click the color box to the right of Fill Color. Choose the white color, which should be in the lower-right corner of the color box. This white background fill will mask the three vertical lines in the background image.
7. Specify a font size of 9 and the color blue.

8. Move to the Format tab. In the Format Category pull-down menu, choose Special.
9. Highlight Social Security Number in the Special Options window.
10. Click Close.

NOTE *Choose View | Show Grid to help align the form fields. You can also enable View | Grid.*

Select the Hand tool, and try entering a Social Security number that doesn't fit the 111-11-1111 pattern. An error message appears if you enter too few numbers, and your computer will beep if you try to enter too many numbers or if you enter letters of the alphabet.

Making Choices: Radio Buttons

I'm going to ask you to set aside your political feelings for a moment and consider the next section purely from the point of view of a form designer. See the Presidential Election Campaign area in the 1040EZ form? We want users to make a choice. They either do want to contribute $3 to the fund or they don't. They can't be politicians themselves, and try to vote yes and no at the same time. We want to force them to make a choice.

TIP *Use the arrow keys on your keyboard to microposition selected form fields. This works best if View | Snap to Grid is off.*

Radio buttons compel users to make one selection. Radio buttons work just like the buttons on your car radio, so you can only have one station playing at a time. A related kind of form field, Check Boxes, allows multiple selections. The following procedure shows how to create radio buttons:

1. Click the Radio Button tool in the Form Toolbar.
2. Marquee around the Yes box across from "Do you want $3 to go to this fund?" Make the box large enough to cover the square on the background image.
3. In the General tab, name the field **Prez1**.
4. Enter a Tooltip of **Presidential Election Campaign**.

5. Move to the Options tab. Change the button style to Square. Make sure the Export Value is set to **Yes**.
6. Click Close.

Now it's time to create the button for the No answer. Although each PDF field should generally have a unique name, in this case, we want the Yes and No fields to have identical names. Follow this procedure to force the user to make a choice:

1. Copy the Prez1 field with CTRL- (Windows) OPTION- (Macintosh) click-drag and release it over the No box.
2. Double-click the field to open it.
3. Go into the Options tab and change the export value to **No**.
4. Click Close.
5. Click the Hand tool and test your work. You can choose either Yes or No, but not both.

TIP *Are some of your fields not aligned? Here's a fast way to line up fields. First, choose the tool that created the form field, and then click on the field that's out of alignment. Now,* SHIFT-*click the field you want to align to. Right-click (Windows) or* CONTROL-*click (Macintosh) and choose the appropriate command from the Align menu.*

NOTE *To show fields of all types in Acrobat 6, choose View | Toolbars | Advanced Editing. Click the Select Object tool. All fields now will be visible in place.*

Add a Reset Button

By this time, you might have input some sample data you want to clear from your form. Let's add a nonprinting Reset button that will leave our form fields in place, but remove the data. Add a Reset button by using the following procedure.

1. If Rulers aren't showing, choose View | Rulers.
2. Select the Button tool in the Form Toolbar.
3. Marquee a 1-inch by .5-inch box in the white space of the upper-right corner.
4. Name the field **Reset**.

5. Add a Tooltip of **Click to Reset Form**.
6. In Common Properties, choose a Form Field type of Visible but Doesn't Print.
7. Switch to the Appearance tab. Set the Border color to none and the Fill to a Yellow color.
8. In the Text area, make the Font Size Auto and the Text Color Black.
9. Move to the Options tab. Set the Layout to Label Only and enter a Label name of Reset.
10. Click the Actions tab.
11. In Select Action, choose Reset a Form and click Add. (Any new fields will automatically be selected for reset.) Click OK and Close.

Tabbing Order

Many users will expect to enter data into a field, and then press the TAB key to move to the next field. Use the following procedure to set the tab order for the 1040EZ form:

1. Click the Pages tab in the Navigation Pane. See Figure 12-2 for an example that shows Page Properties being displayed.
2. Do either of the following:
   - Select a page thumbnail, and choose Page Properties from the Options menu.
   - Right-click (Windows) or CONTROL-click (Macintosh) a page thumbnail, and choose Page Properties.
3. In the Page Properties dialog box, click Tab Order and select Use Row Order.

Combo Box and List Box Fields

You've probably seen what Acrobat calls a combo box at web sites. A *combo box* is a pull-down menu that you select one or more items from. Acrobat also has a field type called list box. A *list box* is similar to a combo box but, instead of displaying all items at once in a pull-down menu, only one item at a time is shown. Most of my students dislike the look of the list box because they've become used to seeing pull-down menus used in web forms.

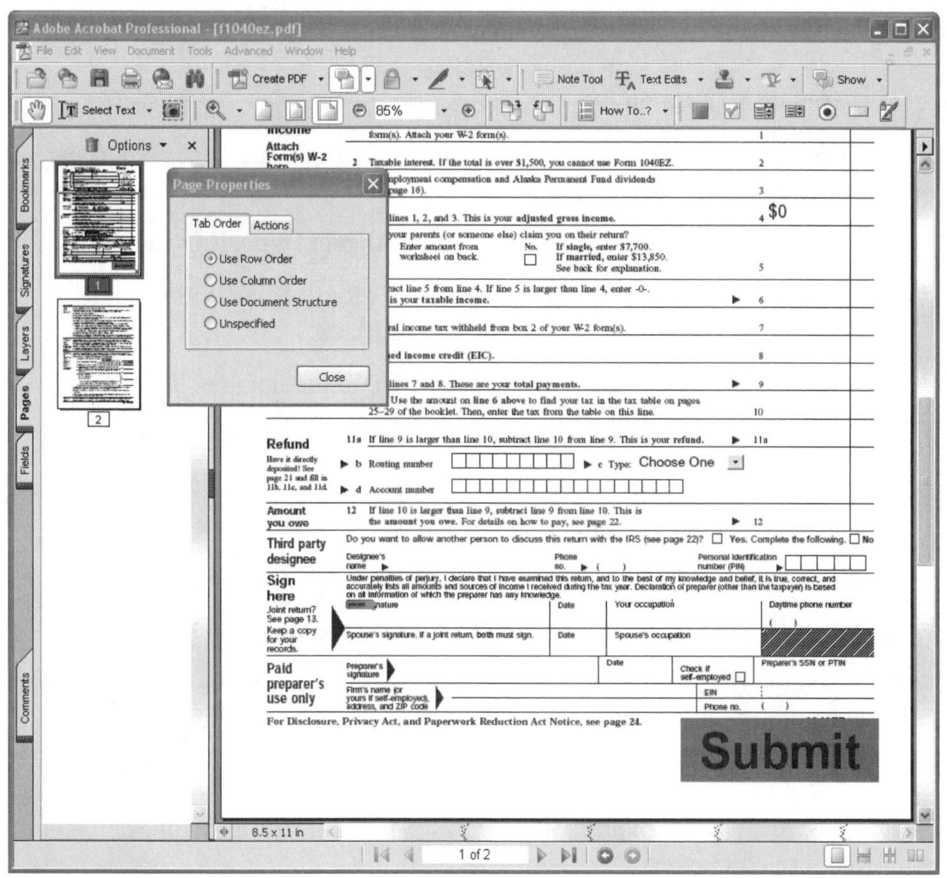

FIGURE 12-2 Page Properties displayed from the Pages tab. Row Order is a common way to set tabbing order in most forms.

> **NOTE** *List boxes have a unique option called Selection Change. When users select an item from the list, a JavaScript can run to show specific options for that item. For example, list box in a catalog might show men's clothing sizes if Men's Shirts were selected in a list box, and women's sizes if Women's Blouses were chosen.*

The procedures for setting up list boxes and combo boxes are nearly identical. We will use a combo box in our form. Because this updated version of 1040EZ doesn't have a built-in place for a combo box, we will improvise. Our combo box will list three refund options: Checking, Savings, and Money Market. Insert the combo box by using the following procedure:

1. Select the List Box tool.
2. Draw a field over Checking and Savings options in the Type area of the Refund section.
3. Name it **Refund**. Add a Tooltip of **Select Direct Deposit Option**.
4. Click on the Appearance tab. Set Border Color to None, Fill Color to White, Font Size to 12, and Font Color to Black.
5. Move to the Options tab. Enter **Checking** into the Item and Export Value fields.
6. Click Add.
7. Enter **Savings** into the Item and Export Value fields. Click Add.
8. Enter **Money Market** into the Item and Export Value fields. Click Add.
9. Enter **Select One** into the Item field. Leave the Export Value blank. Click Add.
10. Highlight Choose One in the Item List and click the Move button until it's the top item.
11. Click Close.
12. Select the Hand tool and test the form. See Figure 12-3 for an example of an open combo box.

Restrict Data Entry in Field

Restricting data entry in some fields is common to minimum and maximum limits. These limits keep users from entering invalid amounts and improve the accuracy of information going into the form. Programming a PDF form to restrict data entry is called Validation in Acrobat.

The 1040EZ has an ideal location for a validated field: Income Line 2, Taxable Interest. The most interest income that can be claimed on this form is $1,500. Any more and you have to use the regular 1040 form. Use the following procedure to restrict data entry in a field:

1. Using the Text Field tool, and then click-and-drag to add a field in line 2. Because the IRS prefers you not to enter cents, you can skip those.
2. Name the Field **Income2**.
3. Add a Tooltip of **Enter Interest Income Up to $1,500**.
4. In the Format tab, choose Number. Set Decimal Places to 0 and Currency Symbol to Dollar.

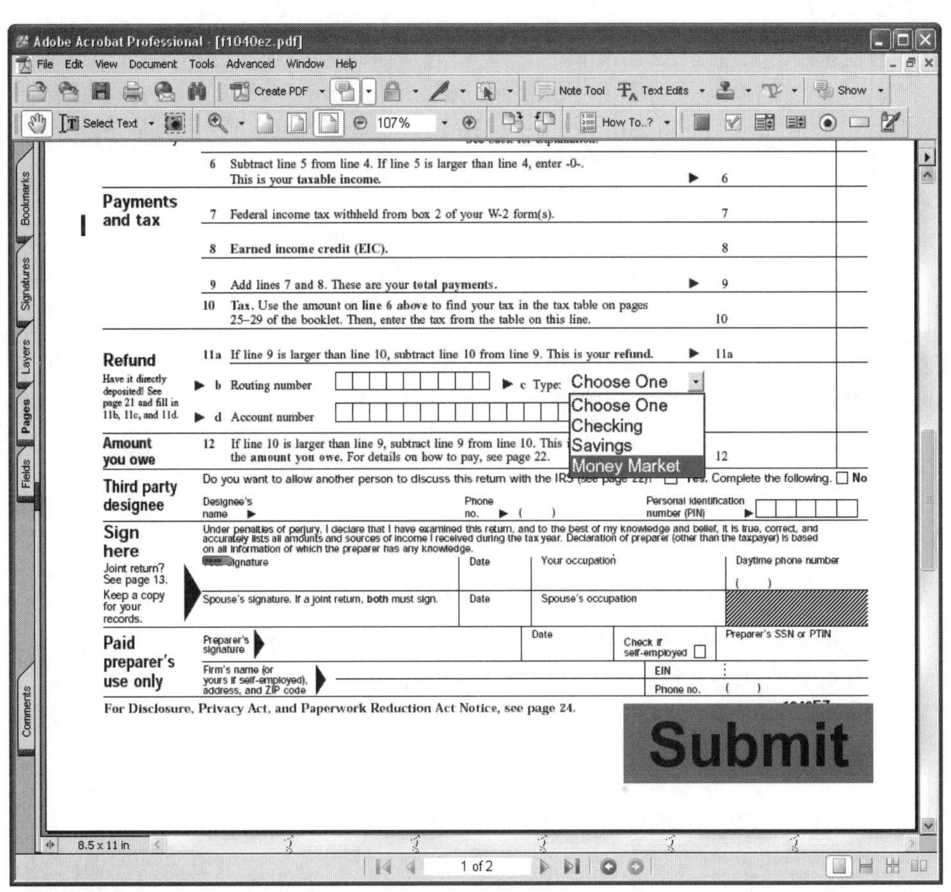

FIGURE 12-3 List box items are displayed as a pull-down menu.

5. Click the Validate tab. Click the radio button to activate Field Value in Range. Enter a range of **0** to **1500**. Don't include commas in the numbers.
6. Click Close.
7. Select the Hand tool, and then test the number field with valid and invalid amounts.

Field Calculation

Acrobat includes a simple point-and-click interface that makes basic calculations easy. More complex calculations require custom JavaScripts, which we discuss in the next chapter.

Before we add a calculation field, we need income fields that we can add. Use the Text Field tool to add number fields to lines 1 and three. By following this procedure, you will sum lines 1, 2, and 3.

1. Use the Text Field tool to make number fields in lines 1 and 3 of the Income section. Name the fields **Income1** and **Income3**. Be sure to set the Currency Symbol to Dollar.
2. Using the Text Field tool again, create a new number field in line 4. Make sure this is a number field and name it **IncomeSum**.
3. Click the Read-only option. We want the form to calculate the sum, not the user.
4. Click the Calculate tab.
5. Select Value is the sum (+) and choose Pick.
6. In the Field Selection dialog box, select fields Income1, Income2, and Income3. Click OK. See Figure 12-4 for an example of selecting fields for calculations.
7. Click Close.
8. Save your work as f1040EZ_Work.pdf.

Test the fields by entering data. Line 4 should update automatically as you set new values in the income fields.

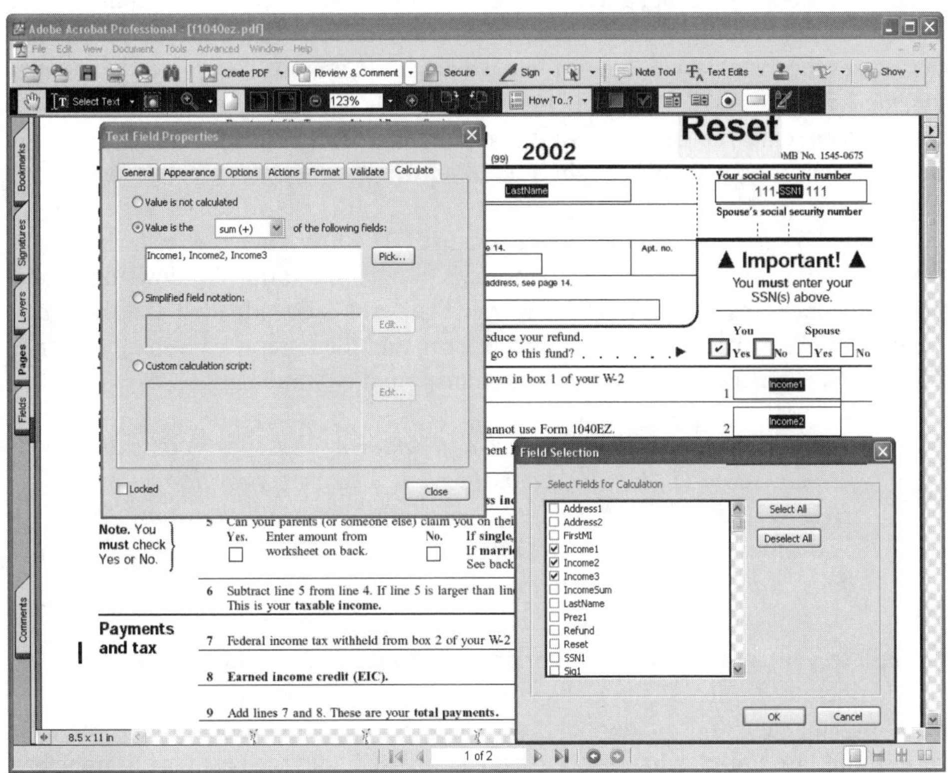

FIGURE 12-4 Fields Income1, Income2, and Income3 are selected for calculation.

Submitting Data

So far, we have a form that holds information, but the information is trapped inside the form. It certainly is a step up for paper-based forms. This PDF form could be printed, and then faxed to a recipient by a user who has the free Adobe Reader.

Just making a form fillable can be a major step for many organizations. However, Acrobat Professional enables you to go beyond simple fill and print forms. PDF Forms can submit form information via e-mail, in a structured text file called Forms Data Format (FDF), HTML, or an XML-like structure called XFDF. For details on XFDF, see the Adobe Technical Note XML Forms Data Format Specification, Version 2.0.

In a client-server setup, a user would enter data into a PDF form running inside a web browser. When they press Submit, the data is transmitted to a server-side script that parses the form data and puts it into a database. Common server-side languages include ASP, ASP.NET, CGI, Cold Fusion, JSP, PHP, and Perl. The server typically accepts form data via a URL. If your company is a Microsoft shop and uses Active Server Pages, a typical URL might look like **http://www.pdfconference.com/register.asp**.

Here's how such a workflow looks to a user. The user navigates to a web page where a PDF form is posted. The user clicks to open the form. Windows users see the form appear inside their web browsers. The form is downloaded as a file for Macintosh users. The user completes the form, and then presses a Submit button. The data is extracted from the form and transmitted onward.

NOTE

Adobe Reader users cannot save data in form fields. They can print the form or submit it, but they cannot save it. The exception: PDF Forms created with Adobe Document Server with Reader Extensions. These extensions can turn on hidden functionality inside of Adobe Reader that does let users save information entered into form fields.

Talk to your system administrator about how the form submission process should operate. Typically, the IT department has strong preferences on which scripting language to use, how fields should be named, how the data from the form should be stored, what data format can be used, and the best way to transfer the data from the form to the database.

Because many IT departments aren't familiar with PDF Forms, you can help them get up-to-speed by referring them to the FDF Toolkit SDK from Adobe. In addition to containing documentation on FDF, the Toolkit provides an Application Programming Interface (API) for writing server-side applications that generate or parse FDF files. The FDF Toolkit supports Windows, Solaris, AIX, or Linux and is available from the Adobe Solutions Network at **http://partners.adobe.com**.

The form designer can create the form, add the correct settings to the Submit button, add a Reset button, and coordinate with IT on field-naming conventions. Distributing the form and producing instructions on how to use it could be a joint effort of the designer and IT.

Setting up client-server web forms goes beyond the available space here. See **www.planetpdf.com** and **www.pdfzone.com** for companies that provide such solutions. Instead of setting up a complex client-server application, we'll insert a Submit button that sends form data via e-mail.

Adding a Submit Button

Our Submit button will strip the data from the form, attach it to an e-mail, and address the e-mail to a specific recipient. The user will have to click Send to transmit the data. Use the following procedure to create a Submit button:

1. Select the Button tool and create a field in the lower right-hand corner of Page 1. Feel free to obscure any of the small type at the bottom of the form.
2. Name the field **Submit** and add a Tooltip of **Click to Submit Form Data Via e-mail**.
3. In the Appearance tab, change the Fill color to red.
4. Change the Font Size to Auto and change the color to black.
5. Move to the Options tab and change the Layout to Label Only.
6. Enter **Submit** in the Label field.
7. Switch to the Actions tab and make sure the Trigger is set to Mouse Up.
8. In Select Action, choose Submit a Form from the pull-down list.
9. Click Add.
10. Enter **mailto:username@companyname.com** in the Enter URL for this Link field.
11. Select FDF Include under Export Format.
12. Make sure Field Selection is set to All Fields.
13. Click OK and Close.
14. Save the file.

NOTE *Adobe Reader doesn't support JavaScripts that add a subject line, cc:, bcc:, and other features.*

To test the form, upload the completed form to a web server, browse to the form, open it inside a web browser, fill in some sample data, and then press the Submit button.

TIP *Check your browser settings to make sure your browser is set up to send e-mail. If it isn't, refer to your browser documentation.*

Receiving Form Data

What do you do if someone e-mails form data to you? The data most likely will arrive in the form of an attachment. (If they send the entire PDF, you simply open the file in Acrobat Professional.)

If they sent only the form data, as we did in the previous section, then it's a bit trickier. The form data has a file extension of *.fdf, or Form Data Format. An *FDF* is a text file with the information organized in a special way.

To view the form data, open your version of the PDF form on your desktop. If necessary, download the form from the Web and save it. Open the form on your computer in Acrobat, not in a web browser. Once the form is open, it's time to bring in the data. Choose View | Navigation Tabs | Fields to open the Fields tab. In the Fields tab, choose Options | Import Form Data and browse to the location of the attached form data file. Highlight the file and click Select. Your blank form will be populated with the sender's form data.

Field Signing

Digital signatures are closely related to Security and are covered in Chapter 9. We'll finish this form by adding a Digital Signature field that locks all the form fields in our 1040EZ. By locking the fields with your digital signature, you prevent someone from changing your field entries after you sign it.

A Digital Signature field controls all or a specific number of fields. A blank signature field appears on the form, and the signature is filled in as a requirement for completing the form. To add a Digital Signature field, follow these steps:

1. Select the Digital Signature Field tool.
2. Draw a field over the Sign Here area in the Sign Here section of the form.
3. In the General tab, name the field **Sig1**. Add a Tooltip of **Click to sign form**.
4. In the Common Properties area, select Required.
5. Click the Signed tab. Choose Mark as Read-Only: All Fields Except these….
6. Click Pick and select Submit to exempt it from being locked.
7. Click OK and Close.

Select the Hand tool and test the fields you just created.

Secure the Form

The best procedure is to secure the form before you deploy it. By securing the form, someone cannot intentionally, or accidentally, change a field or a calculation. For more information on security, see Chapter 9. To protect a form, use the following procedure:

1. Choose Document | Security | Restrict Opening and Editing.
2. For the highest-level of security, be sure to choose Acrobat 5 and Higher Compatibility.
3. In the Permissions area of Password Security Settings Dialog Box, choose Use Permissions to Restrict Printing and Editing of the Document and Its Security Settings.
4. Set Printing Allowed: to High Resolution.
5. Set Changes Allowed: to Filling in form fields and signing.
6. To meet accessibility requirements, choose Enable text access for screen reader devices for the visually impaired.
7. Enter a password of at least six characters.

TIP *Longer passwords made up of random letters and numbers are more secure than short passwords made up of simple words. I've seen demonstrations of password-cracker software that can retrieve four-letter passwords in about 20 seconds. An eight-character password made up of random letters and numbers would take the same software up to two years to retrieve.*

8. Click OK, and then OK again.
9. Reenter the password.
10. Click OK, save the form, and then close and reopen it.

Users who open this form will see a warning box showing the form has security settings applied to it. To make changes, use your password and turn off security temporarily while you modify the form.

Signing the Form

Before you sign the form, make sure you enter some data.

TIP *All fields will be locked after you apply your signature.*

An example of a signed field is shown in Figure 12-5. Follow these steps to sign a form with Acrobat's built-in security feature:

1. Select the Hand tool.
2. Click on the signature field.
3. When the Alert! - Document is Not Certified warning appears, click Continue Signing. (See Chapter 9 for more about Certified Documents).

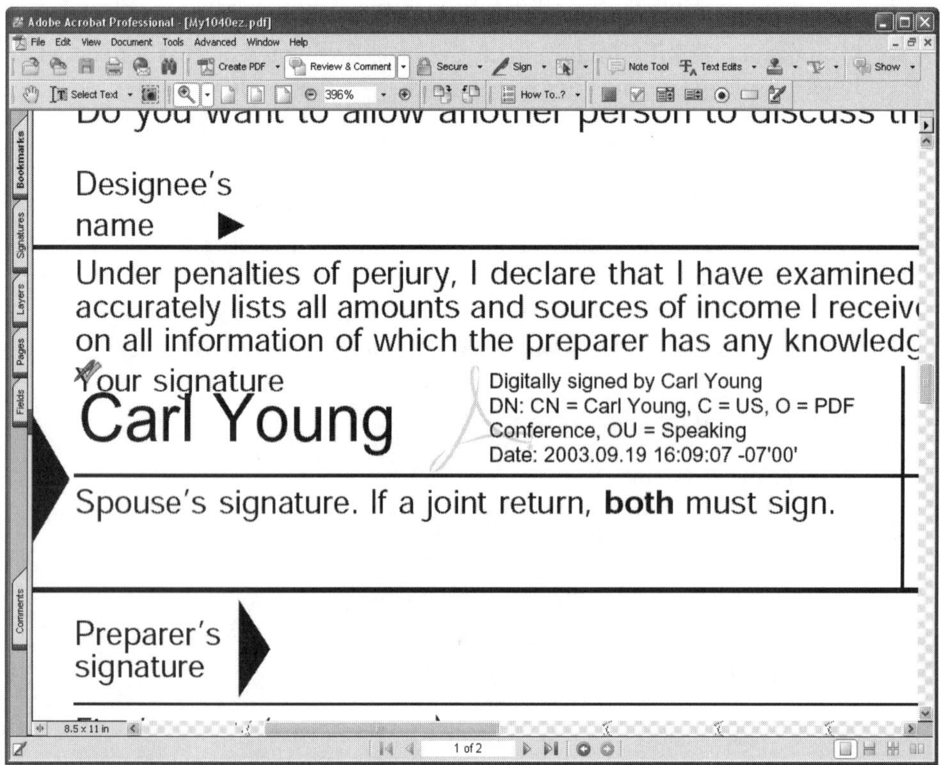

FIGURE 12-5 A form after a digital signature has been applied

4. Select a Digital ID if you have one. If not:

    a. Click Add Digital ID. Your options are to obtain a Digital ID from a trusted third-party source, to create your own with the built-in self-signed ID, or to browse to import an existing ID. In this example, we create our own.

    b. Choose Click Here to Create A Self-Signed Digital ID Now.

    c. Click Continue in the Self-Signed Digital ID Disclaimer dialog box.

    d. Fill in the Create Self-Signed Digital ID dialog box with your name, organization, and e-mail address.

    e. Click Create, and then click Yes to make your new digital certificate available for all applications on your computer.

5. Make sure your certificate name is highlighted in the Apply Digital Signature - Digital Signature Selection dialog box, and then click OK.

6. Enter your password, and then click Sign and Save As....

7. Save the file as My1040EZ. Click Close and reopen the file.

Now, try to change the data in your signed form. You cannot, but the Submit button is still active.

PDF Forms from Other Applications

Although form creation is part of Acrobat 6 Professional, you should know that Adobe, Amgraf, Cardiff, Cerenade, FormRouter, ScanSoft, and other companies make dedicated form creation tools. These companies, as well as activePDF, ARTS, Appligent, Image Solutions, and PDFLib also have products that link PDF Forms to databases.

Add-ons for specific authoring tools, such as "Mapsoft PageForm for Windows" (**http://www.mapsoft.com/products.htm**) let you define PDF fields in PageMaker or "TimeSavers+Form Assistant" for FrameMaker (**http://www.microtype.com**).

Why look at these tools instead of Acrobat? A dedicated form design tool has more design features, an interface devoted totally to form design, libraries of reusable objects, and it might let you output the same form to HTML, XML, and PDF. Some tools also generate JavaScripts that perform form field calculations automatically. (You learn to write some JavaScript calculations in the next chapter).

Do you have a lot of legacy paper or Word forms that need to be converted? Some of the products from these companies will convert your old forms into new, fillable PDF forms.

If You Really Enjoy Creating Forms

Some people find forms fascinating, and they love to put them together just like some people enjoy jigsaw puzzles. If you're one of these people, then you should check out the Business Forms Management Association (BFMA).

BFMA has conferences, workshops, and books on creating forms. It has chapters in most major metropolitan areas that meet regularly. For more information, see **www.bfma.org**.

Company Information

The following companies were mentioned in this chapter:

activePDF, **www.activepdf.com**	Adobe Systems, Inc., **www.adobe.com**
AdLib eDocument Solutions, **www.adlibsys.com**	Amgraf, **www.amgraf.com**
Amyuni Technologies, **www.amyuni.com**	Appligent, **www.appligent.com**
ARTS PDF, **www.artspdf.com**	Cardiff (now part of Verity), **www.verity.com**
Cerenade, **www.cerenade.com**	ScanSoft, **www.scansoft.com**
FormRouter, **www.formrouter.com**	Image Solutions, **www.imagesolutions.com**
PDFlib GmbH, **www.pdflib.com**	

Summary

PDF Forms are relatively simple to create, yet they can save organizations huge sums of money. Savings come because PDF Forms can reduce handwriting mistakes and calculation errors, and they cost nothing to print. PDF Forms can be deployed quickly on web sites, connected to databases, and made to look like the paper forms customers and employees are familiar with.

PDF Forms contain all the common elements found in paper forms: text fields, check boxes, and places for signatures. In addition, PDF Forms have features not found in paper forms: pull-down lists, preset options, digital signatures, and radio buttons that force users to make only one choice.

Chapter 13

Introduction to Adobe Acrobat JavaScript

In this chapter, we will not spend a lot of time in Acrobat itself. Instead, we will take a look at Acrobat JavaScript, which is the programming language for Acrobat. While JavaScript can do other things, it is mainly used for PDF forms. An Acrobat JavaScript can be one simple line of code or many hundreds of lines long.

The uses of Acrobat JavaScript are limited only by your programming skills and the limits of the language. Some common uses include:

- Performing Text form field calculations.
- Validating form input data, such as a telephone number.
- Changing the look of a document on the fly.
- Creating alert boxes that interact with end users.
- Creating a new, blank page or spawning a page of preformatted data.
- Establishing a connection to a repository for group commenting on a document.
- Adding or removing Acrobat or Reader menus or items.

While Reader, Standard, and Professional can execute JavaScripts, only Professional allows programmers to insert JavaScripts into PDF form fields. Standard users can insert JavaScripts into links, bookmarks, page actions, and document actions.

Because Adobe JavaScript is so complex, we only have space to skim the surface of what it can do. You will learn where to put JavaScripts in Acrobat, basic Acrobat JavaScript syntax, and work with a few simple examples in this chapter. If you want to hook Acrobat up with other applications or extend its functionality, see the last section in the chapter on the Acrobat SDK.

About Acrobat JavaScript

Acrobat JavaScript is a powerful programming language that is primarily used to make PDF forms more powerful. It is based on the JavaScript language developed by Netscape Communications that added power and flexibility to its web browsers. (JavaScript is in no way related to the Java programming language, except that the two languages appeared around the same time.)

JavaScript is now a standard (ISO-16262), and is still used extensively in web design. Many mouse rollovers, for example, are written in JavaScript. If you look through the web design section of your local bookstore, you have probably seen half a dozen titles on JavaScript.

If you are starting out to learn JavaScript for Acrobat, here is your first lesson: Acrobat JavaScript works differently than the JavaScript for the Web. In fact, if you pick up a book on JavaScript, it is likely that none of the examples and exercises will work exactly as described. The examples must be modified to take into account the differences between Acrobat JavaScript and HTML JavaScript.

NOTE *Only Acrobat 6 Professional supports the insertion of JavaScript into PDF form fields.*

Adobe is adopting JavaScript in a big way. The newest release of Adobe's flagship page layout program, InDesign CS, can be programmed with Adobe InDesign JavaScript. Like Acrobat JavaScript, InDesign JavaScript is a specialized version of the language with special features just for InDesign.

Acrobat JavaScript and HTML JavaScript

Why is there a difference? The reason is quite simple: a PDF document is not an HTML page. An HTML page cannot create a PDF document, and a PDF document cannot create an HTML page. Because of this fundamental difference, the Acrobat implementation of JavaScript works differently than does the HTML version.

For example, HTML JavaScript can create a new window in a web browser. Acrobat JavaScript cannot, although it can create a new, blank PDF document. HTML JavaScript can't reach inside a PDF to make something happen. Acrobat JavaScript can.

When to use which kind of JavaScript can be confusing because Acrobat contains a plug-in that shows PDF files in a browser window, and HTML pages can link to PDFs (and PDFs to HTML pages). For details, see the Adobe JavaScript Scripting Guide and the Adobe JavaScript Scripting Reference at **http://partners.adobe.com**. A good JavaScript reference also is helpful, such as *JavaScript: A Beginner's Guide, 2nd Edition,* by John Pollock (McGraw-Hill/Osborne, 2004). Just keep in mind that you'll need to modify the samples to run in Acrobat and many of the items may be not applicable.

Where Acrobat JavaScripts Can Be Used

Acrobat JavaScripts can be placed in folders to be loaded at startup—at what is known as the document level, so they are available throughout the PDF document—or in the field level for access by a single form field.

Folder Level Acrobat JavaScript

These JavaScripts run every time Acrobat starts. While Field Level and Document Level JavaScripts go into dialog boxes in the Acrobat user interface, Folder Level JavaScripts are stand-alone files. They are placed in the JavaScripts folder inside the Acrobat installation. Folder Level JavaScripts are plain text files with file extensions of *.js.

If you navigate to your Acrobat installation, you will see a folder called JavaScripts. In Windows, go to C:\Program Files\Adobe\Acrobat 6.0\Acrobat\Javascripts. These are the standard Folder Level JavaScripts that come with Acrobat.

Folder Level JavaScripts generally apply to the application, not to a particular form. For example, you can hide tools and menus with a Folder Level JavaScript.

Document Level

These JavaScripts apply to a particular document and travel with it. Choose Advanced | JavaScript | Document JavaScripts… to add a JavaScript to a document. Give the script a name, and then type, or paste, the script into the JavaScript editor.

Document-level JavaScripts can be accessed by Field Level JavaScripts. Good planning to coordinate Document Level and Field Level JavaScripts can improve the performance of a PDF form. Document Level JavaScripts run when the document opens. Document-level JavaScripts also can be used to change Acrobat and Reader preferences when a document loads. In addition, you may insert JavaScripts that run when something happens to the document. Choose Advanced | JavaScript | Set Document Actions to access this feature.

Field Level

Just as the name suggests, *Field Level* JavaScripts are placed inside form fields. While the types of JavaScripts allowed vary among the form types, each Form tool has one or more places to enter JavaScripts. The most common uses of Field Level JavaScripts are to validate, format, or calculate values.

Field Level JavaScripts probably are the most common type, especially for forms. A Field Level JavaScript is most-often initiated by some kind of user action, most commonly a mouse click. These user events are called *triggers* in Acrobat 6. See Figure 13-1 for an example.

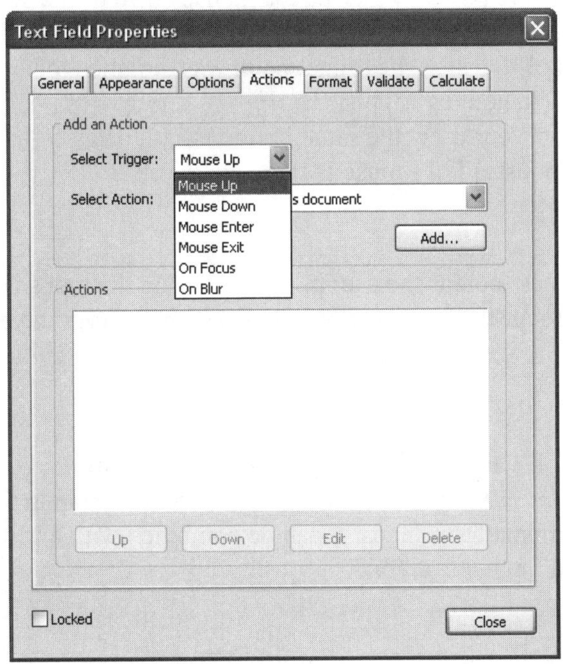

FIGURE 13-1 List of triggers for a Text Field

To set up a form field to accept a trigger, go to the Actions tab in a field's Properties dialog box. The triggers available are Mouse Up (most common), Mouse Down, Mouse Enter, Mouse Exit, On Focus, and On Lose Focus. In Text Fields, you can also add JavaScripts in the Custom calculation script field of the Calculation tab. (For more information on creating form fields, see Chapter 12.)

Additional triggers are available for activating media and are unavailable from form field dialog boxes. These triggers are Page Visible, Page Invisible, Page Enter, and Page Exit. The media triggers are available from the Actions tab in the Multimedia Properties dialog box.

Triggers associated with pages opening and closing are available from Page Properties. Select a page thumbnail in the Pages pane and right-click (Windows) or Option-click (Mac OS) and choose Page Properties | Actions.

Mouse Up

This is the most common trigger. The action takes place when the user releases the mouse. Although most of us think of the action taking place when the mouse button goes down, most programmers use *Mouse Up* as their primary user event. If you think about it, you have probably pushed the mouse down over a selection, realized it was a mistake, pulled the cursor away, and released the mouse button. (And started breathing again, too!) Because the trigger point was designed to be activated by the "up" part of the click, nothing happened.

You should give your users the same option to pull away from the trigger point, and use Mouse Up instead of Mouse Down.

Mouse Down

Mouse Down fires as soon as the user pushes down on the mouse button. There may be certain circumstances where Mouse Down is appropriate but, in general, avoid it.

Mouse Enter

This trigger goes off when the mouse pointer enters a form field or the play area of a media clip. *Mouse Enter* can be used to provide user help in form fields, or to show or hide additional form fields. It can be combined with a Mouse Up trigger to enable a second, optional action.

Mouse Exit

Mouse Exit triggers when the cursor leaves a form field or media play area. If you are using Mouse Enter to display user help when the cursor enters a form field, Mouse Exit can hide the help field when the cursor leaves the field.

On Focus

On Focus is triggered when the user tabs or clicks into a form field. User help could also be activated by this action. On Focus is called *On Received Focus* in the Media Properties dialog box.

On Lose Focus

Formerly known as On Blur, *On Lose Focus* is the opposite of On Focus. Focus is lost when the user clicks or tabs out of a form field.

Multimedia Triggers

The following table shows multimedia triggers available in Adobe Acrobat 6:

Page Visible	Triggers when the page holding the media element appears, even if it is not the current page. An example would be the facing page not on screen when Acrobat is in continuous page mode.

Page Invisible	Triggers when the page holding the media element disappears.
Page Enter	Triggers when the page holding the media element appears as the current page.
Page Exit	Triggers when a user navigates to any page other than the page holding the media element.

Page Actions and Links

JavaScripts can go into the Action tabs of Page, Bookmark, and Link Properties. For example, a JavaScript in a Bookmark could generate an e-mail message containing form data that automatically adds a recipient, subject line, body of the message, and attaches form data.

Finding the Actions tab can take a bit of hunting. Basically, the *Actions* tab is nested inside the Properties dialog box. Details on inserting a JavaScript are listed next.

Pages

To insert a JavaScript:

1. Open the Pages tab.
2. Select the thumbnail of the page you want to apply the action to.
3. Right-click (Windows) or CTRL-click (Mac OS) a page thumbnail and choose Page Properties, or select Page Properties from the Options menu.
4. Click on the Actions tab.
5. Choose Run a JavaScript.

Bookmarks

To insert a JavaScript:

1. Open the Bookmarks tab.
2. Select or create a Bookmark.
3. Right-click (Windows) or CTRL-click (Mac OS) and choose Properties, or select Properties from the Options menu.
4. Click on the Actions tab.
5. Choose Run a JavaScript.

Links

To insert a JavaScript:

1. Choose Tools | Advanced Editing | Link Tool.
2. Use the Link tool to create a new link, or double-click an existing one.
3. Click on the Actions tab.
4. Choose Run a JavaScript.

Naming Fields

Many form designers use description names for form fields. For example, an address block in a form would contain the fields FirstName and LastName. Another typical approach is to label the field for its type. A button field would be btSubmit. In Acrobat JavaScript, it is best to avoid flat names and to use a hierarchal structure that associates the fields.

Instead of FirstName and LastName, the preferred format is Name.First and Name.Last. *Name* is the parent, and *First* and *Last* are the children. There is no theoretical limit to the depth of the hierarchy. Adobe recommends that the hierarchy be "manageable."

Using the hierarchy can speed authoring and improve the performance of the form. By connecting fields in a hierarchy, the grouped fields can be more easily manipulated. For example, we could simultaneously manipulate both Name.First and Name.Last by referring to "Name."

Terms

JavaScript uses terms that most programmers will readily understand. If you are not a programmer (which is my case), here are some terms you will come across and their meanings:

- **Events** User activities that trigger the execution of a JavaScript. MouseUp (clicking on a button, for example) is a common event that triggers a JavaScript.
- **Conditions** Events that can happen depending on user selections or calculated values. For example, negative numbers could be colored red.

- **Loops** Lines of code that perform the same action over and over, such as searching for information in a table or group of form fields.
- **Objects** Objects include buttons, form fields, and documents.

NOTE *If you are unable to enter JavaScript into your PDF document, then JavaScript has been disabled. Enable JavaScript by choosing Edit | Preferences | General. In the list on the left, select JavaScript. Check Enable Adobe JavaScript and click OK.*

Inputting JavaScript into Acrobat Professional

Acrobat 6 Professional includes a JavaScript Editor for inserting JavaScript. There are two primary methods of accessing the JavaScript Editor. One is from the "Run a JavaScript" or "Custom Script" options in a form field, and the other is from the Advanced | JavaScript | Document JavaScripts menu options.

In addition, you can test JavaScripts in the *JavaScript Debugger,* which is an updated version of the JavaScript Console found in earlier versions of Acrobat. The JavaScript Debugger is available from Advanced | JavaScript | Debugger. The keyboard shortcut is CTRL-J for Windows and CMD-J in Mac OS. The Debugger includes a script editor and a console. It can display all the JavaScripts in a document or in the application folder.

NOTE *Use the console.show() command to open the console programmatically.*

Syntax

Because it is a scripting language, JavaScript looks at all the code on a line as input. So you don't foul up the interpreter, you need to know a little JavaScript syntax.

First of all, you should document your work with comments:

- To add one-line comments to a JavaScript (*comments* are your notes in the JavaScript code that will be ignored by the interpreter), put a double slash // in front of a line.
- Multiline comments start with a slash-asterisk (/*) and continue until the interpreter reaches an asterisk-slash (*/).

Next comes the actual code. Quote marks, semicolons, and other operators are used, similar to other programming languages.

- Event name values must be enclosed in double quotation marks.
- Quote marks must appear in pairs.
- Double and single quotes must alternate.
- JavaScript statements end with a semicolon. A semicolon at the end of the last statement is optional.
- Use the + operator to combine items.
- Use the equal sign = to assign values to variables and properties.
- JavaScript is case-sensitive, so you must use *this.getField* not *this.getfield.*

Objects

JavaScript is used to manipulate basic components of Acrobat, which are called *objects*. The most common objects are

- **app object** The app object is used to control Acrobat. It can be used to add menu items, access open documents, and to determine which version of Acrobat the end user has.
- **doc object** The doc object is used to work with PDF documents, and to access other objects within a document such as bookmarks, form fields, comments, and media objects. It is commonly used in conjunction with this object to point to a specific document.
- **util object** The util object defines common methods of date and text formatting.

An Example JavaScript

Unless otherwise specified, use a blank document with no form fields or JavaScripts present. Create a blank document from Microsoft Word or any other application. Just print an empty document to the Adobe PDF printer.

TIP *You can store reusable pieces of code, such as an address field with all the state abbreviations, in a reference document. You can then cut-and-paste your reference code into production documents.*

Display the Date in a Field

One of the most common requirements for a form is the display of the current date. The following example automatically displays the current date in a text field.

1. Open your blank PDF document.
2. Turn on Grid, Snap to Grid, Rulers and Guides from the View menu.
3. If the Form Toolbar is not showing, make it visible by choosing Tools | Advanced Editing | Forms | Show Forms Toolbar.
4. Select the Text Field tool.
5. Create a text field called Today.
6. In the Format tab, choose Format Category: Date. Choose the year format as m/d/yyyy. Click Close.
7. Click on the Calculate tab and click Edit in the Custom calculation script. Enter the following code:

    ```
    var f = this.getField("Today");
    f.value = util.printd("m/d/yyyy", new Date());
    ```

8. Click OK, and then click Close.

Select the Hand tool and look at the Today field. The current date should be displayed in the field.

What Just Happened?

Here is how the code works. Look at the first line. The name of the field that displays the date is named Today. It appears in quotation marks and is enclosed in parentheses. The code,

```
var f = this.getField ("Today");
```

creates a variable named *f* and links it with the Today text field. The second line says that the value of variable *f* is today:

```
("m/d/yyyy", date new Date())
```

Using the JavaScript Console/Debugger

While you are not likely to make many mistakes entering two lines of code, the chances of making an error increase as the lines of code go up. The JavaScript Console/Debugger in Acrobat Professional enables you to evaluate the code as you write it. See Figure 13-2 for an example.

To use the Debugger, it must be enabled. Turn it on at Preferences | Enable JavaScript Debugger. Restart Acrobat.

Code is entered in the console Script Editor, and then tested. You can test one line of code or a block of code.

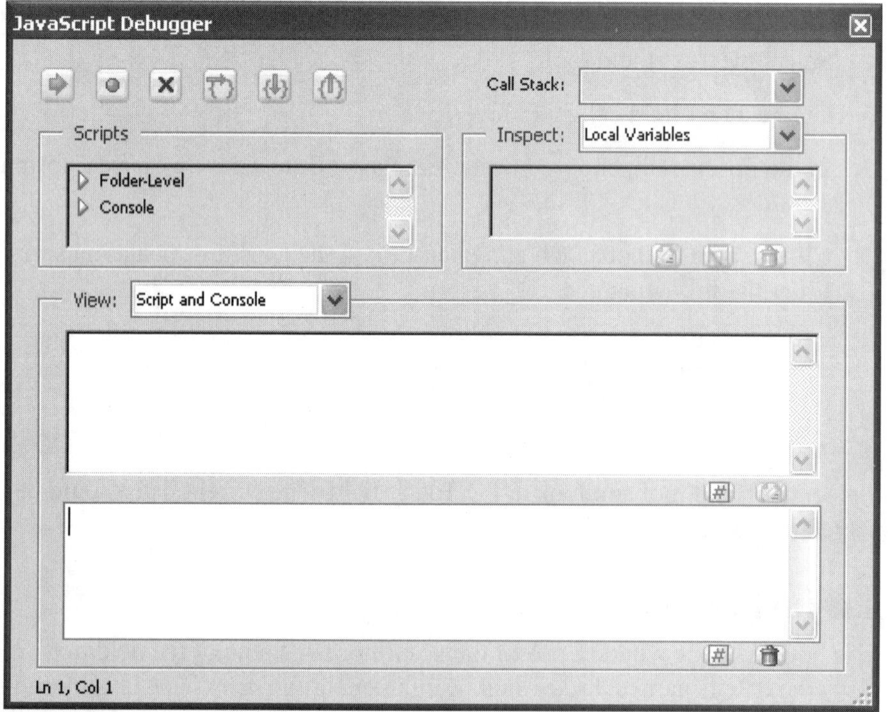

FIGURE 13-2 The Acrobat Debugger and Console can speed the creation of Acrobat JavaScript code.

NOTE *Testing involves the use of the* ENTER *key on the numeric keypad, or* CTRL-ENTER *on the keyboard. Using the* ENTER *key on the keyboard by itself will not work.*

If you would like to test a single line of code, put the cursor on the line and press ENTER on the numeric keypad, or CTRL-ENTER on the regular keyboard. To test a block of code, select the block and press ENTER on the numeric keypad, or CTRL-ENTER on the regular keyboard. The results will appear in the console.

To try it out, follow this procedure:

1. Open a multipage PDF document.
2. Choose Advanced | JavaScript | Debugger.
3. Choose Script and Console from the View pull-down menu in the Debugger window.
4. Delete any text in the Script Editor and replace it with the following:

```
console.println("There are " + this.numPages + " pages in
this document");
```

5. Highlight the text, and type CTRL-ENTER.

You should see a phrase that says, "There are (yournumber) pages in this document."

NOTE *You can specify a JavaScript Editor other than the one built into Acrobat in Edit | Preferences | JavaScript.*

Useful Acrobat JavaScript Examples

Now that we've inserted some JavaScript into both a form field and the Debugger, let's try some more samples.

Performing a Calculation

Let's say you want to add three PDF fields named Income.1, Income.2, and Income.3, and to display the sum in a field name IncomeSum.1. See Figure 13-3 for an example of the completed form.

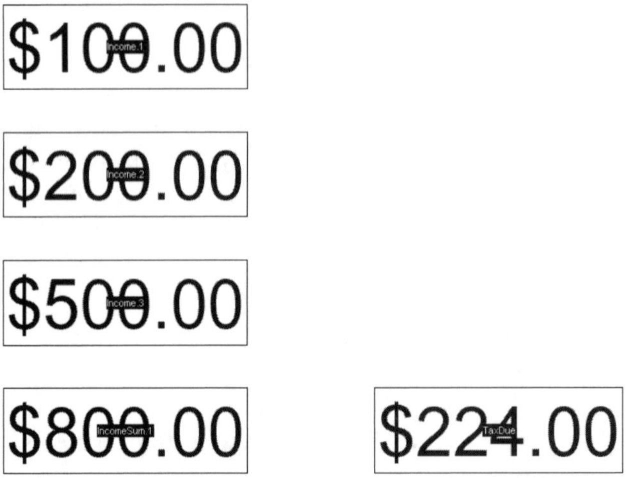

FIGURE 13-3 Fields names are displayed when the Text Field tool is selected.

1. Create Text Fields named Income.1, Income.2, and Income.3. In the Format tab of each field, choose Number from the Select Format Category menu. Add a currency symbol.

2. Create a fourth field named IncomeSum.1. Make sure it has the same format as the other Income fields.

3. Click on the Calculate tab. Choose Custom Calculation Script and Edit.

4. Enter the following text in the JavaScript Editor:

```
// Get field values
var v1 = this.getField("Income.1").value;
var v2 = this.getField("Income.2").value;
var v3 = this.getField("Income.3").value;
// Calculate total
var total = v1 + v2 + v3;
// Set target field value equal to total
this.getField("IncomeSum.1").value = total;
```

5. Select the Hand tool and enter some data into the Income fields. Notice that the total updates whenever you finish entering a value in the first three fields.

NOTE *A good practice is to mark Text fields holding calculations as Read Only. This option prevents users from entering their own values in the field. The Read Only option is available in the General tab of Text fields.*

While this code is a good example to learn from, it is quite long. Acrobat's built-in generator make the fields add in a different way, and does not require scripting by hand. You may remember we did this earlier with the 1040EZ sample in Chapter 12. In the Calculate tab, use the second option and the Pick feature to sum fields.

Perform Another Calculation

Now that we have done some addition, let's try a bit of multiplication. Let's add another field that will calculate a percentage of our field named IncomeSum.1. We will assume our tax rate is 28 percent, and use a JavaScript to calculate the amount of tax due.

1. Use the Text Field tool to create a new field.
2. Name the field TaxDue.
3. In the Format tab, choose Number as the format category. Be sure to include a currency symbol.
4. Click on the Calculate tab. Choose Custom calculation script.
5. Click on Edit.
6. Enter the text:

```
var a=this.getField("IncomeSum.1");
event.value = a.value *.28;
```

7. Click OK and Close.

The new TaxDue field should automatically calculate how much tax is due at a rate of 28 percent.

Automatically Tab from One Field to the Next

You've probably filled out a form that had big black boxes designed to hold one letter at a time. In general, these forms are designed to be scanned by Optical Character Recognition (OCR) software.

Many students are converting these old forms to Acrobat, and they ask for a JavaScript that takes the user from one field to the next.

I usually reply that they should redesign the form to avoid this nonsense. End users of Acrobat forms can enter form data, and then press the TAB key to go on to the next field. If your end user is filling out the form in Acrobat or Reader, then you have captured the text digitally—you don't need to scan the text in and, therefore, the big black box design is a relic from the 1970s. Feel free to design something more visually appealing.

However, I realize that many organizations have to go through long and painful review processes to change the look of a form. Here, then, is an example of how to program form fields so the cursor jumps from field to field.

In this example, you will create three form fields for a U.S. Social Security number. You will then add a document-level JavaScript that moves Acrobat's focus from one field to the next. You finish by adding a Custom Keystroke Script to the first two fields that use the document-level JavaScript.

1. Create a new, blank document without any JavaScripts.
2. Add a new Text field named SSN.1.
3. Go to the Options tab and set a Character Limit of 3.
4. Go to the Format tab and select Custom.
5. Click Edit in the Custom Keystroke Script field and add the following code:

   ```
   AutoTab(this, event, "SSN.2");
   ```
6. Click OK, and then click Close.
7. Duplicate the field and name the copy SSN.2.
8. Go to the Options tab and change the Character Limit to 2.
9. Go to the Format tab and change the Custom Keystroke field to:

   ```
   AutoTab(this, event, "SSN.3");
   ```
10. Duplicate SSN.2. Rename the field SSN.3 and delete the Custom Keystroke Script.
11. Go to Options and set the Character Limit to 4.

Now it's time to insert the document-level JavaScript that moves the focus from field to field.

12. Choose Advanced | JavaScript | Document JavaScripts.
13. Add a new Document JavaScript called AutoTab.
14. Enter this code:

```
function AutoTab(doc, event, cNext)
{
// Use the built-in routine that permits only numbers.
AFNumber_Keystroke(0, 0, 0, 0, "", true);
//When you have completed the field, jump to the next one.
if (event.rc && AFMergeChange(event).length ==
event.target.charLimit)
      doc.getField(cNext).setFocus();
}
```

15. Select the Hand tool and try it. The cursor should jump from field to field when each is complete.

Alert Box

An *Alert Box* will place a dialog box onscreen. It can be a simple warning, such as "You are about to charge your credit card," or it can include an interactive answer. In the following example, you will create an Alert Box that asks a question and provides a response, depending on the answer.

1. Open a blank PDF that contains no JavaScripts.

TIP *Choose Advanced | JavaScript | Edit All JavaScripts to see if any JavaScripts are in your document.*

2. Choose the Button tool.
3. Draw a large button onscreen.
4. Enter a name of Alert.
5. Click on the Options tab.
6. Choose Label Only and Enter a label of Click Me.
7. Move to the Actions tab.
8. Make sure that Trigger is set to Mouse Up.

9. Choose Select Action | Run a JavaScript.
10. Click Add.
11. Enter the following code:

```
/* Create a variable named answer, enter question text*/
/* Add the question icon, Yes/No button. */
var answer = app.alert("Do you like mayonnaise?", 2, 2);
/* 0 = error, 1 = OK, 2 = Cancel, 3 = No, 4 = Yes */
if (answer == 4)
{    app.alert("Then ask for mayo");
} else
{    app.alert("Then ask to hold the mayo");
}
```

12. Select the Hand tool and test the button. The question text should appear in the alert box:

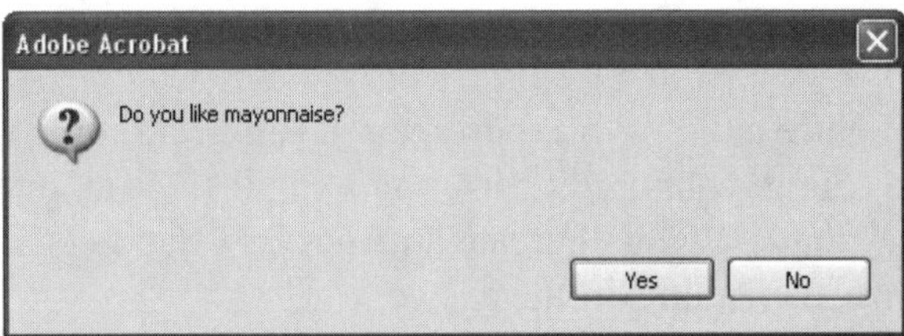

You will receive an answer, depending on whether you choose Yes or No. If your computer has speakers, you will also hear a beep:

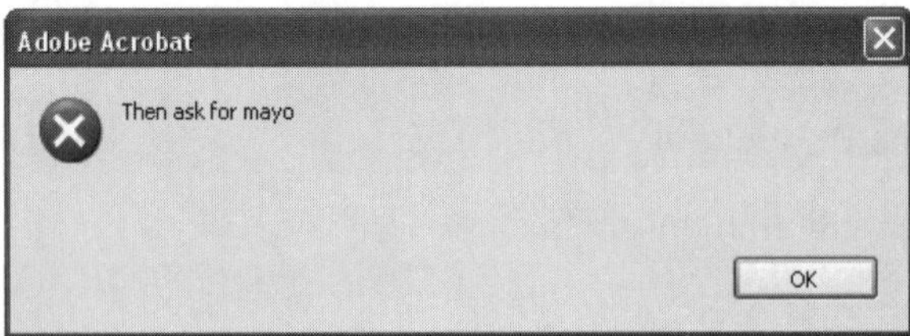

Make Acrobat Bark Like a Dog

Acrobat 6 includes a Read Aloud feature that recites PDFs to end users who are visually impaired, either through loss of sight or a reading disability. Here's a fun JavaScript to make Acrobat sound off.

NOTE *You will need a sound card and speakers to hear Acrobat speak.*

Open the DeBugger by choosing Advanced | JavaScript | DeBugger. Enter the following code into the Script Editor. Remember to activate the code by pressing ENTER on the numeric keypad, or CTRL-ENTER on the regular keyboard:

```
tts.qText("Acrobat says ruff, ruff, like Fido.");
tts.talk();
```

Okay, so maybe your computer's voice doesn't sound much like your dog, but isn't it fun making your computer try?

By the way, cat lovers can use the following:

```
tts.qText("Acrobat says: Meow, Meow, like Kitty.");
tts.talk();
```

Add Voice to the Alert

Now that you know how to make an interactive alert box and make Acrobat talk, let's put them together.

Add the following code to a JavaScript Action in a Button field:

```
/* Create a variable named answer, enter question text*/
/* Add the question icon, Yes/No button. */
/*add speech to text question*/
tts.qText("Do you like mayonnaise?");
tts.talk();
var answer = app.alert("Do you like mayonnaise?", 2, 2);
/* 0 = error, 1 = OK, 2 = Cancel, 3 = No, 4 = Yes */
if (answer == 4)
{
/*add speech to text question*/
tts.qText("Then ask for mayo.");
tts.talk();
app.alert("Then ask for mayo");
} else
{
/*add speech to text question*/
tts.qText("Then ask to hold the mayo.");
tts.talk();
app.alert("Then ask to hold the mayo");
}
```

Pop-Up Menus

Although pop-up menus are easy to create, they are uncommon in PDFs. I've even had students in my class who insist that Acrobat can't do pop-ups!

That's a shame, because pop-up menus can be helpful user aids. For example, if your audience is made up of users who are unfamiliar with Acrobat, you can insert a Button Field with a pop-up menu that can guide users to particular destinations, such as a table of contents, an introduction, or a specific chapter in a long document. Pop-up menus can also be used in forms to refer users to reference materials or web sites.

In the following example, you will create a five-page document, and insert a pop-up menu, like the one shown next, that takes users to each page in the document. I've found that this exercise makes more sense if we work with a brief, multipage document.

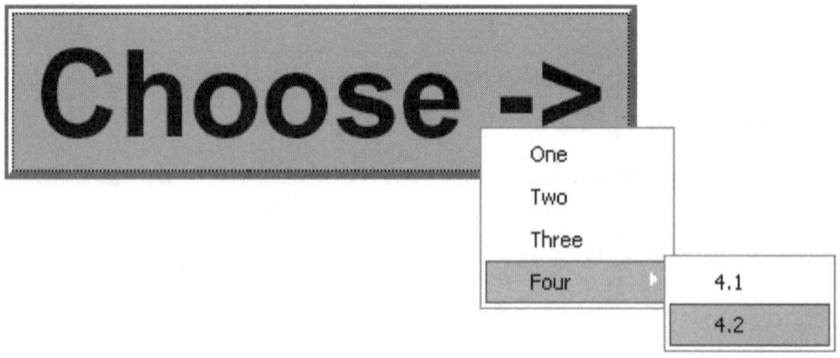

Create a Pop-Up Menu

Begin by creating a five-page document. You can use any word processing or page layout program.

1. At the top of pages 1–3, add a headline of Page One, Page Two, and Page Three.
2. Insert a headline of Page 4.1 on page 4, and Page 4.2 on page 5.
3. Save the file and create a PDF named Pop-up.
4. Open the file in Acrobat and choose View | Navigation Tabs | Destinations.
5. In the Destinations tab, choose Options | Scan Document.
6. Navigate to page 1 of your document and choose Options | New Destination from the Destinations tab.
7. Name the Destination "One."

8. Insert Destinations "Two" and "Three" on pages 2 and 3.
9. On page 4, insert a Destination of 4.1.
10. On page 5, insert a Destination of 4.2.

Now that you have a document with Destinations in it, you will add a Button Field that links to each Destination. You will end by duplicating the Button Field on each page.

1. Select the Button Field tool.
2. Block out a Button Field on page 1.
3. Name the field Pop-Up. Add a Tooltip of Click to navigate to a page.
4. Move to the Options tab in the Button Properties dialog box. Select Label Only. Give the field a label of Choose.
5. Move to the Actions tab. Select a Trigger of Mouse Up and an Action of Run a JavaScript. Click Add.
6. In the JavaScript Editor, enter

```
var cDest = app.popUpMenu("One", "Two", "Three", ["Four", "4.1", "4.2"]);
this.gotoNamedDest(cDest);
```

7. Click OK and Close. Close the Destinations tab.
8. Select the Hand tool and test the pop-up menu. You should be able to navigate to each page of your document by using the pop-up menu. If it works, you are now ready to place the menu on additional pages.
9. Right-click on the Button Field. Choose Duplicate | All | OK.

What Just Happened?

The two-line JavaScript you inserted into the Button Field created the menu and its options.

The first line begins by creating a new variable named cDest, whose value is set through the choice made through the pop-up menu. Each menu item is specified by opening and closing quotes (" ") and is separated by commas. Submenu items are specified with nesting square brackets [ ].

The second line tells Acrobat to go to the Destination specified by the selection cDest.

Specify a User Preference

Students often ask if they can use JavaScript to change preference settings in Acrobat and Reader. The answer is maybe. Check the Acrobat JavaScript Scripting Guide to see if the preference is available.

In the following example, you will create a document level JavaScript that turns off the Open cross-document links in same window in Acrobat Preferences. By default, Acrobat closes one document before it opens another. If you turn off Open cross-document links in same window in preferences, both documents will stay open.

Only the most sophisticated users will ever turn off this setting. See Figure 13-4 for an example of the default setting.

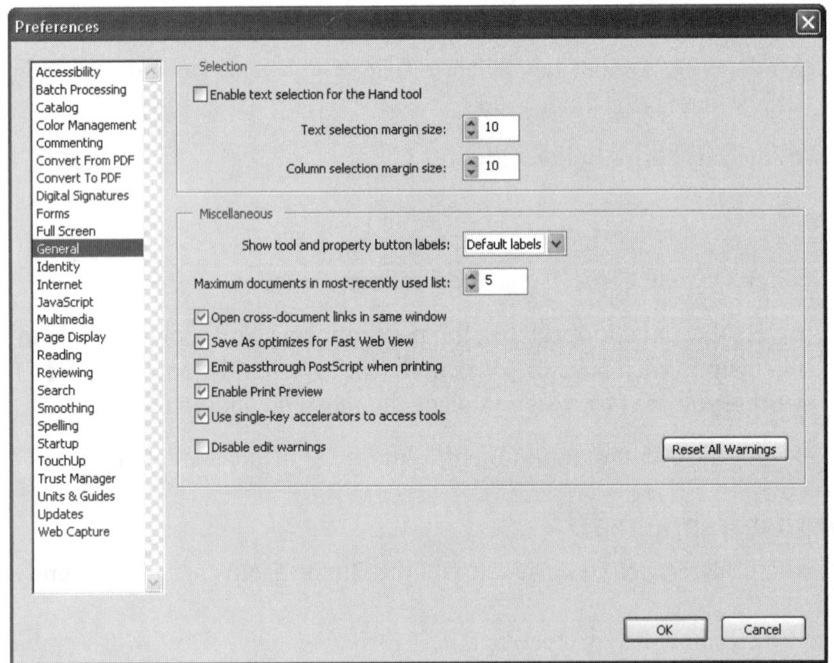

FIGURE 13-4 The Open cross-document links in same window preference is turned on by default.

1. Open a blank PDF that does not contain any JavaScripts.
2. Choose Edit | Preferences | General. By default, Open cross-document links in same window will be on.
3. Close Preferences and choose Advanced | JavaScripts | Document JavaScripts.
4. Enter a name of app.openInPlace and click Add.
5. Replace the automatically placed text with the following line of code:

```
app.openInPlace=false;
```

6. Click OK and Close.
7. Save the file and reopen it.
8. Choose Edit | Preferences | General again. Open cross-document links will be off.

Now, to be good citizens, we should reset Open cross-document links when our file closes. The following procedure uses Document Actions to turn on the Open cross-document links preference. Continue to use the same file.

1. Choose Advanced | JavaScript | Set Document Actions.
2. Highlight Document Will Close.
3. Click Edit and enter the following line of code:

```
app.openInPlace=true;
```

4. Click OK, and then click OK again.
5. Save the file, close it, and reopen it.

Choose Edit | Preferences | General. Open cross-document links in new window should be turned on.

Add a New Menu Item

Something many power users often use is a blank Acrobat page. A PDF document that doesn't contain any JavaScripts, form fields, or text is a "pure" environment in which you can test JavaScripts. It's also handy if you need to insert a blank page into a PDF document to make the pagination turn out right.

The following JavaScript adds a new menu item to the File menu and will create a blank, 8.5- by 11-inch page. Save this code as a text document, and change the file extension to *.js. Close Acrobat, and then place the file in your Acrobat 6\Acrobat\Javascripts folder.

```
/*add New to the File menu*/
app.addSubMenu({ cName: "New", cParent: "File", nPos: 0 })
/*add US Letter to the New submenu and create a new page*/
app.addMenuItem({ cName: "US Letter", cParent: "New", cExec:
"var d = app.newDoc();"});
```

When you restart Acrobat, choose File | New | US Letter. A blank, 8.5- by 11-inch document will appear.

E-mail and Version Sniffing

Two of the most common questions students ask are about sending form data via e-mail and how to check a user's version of Acrobat.

The first example sends an e-mail containing form data to a user. The second looks for the user's version of Acrobat (called *sniffing*), and issues a warning if the version is below 6.0.

E-mail Form Data

For the e-mail example, we will use a Bookmark action that will e-mail form data to a specific user. You could, of course, use a Button field or a link instead.

1. Open a PDF document containing a form field. (See Chapter 12 for more information.)
2. Open the Bookmark tab.
3. Choose Options | New Bookmark.
4. Name the bookmark E-mail Form.
5. Choose Options | Properties.
6. Click on the Actions tab.
7. Delete the Go to Page action.

8. Choose Select Action | Run a JavaScript and click Add.
9. Enter the following code into the JavaScript Editor:

```
/*send form data as fdf* to a specific user*/
this.mailForm(true, "name@address.com", "", "", "Submitted
Form Data");
```

(Note that the empty quotes between commas are for CC: and BCC:.)

10. Click OK, and then click Close.

Check the Version of Acrobat

Some features, such as layers, are not supported in previous versions of Acrobat or Adobe Reader. The script, inserted at the document level, checks the user's system for an older version of Acrobat, and then issues a warning about layers:

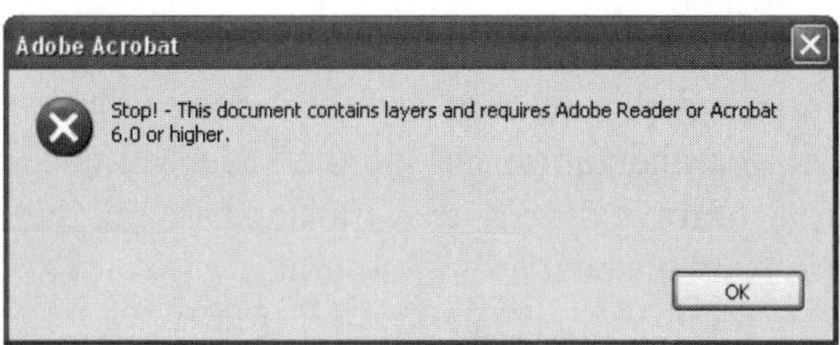

1. Go to Advanced | JavaScript | Document JavaScripts.
2. Give the JavaScript a name, such as Version Check.
3. Click Add and replace the automatically inserted text with the following code:

```
/*check the viewer version and issue an alert if below 6*/
if (app.viewerVersion < 6.0)app.alert("Stop! - This document
contains layers and requires Adobe Reader or Acrobat 6.0 or
higher.");
```

4. Click OK, and then click Close.

Save the document and open it in an older version of Acrobat.

Acrobat 6.0 Software Development Kit

If JavaScript doesn't give you enough horsepower, then you should look at the Acrobat Software Development Kit (SDK). The *SDK* is designed for non-Adobe developers who want to create plug-ins for Acrobat, integrate a PDF solution into another application, or automate a process.

The SDK includes technical documentation and sample code to help you get started. While most people who can follow a recipe can use JavaScript, working with the SDK is a job for a developer who knows the programming languages C and C++. Acrobat Professional, Standard, and Adobe Reader have application program interfaces that can be accessed by the SDK.

Why would you want to do this? Let's say you have a specific business workflow, and you would like to provide new functionality to your users. You could also write a plug-in that could display a PDF in the window of another application. Or, you could write code that tightly integrates PDFs with your document management systems.

You can download the basic Acrobat 6.0 SDK at **http://partners.adobe.com/asn/tech/pdf/acrobatsdks.jsp**. You must join the Adobe Solutions Network (ASN) to obtain the full SDK documentation and sample code. Membership in the ASN also gets you invited to Acrobat developer workshops around the country, and makes it far easier to get into Adobe's beta testing program.

In addition, Adobe has a Forms Data Format (FDF) Toolkit. The *FDF Toolkit* is an application-programming interface that enables Windows and UNIX servers to generate or process PDF form data. Information on the FDF Toolkit can be found at **http://partners.adobe.com/asn/developer/sdks.html**.

Summary

Adobe has taken a web-based scripting tool and modified it to run inside of Acrobat. With JavaScript, form authors can create complex calculations or validate the form's data, technical writers can add pop-up menus to help readers navigate through large documents, and developers can modify or add menu items to Reader and Acrobat.

JavaScripts can be only one line of code or many thousands. Its usefulness is only limited to the imagination and programming skill of the code writer.

For more samples, look at the forums at **www.planetpdf.com** and **www.pdfzone.com**. Adobe also maintains user-to-user forums at **www.adobe.com**.

Chapter 14

A Short Course for System Administrators

As the popularity of Acrobat grows, so do the number of system administrators who have to install and maintain it. Nearly all of them are very sharp at installing and configuring Microsoft products, but many stumble when it comes to Acrobat. After all, it is Adobe Acrobat, not Microsoft Acrobat, so things work a little differently than many administrators are used to.

In this chapter, you will learn what to install from the Acrobat installation CD, the order in which to install applications Acrobat works with, and some common troubleshooting techniques.

An Acrobat on Every Desk

First of all, Adobe is historically focused on the graphics market. Most graphics workgroups are small, only six or seven users each. Most use Macintosh computers. Acrobat, on the other hand, is an enterprise application that often is installed on hundreds, thousands, or tens of thousands of computers. The vast majority are Windows machines.

The users are different, too. A graphic artist might see an application such as Photoshop or Illustrator as their primary workhorse application, but most enterprise users use Acrobat as just another program on the desktop.

When enterprise users want Acrobat to work, they want it to work. They are unwilling to individually spend dozens of hours troubleshooting problems, as a graphic artist might spend tuning up Photoshop. Instead of doing it themselves, the enterprise user calls the system administrator or the help desk.

Many of the students in my classes tell me that their administrators know little about Acrobat. That's unsurprising—I can't imagine many human resources departments specify that their new system administrator hires be Adobe Certified Experts in Acrobat. I've also had a few system administrators in class and have incorporated some of their suggestions into this chapter.

Incorrect Acrobat Installations

Above all, Acrobat must be installed correctly. Why doesn't this happen? Because Acrobat doesn't just sit in isolation from the rest of the programs on a user's computer. Acrobat hooks into the operating system and Microsoft Office products. These hooks include the Adobe PDF printer driver, the macro that enables PDFMaker in the Office product suite, and possibly even your organization's computer security system. (For more information on security, see Chapter 9.)

Installation problems include not installing the basic pieces of Acrobat or installing Acrobat before the applications it connects with. And, if Acrobat isn't installed properly, your organization cannot establish or maintain any PDF publishing standards.

Order of Installation

Because Acrobat extends hooks into other applications upon installation, the other applications have to be installed first. As a practical matter, that means install and update all Microsoft Office Products, Word, Excel, PowerPoint, Project, and Visio before installing Acrobat. The recommended installation order is

1. Update the latest Windows security patches or updates.
2. Update Microsoft Internet Explorer.
3. Install Microsoft Office Products.
4. Install Adobe Reader, if your users want both the Reader and Acrobat available.

NOTE *Adobe does not recommend the installation of both Acrobat and Reader on the same machine.*

5. Install the most up-to-date version of Acrobat. Check for the most recent version by choosing Help | Updates.

Simple? Yes, but the order is critical if you are maintaining hundreds or thousands of desktops. You only want to do this once, not two or three times.

Once the Acrobat installation is complete, check to make sure that the Adobe PDF printer, Acrobat, Distiller, and application-specific macros have been placed on the computer. If you are upgrading from a previous version of Acrobat, the installer will ask to remove the older version. Adobe warns against running Acrobat 6 and earlier versions on the same Windows machine. Mac OS users can easily run Acrobat 5 and 6 on the same computer. If you must run Acrobat 5 and 6 on the same Windows machine, install Acrobat 5 first using a custom installation. Do not install Distiller 5 or PDFWriter. Then install Acrobat 6.

NOTE *What do I do if I want to test my PDFs on an earlier version of Acrobat? Adobe recommends installing the different versions on separate machines. Dual installations of Acrobat tend be highly unstable.*

TIP *The ideal test machine will have no fonts—except for system fonts—installed. Because many applications also install fonts, it is best not to install any applications either.*

What to Install

Basically, you should install nearly all the components of Acrobat. A standard installation should work for most enterprise users. Why doesn't this always happen? Because in this age of attacks by viruses, hackers, and spyware, system administrators are rightly suspicious and take a conservative approach to software installation. If they don't know what a piece of software does, they often won't install it. And because Acrobat doesn't come from Microsoft, a lot of unfamiliar things are going on in an Acrobat installation.

As a result, I've heard from students who don't have the PDFMaker in Microsoft Word, don't have an Adobe PDF printer in their list of printers, and don't even have Acrobat Distiller. Without those basic tools, it is pretty tough to use Acrobat.

In this section, we will go through a typical install. I won't explain how to install Acrobat—it installs like any other piece of Windows software. What I will do is explain what each component does, and tell you why it should be installed. It is my hope this information will let users make the case for getting the proper Acrobat components installed and help some system administrators better understand why Acrobat does what it does.

Components of Acrobat Professional

A default installation should work fine for most users. The only significant options in Acrobat 6 are for Asian language support. The Adobe PDF printer, Acrobat, and Distiller are all installed and placed in the user's list of program files. The following list explains what some of the options are for a Custom Setup.

View Adobe PDF

View Adobe PDF, shown in Figure 14-1, contains the optional features available in either Acrobat Standard or Professional.

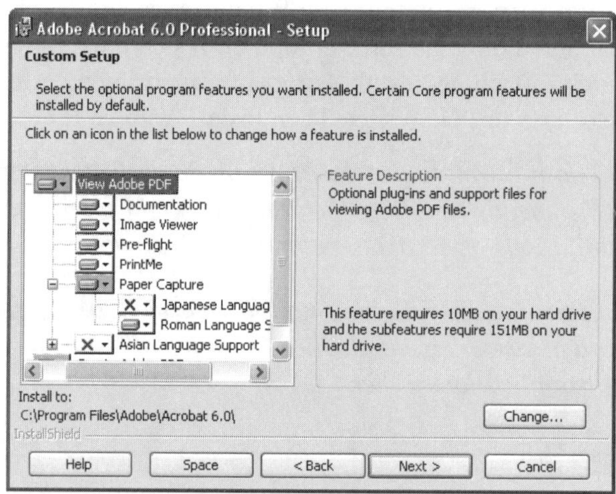

FIGURE 14-1 View Adobe PDF setup installs user documentation, paper capture, and other components.

- Documentation includes both online help and a PDF version of the Acrobat user manual. The user manual is interactive and searchable from within Acrobat. (There is no printed manual.)
- The *Image Viewer plug-in* enables you to see Adobe PDF multimedia slideshows and greeting cards created with Adobe Photoshop Album.
- *Preflight* includes the tools for checking high-end publications and is only found in Professional.
- *PrintMe* is a pay-for-use printing service provided by a third company. Unless the installation is on the laptop of someone who needs to print documents on the road, you can safely disable this option.
- *Paper Capture* turns scanned images of text documents into searchable PDFs. This feature is critical for many users who want to turn paper documents into PDFs. There is an option to include Japanese language support in Paper Capture, and an overall option to support Asian languages in Acrobat.

Create Adobe PDF

Create Adobe PDF, shown in Figure 14-2, includes the options for making PDFs from various applications such as Microsoft Office, Visio, and AutoDesk AutoCad.

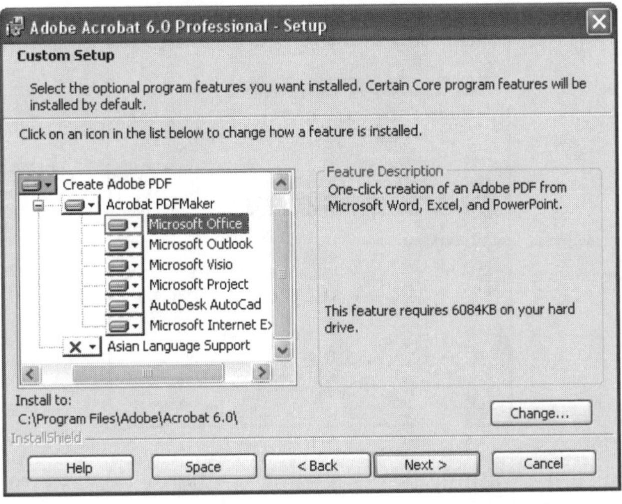

FIGURE 14-2 Create Adobe PDF installs links to popular desktop applications.

Acrobat installs macros in Microsoft Office products, including Outlook, Visio, and Project. In addition, options for installing a PDFMaker macro are inside AutoDesk AutoCAD.

Where Is PDFMaker?

After installation issues, one of the biggest areas of confusion seems to be the PDFMakers installed in Microsoft Office applications, particularly Microsoft Word. As noted in the previous section, Acrobat installs macros inside of the Microsoft Office suite of products by default.

Virus writers often launch attacks from Word macros. As a result, many system administrators lock down Word so it can't see the PDFMaker macro. The PDFMaker icons are shown at right.

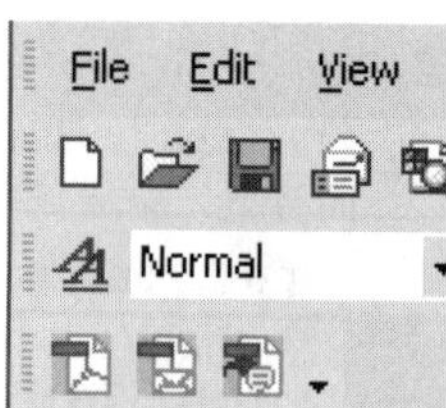

Fortunately, there is an easy fix if you can't see the Adobe PDF icons in your Word toolbar. Keep in mind that the task needs to be performed by someone with Administrator rights.

1. In Microsoft Word, choose Tools | Templates and Add-ins.
2. Enable PDFMaker.dot, shown next, and click OK.

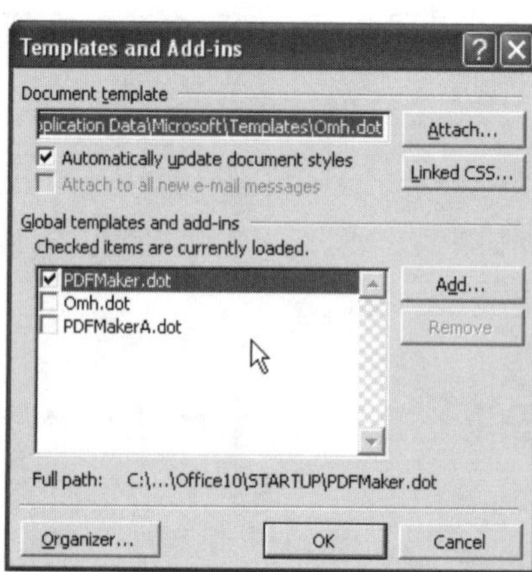

3. In the Security Warning box, shown next, choose Always trust macros from this source. Click Enable Macros.

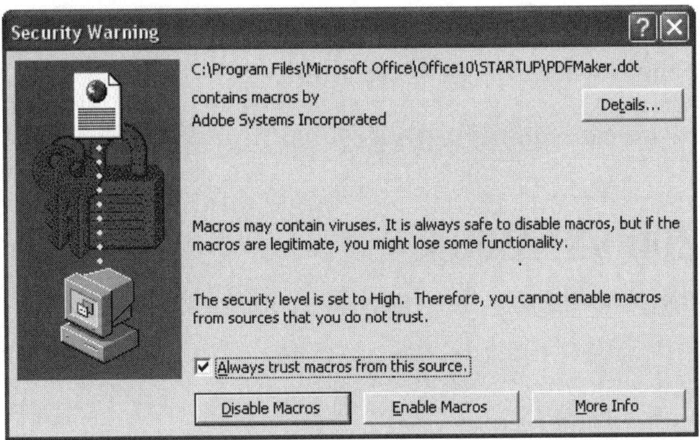

You can verify settings by choosing Tools | Macro |Security. Click on the Trusted Sources tab. You should see Adobe Systems, Inc. listed, as shown here:

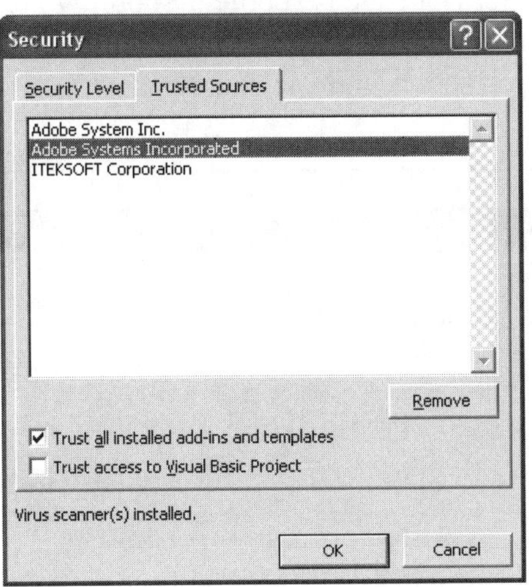

NOTE *The Trusted Sources in Word are shared across the Office suite. Once a macro is set up in Word, it should work in Excel, PowerPoint, Outlook, and Internet Explorer.*

PostScript Driver Setup

Few people know the ins and outs of print driver setup better than Dov Isaacs, one of Adobe's principal scientists. Dov has been working with PostScript and printers for many years, and he is a frequent poster to Acrobat-related newsgroups. Here are Dov's recommendations for going deep inside the Adobe PDF printer and tuning it for the highest-level of PDF creation.

NOTE *Dov's recommendations are not officially endorsed by Adobe.*

Windows 2000/XP/2003

Use the following procedure to fine tune the Adobe PDF printer for maximum performance:

1. Start | Printers and Faxes.
2. Select Adobe PDF | Properties | Advanced.
3. In the Adobe PDF Properties dialog box, shown in Figure 14-3, choose Start printing after last page is spooled. Spooling greatly enhances the user experience because you can continue to work most effectively and efficiently while the print job spools in the background.

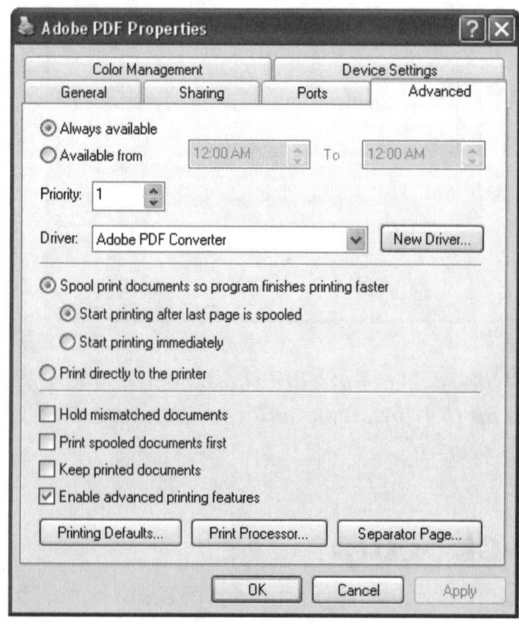

FIGURE 14-3 Change the Advanced settings to start printing after the last page is spooled.

4. Turn on Enable advanced printing features. This activates the Pages Per Sheet option in the Adobe PDF printer. This feature is available at Adobe PDF printer | Preferences | Layout.
5. Click Apply.

Device Settings

Next up are the Device Settings. By default, the PostScript driver is assuming you have a PostScript printer attached to your computer via a parallel port. When working with Acrobat, you are using a virtual printer, not one that is wired to your machine. You will get better results if you modify Device Settings, as shown in Figure 14-4.

1. Switch Output Protocol from ASCII to Binary. A binary-based PostScript fill will be smaller and should Distill more efficiently.

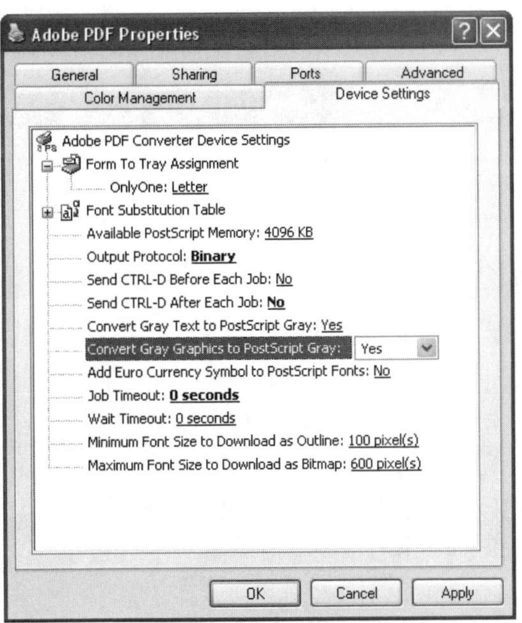

FIGURE 14-4 Change your Device Settings from those meant for a real printer to the virtual printer of Acrobat Distiller.

2. Change Send CTRL-D after each job to No. CTRL-D is necessary for ASCII PostScript, but is a hindrance with Binary.
3. Make sure the Convert Gray Text to PostScript Gray and Convert Gray Graphics to PostScript Gray are set to Yes. These settings produce a better-looking gray, and should be set to Yes by default.
4. Set Job Timeout to 0 seconds. This helps avoid Distiller timeout errors caused by a slow system or network connections.

Properties of the Adobe PDF Converter

The next area is a little deeper inside the Properties of the Adobe PDF Converter. See Figure 14-5 for sample settings.

1. Choose Start | Printers and Faxes | Adobe PDF | Properties | Advanced | Printing Defaults | Layout | Advanced. (Or, choose Printers and Faxes | Adobe PDF | Properties | General | Printing Preferences | Layout | Advanced.)

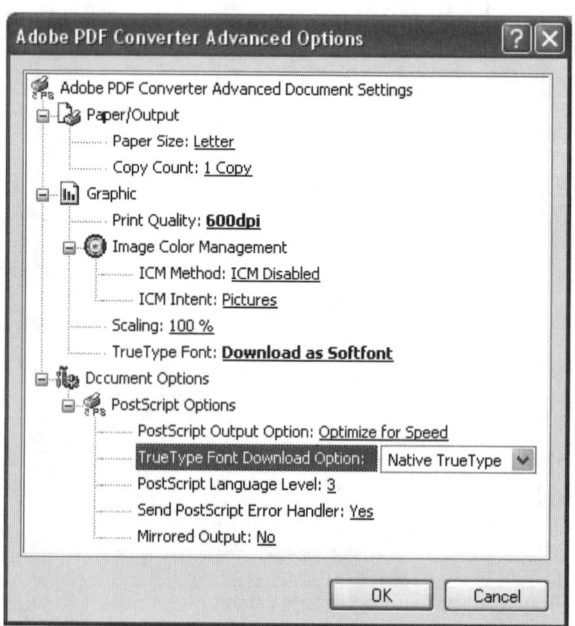

FIGURE 14-5 Several changes recommended for Advanced Document Settings, including changing the print quality from 1200 to 600

2. Change Print Quality to 600 dpi from 1200. This is a workaround for a longstanding bug that shows up in documents that use very large type. This type will not be searchable, cannot be edited with the Touchup Text tool, and may look bad onscreen. The 600 dpi setting generally allows for font sizes up to 144 points.
3. Change TrueType Font to Download as Soft Font. Using the Soft Font option avoids any font substitutions. Font substitutions can result in documents with slight variations in font style and in the character sets that are available.
4. Expand PostScript Options.

NOTE *Leave the PostScript Output Option at Optimize for Speed. The other options are out of date.*

5. Set TrueType Download Option to Native TrueType. Again, this helps to prevent font substitutions. Converting the fonts often yields degraded-looking text that can't be searched or edited with the Text Touchup Tool.
6. Make sure PostScript Language Level is set to 3. Many users will change this to a lower setting to match the PostScript level of the final printer. Both Acrobat and Reader can print to all levels of PostScript devices. Leaving this setting at 3 will produce the highest-possible quality print file for PDF creation.

Adobe PDF Settings

Now it is time to turn your attention to the Adobe PDF Settings. This is found at Printers and Faxes | Adobe PDF | Properties | Advanced | Printing Defaults | Adobe PDF Settings. (Or, at Printers and Faxes | Adobe PDF | Properties | General | Printing Preferences | Adobe PDF Settings.)

This dialog box controls the interaction between the PostScript printer driver and Acrobat Distiller. As shown in Figure 14-6, you can completely control how Distiller will process your PostScript file, including Job Options and Security. (For more information on Job Options, see Chapter 3. For details on Security settings, see Chapter 9.) The recommended settings are to turn on all the options.

View Adobe PDF Results The newly created PDF will open automatically in Acrobat. If this option is not on, you will have to manually open the PDF.

Prompt for Adobe PDF Filename This option lets you set the path and filename for the PDF.

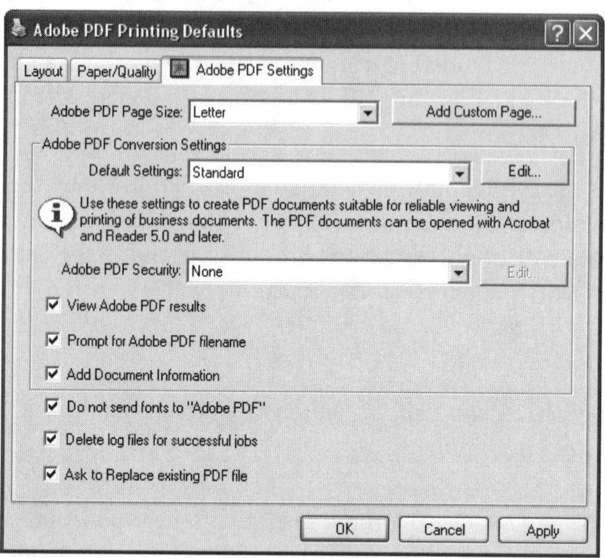

FIGURE 14-6 The Printing Defaults dialog box provides complete control of Acrobat Distiller.

Add Document Information Inserts the filename and the date and time of creation.

Do Not Send Fonts to "Adobe PDF" This sounds counterintuitive but, in general, you should turn this on. Since version 5, Acrobat Distiller locates and inserts Type 1, TrueType, and OpenType fonts available on the creator's computer. By keeping the fonts out of the PostScript file, you will see faster Distiller operation and receive more consistent embedding.

The exception is private, application-installed fonts. An example is Adobe PageMaker 7 running on Windows 2000 or NT, according to Adobe Knowledge Base Article 328684.

Delete Log Files for Successful Jobs Log files are a record of each file that Distiller processes. If everything goes okay, you don't need the log file. If everything doesn't go right, you do need it. Enabling this option keeps log files for unsuccessful jobs so you can troubleshoot.

NOTE *If your jobs are not failing, but you have issues to troubleshoot, keep all log files. Warnings that are not fatal errors may be included in the log files.*

Ask to Replace Existing PDF File This option gives you a chance to stop Distiller from erasing a PDF with the same name as the one you are creating. It prevents accidents, so it's a good idea to keep it on.

Font Issues

One of the most common issues to come up regarding PDF files involves fonts. Users complain that fonts are not embedded. They complain the fonts look different on screen than in print. They complain that fonts turn into Wingding symbols.

Many of these problems are caused by improper setup. First of all, develop a common set of Job Options for your organization and distribute them to each user. (See Chapter 3 for more on Job Options.)

As an administrator, the first thing you should do is change the Standard Job Options in Acrobat Distiller. Most users will gravitate toward Standard as a starting point, but there are two main issues with Standard. First, Standard doesn't embed all fonts—it exempts standard Windows fonts, as shown in Figure 14-7.

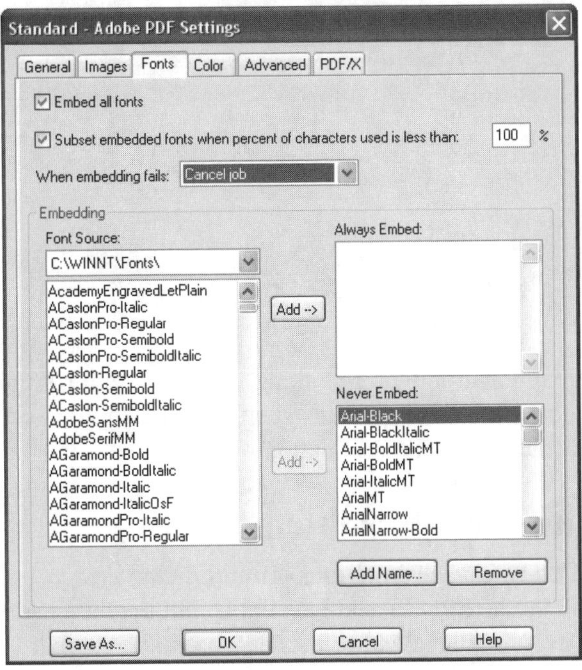

FIGURE 14-7 The Fonts Settings in the Standard Adobe PDF Settings

Because the Standard settings don't embed various flavors of Arial and other common Windows fonts, what happens if a Mac user opens the file? Or someone running Sun Solaris? They will see a substituted font, which may not look much like Tahoma or whatever Windows font didn't get inserted into the PDF.

Never embedding the regular Windows font package is a bad idea. Highlight all those fonts in the Never Embed box and click Remove. That will make those fonts available for embedding.

Next, as discussed in Chapter 3, set the "When embedding fails" option to Cancel Job. Then save the settings as MyStandard.joboptions. Now you have something that really is a standard!

Distiller Can't Find My Fonts

Early versions of Distiller (versions 3 and 4) would occasionally be unable to locate fonts and struggled to handle native TrueType fonts. However, most current applications put fonts in the Windows 2000/XP/2003 Fonts folder, which Distiller automatically adds, as shown here:

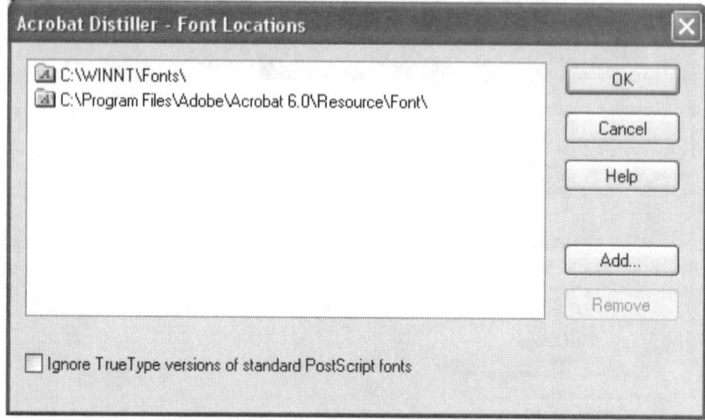

If you have an application that is sticking fonts in an unusual place, go to Distiller | Font Locations and click Add. Then navigate to the location where the fonts are and add those to the Font Locations list.

Fixing Phantom Font Problems

Some printer PPDs can cause mysterious font problems in Acrobat. These show up as phantom fonts that the PPD says are available, but they are not. These printer resident fonts do exist on the actual printer but, because Acrobat Distiller is a virtual printer, it doesn't have access to them. A second issue can show up when certain fonts display onscreen as Wingdings, but then they print correctly.

The fix is not for the faint of heart, though. This cure involves deleting references to all fonts except Courier from all PPD files in the system driver directory. In addition, all *.BPD files in the system driver directory should be eliminated. If you are troubled enough by these problems, follow this procedure:

1. Open every *.PPD file in either C:\WINNT\system32\spool\drivers\w32x86\3 or C:\WINDOWS\system32\spool\drivers\w32x86\3 in a text editor.
2. Search for Font Information.
3. Delete all fonts except Courier, as illustrated in Figure 14-8.
4. Delete all *.BPD files in the folder.

```
*% Font Information ====================
*DefaultFont: Courier
*Font AvantGarde-Book: Standard "(001.002)" Standard ROM
*Font AvantGarde-BookOblique: Standard "(001.000)" Standard ROM
*Font AvantGarde-Demi: Standard "(001.000)" Standard ROM
*Font AvantGarde-DemiOblique: Standard "(001.000)" Standard ROM
*Font Bookman-Demi: Standard "(001.000)" Standard ROM
*Font Bookman-DemiItalic: Standard "(001.000)" Standard ROM
*Font Bookman-Light: Standard "(001.000)" Standard ROM
*Font Bookman-LightItalic: Standard "(001.000)" Standard ROM
*Font Courier: Standard "(001.000)" Standard ROM
*Font Courier-Bold: Standard "(001.000)" Standard ROM
*Font Courier-BoldOblique: Standard "(001.000)" Standard ROM
*Font Courier-Oblique: Standard "(001.000)" Standard ROM
*Font Helvetica: Standard "(001.000)" Standard ROM
*Font Helvetica-Bold: Standard "(001.000)" Standard ROM
*Font Helvetica-BoldOblique: Standard "(001.000)" Standard ROM
*Font Helvetica-Narrow: Standard "(001.000)" Standard ROM
*Font Helvetica-Narrow-Bold: Standard "(001.000)" Standard ROM
*Font Helvetica-Narrow-BoldOblique: Standard "(001.000)" Standard ROM
*Font Helvetica-Narrow-Oblique: Standard "(001.000)" Standard ROM
*Font Helvetica-Oblique: Standard "(001.000)" Standard ROM
*Font NewCenturySchlbk-Bold: Standard "(001.000)" Standard ROM
*Font NewCenturySchlbk-BoldItalic: Standard "(001.000)" Standard ROM
*Font NewCenturySchlbk-Italic: Standard "(001.000)" Standard ROM
*Font NewCenturySchlbk-Roman: Standard "(001.000)" Standard ROM
*Font Palatino-Bold: Standard "(001.000)" Standard ROM
*Font Palatino-BoldItalic: Standard "(001.000)" Standard ROM
*Font Palatino-Italic: Standard "(001.000)" Standard ROM
*Font Palatino-Roman: Standard "(001.000)" Standard ROM
*Font Symbol: Special "(001.001)" Special ROM
*Font Times-Bold: Standard "(001.000)" Standard ROM
*Font Times-BoldItalic: Standard "(001.000)" Standard ROM
*Font Times-Italic: Standard "(001.000)" Standard ROM
*Font Times-Roman: Standard "(001.000)" Standard ROM
*Font ZapfChancery-MediumItalic: Standard "(001.000)" Standard ROM
```

FIGURE 14-8 Printer resident fonts can cause phantom font problems. To fix this, delete all fonts except Courier (highlighted) in your PPDs.

On my computer, I had five *.PPDs and four *.BPDs. The ADPDF6.PPD didn't have any printer resident fonts, but the other *.PPDs did.

Mac OS X Issues

Mac OS X users can work with their PostScript Driver setups from Print | PDF Options. There are far fewer options to choose from, such as:

- You cannot manually select a PostScript language level. This information comes from the PPD.
- You cannot minimize the PostScript file size by removing the fonts from the PostScript file.
- You cannot choose between binary or ASCII format.

NOTE *OS X is relatively new, and its PostScript drivers are immature. Microsoft and Adobe have worked closely to produce the drivers for Windows XP/2003, but Apple has a significant amount of work to do on the OS X PostScript drivers.*

Installing Acrobat Across the Enterprise

Adobe beefed up the tools for system administrators in Acrobat 5 with the release of the Acrobat Enterprise Installation Tool (AEIT). This tool allows your IT department to customize Acrobat installations.

The Acrobat 5 AEIT will not work with Acrobat 6, so Adobe has released a similar tool, called InstallShield Tuner, for the Acrobat 6 product family. It works with Acrobat 6 Professional and Standard, Acrobat Elements 6, and Adobe Reader 6. The *InstallShield Tuner* can modify the Acrobat 6 product installer to meet an organization's needs, including:

- Preventing users from changing settings
- Shutting off online registration and update features
- Detailing silent (no user input) installation, including your company name and a serial number
- Configuring custom job option files in Acrobat Distiller

- Removing the Custom Setup option for users
- Eliminating Acrobat Desktop and Start menu shortcuts

The InstallShield Tuner can be found at **http://www.adobe.com/products/acrobat/deployment.html**.

Acrobat 6 installations also can be managed by two of the more popular enterprise software distribution tools, Microsoft System Management Server (SMS) 2 or IBM Tivoli. By using these tools, Acrobat can be installed remotely. Little or no end user activity is required.

Microsoft SMS

SMS uses the Adobe installer and InstallShield. By combining the functionality of SMS and the Windows-friendly Adobe installer, IT personnel can deploy Acrobat family products by creating an SMS "package."

Previous versions of Acrobat should be uninstalled first. SMS users can create a package that uninstalls the older version of Acrobat. For more information on SMS and Acrobat, see the Adobe white paper Adobe Acrobat 6.0 for Microsoft Systems Management Server at **http://www.adobe.com/products/acrobat/deployment.html**.

IBM Tivoli

IBM Tivoli works similarly to SMS. A system administrator will need to create an Acrobat uninstall software distribution profile and an Acrobat installation software distribution profile. For more information, see Adobe Acrobat 6.0 for IBM Tivoli Software Distribution at **http://www.adobe.com/products/acrobat/deployment.html**.

Keeping Up-to-Date

One of Acrobat 5's annoyances was the frequency at which it checked **www.adobe.com** for updates. You couldn't use the product while Acrobat checked for an update, which it seemed to do everyday.

Fortunately, Acrobat 6 has a friendlier policy on updates. The default setting checks for updates monthly, as shown in Figure 14-9. By choosing Edit | Preferences | Updates, you can change the setting to Manual. Acrobat will then not ever check for updates on its own.

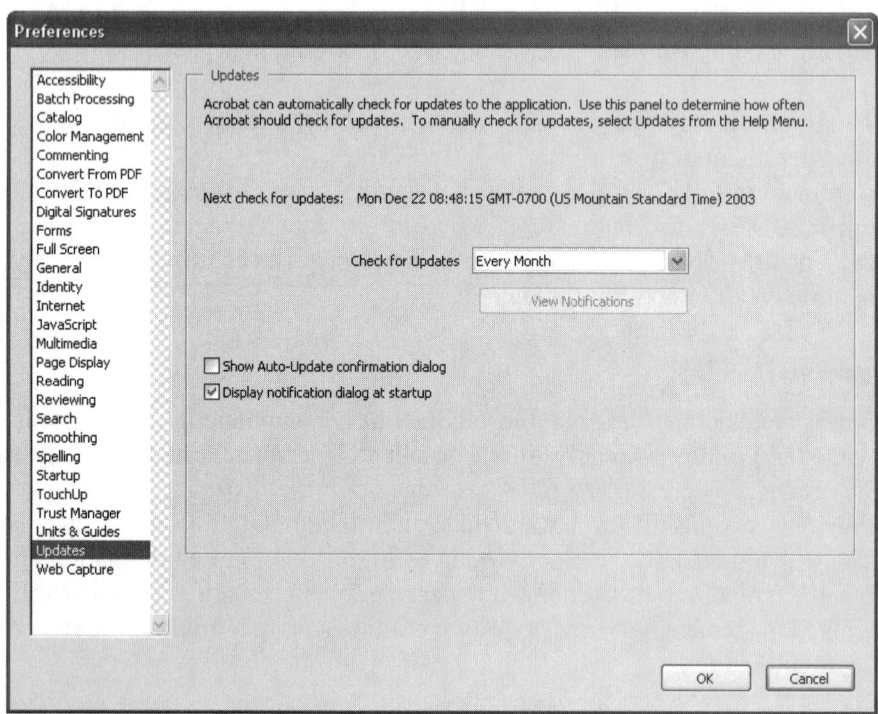

FIGURE 14-9 Web updates keep Acrobat up-to-date.

If you do want to check for an update, choose Help | Update. If an update is available, as shown in Figure 14-10, click Add | Update. You may need to restart the computer after installing an update.

Although no one can predict the future, Adobe has historically released only a handful of updates for each version of Acrobat. Set Acrobat to check for updates monthly or plan on watching for news of updates at **www.adobe.com**, **www.planetpdf.com**, or **www.pdfzone.com** and manually updating Acrobat yourself.

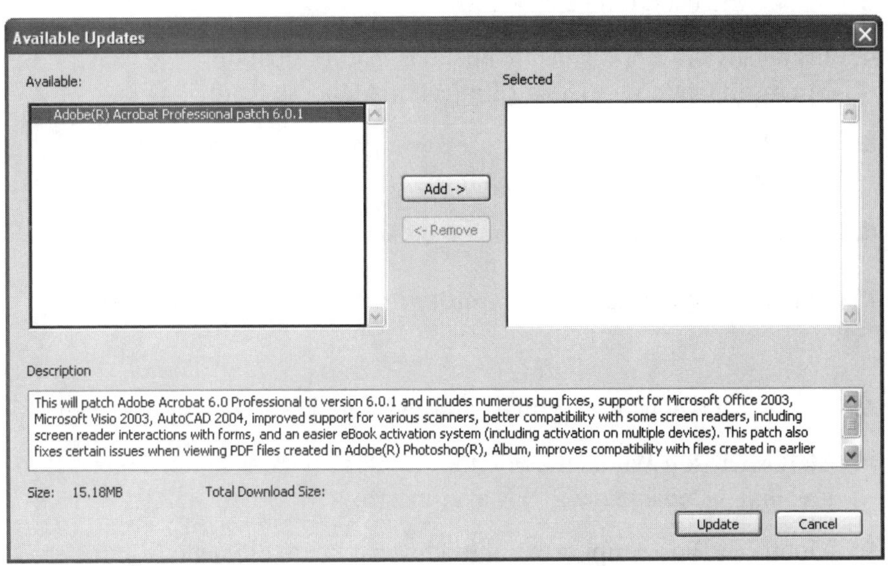

FIGURE 14-10 When updates are available, select the update, click Add, and then Update.

A Checklist for System Administrators

To recap, installing Acrobat isn't any more difficult than installing Microsoft Office products. Acrobat is different from Microsoft products, however, so IT professionals may need a little education to become familiar with the product.

The List

The following is a list of action items that an IT professional should use when installing Acrobat 6:

1. Install the latest Windows security patches or updates.
2. Update Microsoft Internet Explorer.

3. Install Microsoft Office Products.
4. Install any other software applications that Acrobat links to, such as Microsoft Outlook, Visio, or Project or Autodesk AutoCAD.
5. Install Adobe Reader, if your users want both the Reader and Acrobat available.
6. Install the most up-to-date version of Acrobat.

NOTE *If upgrading, Acrobat 6 will uninstall previous versions of Acrobat.*

7. Verify that Adobe PDF Printer, Acrobat, and Distiller were installed.
8. Start Microsoft Word and look for the Acrobat icons in the toolbar. If those are missing, enable the PDFMaker macro.
9. Modify the PostScript driver setup for maximum efficiency.
10. Modify the Standard Job Options to remove the standard Windows fonts from the "Never Embed" list and change the "When embedding fails" option to Cancel Job.
11. Remember that you can use SMS and Tivoli for enterprise installations.

Part III

Acrobat for Creative Professionals

Chapter 15

Adobe Products

In other chapters, you learn how to produce PDFs from Microsoft applications, QuarkXPress, and Corel programs. While PDF is a universal format, and almost every application running on the PC and Mac can produce a PDF, without a doubt, the best PDF creation tools are from Adobe.

Because Adobe controls the PDF specification, its engineers know PDF well. Adobe Photoshop, Illustrator, and InDesign can produce PDFs directly without going through the Adobe PDF Printer. Adobe applications tend to support the newest PDF features, such as layers, while competing products often lag behind. Instead of being an afterthought, PDF production from Adobe FrameMaker, Illustrator, InDesign, PageMaker, and Photoshop is integrated into the products.

Adobe's newest package of products, the Adobe Creative Suite Premium, includes Acrobat 6 Professional along with the Creative Suite (CS) versions of Photoshop, Illustrator, InDesign, and GoLive. (The Creative Suite file management program, Version Cue, doesn't work with Acrobat 6.)

In this chapter, you will learn how to create PDFs from Adobe products that are engineered to produce great print and onscreen PDFs.

Adobe Illustrator CS

Adobe Illustrator is a wonderful application to use for creating PDFs. Illustrator is a *vector graphics* program, meaning its art is made up of lines. Vector graphics produce smooth lines that are ideal for logos, illustrations, and technical drawings. Vector art scales smoothly and does not pixellate as it is enlarged, as do bitmap graphics, such as digital photographs.

TIP *Many Illustrator CS users report that files become corrupt when saving across network drives. Save Illustrator files to local file systems before creating PDFs.*

Vector art exported as PDF is compressed easily, without any loss of data. In general, a PDF from Illustrator will be smaller than a native Illustrator file. Smaller files are easier to manage in a workflow, and can be easily e-mailed or posted to web sites.

You can use Illustrator to create graphics that can be exported as PDFs, and then placed into other applications. Or, the PDF from Illustrator can be sent directly to a printer for traditional publication. The latest version of Illustrator also supports layered PDFs.

PDFs also can be placed into Illustrator, and Illustrator PDFs can be round-tripped. One Illustrator option embeds all data in exported PDFs, so you can reopen the file in Illustrator without any loss of data.

CAUTION *Many graphic artists expect to be able to open any PDF, including those created from scanned images, for editing in Illustrator. If it works, fine, but realize what you are doing is not supported by Adobe and cannot be recommended. You can only reliably edit PDFs that have been saved with Illustrator's Presets that embed Illustrator data.*

The best editing procedure is to go back to the source file and make changes there, and then generate a new PDF.

Illustrator File Formats

Illustrator files can be saved in four basic formats: native Illustrator (AI), PDF, Encapsulated PostScript (EPS), and Scalable Vector Graphics (SVG). Files saved in these formats can be brought back into Illustrator and be fully editable.

In addition, Illustrator can export a variety of formats that are not easily "re-editable." These include bitmap formats, such as Tagged Image File Format (TIFF) and Joint Photographic Experts Group (JPEG), and many kinds of PDFs. Because Illustrator uses JPEG compression, keep in mind that JPEG throws out data to create smaller files. In general, you should preserve your art in the AI format until you are finished, or you are at a point where you need to export the art in a format clients or reviewers need, such as PDF.

Something you will not see in Illustrator is Acrobat Distiller. Illustrator has the capability of creating PDFs directly without going through Distiller, although you certainly can use Distiller if you want.

TIP *The Presets in Illustrator will not create multipage PDFs. To create a multipage PDF from Illustrator, choose File | Print | Adobe PDF and create the PDF via the print process. For best results, make sure your multipage tiles are aligned properly.*

Creating a PDF from Illustrator

Just as Adobe preloads Distiller with a number of standard job options for you to choose from, Distiller includes a number of what Adobe calls "presets." These *presets* offer you a choice of output options, and all include the data Illustrator needs to preserve editing capabilities.

The presets, which are available when you choose File | Save As | Adobe PDF | Save, are listed here:

- **Illustrator Default** This option preserves all Illustrator data, so the PDF can be reopened and edited. No Illustrator data will be lost if this option is selected. The file will be Acrobat 5-compatible, Page Thumbnails will be embedded into the PDF, bitmap images will not be downsampled, compression will be ZIP (which preserves all data), no marks and bleeds will be inserted, all fonts will be subset, and no security will be applied.
- **Press** The file will be compatible with Acrobat 4, Illustrator file-editing capabilities will be preserved, the file will be set up for Fast Web View, and you will see the PDF in Acrobat right after it is produced. Color and black-and-white bitmap images will be downsampled to 300 ppi, if the original resolution is greater than 450 ppi, and the bitmaps will be compressed as JPEGs. Some data loss in the bitmaps may occur, even though the quality is set to Maximum.

NOTE *I would not reopen a file in Illustrator and export it with the Press settings again. Any bitmap images would be run though JPEG compression again. In general, it is not a good idea to apply JPEG compression to a graphic twice. You may see a noticeable loss of image quality.*

Printer's marks will be added to the PDF, no security will be applied, and all fonts will be subset.

- **Acrobat 6 Layered** As the name indicates, this file is compatible with Acrobat 6 layers. Layers will be grouped under top-level layers. Illustrator editing capabilities are preserved, page thumbnails are created, and the PDF will pop up in Acrobat following creation.

Compression is identical to the Press preset, so be aware that JPEG compression is being applied. No Printer's Marks are included, fonts are subset, and no security is applied.

Illustrator Presets Compared

You can see how well these presets work by using them on one of the sample files Adobe includes in the Illustrator CS installation on your computer. Look inside the Sample Files / Sample Art subfolder for the Yellowstone Map file. This file in AI format is 2.7MB.

Illustrator's Default PDF Setting

Choose File | Save As | Adobe PDF | Save and save the file as Yellowstone Map AI Default. Choose the Illustrator Default settings and click Save PDF. Close the file in Illustrator and open it in Acrobat.

The PDF is slightly larger at 3.6MB. Zoom into a high level, such as 1,000 percent. All detail is sharp and crisp, and the text shows no sign of being jagged.

Now close the file in Acrobat, and reopen it in Illustrator. Zoom in to 300 percent and grab the Type tool. Edit some text (look in the Text layer group for the color of text you want to edit), save, close, and reopen the file in Acrobat. Amazingly enough, you can. The integrity of the file is intact.

TIP *Use Acrobat's Search tool to look for the text edit you made in Illustrator.*

Illustrator's Press Preset

Now open the original Yellowstone Map, and use the Save As function to save the file as Yellowstone Map Press, using the default Press Preset option.

This time, the file opens in Acrobat, as well as in Illustrator. Again, the image and text quality are excellent, and Printer's Marks and Color Bars are printed on the PDF. This file size is 3.4MB.

TIP *You can add Printer's Marks, Color Bars, and Page information from within Acrobat 6 Professional. Choose File | Print | Advanced | Marks and Bleeds. See Chapter 18 for more information.*

Close the file and reopen it in Illustrator. Save the file with a new name, such as Press AI Default, and use the AI Default settings. Open this new file in Acrobat. The Printer's Marks are gone.

While this round-tripping of PDFs back and forth into Illustrator is a wonderful feature, I repeat that you must take care when you include bitmap file formats in your illustrations. The JPEG compression format used in the Press and Acrobat 6 Layered presets can degrade the quality of bitmap images.

Acrobat 6 Layered Preset

This option uses the new layers creation feature in Acrobat 6. With layers, users can show and hide layers, just like creators can when using Illustrator and InDesign. (Photoshop CS doesn't do Acrobat layers.)

NOTE *Older versions of Acrobat and Reader (versions 5 and earlier) display all layers in a layered PDF.*

To give this feature a try, open the native Illustrator Yellowstone Map file, and use Save As and the Acrobat 6 Layered preset option to create a new file.

Although this file contains several layers, it is 3.6MB, about the same size as the other PDFs you've created from Illustrator CS. Click the Layers tab to display the layers, which are shown in Figure 15-1.

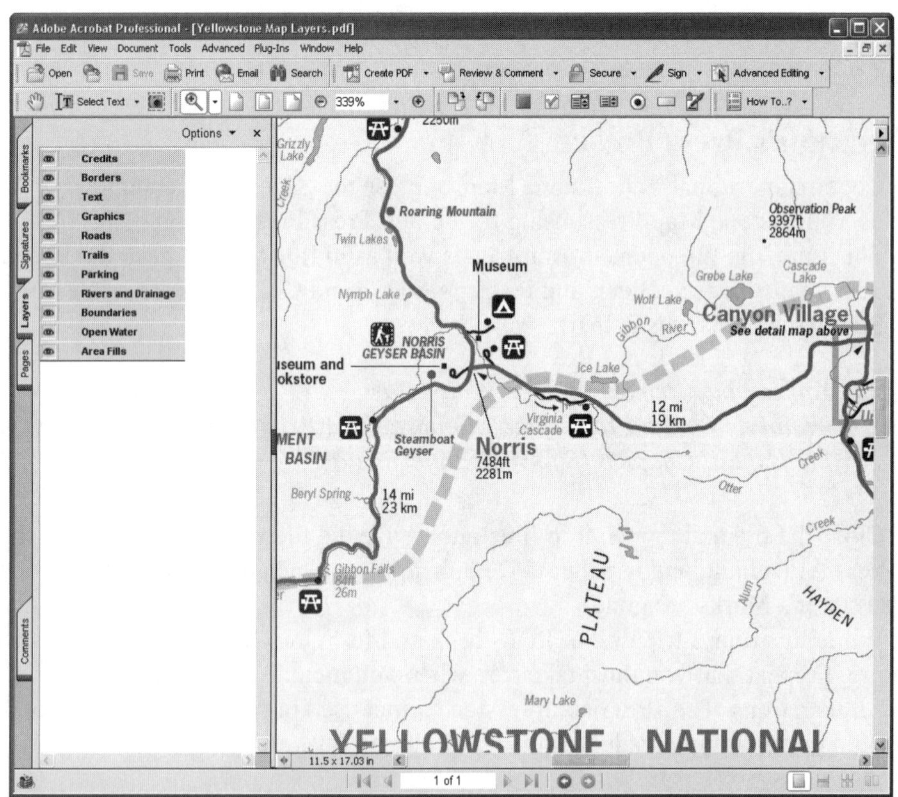

FIGURE 15-1 This is a layered PDF produced by Adobe Illustrator CS. Note the layer cake icon in the lower-left corner, signifying the presence of layers.

Use the Zoom tool to increase magnification so you can read the text and see details in the map. Click the Text and Roads layers to turn those layers on and off. As with the other presets, you can reopen the file in Illustrator CS and make edits.

TIP

Some users report that the PDFs created from Illustrator CS have page sizes that are different than the native Illustrator file. Illustrator CS uses the bounding box of the artwork to set the boundaries of a PDF. Earlier versions used the artboard and printable area. Adobe recommends setting crop marks in Illustrator to fix the problem.

1. *Select the Rectangle tool.*
2. *Use the Rectangle tool to draw a rectangle the size of the boundaries you want to see in the PDF.*
3. *Choose Object | Crop Area | Make.*
4. *Save the Illustrator file, and then create a new PDF.*

Suggested Changes to the Illustrator Presets

For the most part, I agree with Adobe's selections in the presets. However, there is no need for the Embed Page Thumbnail options to be selected in the Illustrator Defaults or the Acrobat 6 Layered presets. Acrobat 5, the compatibility level in Illustrator defaults, creates thumbnails of page images on the fly, as do Acrobat 6 and Adobe Reader 6.

Embedding these images makes the files larger and adds nothing to the end user's experience. You can create your own settings by disabling the Embed Page Thumbnail option and clicking the Save Presets button.

NOTE

The Acrobat 5 plug-in for Internet Explorer (Windows) does not create thumbnails on the fly, although Acrobat 5 running outside of IE will.

Printing to Adobe PDF

Using the preset export function is not the only way to create a PDF from Illustrator, of course. If you have Acrobat 6 and Distiller, you can create a PDF via the Adobe PDF printer.

1. Choose File | Print. Select Adobe PDF as the printer and the PPD as Adobe PDF.
2. Check the options in the General section of the print dialog box to make sure they are correct. If you have produced a layered illustration, be sure the Print Layers selection is correct. See Figure 15-2 for an example configuration for creating layers.

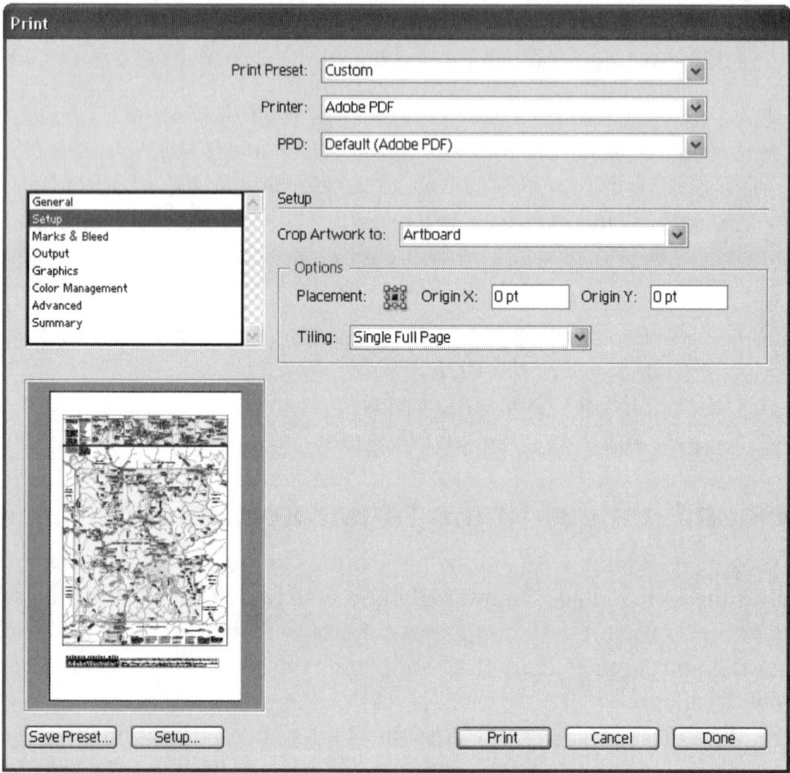

FIGURE 15-2 You can create layers from Adobe Illustrator by using present options, or by printing to the Adobe PDF Printer.

3. Move to Setup. Choose the correct crop settings for your document.
4. Move to the Output section. Enter the Output settings requested by your print vendor, or accept the default values.
5. Move to Graphics. Accept the defaults. The Compatible Gradient and Gradient Mesh Printing option is unnecessary with the Adobe PDF printer.
6. Accept the defaults in Color Management and Advanced sections.
7. Click on Setup and Continue. You can now access the settings in Distiller via the Adobe PDF printer. You can create a PDF/X-compliant file, for example, or use settings provided by a print vendor.

I used the default Press Quality settings in the Adobe PDF printer to see what would happen to the Yellowstone Map file. The file looks great and is 977KB in size, the smallest of any files produced.

However, you cannot easily round-trip this file back into Illustrator. If you open the PDF in Illustrator, you can edit it, but all layer information has been lost. You can make small text changes, but I would not recommend trying any significant editing with a PDF of this sort.

Adding File Information for Acrobat

You can use Illustrator's File Info feature to add information to the Document Properties fields in Acrobat. Choose File | File Info and add information to be passed along to Acrobat, as shown in Figure 15-3.

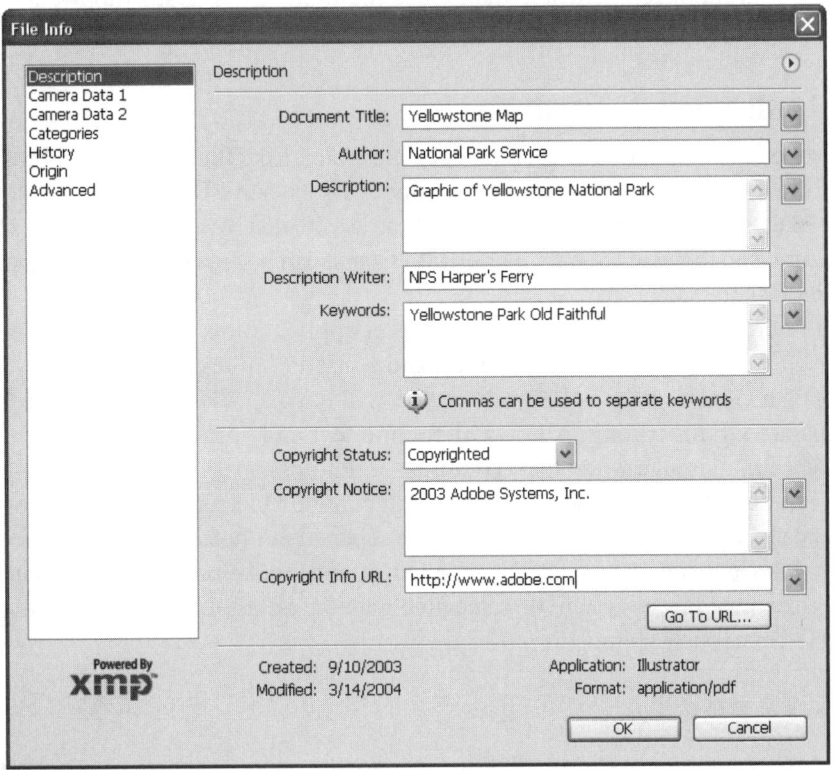

FIGURE 15-3 The XMP data in File Info is passed along to Acrobat's Document Properties.

This information will be shown in Document Properties, and in the Document Metadata section of Acrobat. Choose Advanced | Document Metadata to see the identical information in Acrobat.

NOTE *Web search engines display the information in the Title field of Document Properties when displaying the results of a search.*

PDF and Photoshop CS

As with Illustrator CS, Photoshop CS seamlessly works with PDF. You can place PDFs inside Photoshop; export PDFs with all the usual options; import and export PDF comments, include metadata; import images from a PDF; and even create multipage presentations of Photoshop documents in PDF.

What you cannot do is create a layered PDF from Photoshop. Photoshop's layers are far more sophisticated than those found in Acrobat, so Adobe chose not to make PDF layers an export option.

Photoshop PDF Format

Photoshop has its own PDF format, as does Illustrator. Like Illustrator, the Photoshop PDF format preserves some editing capability. A Photoshop PDF is simply a single-image (and, therefore, single-page) PDF. These are created by using Photoshop's Save As feature, and they are the only kinds of PDFs that can be created and later edited with Photoshop.

To Photoshop, any PDF created in another application is called a Generic PDF. *Generic PDFs* can have multiple pages, and a mixture of text and images. When you open a Generic PDF in Photoshop, you will have to select a single page from a multipage PDF for editing. All data, including text and vector art, are converted to a single bitmap image when the PDF opens in Photoshop.

A Photoshop PDF, on the other hand, will continue to keep the text unrasterized, so you can make edits in Photoshop. When reopened in Photoshop, a Photoshop PDF will keep text on a separate layer. When opened in Acrobat 6, the text will not be on a separate layer, but will be selectable with the Select Text tool, and editable with the Text Touch-up tool.

Save As PDF

Although opening or placing a PDF into Photoshop creates a raster image, you can preserve text and vector art from PSD files that are being Saved As PDF files.

1. Choose File | Save As Photoshop PDF (*.PDF, *.PDP).
2. Select the appropriate options, such as annotations.
3. Click Save.
4. PDF Options dialog box appears with several options.
5. You can select a compression type (called "encoding" here). Use JPEG for photographs, or ZIP for TIFF images.
6. Image Interpolation applies anti-aliasing to low-resolution images. It is unnecessary for Acrobat 6.
7. Downgrade Color Profile is unnecessary if you plan on opening the file in Acrobat 6.
8. PDF Security | Security Settings permits you to secure the PDF. See Chapter 9 for details.
9. Enable Include Vector Data and Embed Fonts. This will create a PDF with embedded fonts, and vector art will not be rasterized in the PDF.

CAUTION *If you select the Use Outlines for Text option, the resulting PDF will not be searchable and the text will not be selectable in Acrobat or Adobe Reader. The text will still be editable in Photoshop, however. In general, it is best to avoid converting text to outlines when creating PDFs.*

10. Click OK.

Placing PDFs in Photoshop

You can place PDFs into Photoshop, but don't expect even the minimal editing capabilities you will have with Illustrator. As with Illustrator AI and EPS files, placed PDFs are rasterized, or turned into bitmap images. You will be unable to edit text or manipulate vector images because those are converted to bits, just like in a photograph.

However, you can extract bitmap images from PDFs for editing in Photoshop. See the "Importing Images from a PDF" section that follows for details.

Placing a PDF is straightforward. Use the File | Place command and place the PDF in a new layer. What happens next is a bit more complex, as you can see in the following:

- If you are placing a multipage PDF, Photoshop asks which page you want to place. If you are placing a one-page PDF, the file appears in the middle of the Photoshop screen.
- You can scale or move the PDF on the import layer.
- You also can rotate the PDF, but this often results in more pixilation of the document.
- Enabling Anti-Alias will smooth the text and lines in the PDF.
- Complete the placement (and rasterization) by clicking the Commit button (this looks like a check mark) or striking the ENTER (RETURN, Mac OS) key.

Opening a PDF in Photoshop CS

Opening PDFs in Photoshop is similar to placing PDFs. Again, don't expect to be able to edit text and vector graphics in PDFs you open in Photoshop.

1. Choose File | Open.
2. If you are opening a multipage PDF, Photoshop asks which page you would like to open.
3. Photoshop asks what rasterization options you would like to select. You can set the page size, resolution, and color model.
4. You can enable Anti-Alias to smooth text and lines.

Importing Images from a PDF

While you cannot edit text or vector graphics in Photoshop, you can extract bitmap images from PDFs and edit those (see Figure 15-4). Use the following procedure to import PDF images into Photoshop for editing:

1. Choose File | Import | PDF Image and navigate to the folder where the file you want to import images from resides.
2. Select the file.

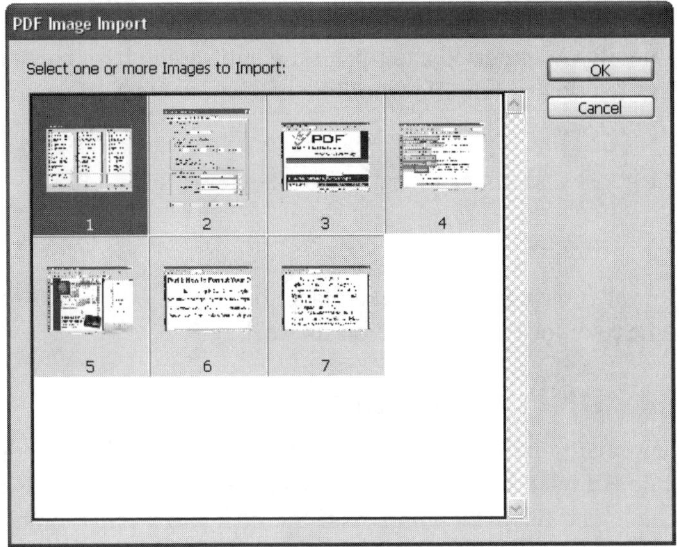

FIGURE 15-4 You can import images from PDFs into Photoshop. Select one or more images to import.

3. When the PDF Image Import dialog box opens, select one or more files for importation. Use SHIFT-click to select contiguous images; use CTRL-click (Windows) or CMD-click (Mac OS) for noncontiguous images.

You can now edit the images in Photoshop.

Automating PDF to PSD Creation

You can use Photoshop's automation features to turn a multipage PDF into a series of Photoshop PSD files. You don't have to build this action from scratch. Adobe includes it as a default option available from the Automate submenu.

Use the following procedure to create PSD files from a multipage PDF:

1. Choose File | Automate | Multi-Page PDF to PSD.
2. In the Convert Multi-Page PDF to PSD dialog box, click Choose and select the file to be converted.
3. Specify a page range.
4. Set your import options, including resolution and color model. Enable Anti-aliased to smooth text and lines.

5. Enter a base name for the files Photoshop will create. The names of the new files will be the base name plus the page number of the PDF. For example, if you imported a ten-page file and set the base name to chpt11, the first new Photoshop file would be named *chpt110001.psd* and the last *chp110010.psd.*
6. Click Choose and select a location for the new files.
7. Click OK.

You get to watch the conversion take place. If you selected a 100-page PDF, it could take some time for Photoshop to do its work.

Creating a PDF Presentation

This feature automates the creation of PDF slide shows from Photoshop images. You use the File Browser in Photoshop to select the files you want to include in your presentation, and Photoshop processes the files into a self-running PDF presentation. Use the following procedure to create a PDF presentation:

1. Although you can start from the File | Automate | PDF Presentation, a better approach is to start from the File Browser. Open the File Browser and navigate to the location of the images you want to include:

NOTE *All images in the File Browser will be included in the PDF presentation unless you specify which images you want to include.*

2. Choose which files to include.
3. Select Automate | PDF Presentation from the File Browser menu.
4. In Output Options, choose Presentation and View PDF After Saving.
5. In Presentation Options, choose the ones most appropriate for your presentation. *Advance Every* creates a self-running presentation that advances pages at the rate you specify. *Deselecting* means you manually advance the presentation. *Loop after Last Page* restarts the presentation after the last page. *Transition* includes a number of Acrobat-compatible transitions effects.
6. Click Save. Give the new PDF a name and click Save again.
7. Set the PDF Options as required. See the preceding section in this chapter on Save As PDF options.
8. Click OK.

Photoshop now cycles through each image and creates a multipage PDF that opens in full screen mode in Acrobat. Use the Page Up/Down keys to navigate through the presentation. Use CTRL-L (Windows) or CMD-L (Mac OS) to drop out of full-screen mode.

Layer Comps to PDF

Graphic artists and photographers use Photoshop's Layer Comps feature to create multiple compositions for clients. Clients can then review the comps and decide which one they like best. By outputting Layer Comps as PDFs, clients can use Acrobat's Commenting features to review and mark up the various compositions.

You will need to add Layer Comps to your Photoshop file before exporting them. Use the following procedure to output Layer Comps to PDF:

1. Choose File | Scripts | Layer Comps to PDF.
2. In the Layer Comps to PDF dialog box, click Browse and navigate to a folder where the new PDF presentation will be created.
3. Enter a filename and click OK.
4. Select your slide show options. You can have the show advance every few seconds, or have the user manually click to advance.
5. Click Run.

As with the Automate command, you now watch as Photoshop creates the slide show. At the end, Photoshop says Layer Comp to PDF is Complete. Click OK.

The PDF slide show pops up in full-screen mode. Use the Page Up/Down keys to navigate through the presentation. Use CTRL-L (Windows) or CMD-L (Mac OS) to drop out of full-screen mode.

Importing and Exporting PDF Text and Audio Comments

Photoshop contains some basic commenting tools. These annotation or commenting tools are not as extensive as in Acrobat, but text and audio comments can be transferred between Photoshop and Acrobat.

Other Acrobat Comments, such as Stamps or Text Boxes, will come in as rasterized images. These images will be a permanent part of any exported PDF.

If you open a PDF in Photoshop, any Note or Audio comments will come in as Photoshop comments. Likewise, any Note or Audio comments placed in a Photoshop file will appear as comments in Acrobat.

You also can choose File | Import | Annotations, and import Note and Audio comments from Acrobat into a Photoshop file. The comments will appear in the same locations as in the PDF.

Transferring Photoshop Metadata to PDF

In a preceding section, you learned to add metadata to Illustrator files. You can do the same thing for Photoshop files and, likewise, have that metadata exported to the PDF.

To add metadata, choose File | File Info and fill in the Description dialog box.

NOTE *The Camera Data 1, Camera Data 2, AP Categories, History, and Raw Data metadata categories are not editable.*

This information will be shown in the Document Properties dialog box in Acrobat, and in the Document Metadata section. Choose Advanced | Document Metadata to see the identical information in Acrobat.

Adobe InDesign CS

Adobe InDesign CS is tightly integrated with Acrobat 6. PDFs can be placed in InDesign. InDesign can export layered PDFs, multimedia elements, and secured PDFs. In addition, InDesign can automatically create bookmarks, links, rollover buttons, tagged PDF for accessibility, and, of course, pass document metadata to the PDF.

TIP *Many Acrobat users like the hand tool for navigating within documents. Hold down the* SPACEBAR *in InDesign to change any tool to the Hand tool.*

Importing PDFs into InDesign CS

While you can place PDFs into InDesign, you cannot open PDFs in InDesign, as you can Photoshop and Illustrator. Placed PDFs are not rasterized as happens in Photoshop, but they are placed as native PDF files with text and vector art intact. Interactive elements, such as movies and sounds, are not retained. However, links (within certain restrictions) are carried over into InDesign.

You can place individual pages from a multipage PDF into InDesign. You cannot import the entirety of a multipage PDF and have it flow page-to-page, as you can placed text. Each page must come in separately.

To place a PDF, choose File | Place and select the PDF you want to place in InDesign. When you choose the Place command, you are given the following options if Show Import Options is turned on:

- **Preview** *Preview* shows what the PDF document looks like. In a multipage PDF, this view gives you the capability of selecting which page you want to place.
- **Crop to** *Crop to* lets you select how you want the PDF cropped. *Bounding box* is the minimum area that encloses the objects on the page. *Art box* defines the content of the page, including white space. Art box can be defined by a document's creator. *Crop* places only the area that was cropped in Acrobat. *Trim* places the part of the page that would remain after pages were cut to trim marks. *Bleed* includes any bleed marks. Media places the original paper size.
- **Transparent Background** Enable this option to permit InDesign page elements to shine through the background of the PDF. Deselecting turns the background opaque.

When working with placed PDFs, keep these facts in mind:

- *Placed PDFs print at the best available resolution.* For a PostScript output device, the placed PDF would print at the resolution of the device. For non-PostScript output devices, placed PDFs print at the same resolution as other InDesign objects.
- *Placed PDFs are linked, not embedded.* What you see in InDesign is a preview image. Moving, renaming, and deleting the linked PDF will break the link. InDesign will ask you to fix the broken links. Inserting, deleting, or added pages within a linked PDF can change the PDF page that appears in InDesign.
- *Security settings are respected in InDesign.* You will need the PDF password to place a PDF that has security settings.

Exporting to PDF

PDFs can be created from a single document or from InDesign Book files. Unlike Photoshop and Illustrator, PDFs are created from InDesign through Export, rather than Save As.

To create a PDF from a document or book file, choose File | Export | Adobe PDF. You can then choose from a selection of preset options, or create your own. Click Save (Windows) or Export (Mac OS) to complete the process. (You also can choose File | Print and print to the Adobe PDF printer to use Distiller as the creation mechanism, but you will lose all interactive features in the PDF.)

You can see what PDF export settings are available by choosing File | PDF Export Presets | When using the export function, you can choose from one of the following presets:

- **eBook** This setting compresses color and grayscale graphics to 150 dpi and uses medium-quality JPEG compression to create an Acrobat 5-compatible file. Colors are converted to RBG, and fonts are subset. Bookmarks and hyperlinks are created, and tagged PDF is generated, so the PDF will easily reflow on the small screens usually found on eBook devices.
- **Screen** This setting creates an Acrobat 4-compatible file that uses a high degree of compression. Color and grayscale graphics are downsampled to 72 dpi and a medium level of JPEG compression is applied. The file is optimized for fast web view, hyperlinks and bookmarks are created, and fonts are subset.
- **Print** Print PDFs from InDesign are Acrobat 4-compatible. Although the name implies that the PDF would be used for paper output, electronic publishing features, such as bookmarks and hyperlinks, are created and the file is optimized for fast web view. Tagged PDF for reflow and accessibility are omitted. Color and grayscale graphics are downsampled to 300 dpi, and JPEG compression for maximum quality is used. Fonts are subset.
- **Press** Press PDFs from InDesign are Acrobat 4-compatible. Press files are optimized for fast web view, but no hyperlinks, bookmarks, or tagged PDF are created. Color and grayscale graphics are downsampled to 300 dpi and compressed with JPEG for maximum quality. Fonts are subset.
- **PDF/X-1a** and **PDF/X-3** are standards for the printing industry. See Chapter 18 for more information on PDF/X.

Acrobat 6 Layered creates Acrobat 6-compatible files with layers. Files are optimized for fast web view, but no bookmarks or links are created. Graphics are downsampled to 300 dpi and JPEG compression is set for maximum graphics quality. Fonts are subset. Tagged PDF is not created, and multimedia elements are not exported.

Changing Presets

While the presets are fine for many uses, you can create your own presets. Refer to the recommendations in Chapters 3 and 4 for ideas on modifying the presets that come with Acrobat.

For example, the Acrobat 6 Layered PDF doesn't include any interactive elements, yet layers are only useful to the onscreen reader. Why not include bookmarks and hyperlinks to make the onscreen experience a better one? And why not include multimedia elements as well?

To change the options, choose File | PDF Export Presets | Define. You can select a preset that closely matches your requirements, and then choose New. You can then use the existing presets as a starting point for creating new settings.

NOTE *To restore the default presets, choose File | PDF Export Presets | Define and hold down* ALT *(Windows) or* OPTION *(Mac OS) and click Reset.*

InDesign PDF Presets are stored PDFS files, which have a file extension of *pdfs*. You can share these files with other users. To export a PDFS:

1. Choose File | PDF Export Presets and click the Define button.
2. Select a Preset to export.
3. Click Save.
4. Save the file in a convenient location.

To load a PDFS:

1. Choose File | PDF Export Presets and click the Define button.
2. Click Load.
3. Locate the PDFS file you want to load. Click Open.

Creating Interactive PDFs with InDesign CS

InDesign CS includes new features for creating interactive PDFs. Not only can you create bookmarks and hyperlinks automatically (and manually), but you can add buttons in InDesign that will activate links, media clips, and even mouse rollovers.

About InDesign Buttons

If you create an interactive button in Acrobat, you use the Button tool. In InDesign, you create a button with the Button tool, or by converting other objects to buttons. There is no mention in InDesign of form fields, although that is what is created during the PDF Export process.

In the following sections, you will learn how to create InDesign buttons designed specifically to add interactivity to onscreen PDFs.

The Button Tool

The most straightforward way to create an InDesign button is to use the Button tool, which looks like a pointy finger on top of a rounded rectangle. Click-and-drag with the *Button tool* to create buttons on body pages or master pages. For example, you could add forward, back, and home navigation buttons to an onscreen newsletter by placing buttons on a master page. To use the Button tool:

1. Select it from the Tool palette.
2. Click-and-drag to create a button, or click once and specify a width and height.
3. Use the Selection tool to reposition a button.

NOTE *Remember, you can hold down* SHIFT *to constrain the Button tool to drawing a square. In addition, you can hold down* ALT *(Windows) or* OPTION *(Mac OS) to draw a square from the center.*

4. Double-click a button to name it and set its properties. Or right-click (Windows) or CTRL-click (Mac OS) and choose Interactive | Button Options. From the main menu, choose Object | Interactive | Button Options.

Converting Objects to Buttons

You can convert text frames, a graphics frame, or a drawn shape to buttons. When converted, these objects become the button's up state.

To convert an object to a button, use the Selection tool. Select the object and right-click (Windows) or CTRL-click (Mac OS) and choose Interactive | Convert to Button, or choose Object | Interactive | Convert to Button.

Button Options

If you've ever created a button form field in Acrobat, you will feel right at home with the InDesign Button tool. Just as Button field in Acrobat has Properties, the Button objects in InDesign have button options, which are a simplified version of the button field properties available in Acrobat. (See Chapter 12 for more on form fields.)

In the General section of InDesign button options, you name the button, set whether the button is visible in the PDF, and add a description. The description is translated to a tool tip in Acrobat, which may also be used by screen readers used by the visually impaired.

The Behaviors section is much like the Actions tab in the Acrobat button field. You set an event (trigger in Acrobat), such as mouse up or mouse enter, add a behavior (or action in Acrobat), and specify a zoom level (if appropriate for the behavior).

If you have created form fields in Acrobat, then you know how important the tab order of form fields is. You can specify the tab order of buttons on an InDesign page with the following procedure:

1. Navigate to the page where the buttons are.
2. In the main menu, choose Object | Interactive | Set Tab Order.
3. In the Tab Order dialog box, shown next, drag a button name to a new position, or select the button name and use the Move Up and Move Down buttons.

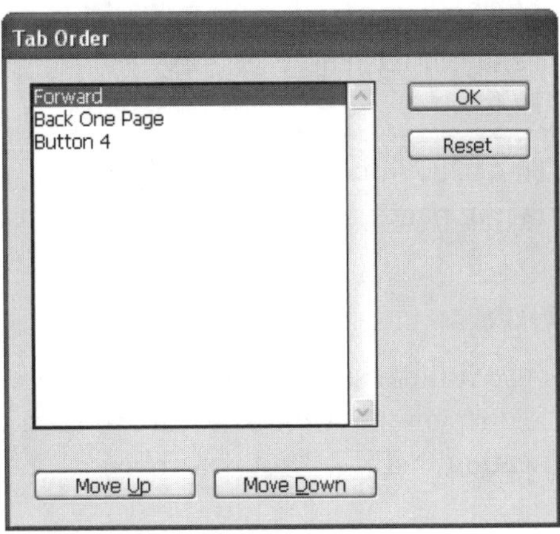

4. Click OK when you finish.

The events in InDesign buttons are Mouse Up/Down/Enter/Exit and On Focus and On Blur. Most behaviors will take place on Mouse Up, except for rollovers, which also will include a Mouse Enter.

Button Behaviors

The behaviors available in InDesign are extensive. They are

- **Close** This behavior closes the PDF in the viewer.
- **Exit** This behavior exits the PDF viewer.
- **Go to Anchor** This behavior takes users to a specified bookmark or hyperlink destination.
- **Go to...** These options are used to help end users navigate. Go to Previous View and Go to Next View work like the forward and back buttons in a web browser.
- **Movie** This behavior lets end users play, pause, stop, or resume movies placed in the InDesign document.
- **Open File** This behavior opens a specified file. Absolute, not relative, pathnames are required. Remember that end users will need an application installed on their machines to open the files specified with the Open File behavior.
- **Show/Hide Fields** This behavior is used with rollovers to make fields appear and disappear.
- **Sounds** This behavior lets end users play, pause, stop, or resume sounds placed in the document.
- **View Zoom** This behavior controls zoom settings, page layout in Acrobat (continuous or facing pages), and page orientation.

Creating Rollovers

InDesign can create mouse rollovers that make buttons more interactive. Rollovers in Acrobat work like the ones on the web——your mouse goes over a button, and the button changes, indicating that it is "hot" or linked.

To begin, you will need a button. Use the File | Place command to insert a graphic, and convert the graphic to a button. Or, use the Button tool, and click-and-drag to create a button.

To add a rollover to a button created by the Button tool:

1. Choose | Window | Interactive | States to open the Interactive States palette.
2. Use the Selection tool to select the button.
3. In the States palette, choose a preset option.
4. Add behaviors to the button.

You can also use graphics to represent various states. Use the following procedure to add new graphics to each state:

1. Place a graphic in InDesign. Convert it to a button.
2. In the States palette menu, choose New State.
3. Create States for Up, Rollover, and Down. The states will look exactly like the original placed graphic.
4. Select the state you want to use a new graphic for.
5. Copy the graphic for the new state to the clipboard.
6. Choose Edit | Paste Into.
7. Add appropriate behaviors to the button.

Adding Hyperlinks and Bookmarks

InDesign can create hyperlinks and bookmarks from InDesign documents and book files. These interactive elements are a great aid to end users who need to navigate in your PDF document.

You can manually add hyperlinks, and hyperlinks can be automatically generated from a book's table of contents. You can manually add bookmarks, and bookmarks will be automatically generated from a book file's table of contents.

NOTE *Your custom bookmarks will be forced to the end of the bookmark list after the table of contents is updated.*

Adding Hyperlinks

InDesign has a Hyperlink palette to help you manage your InDesign bookmarks. Choose Window | Interactive | Hyperlinks to bring up the Hyperlinks palette.

Creating manual hyperlinks in InDesign is a two-step process. First, you add a hyperlink destination, and then you add a link to the destination. You must add destinations for pages, specific paragraphs (text anchors), and web links.

To create a hyperlink destination, choose New Hyperlink Destination from the Hyperlinks Palette. Choose Page, Text Anchor, or URL from the Type pull-down menu. You should name your destinations.

Once the destinations are set, you can use the Hyperlink palette to create hyperlinks to the destinations. Use the New Hyperlink command from the Hyperlink palette, as shown here:

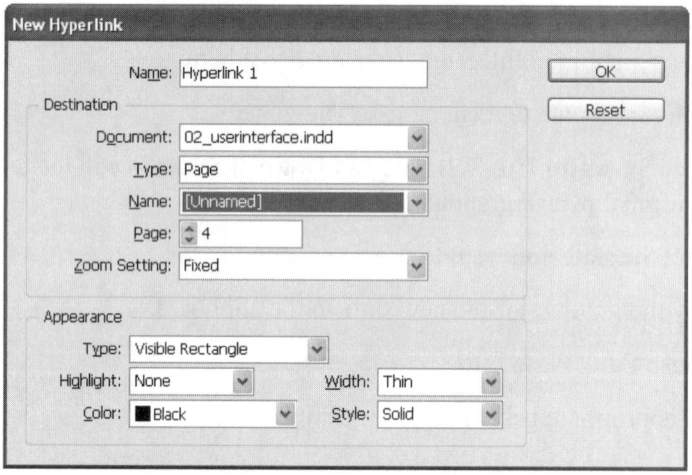

Your hyperlink options are

- **Pages** You can specify which page to link to, which document in a book you are linking to, the zoom setting, and the appearance of the link.
- **Text Anchor** These links go to specifically named destinations. Select the name of the text anchor and set the link appearance.
- **URL** Specify the web page you are linking to and set the link appearance. The links can include http://, file://, ftp://, or mailto:*username*@*company*.com.

Adding Bookmarks

Bookmarks will be created automatically from a table of contents generated by an InDesign book file. In addition, you can add manual bookmarks to individual documents or to content inside of InDesign books.

Manually created bookmarks are inserted with the bookmarks palette. Choose Window | Interactive | Bookmarks to display it. Use the Bookmarks palette menu and choose New Bookmark to create a new bookmark.

When manually creating bookmarks, keep these points in mind:

- Selected text will become the name of bookmark.
- Graphics will be named Bookmark1, 2, 3, and so on. Double-click the bookmark name in the Bookmark palette and rename it.
- If you click in text without highlighting, the bookmark will be named Bookmark1, 2, 3, and so on. Double-click the bookmark in the Bookmark palette and rename it.

Considerations for Creating Interactive PDFs from InDesign

When you produce PDFs from InDesign, you should keep several points in mind:

- You can use InDesign's File Info feature to add information to the Document Properties fields in Acrobat. Choose File | File Info and add information to be passed along to Acrobat.
- When exporting a book to PDF, InDesign uses the File Info of the first document in the book.
- InDesign adds Acrobat page labels to the PDFs. Page labels, which accurately reflect the page numbers displayed on PDF document pages, are created when page numbering starts with a number greater than one; when page numbering uses non-Arabic styles, such as roman numerals or letters of the alphabet; or when section numbers are used with page numbers.
- The PDF export option ignores the expanded/nested state of bookmarks in InDesign. All bookmarks will be expanded in an InDesign CS exported PDF.
- Some special characters, such as copyright and trademark symbols, are stripped from bookmarks.

Adding Movies and Sounds

Movie and sound files cannot be played in InDesign, but will be available when you create an Acrobat 6-compatible PDF. You can link or embed streaming media, QuickTime, AVI, MPEG, and SWF files, and WAV, AIF, and AU sounds.

You can add multimedia elements with the File | Place command, or by dragging and dropping elements into InDesign. Or, you can convert a frame to a media object with the Object | Interactive | Movie (or Sound) Options.

When you place a movie or sound file into InDesign, you have the following options (shown in Figure 15-5):

- **Description** Enter alternative text for screen-reading software here.
- **Embed Movie in PDF** This option only works in Acrobat 6. Earlier versions can only link to multimedia files.
- **Specify a URL** Enter the address of streaming media here.

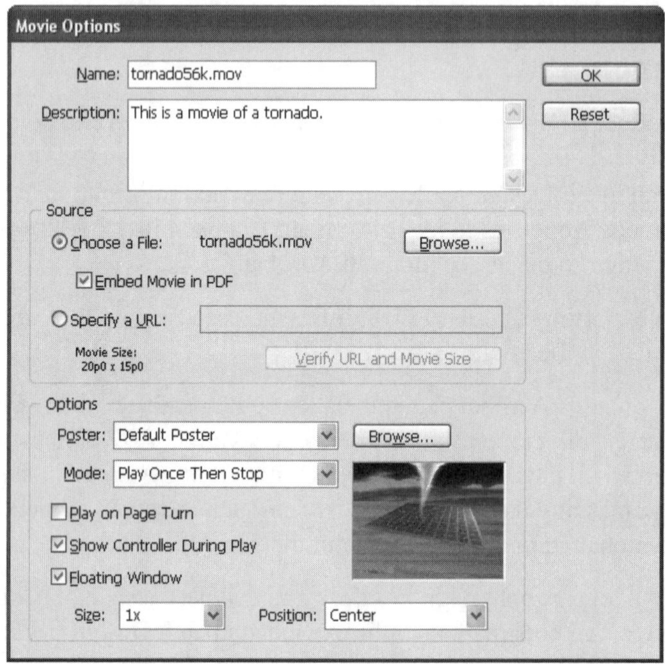

FIGURE 15-5 The Movie Options dialog box lets you embed movies in Acrobat 6 files.

- **Poster options inserts an image into the PDF** *None* keeps it empty, *Standard* inserts a generic image, *Default Poster* retrieve the first frame of the movie, *Choose Image* as poster lets you choose an image to represent the movie, and *Choose Movie Frame as Poster* lets you choose a frame from the movie.

Creating Tagged PDF

Tagged PDF is used for creating PDFs that are accessible to screen-reading software used by the visually impaired. Tagged PDF also reflows easily and aids in repurposing PDF data.

InDesign permits you to map InDesign styles to tags that will be used in Acrobat. (XML tags also can be used.) To map styles to tags, choose Window | Tags. From the Tags palette, choose Map Styles to Tags. Then use the Map Styles to Names feature to set up a logical reading order.

Adobe PageMaker

Adobe has announced that PageMaker is being discontinued, and is encouraging PageMaker users to migrate to InDesign. Adobe has produced a special version of InDesign CS for PageMaker users, and offers the PageMaker Plug-in Pack for existing InDesign CS customers.

The plug-in pack adds PagerMaker formatting features missing in InDesign, such as autonumbering and bullet-list creation. It also includes a filter for importing PageMaker files into InDesign. The PageMaker plug-ins make no changes to InDesign's PDF-export capabilities.

The last release of PageMaker, version 7, includes a PDF export feature. You can automatically create bookmarks and hyperlinks from a PageMaker table of contents. You also can create tagged PDF for accessibility and text reflow.

Adobe FrameMaker 7.1

Although little-known outside of the technical publishing community, *Adobe FrameMaker* is the leading product in the world of technical documentation.

I'm often asked what the difference is between InDesign and FrameMaker. InDesign is best used for book-length publications that involve lots of design elements. FrameMaker is best used for book-length publications that have a uniform look, as most reference or user guides do.

FrameMaker has a long history of integration with Acrobat. An earlier version of FrameMaker shipped with Acrobat 3.0, making the FrameMaker community one of the oldest and most experienced groups of PDF creators.

FrameMaker documents tend to be long and complex—often running into thousands of pages. For example, the longest FrameMaker document I've worked on was 30,000 pages. FrameMaker has excellent autonumber, cross reference, and hyperlinking capabilities. These features make FrameMaker a popular choice for preparing government proposals, and military and aerospace documents that use lots of numbered headings and step procedures.

Importing PDFs into FrameMaker

PDFs can be placed as graphics inside of FrameMaker. As with other Adobe applications, only one page of a multipage PDF can be inserted into a FrameMaker page. To insert a PDF into FrameMaker, choose File | Import File and select the PDF you want to import from.

FrameMaker does not support PDFs that use Asian-language fonts. PDFs with transparency may not print as you expect to PostScript Level 1 printers or to non-PostScript printers.

Creating PDFs from FrameMaker

PDFs can be created from individual FrameMaker files, or from FrameMaker book files. Tables of contents, tables of figures, tables of tables, index entries, cross references, web URLs, and other links are automatically passed on to PDFs. Bookmarks are created from styles (called *tags* in FrameMaker).

Although other Adobe products incorporate the PDF Library for direct PDF output, FrameMaker relies on Acrobat Distiller for PDF Creation. FrameMaker 7.1 ships with Distiller 6, but not Acrobat 6. You must buy Acrobat 6 separately for PDF editing capabilities.

Setting Up FrameMaker for PDF Generation

There are two menus for setting up FrameMaker files for PDF generation. The first is the PDF Optimization menu, available at Format | Document | Optimize PDF Size | Options. While this feature will reduce the size of PDFs produced by older versions of FrameMaker by removing named destinations for all paragraphs, optimization may result in some cross-references and links failing or pointing to wrong locations.

The next PDF-related menus are the PDF Setup dialog boxes, which are found at Format | Document | PDF Setup. These dialog boxes permit great control over PDF generation.

PDF Settings

The PDF Settings dialog box in PDF Setup gives you an opportunity to select the JobOptions that Acrobat Distiller will use. You also can set the page the document will open to, the zoom setting at opening, whether to view the file after PDF creation and whether to create a series of linked PDFs from a book or a single large file. You also can add Registration Marks to the PDF.

PDF Bookmarks

You create bookmarks, and a hierarchy of bookmarks, from this dialog box. In the Bookmarks Expanded Through menu, you can choose to have all the bookmarks expanded or just to display the top level.

There is seldom a reason to include the paragraph tag name in the bookmark. Be sure this option is deselected, unless you have some reason to insert the paragraph tag name in the bookmark.

You also can activate Acrobat's article-threading features here. *Article threading* can be useful for reading multicolumn PDFs onscreen, but I prefer to avoid it for one-column documents. If you add article threading, be sure to enable Thread by Column for multicolumn documents.

PDF Tags

If your PDFs need to reflow or meet Section 508 requirements, create tagged PDF. Be aware that creating tagged PDF can greatly increase the size of FrameMaker files.

To create *tagged PDF,* set up a logical hierarchy of paragraph tags. For example, a chapter or section title might be the top level in a document, followed by Heading1, Heading2, Heading3, and so on. An example is shown in Figure 15-6. Click set when you are done.

Be sure to put header and footer tags in the Don't Include side. You want screen readers to skip this information. For more information on accessibility, see Chapter 5.

Links in PDF Setup

I find the name of this dialog box confusing. When I first saw it in an earlier version of FrameMaker, I thought this was the place where I would control hyperlinks. Instead, the only purpose of this screen is to enable or disable the creation of named destinations for linked paragraphs in a FrameMaker publication.

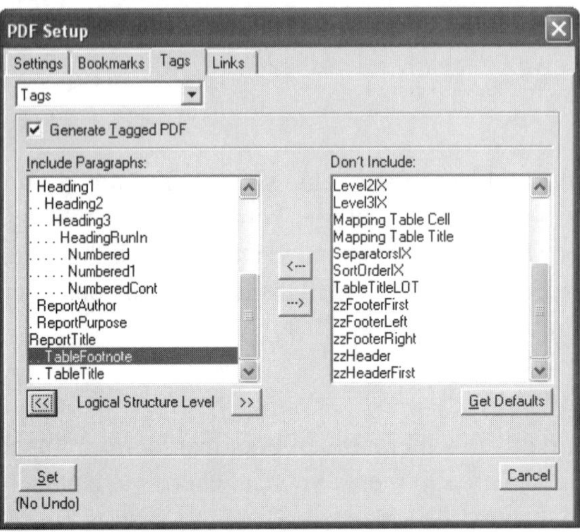

FIGURE 15-6 FrameMaker can create tagged PDF for making PDFs accessible for the visually impaired.

You should enable Create named destinations for paragraphs. While the dialog box indicates you only need this feature if you are manually creating links after creating a PDF from FrameMaker, for practical purposes, you should enable it. For more information, see the list of FM bugs/issues at **www.microtype.com**.

Generating a PDF from FrameMaker

To create a PDF from FrameMaker, choose File | Print and print to the Adobe PDF printer. When printing to Adobe PDF, be sure to enable the Generate Acrobat Data option, and to deselect the Print to File option, as shown in Figure 15-7.

NOTE *When printing book files to multiple PDFs, you should choose the Print to File option, in addition to the Generate Acrobat Data option. Drag the *.ps files you create with this option and drop them on Acrobat Distiller. Distiller will convert the PostScript files to PDF.*

Alternatively, you choose File | Save As, and then select PDF as the file type. However, this process has historically been problematic, and technical editor Shlomo Perets advises against using it, even in FrameMaker 7.1.

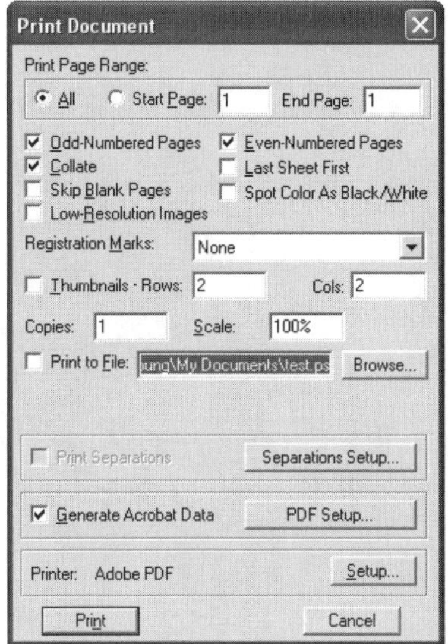

FIGURE 15-7 When printing to Adobe PDF from FrameMaker, enable Generate Acrobat data to include interactive features, such as hyperlinks and bookmarks.

You can click PDF Setup to review your PDF creation options, or click Print to create a PDF.

Summary

Adobe has tightly integrated PDF creation with most of its tools. Unlike products from other software vendors, PDF creation from Adobe is clearly not just an afterthought, but is a tightly integrated part of the production process.

Adobe InDesign CS and FrameMaker 7.1 can create book-length PDFs with automatically generated links and bookmarks. InDesign CS and Illustrator CS can create layered PDFs, the first tools for graphic designers to do so. The Creative Suite versions of InDesign, Photoshop, and Illustrator export PDFs directly without having to go through Acrobat Distiller. Adobe FrameMaker 7.1 relies on Distiller for PDF creation, but includes a copy of Distiller 6.0.

Chapter 16

Corel Applications

Ventura Publisher is Corel's long-document page layout application. Ventura is used to produce books (including this one), and book-length documents, such as user and reference manuals.

Corel Ventura 10

Ventura 10 for Windows, released in 2002, includes extensive built-in PDF generation capabilities. There are five outputting settings, including one for the industry standard PDF/X-1 format for magazine ad submission. Also included are the capabilities to generate hyperlinks, bookmarks, and thumbnails in your PDFs.

Unfortunately, the built-in Publish to PDF feature has some limitations, as you will see later in the chapter. But, first, let's begin with the good news.

Ventura Publish to PDF Capabilities

The PDF output capabilities in Ventura are some of the most ambitious of any non-Adobe application. Corel has certainly tried to provide Ventura users with a robust set of options, including:

- Color management
- Preflight summaries
- Passing document information onto the PDF
- Control over graphics compression
- Control over embedding fonts
- Setting the number of fountain steps (gradients, for Adobe application users)
- A set of predefined PDF output styles, and the capability to create your own
- Interactive PDF features, such as hyperlinks and bookmarks

PDF output can be either Acrobat 3- or Acrobat 4-compatible. No provision is made for Acrobat 5-level PDFs. The output is directly from the application—no PostScript file is created and processed, as happens with Acrobat Distiller. Ventura uses Corel PDF Engine 10 as its creation mechanism.

Online PDFs from Ventura

Ventura's built-in PDF generator looks promising for online PDF creators on the outside, but is a disappointment on close examination. Among your output choices are options to convert hyperlinks and bookmarks to PDF, as shown in Figure 16-1.

You insert a hyperlink in Ventura by choosing Insert | Hyperlink, and then choosing the type of link, as shown in Figure 16-2. You can link to a web address, insert a command to send e-mail, link to a chapter in your book, or link to a file outside the book.

As with most other applications, including Adobe's, you must use the built-in PDF creator rather than using Print | Adobe PDF to preserve hyperlinks.

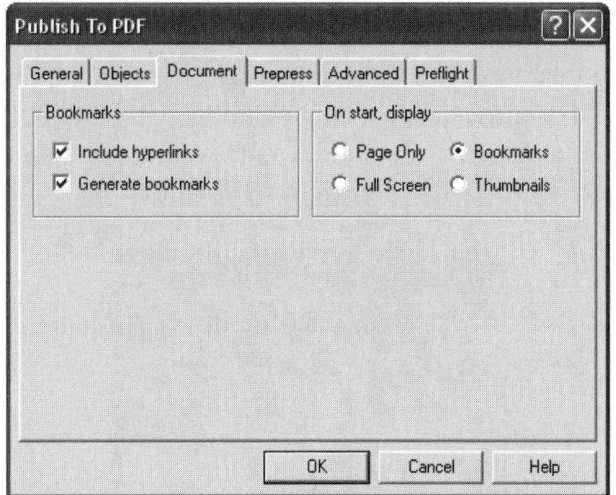

FIGURE 16-1 Publish to PDF includes options to create hyperlinks and bookmarks.

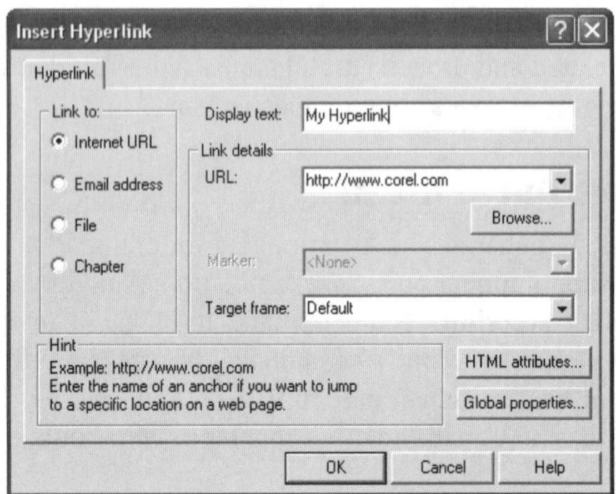

FIGURE 16-2 Ventura hyperlinks are passed on to PDFs created with Publish to PDF.

Invisible hyperlinks in tables of contents and index entries generated by Ventura also can be passed on to PDF. As discussed in Chapter 4, online readers should be able to navigate within a book-length PDF by using hyperlinks from a table of contents and from index entries. Choose Publication | Update Publication and be sure to enable the Generate hyperlinks for Adobe Acrobat option, as shown next. Hyperlinks are inserted into tables of contents and index.

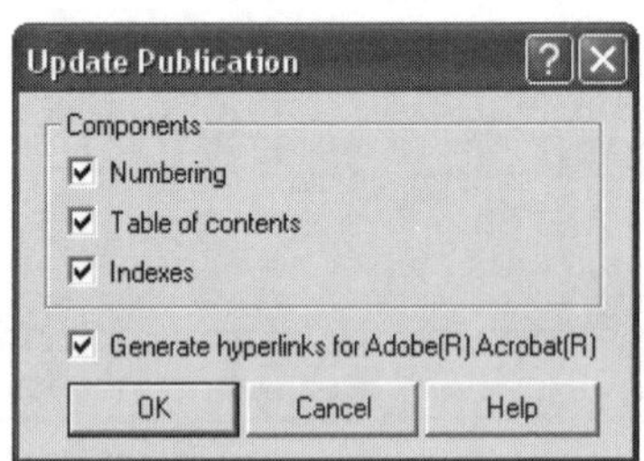

The implementation of bookmark creation is quite interesting in Ventura. The approach of Adobe and most other vendors is to generate bookmarks based on heading styles used inside a document. You can specify that all headings with the H1 style produce bookmarks, for example.

Corel, in Ventura, creates PDF bookmarks from tables of contents and indexes. This means an entire index could appear in the Bookmark tab of a PDF—an intriguing concept, but not one that I can generally recommend. Shown here is an example from a Ventura sample file. And, once inserted, the hyperlinks are there to stay in the index, even after you replace the contents of the index with the Delete Index/Create Index commands. You can, however, easily get rid of the index and all entries by deleting them.

Ventura's way of creating bookmarks doesn't help if you have a multipage document, but you don't have a table of contents. You can't generate bookmarks based on heading styles alone—you must create them by hand. Overall, Ventura's online PDF hyperlinking and bookmark creation features are useful, but pay close attention when using them.

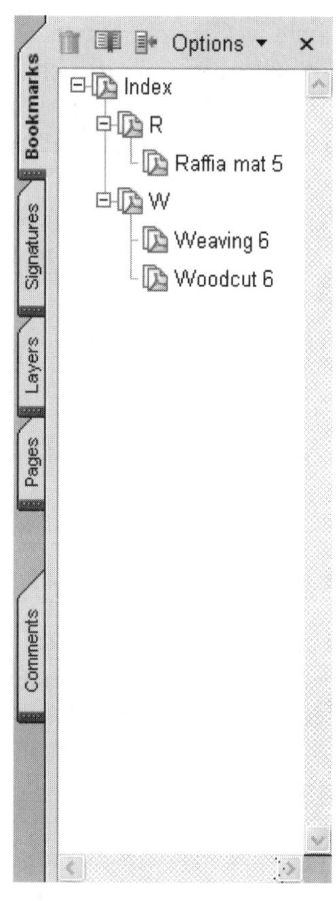

Creating PDFs for Specific Uses

The interface for creating PDFs is straightforward. Simply choose File | Publish as | Publish to PDF and choose an output setting. The output settings (called styles in Ventura) and their Acrobat 6 equivalents are

- PDF for document distribution
- PDF for editing
- PDF for prepress
- PDF for the Web
- PDF/X-1
- PDFX1a
- Standard
- Standard (with all fonts embedded)
- High Quality
- Smallest File Size

Now let's take a closer look at each of the default PDF settings, and discuss some recommendations for tuning them up. The Publish to PDF dialog box contains General, Objects, Document, Advanced, and Preflight tabs, which allow for customization of each of these styles.

The modified styles can be saved with new names, or you can create entirely new styles. To create a PDF style:

1. Choose File | Publish as | Publish to PDF.
2. Click the Settings button.
3. Modify any settings in the first four tabs in the Publish to PDF dialog box.
4. Go to the General tab.
5. Click on the plus sign (+).
6. Enter a name for the style in the Save PDF style as dialog box.

PDF for Document Distribution

This PDF style produces an Acrobat 4-type PDF file. Graphics are downsampled to 200 dpi, and bitmaps such as photographs are compressed with the JPEG format set to High Quality. All fonts are embedded and subset. Unfortunately, TrueType fonts are converted to PostScript Type 1 fonts, and all the base 14 fonts are embedded as well.

As discussed in Chapter 3, I advise against converting TrueType to Type 1 fonts. The base 14 fonts, which were the original PostScript fonts that shipped with the earliest laser printers, are unnecessary and bloat the file. These options should be deselected.

Hyperlinks and bookmarks are created, and the PDF is linearized, or set up for one-page-at-a-time downloading from the Web. Adobe calls this *Fast Web View.*

PDF for Editing

This style produces an Acrobat 4-type PDF. Bitmap graphics are compressed with the LZW algorithm, which shrinks the file size without throwing away any data. Fonts are embedded, but TrueType fonts are converted to PostScript Type 1 fonts, and all of the base 14 fonts are also embedded. Deselect Convert TrueType to Type 1 and Embed base 14. You should enable the Subset fonts option.

Hyperlinks and bookmarks are created, but the file is not linearized for Fast Web view. It should be. Advanced settings enable this file to be placed in a high-end production environment, which is fine.

PDF for Prepress

This PDF Style produces an Acrobat 4-level document. ZIP compression is applied to bitmap graphics, and graphics are downsampled to 300 dpi. Fonts are embedded and subset. Deselect Convert TrueType to Type 1 and Embed base 14 options. No hyperlinks or bookmarks are created—this is appropriate for a PDF that is not intended for onscreen reading.

The bleed limit (how far an image can extend beyond the page crop marks) is set to 0.125 inch. Check with your print provider to see if this is an appropriate amount, and increase or decrease the limit to the print provider's recommendations.

You have a choice of selecting an ICC color profile in the Advanced tab. Check with your print provider to see whether the Composite Printer Profile or the Separations Printer Profile is appropriate for your job.

CAUTION *Be careful when using an option such as Color Management because unexpected color shifts can occur. For example, if you use some RGB graphics (the kind of graphics displayed on computer screens) in your Ventura file, you may see color shifts if you choose a different color model for PDF output, such as CMYK (the four-color print model used in traditional printing).*

PDF for the Web

This produces an Acrobat 3-level file. Acrobat 3 was introduced in 1996 and replaced when Acrobat 4 was launched in 1999. Unless you know your customers are using computers more than five years old, I would stay away from Acrobat 3-type files and set the version level to Acrobat 4. After all, Acrobat 4 will operate on PCs running Windows 95.

Images are downsampled to 96 dpi, which is fine for onscreen viewing on a PC. Graphics are compressed to a mid-level JPG, which should look fine on a screen.

Oddly, no fonts are embedded. This means a high likelihood exists that a font substitution will be on the user's end—you don't ever want that to happen. Embed and subset the fonts.

Although web-based PDFs are destined to be viewed online, for some reason the default PDF for the web settings do not insert Bookmarks to help online readers navigate through long documents. This is a bad idea. Enable bookmark creation. Hyperlinks are already selected. Optimize for Web is already enabled, which is a must to enhance the online viewing experience.

PDF/X-1

Hats off to Corel for including this important industry standard as a predefined PDF output style. *PDF/X-1a* is a production standard for the printing industry intended to make the exchange of high-quality PDF files more uniform. For example, starting on January 1, 2004, all Time, Inc., magazines are requiring that every ad be submitted in PDF/X-1a format. (For more on PDF/X-1a and related PDF/X standards, see Chapter 18.)

NOTE *Ventura calls its PDF style PDF/X-1. The Adobe PDF job option is named PDFX1a. Most authorities write the standard as PDF/X-1a.*

The PDF/X-1 setting creates an Acrobat 3-level PDF. Graphics are compressed with the ZIP algorithm, fonts are embedded, and color output is set for CMYK.

Unfortunately, the Corel-supplied Ventura sample documents output to PDF with the built-in PDF/X-1 style failed the Acrobat 6 prepress flight check. Even though the instructions are to convert RGB colors to CMYK, that did not happen with the test files. RGB color images, such as a scanned color photograph, were still RGB in the PDF. To see a portion of the report, refer to Figure 16-3.

Suggested Alternatives to Publish to PDF/X

I recommend that you use Acrobat 6 or Jaws PDF Creator to produce PDF/X-1a-compliant files from Ventura. The same test files printed to Adobe PDF using the PDF/X-1a setting produced a file that easily passed the Acrobat 6 PDF/X-1a preflight check. Both Acrobat and Jaws PDF Creator are widely used in the printing industry, and they can be expected to produce high-quality results.

Fonts and Publish to PDF

While I am sure many Ventura users are pleased with the application's built-in PDF generator, you should be aware that the Publish to PDF feature can have trouble embedding fonts. I'll walk you through a brief test case.

My test file is made up of the following characters:

abcdefghijklmnopqrstuvwxyz 0123456789 ~!@#$%^&*()_+|[]{},./<>?—
"®©¶üæ

FIGURE 16-3 A PDF created with PDF/X-1 setting in Ventura 10 does not pass a test for PDFX-1a compliance in Adobe Acrobat 6. For example, a preflight check in Acrobat 6 Professional points out that a graphic is neither four color nor a spot color.

The characters include the German language umlaut vowel *ü,* and the *æ* diphthong. These characters are part of the standard ASCII character set, which many fonts include. The size used was 24 points, and I used eight lines of text with the following TrueType fonts applied, one font for each line:

- Times New Roman
- WP Arabic Sihafa
- Script MT Bold
- Weltron Urban
- OCR A Extended
- TypoUpright BT
- Smudger LT
- Amaze

NOTE *Smudger and WP Arabic Sihafa do not contain the complete ASCII character set, and missing characters appear as square boxes in Ventura. You would expect to see square boxes in the same locations in the resulting PDF.*

None of the default Publish to PDF settings produced an acceptable PDF. None of the settings could embed Weltron Urban, and many could not embed Amaze or Smudger LT. Not a single file looked liked the original Ventura file.

On the other hand, when I printed the Ventura file to Adobe PDF using the settings recommended in Chapter 3, the resulting PDF looked just like the original. The fonts were embedded and displayed well onscreen. It also printed well.

If you use the Publish to PDF features in Ventura, I would stick with well-known TrueType fonts, such as Times New Roman, Arial, and Type 1 PostScript fonts. Test with sample files before you write a 400-page book with an unfamiliar TrueType font that might not display or print correctly!

CorelDRAW 11

CorelDRAW has long been a favorite drawing package for many technical writers and others who need to produce high-quality graphics quickly and easily. CorelDRAW 11 uses Corel PDF Engine 11 as its creation mechanism.

What you may not know is that CorelDRAW can produce PDF forms—this does not appear to be documented anywhere in the application or at **www.corel.com**. This is particularly good news for Mac users because nearly all form creation tools are Windows only, and CorelDRAW runs on both platforms.

CorelDRAW is not a full-featured form designer, but you can create sophisticated form layouts and add form objects to them.

Like other Corel products, CorelDRAW includes a Publish to PDF feature. This is similar to the one in Ventura, with five preset PDF output styles. Unlike Ventura, CorelDraw 11 will output Acrobat 5-level PDFs. Available styles are

- PDF for document distribution
- PDF for prepress
- PDF for the Web
- PDF for editing
- PDF/X-1

Using the Publish to PDF feature is simple:

1. Choose File | Publish to PDF.
2. Pick a PDF output Style.
3. Save the file.

Corel also has its own "Create from Multiples" feature that gives you the capability to combine multiple CorelDraw files into a single PDF.

1. Open the files you want to combine.
2. Choose File | Publish to PDF.
3. Click Settings | General.
4. Select the Documents option.
5. Choose each document you want to save as a PDF.
6. Click OK, specify a file name, and Save.

Creating Online PDFs with CorelDraw

Like Ventura, CorelDraw includes features for creating PDF bookmarks and hyperlinks. Unlike Ventura, CorelDraw users have greater control over these features.

For those who want to create bookmarks, I have some bad news. Unfortunately, by default, the top-level PDF bookmark will be the page number of the document, as shown in Figure 16-4.

To create a bookmark, you use the Internet feature inside the software. To assign a bookmark name:

1. Right-click (Windows) or CTRL-click (Mac OS) an object on the page, and choose Properties.
2. In Windows, click the Internet tab. In Mac OS, choose Internet from the list box.
3. Choose Bookmark from the Behavior pull-down menu.
4. Enter the name of the bookmark.

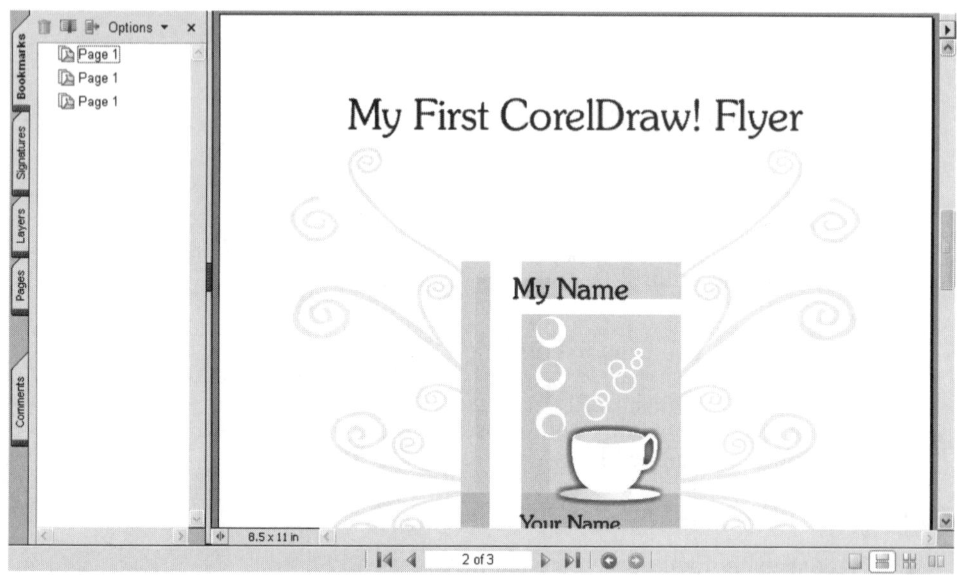

FIGURE 16-4 Acrobat Bookmarks from a multipage PDF created with CorelDRAW include a page number.

Hyperlinks are passed on to the PDF as well. While you can't link specific zoom levels, you can link from an object to a page, or to a web address. To add a link to a multipage CorelDRAW file:

1. Right-click (Windows) or CTRL-click (Mac OS) an object.
2. Choose Internet Links | Page and select the page you want to link to.
3. Publish the file to PDF.

NOTE *The Alt Text field in the Behavior | URL window produces a Note comment in PDF.*

Creating Prepress PDFs from CorelDRAW

The Publish to PDF feature in CorelDRAW is an updated version of the one in Ventura. PDF/X1-and PDF/X-3 support were added with Service Pack 1, which is available for download from **www.corel.com**.

The setup and output from CorelDRAW are similar to those in Ventura. The main exception is that you can output Acrobat 5-level PDFs, which support transparency.

Problems with the default settings are the same as Ventura. The default settings unnecessarily embed the Base 14 fonts, and Convert TrueType to Type 1 fonts. These should be deselected.

CorelDRAW had similar difficulties handing the font test previously described in the Ventura section of this chapter. While there were fewer errors, you should still consider using File | Print | Adobe PDF to output any files with unusual or troublesome fonts.

Creating PDF Forms with CorelDRAW

The PDF form capability inside CorelDRAW is a byproduct of its web page creation tools, and not all web functionality is implemented in a PDF form. Many heavy-duty form designers will be pleased to learn you can insert bar codes into PDF forms with CorelDRAW.

Form objects are inserted with the Edit | Insert Internet Object command. The first two objects, Java applet and Embedded file, don't apply in the PDF form world. Eight of the next nine choices do apply to PDF forms. CorelDRAW objects and their PDF form equivalents are listed in the following table:

CorelDRAW	PDF Form
Simple Button	Button field
Submit Button	Button field programmed to submit a form
Reset Button	Button field programmed to reset the entire form
Radio Button	Radio button field
Check Box	Check box field
Text Edit Field	Text field
Text Edit Box	Does not pass to PDF, although it appears to be equivalent to a Text field with the Multiline option enabled
Pop-Up Menu	Combo Box field. Note that list items do not pass to PDF
Options List	List Box field. Note that list items do not pass to PDF

For details on creating PDF forms, see Chapter 12.

To create a PDF form in CorelDRAW, use the Text Tool to add field labels and instructions to the form. Then add the form fields and choose Publish to PDF.

You probably will need Acrobat to finish the PDF form. Radio buttons and check boxes don't keep arbitrary name assignments made in CorelDRAW. You'll have to rename those in Acrobat, as well as specifying the field export values.

As noted in the table, you must add items to combo and list boxes, and program functionality into the Button fields.

Last, you should add a Tooltip to each form field for accessibility and usability.

Corel DESIGNER 10

DESIGNER is a technical illustration program originally developed by Micrografx, and then acquired by Corel. DESIGNER uses Corel PDF Engine 10, the same as Ventura. But, unlike the version 10 PDF Engine in Ventura, the DESIGNER engine does produce Acrobat 5-compatible files.

Creating online PDFs is exactly the same as in CorelDRAW. You can insert hyperlinks and create bookmarks, and do so in the same way. The problems are also the same as in CorelDRAW. When you create bookmarks, DESIGNER automatically inserts a page number at the top of each set of bookmarks.

Output options are more limited in DESIGNER. Only three preset styles are available: PDF for Document Distribution, PDF for Editing, and PDF for the Web. The default settings are similar to those in Ventura and CorelDRAW. You should modify the settings so that fonts are embedded and subset, but no text is converted to curves and TrueType fonts are not converted to Type 1.

DESIGNER had the same issues with the font test as did Ventura and CorelDRAW. Although it is unlikely that you would insert lots of wild fonts in a technical drawing program, you should be careful about using fonts in DESIGNER. Test fonts before going to final output. Unless you need hyperlinks and bookmarks, you should consider printing directly to the Adobe PDF printer.

Summary

Corel recognizes the importance of PDF to its users, and has done a real service in providing a free PDF generator inside of Ventura, CorelDRAW, and DESIGNER. The company is among the first to provide tools to support the printing industry standard PDF/X-1a. The Corel PDF Engine will work acceptably for many users but, when in doubt, you should use Print | Adobe PDF to fix font issues.

Chapter 17

PDF from QuarkXPress

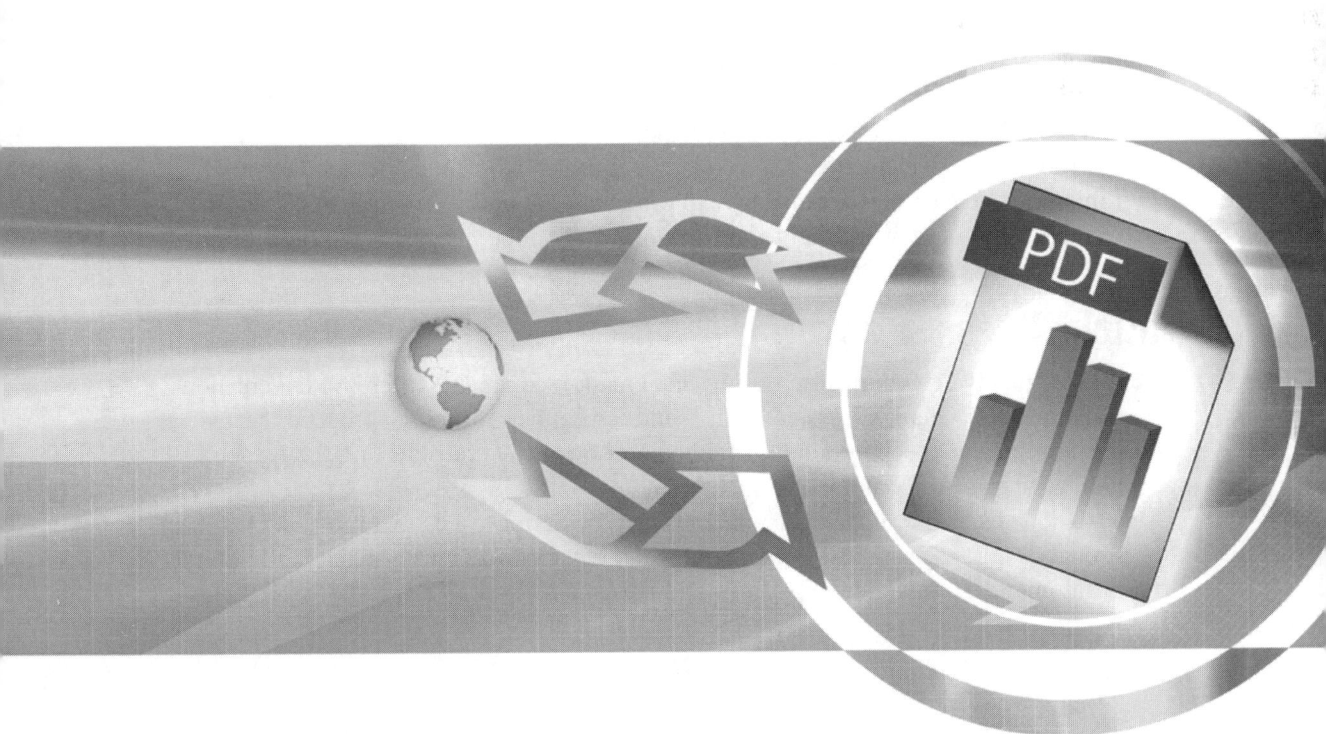

At times, it seems as if the creative world is split into two camps: the QuarkXPress people on one side, and the Adobe people on another. A history of fierce competition exists between the two companies, and that rivalry sometimes filters down to the users.

As a practical matter, many Adobe Photoshop and Illustrator users place their art into QuarkXPress for layout and production. Many printing companies have workflows built on handling native QuarkXPress files filled with embedded graphics produced by Adobe graphics programs.

Perhaps because Adobe developed the PDF standard, many QuarkXPress users have been slow to adopt PDF. Early QuarkXPress moves to incorporate PDF into XPress workflows were a bit awkward, as you will see in the following. Fortunately, Quark has incorporated a fine PDF-generating solution in version 6, making it much easier to produce high-quality PDFs directly from QuarkXPress.

Overview

There are two basic approaches to produce PDFs from QuarkXPress. The first method is to generate a PostScript print file, and to turn that PostScript file into a PDF with Adobe Acrobat Distiller. The second method is to use the PDF generation capability incorporated into XPress. The QuarkXTensions PDF Filter in versions 4 and 5 is a simpler way to create PDFs, and can do so quite capably by working behind the scenes with Acrobat Distiller. In essence, a PostScript file is still created—it's just that the PDF Filter automates the process.

The best implementation is in version 6, however, which includes the Jaws PDF Library. In Version 6, it is quite easy to produce print and interactive PDFs. From Quark's point of view, it is an ideal solution—no Adobe product is required at all!

QuarkXPress 4 and 5

As with nearly everything else, Adobe and Quark recommend different PDF creation techniques for QuarkXPress versions 4 and 5. If either of these approaches seems too complicated, keep in mind that choosing File | Print and selecting the Adobe PDF printer in Acrobat 6 works just fine, too.

Adobe technical support recommends the PostScript-to-Distiller method. Quark strongly suggests using its PDF Filter QuarkXTension. You must use the PDF Filter to automatically generate hyperlinks and bookmarks in the PDF.

NOTE *These recommendations apply to both the Windows and Mac OS versions of QuarkXPress. Platform and operating specifics will be noted.*

Adobe's Recommended Solution

Adobe technical support recommends installing an Adobe PostScript printer driver (AdobePS), and then configuring AdobePS to use the Adobe Acrobat Distiller PostScript Printer Description (PPD) file. You then generate a PostScript print file from Express, which Acrobat Distiller automatically turns into a PDF.

While these steps are a bit tedious, remember you only have to do it once. After your settings are configured, you can use them over and over again.

NOTE *This process is best for creating a document destined to be printed. The PDF Filter adds interactive hyperlinks from QuarkXPress lists, making the PDF Filter method a better choice for online documents.*

Installing and Configuring the PPD for Windows

In general, installing Acrobat 6 will update the printer driver on your Windows machine to correctly use the Adobe PDF printer driver. You should not need to do anything special.

Next, download Adobe's universal PostScript driver from **www.adobe.com/support/downloads/main.html**. Adobe provides a universal PostScript driver for Windows 95, 98, 98SE, and Me; Windows NT 4 with SP6 or later; and Windows XP and 2000. Follow the wizard to install it.

NOTE *Be sure to select the Acrobat Distiller PPD when the wizard prompts you to select a PPD.*

CAUTION *Selecting the default "Generic PostScript Printer" PPD may result in color and font problems in the PDFs produced.*

In QuarkXPress, go to Utilities | PPD Manager. You should see Adobe PDF listed in the PPD Manager window, as shown in Figure 17-1. If it isn't showing, click on Browse and navigate to C:\Program Files\Adobe\Acrobat 6.0\Distillr\Xtras. Click OK, and then click Update. Adobe PDF should now show as a valid PPD.

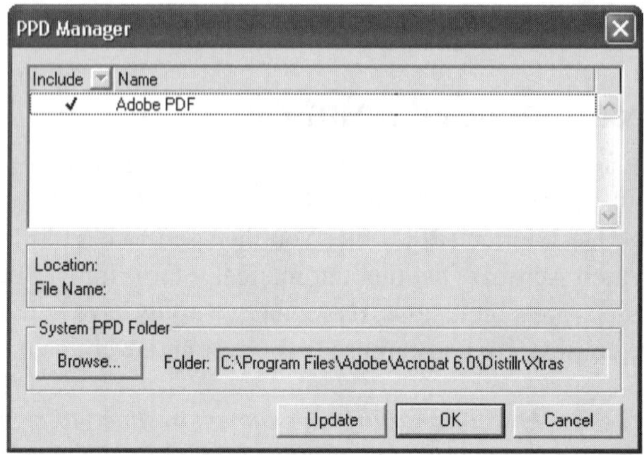

FIGURE 17-1 The PPD Manager in QuarkXPress should list Adobe PDF as being available.

Installing and Configuring the PostScript Print Driver for Mac OS

NOTE *Acrobat 6 and QuarkXPress 6 run on Mac OS X only. QuarkXPress 4 and 5 run in Classic mode.*

If you cannot see the Adobe PDF printer from the QuarkXPress 4 or 5 Print dialog box, you will need to follow these steps:

1. Download AdobePS Printer Driver from Adobe's web site at **www.adobe.com/support/downloads/product.jsp?product=44&platform=Macintosh**.
2. Download the Acrobat Distiller PPD from Adobe's web site at **www.adobe.com/support/downloads/main.html**. Copy the Distiller PPD to the Mac OS 9 System Folder/Extensions/Printer Descriptions folder.
3. Start QuarkXPress.
4. In the Chooser, select AdobePS.
5. Click Setup, and then click Select PPD.

6. Select Acrobat Distiller from the list of Printer Descriptions, click Select, and then click OK.
7. In QuarkXPress, choose Utilities | PPD Manager.
8. In the System PPD Folder section, click Select.
9. Navigate to the Mac OS 9 System Folder/Extensions/Printer Descriptions folder.
10. Click Select Printer Descriptions and choose Acrobat Distiller.
11. Click OK.

Printing to Adobe PDF from QuarkXPress 4 or 5

NOTE *Always use the Acrobat Distiller PPD and AdobePS print drivers to create PostScript files for processing by Acrobat Distiller. Using other PPDs or PostScript drivers can result in low quality PDFs. Never use PDFWriter, which has been discontinued by Adobe.*

Once the PPD and print driver are installed, you can start to produce PDFs. These procedures apply to both Mac OS and Windows.

To create a PDF file in QuarkXPress 4 or 5:

1. In QuarkXPress, open the document and choose File | Print.
2. Click the Document tab. Make sure Separations and Back to Front are deselected, as shown in Figure 17-2. Set other options as necessary.

TIP *Do not print blank pages if the document will be published online.*

3. Click the Setup tab. Choose Adobe PDF from the Printer Description pop-up menu, and then choose the correct paper size and page orientation.
4. Click the Output tab. Choose Composite CMYK from the Print Colors pop-up menu, choose Conventional from the Halftoning pop-up menu, and then choose the resolution that matches the final output device. An example is shown in Figure 17-3.

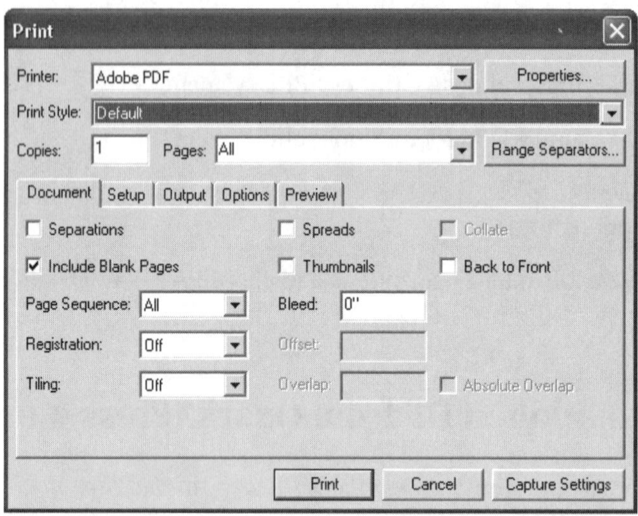

FIGURE 17-2 Document tab in the Print dialog box in QuarkXPress 5

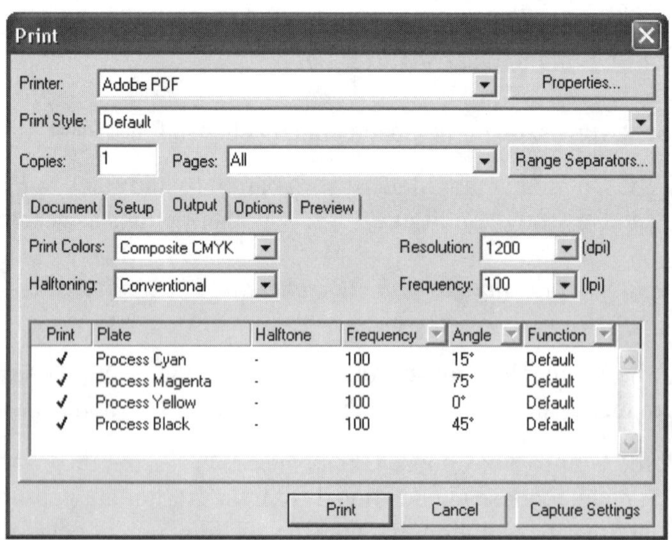

FIGURE 17-3 Sample Output settings. Your print provider should provide exact settings for Halftoning, Resolution, and Frequency.

5. Click the Options tab. Choose None from the Page Flip pull-down menu, choose Normal from the Output pop-up menu, and then choose Binary from the Data pop-up menu, as shown in Figure 17-4.

6. Click Capture Settings to preserve your options.

NOTE *If you use OPI options, choose Include Images from the OPI pop-up menu. If this menu is dimmed, click the OPI tab, and then select Include Images.*

Check Page Setup to ensure that your settings are still valid. Choose File | Page Setup. If the settings do not match those established in the previous procedure, reset them.

Creating the PDF

Once the setup is complete, you are ready to begin PDF production. As you can see from the following procedure, it's an easy five-step process.

1. Open the document in QuarkXPress and choose File | Print.

2. Select Adobe PDF. Verify that the Document, Setup, Output, and Options settings are correct.

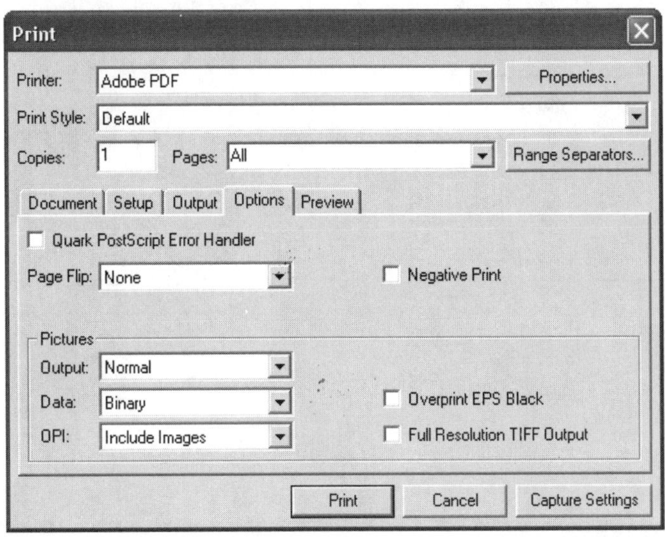

FIGURE 17-4 Options setup for a typical print-quality PDF

3. Click Properties.
4. Select the Adobe PDF Settings appropriate for the job (Refer to Chapter 3 and Chapter 18 for more information). See Figure 17-5 for an example.
5. Click Print, give the PDF a name, and save it in a location you can find later.

QuarkXPress will work with Acrobat 6 to create a PostScript file that is automatically turned into a PDF.

Quark's PDF Solution

Quark created a QuarkXTension module called the *PDF Filter* that gives QuarkXPress 4 and 5 the capability to import and export PDFs. PDF Filter is available as a free download from **www.quark.com**, or from the installation CD.

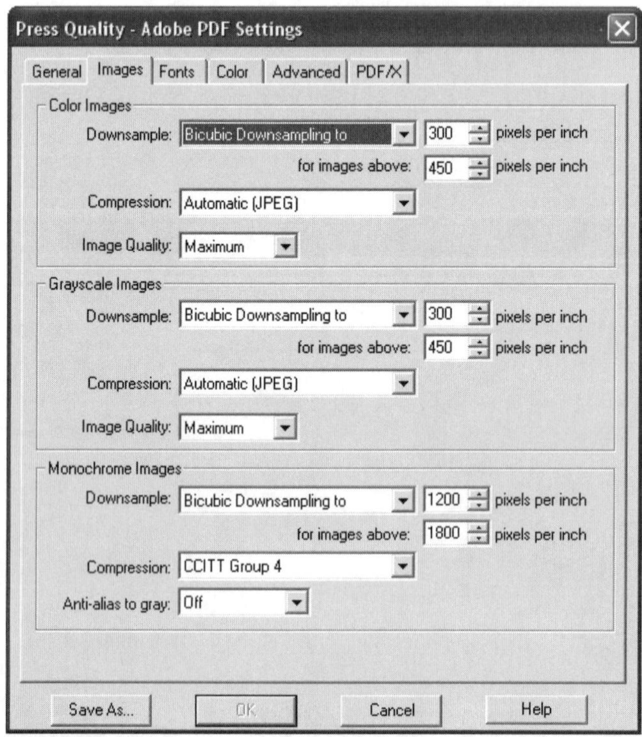

FIGURE 17-5 Sample Distiller Job Settings to create a press-quality PDF.

Installing the PDF Filter

Once the PDF Filter is downloaded, different methods are required for installation in Mac OS and Windows. For Mac OS, copy the PDF Filter into the XTension folder within the QuarkXPress application folder. For Windows, run the Install.exe file inside the Freebies folder on the QuarkXPress installation CD.

Both Windows and Mac OS versions of the filter require that you accept the end-user license agreement. Make sure the Adobe PDF PPD is available in the PPD Manager. (For details on installing PPDs, see the earlier section "Installing and Configuring the PostScript Print Driver for Mac OS.")

Using the PDF Filter QuarkXTension

Just as Acrobat Distiller has job options, the PDF Filter has preferences. To set the PDF Filter preferences, choose Edit | Preferences | PDF Export.

As shown in Figures 17-6 and 17-7, the PDF Export Preferences dialog box includes the basic features suggested for an online document. Metadata about the

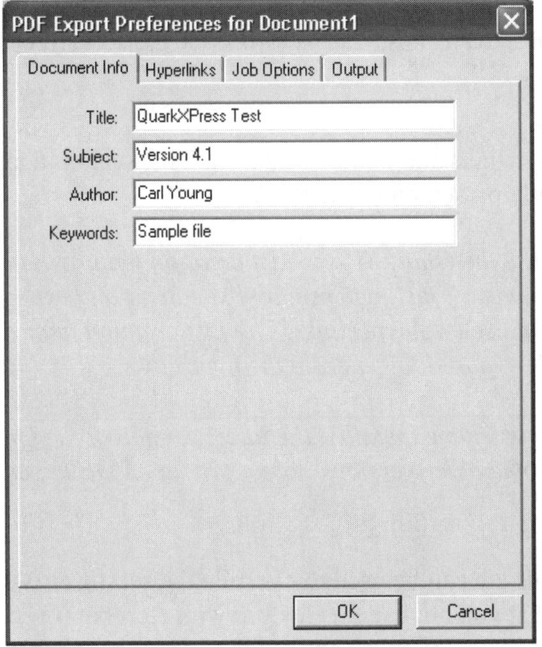

FIGURE 17-6 PDF Export Preferences include the capability to create metadata in PDFs.

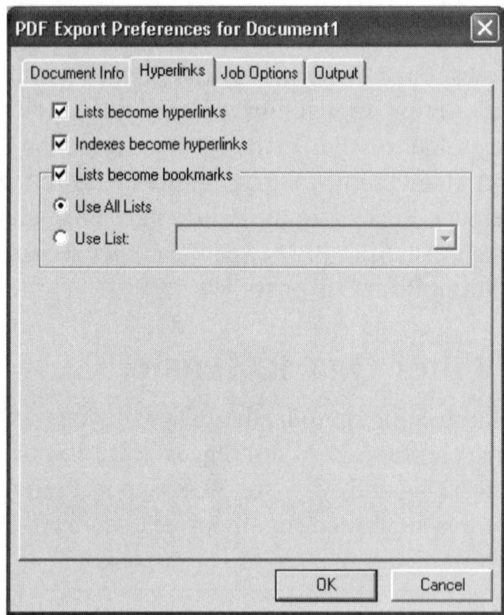

FIGURE 17-7 QuarkXPress lists can be used as the basis for hyperlinks and bookmarks in a PDF.

document, and hyperlinks and bookmarks from lists, such as a table of contents, can be automatically passed on to the PDF.

CAUTION *You must use the QuarkXPress List creation feature to get the hyperlinks to work. You can't just type pseudo list entries and expect the PDF Filter to convert those into hyperlinks. The List creation feature inserts the commands required to generate the hyperlinks.*

NOTE *Make sure you have installed the latest version of the QuarkXTension for Indexes. Some older versions do not produce PDF hyperlinks from index entries.*

The Job Options tab can be used to override the settings in Acrobat Distiller. It is recommended that you not use this feature with Acrobat 6 because the newest version of Distiller has many more options than are available here.

Last, go to the Output tab and select Adobe PDF as the Printer Description.

Exporting the PDF

Once you have set your preferences, you are ready to export the PDF. Versions 4 and 5 rely on Acrobat Distiller to create the PDF. Unfortunately, QuarkXPress may not find Distiller immediately. When you choose Export | Utilities, you may see the Locate Acrobat Distiller dialog box shown in Figure 17-8.

Navigate to your Acrobat installation directory, and go into the Distillr folder. Select the acrodist.exe file to tell QuarkXPress where Distiller can be found. Now that QuarkXPress knows where Acrobat Distiller is located, you can export your PDF. Simply save the PDF in a location and with a name you can remember.

As shown in Figure 17-9, you can also access your PDF Export Preferences from the Export as PDF dialog box. If you want to export only a range of pages, enter the page numbers in the Pages field. Another option is to export facing pages as a single spread.

A 100-Percent Non-Adobe Solution

QuarkXPress version 6 comes with its own PDF-generating capability, eleminating the need for the user to have Acrobat 6 installed. Version 6 includes Jaws PDF

FIGURE 17-8 Look for the file acrodist.exe in the Acrobat 6 Distillr folder.

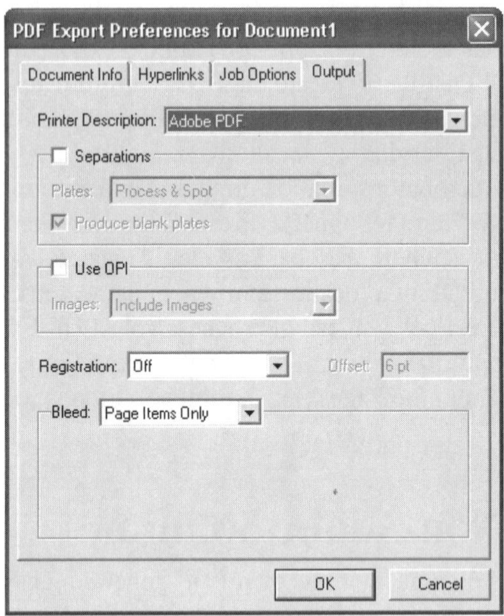

FIGURE 17-9 The Export to PDF dialog box gives you access to PDF Export Preferences.

Library, which brings Jaws PDF Creator technology to QuarkXPress users. As you may have noticed from all the previous steps, quite a bit of user configuration was required to export PDFs from previous versions of QuarkXPress. The process is something like installing an after-market sunroof on your car.

QuarkXPress 6 makes PDF export much simpler because PDF creation was installed at the factory. Just choose Export | Layout as PDF to bring up a screen similar to the one shown earlier in Figure 17-9. The only difference is the Preferences button has been relabeled Options. Or, if you prefer to continue to create using Acrobat Distiller, you can certainly do that instead. The process is the same as described for the previous versions 5 and 6.

As shown in Figure 17-10, setup is accomplished from Preferences (Windows: Edit | Preferences | PDF | Options, or Mac OS: QuarkXPress | Preferences | PDF | Options).

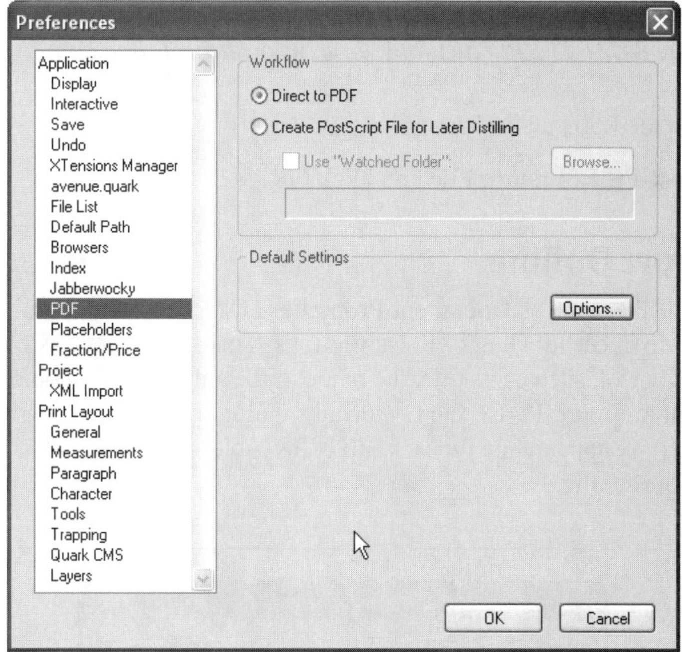

FIGURE 17-10 Version 6 users can directly export PDFs, or create PostScript files to be processed by Acrobat Distiller.

Print Driver Configuration

Users of the Windows version of QuarkXPress 6 will still need to install a PostScript Print Driver to make the direct to PDF export function work. (See the earlier section "Installing and Configuring the PPD for Windows" for details. Use the latest Adobe PostScript driver.)

Mac OS users do not have to add a special print driver if they have Acrobat 6 installed on their machines. The print driver must be configured to print to a file, as shown in Figure 17-11.

Follow these steps to configure a Windows printer to print to a file:

1. Go to Start | Printers and Faxes.
2. Right-click the Generic PostScript Printer and choose Properties.

Selecting the default "Generic PostScript Printer" PPD may result in color and font problems in the PDFs produced. Use the Distiller PPD, or the DDAPv3 PPD available from ***www.direct2.time.com****.*

3. Go to the Ports tab in Properties.
4. Choose FILE: Print to File and click OK.

PDF Export Options

Layout Info is the same as Document Properties | Description in Acrobat, or Document Info in earlier QuarkXPress versions. This field is for basic metadata about the document, such as its title, the name of the author, subject, and keywords.

As shown in Figure 17-12, the Hyperlinks dialog box has been expanded to include basic link appearance types: visible, invisible, and so on. Also included is a default Zoom setting.

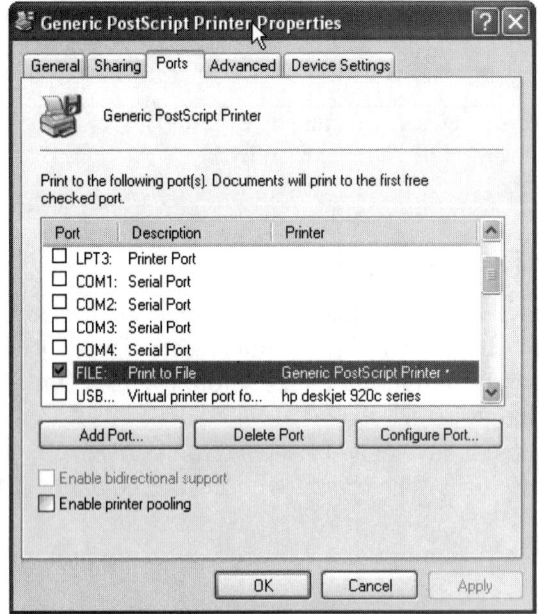

FIGURE 17-11 Windows PostScript Printer configured to print to a file.

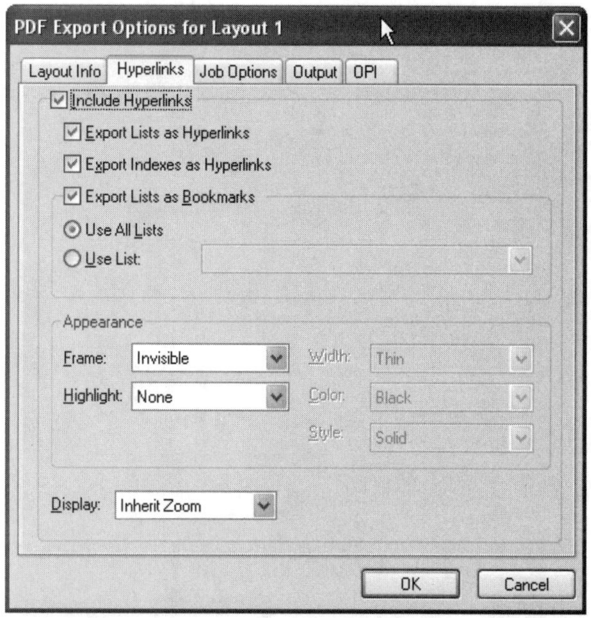

FIGURE 17-12 PDF Export Preferences include choices for visible or invisible hyperlinks.

Unlike earlier versions that depended heavily on Acrobat Distiller, the direct export feature of QuarkXPress 6 does require careful attention to the Job Options dialog box, as shown in Figure 17-13. These options will be used to create the PDF, so be sure to set them as the job requires. (For tips on Job Options settings, see Chapter 3.)

The Output dialog box is for specifying color type. In general, you will want Composite for nearly all PDF creations. Acrobat 6 Professional includes options for previewing and printing color separations. (See Chapter 18 for more information.)

Other options give you a choice for the appropriate color model, such as CMYK or RGB, and whether to include blank pages and registration marks. Set the Bleed Type to whatever is required by the job. Only use Open Prepress Interface (OPI) if that is what your process uses.

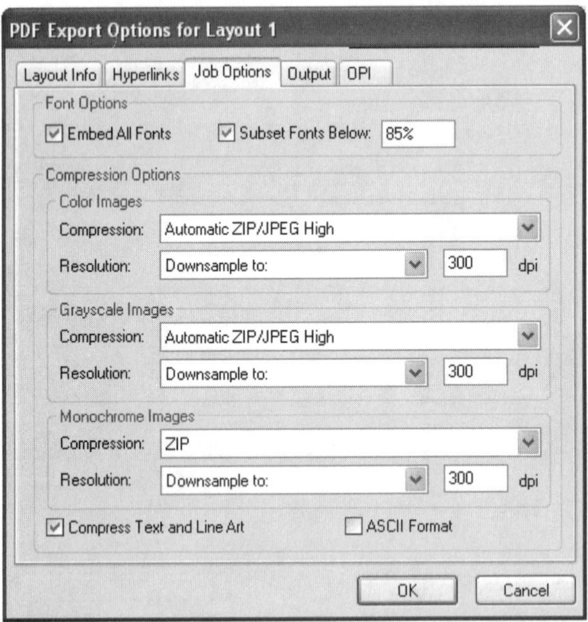

FIGURE 17-13 Sample Job Options for a high-quality PDF to be printed on an imagesetter.

Summary

QuarkXPress 6 has greatly simplified the process of creating PDFs, especially for users of the Macintosh. Users of earlier versions can use Acrobat Distiller to turn PostScript files into print-ready PDFs, or they can use the PDF Filter and Distiller to create interactive PDFs for online delivery. However, some configuration of printer drivers is required to produced PDFs from Version 6 in Windows and for all earlier versions of QuarkXPress.

Chapter 18

Preflighting and Color Printing

Acrobat 6 Professional includes new tools for the publishing industry. On the creation side, Acrobat 6 includes preset capabilities to create industry-standard PDF/X files.

Creators and publishers also can check the readiness of their PDFs for printing by using new preflighting tools built into Acrobat 6 Professional. These tools permit Acrobat users to perform sophisticated file inspections that were once limited to only prepress experts.

Color Printing and PDF

The use of Acrobat is exploding in both the business world and in government as businesses see how much money they can save with electronic documents. Ironically, the acceptance of Acrobat is moving more slowly in the industry that gave Adobe its start: publishing.

Many in the publishing world, especially printers, have been wary of Acrobat. Some have only recently recouped their investments in updated workflow and printing technologies, and they are reluctant to invest more to incorporate PDF. Others have lost lots of business as customers dropped paper in favor of electronic formats, such as the Web and Acrobat, and they hesitate to use a technology that can be a competitor.

Even with these handicaps, PDF use is growing in the publishing world. It is poised to become the industry standard for file exchange among customers, the design community, and the publishing world.

PDF/X: The PDF Publishing Standard

For proof of this trend, put yourself in the position of being a Madison Avenue advertising agency. If your Global 500 client wants to place an ad in one of Time, Inc.'s stable of magazines, you can't follow your existing practice and submit the ad in QuarkXPress anymore.

Instead, you have to submit a PDF (which QuarkXPress can, of course, produce). You can't even use a rival standard, *TIFF/IT,* which is a bitmap format similar to the TIFF image your scanner produces.) And you can't submit any old kind of PDF. It has to be a specific kind, known as PDF/X-1a.

The digital production staff at Time, Inc., has created a web site, **www.direct2.time.com,** that details how to create a PDF/X-1a for submittal. In bold, red type, the site announces **2004: 100 percent PDF/X.** See Figure 18-1 for an early 2004 view of the web site.

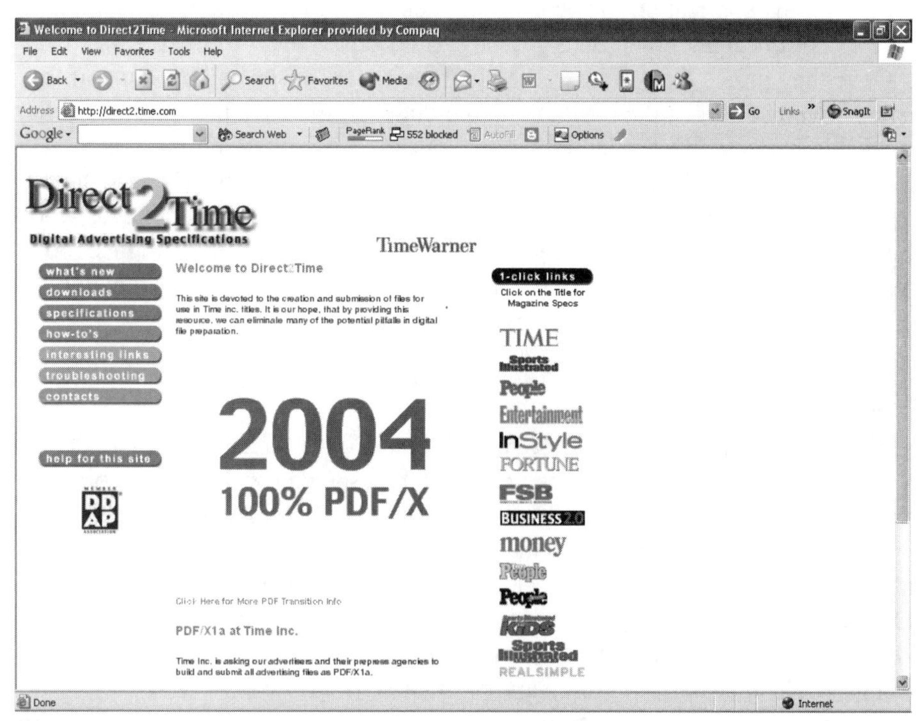

FIGURE 18-1 Direct2.Time.com provides information on how to create PDF/X files from the most commonly used advertising design applications.

"Time, Inc., being the 900-pound gorilla in the magazine industry, helps pave the way for new technology adoption." Erik Cullins, Associate Director of Digital Development at Time, Inc., explains. "If you have doubts about whether it works, I suggest you pick up a copy of *Sports Illustrated* some time and see for yourself."

I've had the pleasure of having Erik on a conference panel I hosted, and he does a great job of explaining why the publishing industry is moving to PDF.

First of all, PDF/X1-a is a package of fonts, text, and graphics. If you submit application data, such as an Adobe Illustrator or QuarkXPress file, you have to work to make sure the fonts, text, and graphics are properly bundled on your end, and then hope that the fonts, text, and graphics are correctly unbundled at the receiver's end. Put yourself in the place of Time, Inc.'s production staff, and consider your workflow. You are receiving tens of thousands of ads each year, which have to be placed in more than a dozen magazines printed at many different sites around the world. Before Time, Inc., started using PDF/X, the company had to check all the application files containing ads that came in, move the application files into the magazines, and then get magazines out to the printing plants.

Once they pulled that off, then they had their work inspected by some of the sharpest-eyed editors in the business, and by clients that have multimillion dollar advertising budgets. It's a relentless workflow, loaded with potential pitfalls.

By standardizing on PDF/X-1a, Time, Inc., is asking its advertisers to supply files in a uniform way. Even though PDF works today, Time, Inc., believes Adobe when Adobe says PDF will be improved to work with future technologies, too. This means Time, Inc., will be able to move its publications into a completely digital world, if that is where the market ends up.

What Is PDF/X?

As you learned in previous chapters, you can create PDFs in many ways. A PDF/X (Portable Document Format Exchange) is a PDF designed specifically for print publishing and approved by the ISO. PDF/X isn't just an Adobe or Time, Inc., format. Members of the committee that established PDF/X include Creo, Callas, Enfocus, RR Donnelley, Hewlett-Packard, Heidelberg, Apago, Kodak, IdeaAlliance, DDAP, and Young & Rubicam. No interactive features are allowed—sounds, movies, and form fields are unnecessary for print publishing, and they can even be a hindrance. The files must be Acrobat 4-compatible (PDF 1.3).

The most common problems reported in a recent Seybold Report were missing fonts, graphics, page size, missing bleeds, and incorrect color spaces. PDF/X goes a long way to resolving those problems.

A PDF/X-1a is created by following a set of rules, as you can see in Figure 18-2. Fonts must be embedded and the file must be Acrobat 4-compatible. Trapping and the TrimBox or ArtBox must be specified. Transfer functions and halftone screen frequencies are not permitted. In Figure 18-2, you can see this PDF/X-1a is built for output on a SWOP web color press.

Another version of PDF/X is called PDF/X-3, which is similar to PDF/X-1a. The main difference is that the color can be managed by several common methods, such as ICC-based color spaces. PDF/X1-a is most commonly used in the United States and Canada, and PDF/X-3 is most often used in Europe, particularly Germany.

Creating a PDF/X-1a

To create a PDF/X-1a, you can use Acrobat Distiller 6. From your application, choose File | Print | Adobe PDF.

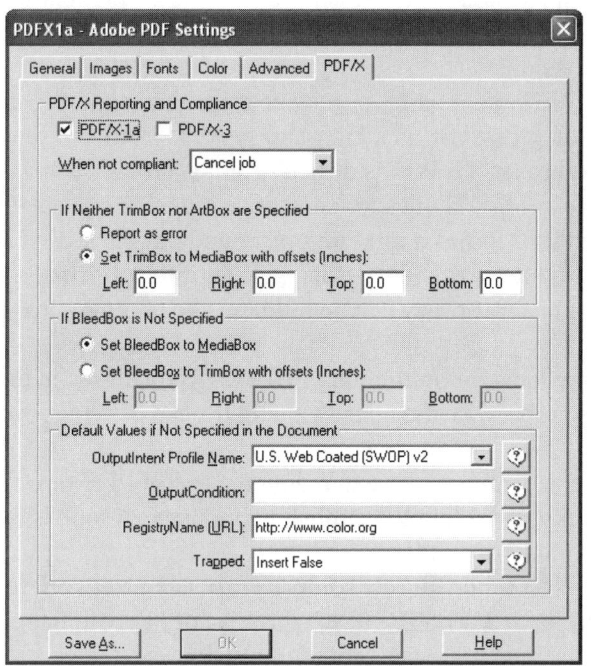

FIGURE 18-2 PDF/X-1a Adobe PDF Settings from Adobe Acrobat Distiller 6

In Windows, click Properties. In Adobe PDF Settings, choose PDFX1a (Adobe omits the slash and dash from the name) from the Default Settings pull-down menu. In Mac OS, choose PDF Options | Adobe PDF Settings | PDFX1a.

If you are going to create a PDF/X for Time, Inc., you should download the job options from **www.direct2.time.com**. Uncompress the files and drop them on your copy of Distiller.

TIP *Only the Distiller in Acrobat 6 Professional ships with PDF/X Job Options already predefined. However, you can create PDF/X-1a files from the Distiller in Acrobat Standard by using the Time job options, by creating your own, or by using the PDF/X job options supplied by your print vendor.*

Advantages of PDF/X

Although many in the publishing world send application files, fonts, and graphics for printing, there is another widely used format. This format is TIFF/IT, a bitmap format. TIFF/IT can accurately represent images and colors, but it is still a bitmap, or an image file. TIFF/IT files can be extremely large, so they are difficult to manage and to transmit.

Creating a TIFF/IT file requires specialized tools and expertise—creating TIFF/IT generally can only be done on a high-end system. There are few preflighting tools, and fixing a broken TIFF/IT is difficult. While TIFF/IT can work today, it is difficult to repurpose TIFF/IT files for alternative digital formats.

PDF, on the other hand, is a mixture of text and graphics. Text is still text, and isn't converted into lots of tiny dots as happens in bitmap formats. Graphics can remain as vector objects, or they can be bitmaps like photographs. File sizes are relatively small.

There are many tools for preflighting PDFs (as you will see in the section "Preflighting in Acrobat 6 Professional") and PDFs can be repurposed for alternative media.

Lastly, Adobe is committed to expanding the use of PDF throughout the business community, including the publishing industry. Adobe is buying network TV ad time to promote PDF adoption.

When was the last time you saw someone produce a network television commercial to promote TIFF/IT? Never, and it's not likely to happen. But you and your clients will see more ads promoting PDF.

Use PDF/X-1a, and you will have a format that will make it easy for you to reliably deliver content to your print provider. If you are a print provider, show your customers how to create PDF/X-1a files. Acrobat 6 Professional has made this easy. You will save yourself a lot of headaches, and probably save some time and money, too.

PDF/X Resources

For more information, make use of the following sites:

- **www.ddap.org/resources/pdfx_imp.html**
- **www.pdf-x.com**
- **www.iso.org**
- **www.gentpdfworkgroup.org**
- **www.planetpdf.com**
- **www.pdfzone.com**
- **http://Direct2.Time.com**

Quality Assurance

When creating PDFs for print, you should perform some specific quality checks. This process is called *preflighting.*

Because of the wide adoption of PDF, several companies have produced software tools for preflighting PDFs. In the section "Preflighting with PitStop Professional," you will learn more about Enfocus PitStop Professional (**www.enfocus.com**), but you should also know that callas (**www.callassoftware .com/en/**), Markzware (**www.markzware.com**), ARTS PDF (**www.artspdf.com**), and others make PDF preflighting software as well.

Preflighting in Acrobat 6 Professional

Acrobat 6 Professional includes a new set of preflighting tools that helps you verify your output. There are some specific tools for verifying that a PDF is PDF/X-compliant. Use the following procedure to start your PDF/X-1a preflighting process. The process is similar for PDF/X-3, but it includes the color management features allowed in PDF/X-3.

1. Open the document to be checked.
2. Choose Document | Preflight | PDF/X button.
3. Select either PDF/X-1a or PDF/X-3, as shown in Figure 18-3.
4. Click Done.

NOTE *Acrobat Professional Preflight will not fix major problems, such as RGB color or missing fonts, to make the files PDF/X-compliant.*

Save As PDF/X-1a

The *Save As PDF/X-1a* option runs a preflight check, embeds an ICC color profile, and then saves the file as PDF/X-1a. In the Save As PDF/X-1a dialog box, you can select a selection of subsets. SWOP_CGATS-TR001 is a good choice for marketing collateral printed on coated stock. A similar option exists for PDF/X-3.

In addition in the Profiles window itself, you can run additional checks that go beyond the PDF/X-1a standard, such as PDF/X Plus. You can set the maximum number of color plates, and the minimum resolution of halftone and bitmap images.

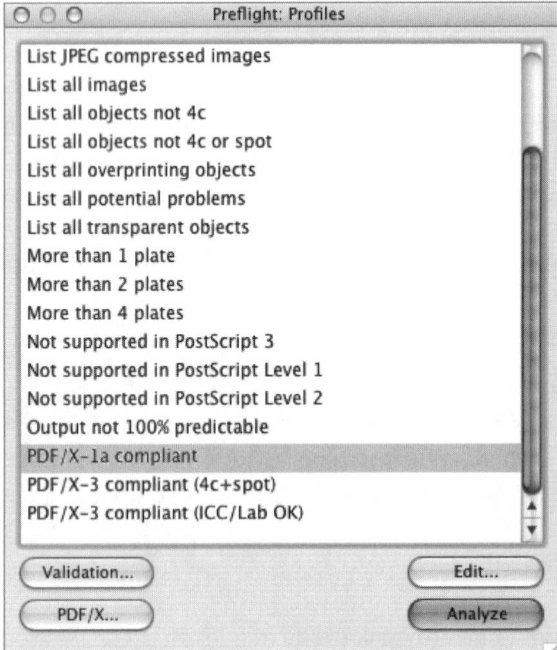

FIGURE 18-3 Preflighting options in Adobe Acrobat 6 Professional for PDF/X files

Once the check is run, you will see the results:

- An embossed red circle indicates the check failed. Click the Report button to see the details of the preflight check.
- If the report is successful, you will be asked for a location to save the document, and a green embossed circle appears. Click OK to close the window.

Verify

The *Verify* option runs the PDF/X preflight report, but it does not save the file or insert an ICC profile. You also can apply a stricter set of standards, such as checking the number of color plates required and the minimum resolution of images.

Extract ICC Profile

This option will remove an embedded ICC profile. You can then use the Save As PDF/X-1a option to add a new one.

Remove PDF/X

This option will remove PDF/X-specific information from a PDF if you have changed the file in some way to make it no longer PDF/X-compatible. If any PDF/X information is in the file, a dialog box will appear and ask you if you want to remove this information. Click Yes.

PDF/X-1a Sets

You can use this option to create a customized conversion set that is optimized for your specific needs. These sets include output intent and a printing profile. Use the following procedure to create a customized PDF/X-1a conversion set:

1. Click the PDF/X-1a Sets button.
2. Click New.
3. Enter a name for the set. You have the option to add other validation criteria, such as the number of color plates allowed, and the minimum resolution for halftone and bitmap images.
4. To add an ICC profile, click Browse (Windows) or Choose (Mac OS) and select the profile.
5. Enter a description of the intended printing condition. This informational text is required.
6. Enter additional information for the recipient. This field is optional. Click OK.

Previewing Color Separations

You can preview color separations in Acrobat Professional, as shown in Figure 18-4. Remember that onscreen separation preview may not be accurate unless you are using a color management system and if you have calibrated your monitor to match your color system.

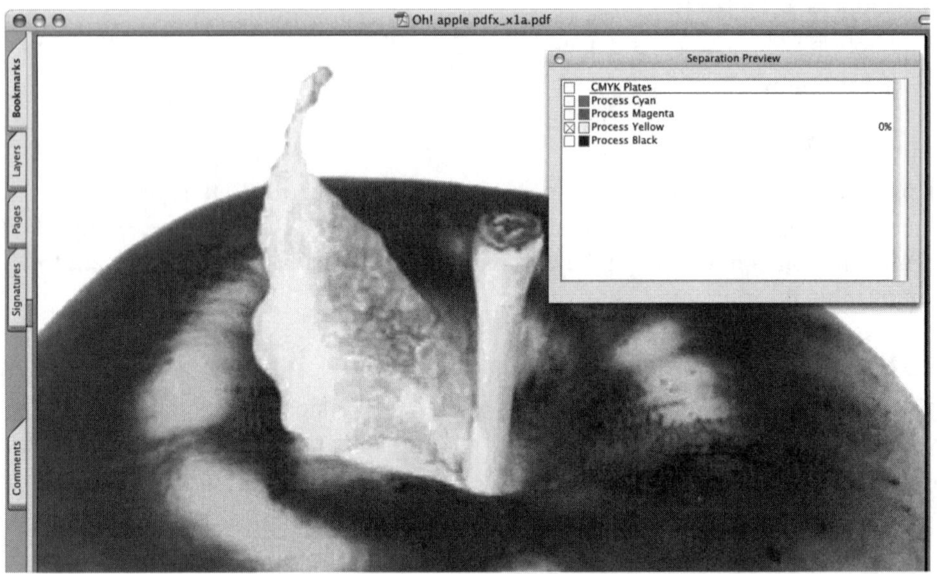

FIGURE 18-4 Separation preview

NOTE *Single process plates appear in grayscale.*

Use the following procedure to preview color separations onscreen:

1. Choose Advanced | Separation Preview.
2. Deselect colors to no longer see those onscreen.
3. Move your cursor over an area on the PDF. The percentage of the selected color will display next to the color.
4. You can convert a spot color to process by clicking on the name of the color until the process color icon appears. The icon is the four process colors arranged as interlocking triangles that form a square.

NOTE *If separation preview is a key part of your workflow, you should consider ARTS PDF Crackerjack. Crackerjack can map spot colors and convert RGB color to CMYK. For more information, see* ***www.artspdf.com****.*

Previewing Transparency Flattening

Another common problem for PostScript printers is transparency in artwork. Adobe and other companies that make graphics programs have made it easy for designers to use transparency in their artwork, so they do. To print correctly on some PostScript printers, transparency must be flattened, or turned into raster images. See your vendor for requirements.

You can take an advance look at the results of transparency flattening in Acrobat Professional.

1. Choose Advanced | Transparency Flattener Preview.
2. Click Refresh to display a preview in the blank space below the flattener settings.
3. Zoom in by clicking in the preview area. Press the spacebar and drag to pan.
4. Specify your Preview options. The settings available become active, depending on the content of the art and the settings in the Advanced Print Setup dialog box.
5. Set the degree of rasterization in complex areas of the art in the Flattener Settings.
6. Set a resolution for the degree of rasterization in complex areas.
7. Specify your flattening options:

    - **Convert Text to Outlines** turns text into graphics. This makes the text unsearchable and may make small fonts appear larger. Text width will stay consistent. Flattening performance will be degraded.
    - **Convert All Strokes to Outlines** keeps stroke widths consistent. Thin strokes, like small fonts, may appear larger.
    - **Clip Complex Regions** preserves the boundaries along object paths between vector and raster art. It can create complex clipping paths that can take a long time to compute.

Preflight Profiles

Acrobat Professional includes 21 preflight profiles, and a set of more than 150 conditions you can assemble into your own, customized profiles. As discussed in a preceding section, these profiles can check for PDF/X-1a compliance, but they also can be used for much more.

For example, let's say a manager wants to know if a design project is going to cost more than the estimate. Assume the estimate was based on using four colors and, therefore, four color plates. You could run the "More than four plates" profile to see if a designer had used a process color in addition to the four colors specified in the estimate.

Another common question is whether fonts are embedded in a PDF. You can build a custom report that will check your PDFs for font embedding.

To run a profile, choose Document | Preflight. Then select your profile and click Analyze. The profile will check the PDF and display the results. You can use the Preflight: Results dialog box to save the analysis. Click Done to close the Results dialog box.

Keep the following points in mind when working in the Preflight: Results dialog box:

- Use Active Snap to isolate problems. When you select a problem in the Preflight:Results dialog box, snap will display the problem area on the right side of the screen.
- Click the plus sign (+) adjacent to a page number in the Problems part of the report. Double-click to see the item on the PDF page. A red dotted line will be around the object in the main document window. You may need to move the Result screen to see the red line in the main document window.
- Use Hits per Rule to cut down on the number of times a violation shows up in the report.

Creating a Preflight Profile

You can modify existing profiles by adding, changing, and deleting rules of existing profiles, or you can create a new one by defining your own. For example, one common area of concern is whether fonts are embedded in a PDF. You can create a preflight profile to check for embedded fonts, and use this profile on all kinds of PDFs, not just ones designed for print.

NOTE *The PDF/X profiles are locked and cannot be edited.*

A new profile is required to have one rule and one condition. A rule and a condition for checking font embedding already exist, but not a profile. Use the following procedure to create a profile that uses the existing rule:

1. Choose Document | Preflight if the Preflight: Profiles dialog box isn't already open.
2. Click Edit.
3. Click the New Profile icon below the Profiles column.
4. Enter **Check for font embedding** in the Name box. You also can enter a description. Click OK.
5. Select Fonts not embedded in the Rules column.
6. Click the plus sign to the left of the rule. Notice that the condition attached to this rule is not embedded.
7. Click the green, left-pointing double chevron between the Profiles and Rules columns to attach the rule to the new profile.
8. Click OK.

To use your new profile, highlight it in the Preflight: Profiles window and click Analyze. You then can create a report of the fonts embedded (or missing!).

Exporting and Importing Preflight Profiles

New or customized profiles can be shared within your organization, with clients or with vendors. You export the profile as a package, which is then imported by others who want to use it. Use the following procedure to export, and then import the profile:

1. Select the profile in the Preflight: Profiles dialog box.
2. Click Edit.
3. Click the Export icon. Be careful to select the icon with the arrow pointing into the floppy disk.
4. Specify a location and click Save. The Profile is saved with a file extension of *.kfp.

5. To import, click the Import button below the Profiles column in the Preflight: Edit profiles.
6. Navigate to the location of the profile, select it, and click Open.
7. You can rename the profile and add a description. Click OK. The imported profile appears in the Profile column with a lock on it.

Preflighting with PitStop Professional

Enfocus PitStop Professional will run preflight checks like Acrobat 6 Professional, but PitStop can go beyond Acrobat to fix many common problems. For complete information on PitStop and other tools, see **www.enfocus.com**.

PitStop Professional, available for Windows and Mac OS, is a plug-in that integrates with Acrobat 6. More menu choices will appear after installation, and PitStop adds several new groups of icons to your Acrobat taskbar.

Many of PitStop's most powerful features are displayed from the Window menu. For example, the PitStop Inspector provides information on PDF objects you select with PitStop's tools. In many instances, you can edit a PDF object, such as a graphic or text, by using the Inspector and the appropriate PitStop tool.

PitStop PDF Profile Control Panel

PitStop supplies a number of default profiles you can use to preflight PDFs, including several for PDF/X. You can, of course, create new profiles as well. As industry bodies adopt or create subsets of PDF/X, Enfocus publishes updated profiles at its web site, **www.enfocus.com**.

Unlike Acrobat, PitStop preflight profiles can include options to fix problems that it detects. For example, if you use one of PitStop's PDF/X profiles and the profile finds that a font is not embedded, PitStop can embed the font. See Figure 18-5 for an example of a PitStop profile.

The following example shows how to use PitStop to preflight a PDF/X for magazine production:

1. Choose Window | Show PitStop Preflight Panel. This opens the PDF Profile Control Panel.
2. Select PDF/X-1a PLUS Magazines v3.
3. Choose Regular Preflight. Specify whether to check the entire document, a page range or the current page.

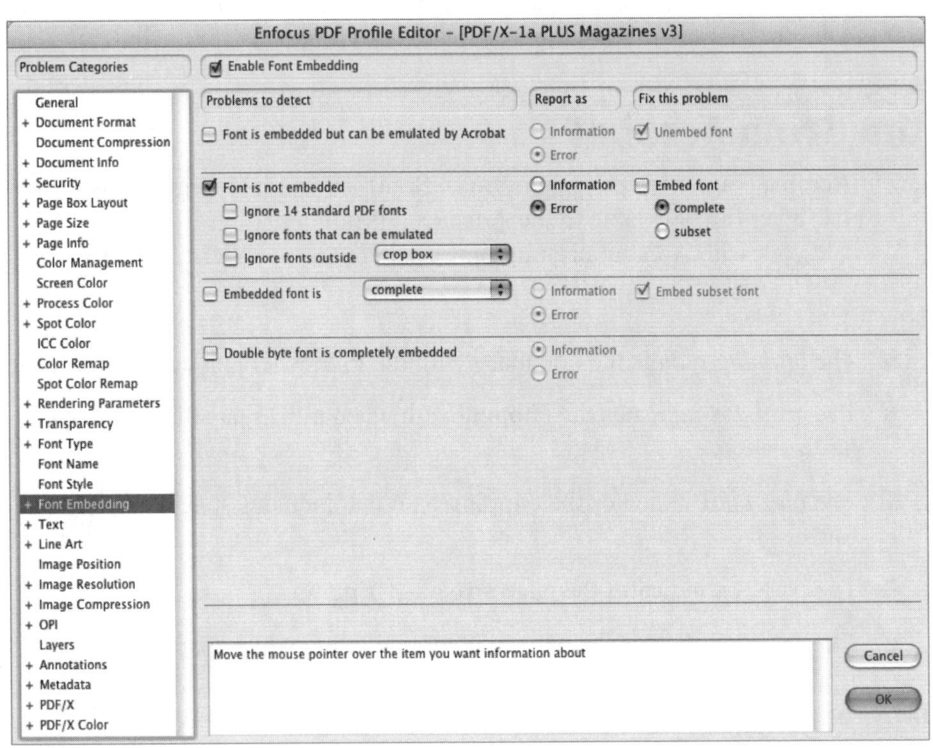

FIGURE 18-5 PitStop profiles can report, and fix, many problems that crop up in PDFs, such as missing fonts.

4. Click Create Report.

The profile runs, and then generates a report. The first page of the report displays the severity of the problems encountered, and whether PitStop has found a problem and fixed it. These errors and warnings are all hyperlinked back to the preflighted PDF.

NOTE *Enfocus has long used the term "Certified PDF" to mean a PDF that has met its preflight testing requirements and is ready to be moved along in the Enfocus Certified PDF workflow. A Certified PDF is indicated by a green check mark in the Acrobat toolbar. This kind of Certified PDF is not to be confused with the Certified Document terminology used by Adobe. In Acrobat 6, Adobe defines a Certified Document as one that is trustworthy.*

Many design firms, prepress operations, and print facilities use PitStop Professional for routine preflighting and for fixing problem PDFs.

Printing from Acrobat

New in Acrobat 6 are more printing options. Some are available right in the Print dialog box, others are available in the Advanced Printing dialog.

As you work with Acrobat printing options, here are some terms you should know:

- The *clipping path* is the boundary within a PDF where objects may appear.
- The *crop box* indicates the clipping path when a PDF page is first opened or displayed.
- The *bleed box* indicates the clipping path that includes space for bleeds and folds.
- The *trim box* indicates the page size after trimming.
- The *art box* indicates the page content, including white space.

Print Options

Choose File | Print and you will see a large dialog box with many options. Prominently displayed in the lower-right corner is a thumbnail picture of the document, including the page size and how the document will print on the selected printer.

By default, Acrobat will automatically rotate and center pages, and scale pages to fit on the default page size of the selected printer.

When printing from Acrobat, you can choose from the following options:

- *Subset* pull-down menu prints all pages in the print range, or odd or even pages.
- *Print What* pull-down menu will print just the document, the document and comments, or Form Fields only.
- *Page Scaling* pull-down menu includes None; Fit to Paper; Shrink Large Pages, Tile Large Pages; and Tile All Pages. For a preview of how tiling works, see Figure 18-6.

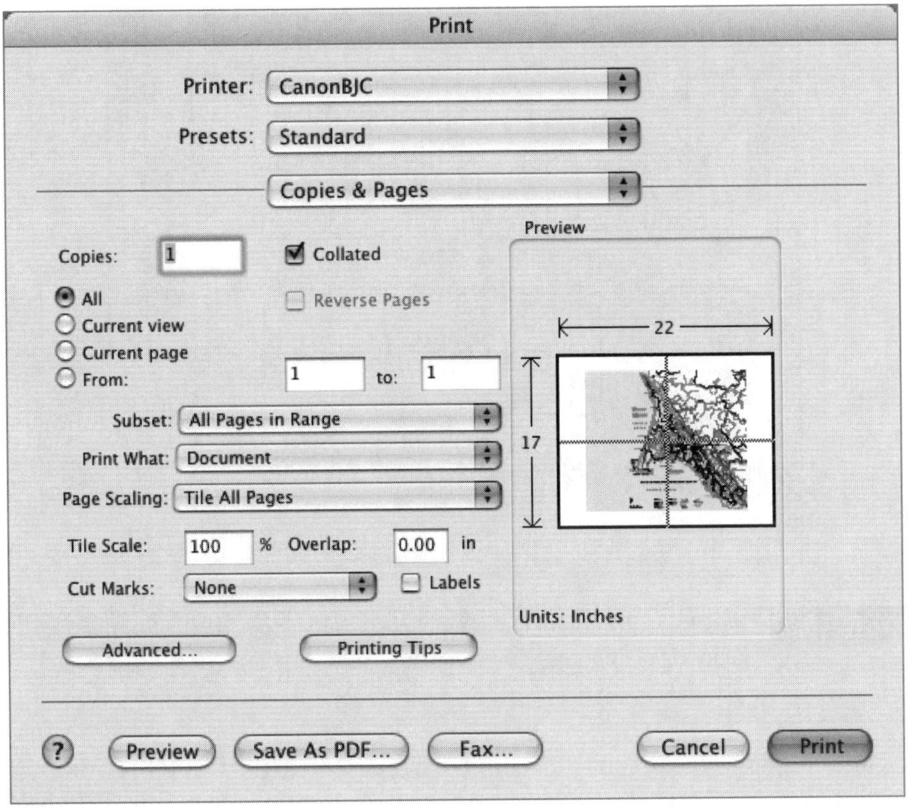

FIGURE 18-6 Acrobat 6 Print dialog box. The preview image shows how a 22-inch by 17-inch drawing will be printed on four 8.5-inch by 11-inch pages.

Click Print to send the print job to the printer you specified in the Printer: pull-down menu.

Print with Comments

When you choose File | Print, and choose Document and Comments from the Print What pull-down menu, Acrobat prints a document that is a composite of the comments and the PDF.

Choosing File | Print with Comments gives you much more control over how the PDFs and comments are printed, as shown in Figure 18-7.

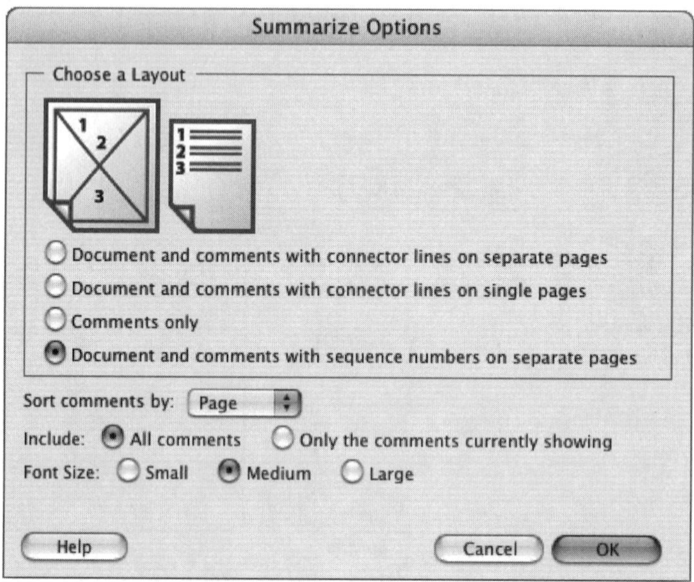

FIGURE 18-7 The File | Print with Comments command brings up the Summarize Options dialog box. You can print Comments in several different formats.

For example, you can send a PDF of a magazine ad to a client for review. The client can use Acrobat 6 to make comments. When you receive the PDF back from the client, you can use this feature to print the client's comments. For more information on commenting, see Chapter 7.

You can choose from four different layouts, including one option to print only the comments.

You also can sort comments by page, author, date, and type; screen out comments not showing in the document; and pick a font size for the printed comments.

When you click OK, you see a preview of your selected layout. Click Cancel to choose a new layout, or click Print to send the document and comments to the printer.

Advanced Printing

Adobe has greatly increased the functionality inside the Print dialog box in Acrobat 6 Professional. If you select a printer and choose Advanced, you will see a large selection of output options for printing directly from Acrobat.

You can use these output settings in a variety of ways. For example, you could take a PDF designed for a high-end printing system and convert the colors for proofing on a desktop printer. While designers and others may find these options helpful, for the most part, these options are for use inside commercial printing operations.

Choose File | Print | Advanced to display the Advanced Print Setup dialog box. The dialog box has four setting groups on the left, and details about each setting on the right. A preview image displays in the lower-left corner. These settings can change the output from the PDF, but do not change the file itself.

Output Settings

You can override the printing profile of the PDF in the Advanced Printing dialog box. This setting controls color output.

TIP *Use the Print As Image option for printing to a desktop printer only if all other options have failed. The image this option creates is a bitmap.*

Your color output options are

- **Composite**, which prints all colors on a single plate to a PostScript printer.
- **Composite Gray**, which is used to print to non-PostScript devices.
- **Separations**, which prints separations to PostScript devices.
- **In-RIP Separations**, which sends data to a PostScript Level 3 device. The device then creates the separations.

The *Screening* option applies to halftone screen frequency. The options you have available here come from the PPD of the selected printer, and are specified as lines per inch (lpi) and dots per inch (dpi).

The *Flip* options are used for creating film. Check with your service provider on which options to use.

Printer Profile lets you select the profile for your printer. You should generally select the profile that comes with the printer you have selected, unless otherwise directed by your service provider.

Apply Working Color Spaces lets you apply a color profile to uncalibrated colors in the document.

Apply Proof Settings lets you simulate the proofing device specified in Advanced | Proof Setup. Available only for composite color.

Simulate Overprinting displays how spot colors will display in composite color documents. Do not use this option if your printer supports overprinting.

Use Maximum Available JPEG2000 Image Resolution controls JPEG2000 image resolution. When enabled, the maximum resolution in the image is used. When deselected, the resolution will be set by the Transparency Flattener.

Ink Manager

The *Ink Manager* lets you override the colors used in the PDF document. For example, if your document uses a spot color, you can use the Ink Manager to change the color to CMYK process color.

To use Ink Manager, you use the check boxes next to the ink name. To include the plate, enable the box. To omit the plate, disable the box. To change a process color to CMYK, click until a four-color box appears. For more on Ink Manager, see the previous section on previewing color separations.

Marks and Bleeds

The next group of options is for placing Marks and Bleeds on pages. *Marks* are printer marks for registration, trimming, or cropping pages. *Bleeds* are objects that extend beyond the page. When the pages are cut, or trimmed, the object then appears flush with the edge of the page.

When working with this dialog box, you have the following options:

- **Emit Printer Marks** turns on marks that the authoring application embedded in the PDF.
- **All Marks** prints all available marks.
- **Marks Style** gives you the option of choosing either Western marks or Eastern printer marks for use with Asian languages.
- **Crop Marks** places marks at the corners of each page to show PDF crop box boundaries.
- **Trim Marks** displays marks at the corners to indicate the PDF trim box boundaries.
- **Bleed Marks** puts marks beyond the page boundaries at corners to indicate where the PDF bleed box is located.
- **Registration Marks** puts marks outside the margin for aligning separations.

- **Color Bars** are used to adjust ink density, contrast, and other printing variables. This option puts a sample of each color outside the printable (crop) area.
- **Page Information** includes basic data about the file, including time, date, filename, page number, and name of the plate.

Transparency Flattening

Art containing transparency must be flattened before it can be printed. Examples of transparency are many kinds of drop shadows, Illustrator objects with feathering, and many layer effects.

Flattening divides overlapping transparent objects into separate pieces, so they can be printed. These new pieces can be rasterized bitmap images or vector objects.

When the Transparency Quality/Speed slider is all the way to the right, as many vector objects as possible will be preserved. When the slider is all the way to the left, entire images with transparency are rasterized.

Using this setting may mean trading print speed for quality. For example, if you push the slider all the way to the right, Acrobat will preserve as many objects as possible as vectors. This can make the print file huge, which can mean slow print times.

Moving the slider to the left will make the file size smaller and it will print faster. However, you may see noticeable loss in image quality in the print file. Using this setting is a trade-off between speed and image quality. If you experiment with the output, you should be able to find a balance that suits your job requirements.

For more information, see "Previewing Transparency Flattening" in a previous section.

PostScript Options

The Font and Resource Policy options give you control over the downloading of fonts and other PostScript resources. You also can set the PostScript language level in the Print Method pull-down menu.

Choosing a policy of *At Start* sends resources and fonts used on multiple pages at the beginning of the print stream. This option requires more printer memory, but it is the fastest method. To use less memory, use the slower *At Range* option to download fonts and resources at the time they are needed. Choose *Each Page* to download fonts and resources a page at a time for the lowest use of printer memory.

Printing Layers

Acrobat 6 generally prints visible layers. For example, if you are working with an ad that has text in different languages, the visible English layer would print, and the hidden German and French layers would not.

PDF creators also can specify whether layers print. For example, a graphic artist wanting to protect a copyright could set a hidden layer containing a watermark to always print.

You can change layer settings in Acrobat 6, assuming the file is unsecured. To change printing properties, use the following procedure:

1. Open the Layers Palette.
2. Select a layer.
3. Choose Options | Layer Properties.
4. Change the Print setting. Your options are Always Prints, Never Prints, and Prints When Visible.

Measuring Tools

Although there are many uses for Acrobat's measuring tools, they can be helpful for commercial printing.

First of all, you can turn on rules to give you some perspective. Choose View | Rulers to display rulers. Change ruler units by choosing Edit | Preferences | Units and Guides. You can choose from inches, centimeters, millimeters, picas, and points.

You can access the measuring tools by choosing Tools | Measuring | Show Measuring Toolbar. The Properties toolbar will appear as soon as you select a measuring tool and will display the results. Be sure to set the appropriate units on the right side of the Properties toolbar for accurate scaling.

The *Distance* tool is used to measure the distance between two points. Click to establish the first point. Position the mouse at the next point and click again. You can hold down SHIFT to draw a straight line.

The *Perimeter* tool measures angles and the outside perimeter polygons. To finish using the tool, click once to establish the endpoint, and then click a second time to end measuring.

The *Area* tool measures the inside area of polygons. End by positioning the circle over the starting point and clicking.

TIP *Turn on the Annotate option to create comments from the measured areas. Otherwise, the values in the properties bar disappear when you select a new tool.*

Cropping Pages

Although it's best to always set the proper margins in the authoring tool, you may have to trim pages after the PDF arrives at your workstation.

1. Choose View | Page Layout | Single Page to put Acrobat into single-page mode. This is the recommended view setting for cropping pages.
2. Choose Document | Pages | Crop. The crop pages dialog box shown in Figure 18-8 will appear.
3. You can display a PDF's document's crop box, bleed box, trim box, and art box. In many cases, these will be the same values.

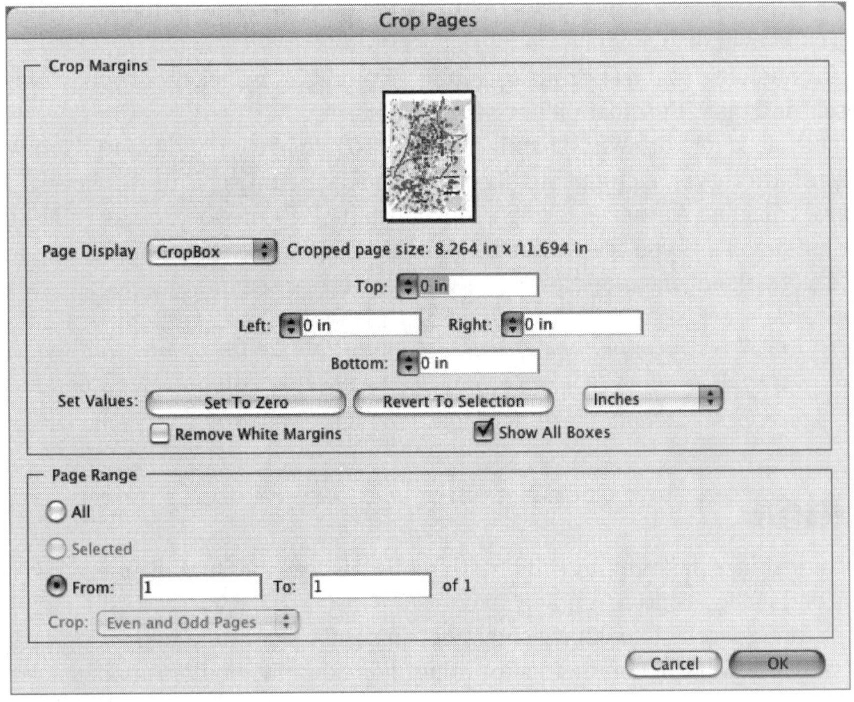

FIGURE 18-8 You can define crop margins and page ranges in the Crop Pages dialog box.

TIP *Use Remove White Margins if you want Acrobat to automatically trim white margins from the PDF.*

4. Use the Top, Left, Right, and Bottom settings to specify how much of the page you want to crop. The preview window shows the cropped area.
5. Specify a page range for which you want these settings to apply.
6. Click OK.

TIP *You also can use the Crop Tool (Tools | Advanced Editing) to visually crop pages.*

Job Definition Format (JDF)

Job Definition Format (JDF) is an XML-based standard for electronic job tickets. A JDF file can be inserted into the original page layout program, passed on to Acrobat, and then retrieved when the file reaches the print production facility.

The JDF standard is supported by major vendors, and is maintained by a group called CIP4. JDF incorporates features of two earlier technologies: the Print Production Format (PPF) and Adobe's Portable Job Ticket Format (PJTF). You can find more information at **www.cip4.org**.

You'll need to work with Distiller to put a JDF inside a PDF. Go to Acrobat Distiller (Advanced | Acrobat Distiller) and choose Settings | Edit Adobe PDF Settings. Click the Advanced tab and click Create Job Definition Format (JDF) file.

Alternatively, if you are working in an all-Adobe workflow, you can use Adobe's XMP metadata format to pass along information.

NOTE *You also can embed the Distiller Adobe PDF Settings (Job Options) inside the PDF. In the Advanced tab of the Adobe PDF Settings, enable the option Save Adobe PDF Settings.*

Imposition

Acrobat displays pages in logical order. In other words, the first page is the cover, the second is the inside cover, and so on.

This order works fine for onscreen viewing and for printing to desktop printers, but it may not work in commercial printing. For example, book printers use large sheets of paper for printing books. To make the best use of the paper, the pages will be printed out of logical order, but in a way that when the pages are printed, folded, and cut they will appear correctly in the book. This process is called *imposition.*

You cannot impose pages within Acrobat. You need a plug-in for that, and one of the most popular is Quite Imposing and Quite Imposing Plus from Quite Software (**www.quite.com**).

With these products, you can put any number of PDF pages on a single sheet, create booklets, and add and remove page numbers.

Summary

Adobe Acrobat 6 Professional includes a range of tools for creating and preflighting PDFs for print. In addition, there are a number of products for fixing PDFs, such as PitStop from Enfocus, and specialty tools, such as Quite Software's Quite Imposing, for specific uses.

Index

References to figures and illustrations are in italics.

A

Accelio, 7
accessibility
Accessibility checker, 105
Accessibility FAQ, 98-99
Auto Scroll, 25, 93
considerations, 97
creating accessible PDFs, 26-27
for Japanese, 27, 93
keyboard shortcuts, 93
new features in Acrobat 6, 93
Quick Check, 25
Read Out Loud, 25, 93, 94
reflow, 25, *26*, *27*, 93, 95-96
screen readers, 24
testing for accessibility, 106
for visually impaired, 25
Acrobat 6.0 Software Development Kit, 272
Acrobat Capture. *See* Capture
Acrobat Distiller, watched folders, 216
Acrobat eBook Reader, 7
Acrobat JavaScript, 248-249
adding a new menu item, 269-270
adding voice to an alert, 265
Alert Box, 263-264
automatically tabbing from one field to the next, 261-263
bookmarks, 253
displaying the date in a field, 257
Document Level, 250
e-mailing form data, 270-271
examples, 256-257, 259-270
Field Level, 250-253
On Focus, 252
Folder Level, 250
vs. HTML JavaScript, 249
hyperlinks, 254
inputting into Acrobat Professional, 255-256
JavaScript Console/Debugger, 258-259
On Lose Focus, 252
making Acrobat bark like a dog, 264-265
Mouse Down, 252
Mouse Enter, 252
Mouse Exit, 252
Mouse Up, 251-252
multimedia triggers, 252-253
naming fields, 254
objects, 256
page actions, 253
performing a calculation, 259-261
pop-up menus, 266-267
specifying a user preference, 268-269
syntax, 255-256
terminology, 254-255
triggers, 250-253
version sniffing, 271
where to use, 250-255
Acrobat Professional. *See* Professional, Acrobat
Acrobat Standard. *See* Standard, Acrobat
activePDF, 55
Adaptive Compression, 56
See also compression
AdLib eDocument Solutions eXpress & OCR, 58, 85, 221-222
Adobe Acrobat Capture. *See* Capture
Adobe Acrobat Distiller, 45
creating PDFs, 44
PostScript Printer Driver installation and configuration, 343-345
Adobe Acrobat version 6, 4
new language features, 194-197
product comparison, 5
Adobe Distiller Server. *See* Distiller Server

Adobe Document Server. *See* Document Server
Adobe Form Designer. *See* Form Designer
Adobe FrameMaker, 321-322
 bookmarks, 323
 creating PDFs from, 322
 creating Tagged PDFs, 102-103
 generating PDFs from, 324-325
 importing PDFs into, 322
 Links in PDF Setup, 323-324
 setting up for PDF generation, 322-324
 settings, 323
 Tagged PDFs, 323, *324*
Adobe Illustrator CS, 296-297
 creating PDFs from, 297-298
 file formats, 297
 File Info feature, 303-304
 presets, 297-301
 printing to Adobe PDF from, 301-303
Adobe InDesign, 310
 adding movies and sounds, 320-321
 behaviors, 316
 bookmarks, 317, 319
 Button tool, 314
 buttons, 314-316
 converting objects to buttons, 314
 creating interactive PDFs, 313-321
 creating Tagged PDFs, 103-105
 exporting to PDF, 311-312
 hyperlinks, 317, 318
 importing PDFs into, 310-311
 presets, 312-313
 rollovers, 316-317
 Tagged PDFs, 321
Adobe PageMaker, 321
Adobe PDF Settings, changing, 47
Adobe Policy Server, 175
Adobe Reader, 7
applications, creating PDFs from, 44-45, 54
Area tool, 378
arrowheads, 15
ARTS Link Checker, 40, 75
Auto Scroll, 25, 93
Autodesk AutoCAD, 129-130

B

backgrounds, 23-24
batch processing, 202-203
 compared to manual input, 206-208
 defined, 203-204
 preferences, 209-210
 procedure, 205-206
batch sequences, 203, 204
 on the Acrobat 5 CD, 205
 creating a custom batch sequence, 208-209
 prebuilt, 204-205
 running, 204-210
Beauty and the Beast PDF, 36
 checking for problems, 41
 in onscreen PDFs, 69, 82
Betrayal PDF, 35
 checking for problems, 40
 in onscreen PDFs, 68, 75
bitmap art, 60, 61, *62*
 See also graphics
bleeds, 376-377
bookmarks
 in Acrobat, 157
 in Adobe FrameMaker, 323
 in Adobe InDesign, 317, 319
 in CorelDRAW, 337-338
 creating, 70-72
 inserting a JavaScript, 253
 in non-Western languages, 196-197
 in onscreen PDFs, 69-73
 preserving, 75-76
 setting up in PDFMaker, 119-120, *121*
 size of text, 13
 in Ventura, 330-331
 in WordPerfect, 157
 wrapping, 13
books in PDF, 89-90
browsers
 browser-based reviews, 146-150
 viewing PDFs in, 111-113
Business Forms Management Association, 246

C

Capture, 7, 55-57, 82-85, 217
 alternatives to, 85, 221-222
 Searchable Image, 57, 217, 219
 Suspects, 217
Capture "Lite," 218-221
Catalog, 6
Certified PDFs, 21
certifying documents, 186-189
Changes Allowed option, 173-174
CID (Character ID) font technology, 198
cloud tool, 15
Color Management option, 333
color printing, 358
 previewing color separations, 365-366
 See also preflighting

Color Purple PDF, 35
- checking for problems, 41

combined PDFs, 23
comments. *See also* editor's marks
- commenting tools, 134-135
- importing into Word, 150-152
- importing/exporting comments in Photoshop, 309-310
- inserting a new Acrobat note, 136
- preferences, 134-135
- printing with, 373-374
- receiving and reconciling e-mail-based comments, 146
- reporting on, 140, *141*
- Review & Comment button, 133
- sorting and filtering, 139
- toolbar, 135
- working with, 138-139

Compare Documents feature, 153-154
compatibility
- Compatibility settings, 53
- and security, 172

compression, 20
- Adaptive Compression, 56
- lossy, 61
- ZIP, 61

Connolly, Bob, 87-88
CONTROL-click combine, 24
copying. *See also* repurposing PDFs
- options, 174
- from PDFs, 124

Corel Designer 10, 340
Corel Ventura. *See* Ventura
CorelDRAW 11, 336-337
- bookmarks, 337-338
- hyperlinks, 338
- online PDFs, 337-338
- PDF forms, 339-340
- prepress PDFs, 338-339

Create Adobe PDF option, 277-278
Create from Multiples command, 129
cropping pages, 379-380
CZ-Pdf2Txt, 124

D

default settings
- Compatibility settings, 53
- High Quality, 46, 53-54
- PDF/X-1a, 46-47
- PDF/X-3, 47
- Press Quality, 46
- Smallest File Size, 46, 49-53
- Standard, Acrobat, 45-46, 48-49
- suggestions for improving, 47-53

desktop alternatives, 55
diagnosing problem PDFs, 36-38
digital identities, 175-176
- assembling a list of trusted identities, 178-180
- configuring identity search directories, 180
- creating, 176-177
- encrypting documents for a group of users, 180-181, *182*
- requesting digital certificates, 177-178, *179*
- sharing, 177
- *See also* security

digital signatures, 181-182
- adding a Digital Signature field to a PDF Form, 242
- applying invisible digital signatures, 183
- configuring the appearance of, 185-186
- creating a form field, 184
- displaying invisible signatures, 183, *184*
- signing a digital form field, 184-185
- using your signature, 182-183
- visible and invisible, 182
- *See also* security

Distance tool, 378
Distiller Server, 8
Document Open Password, 172
Document Properties, 36-38, *39*, 119, *120*
Document Server, 8
- for Reader Extensions, 8-9

double-byte fonts, 198
Drake, 124
Dynamic Zoom tool, 13

E

easyPDF, 55
eBinder, 129
eBook Reader. *See* Acrobat eBook Reader
eBooks, security, 170-171
editor's marks, 13-15, 136-137
- *See also* comments; reviewing

Elements, 5
e-mail-based reviewing, 142-146
e-mailing form data, 270-271
encrypting documents for a group of users, 180-181, *182*
Enfocus, 21
- PitStop Professional, 370-372

engineering drawings, 16-17
Excel. *See* Microsoft Excel
export options, 125-126

F

Fast Web View, 35, 38, 77, 332
Fat Albert PDF, 35
    checking for problems, 40
    in onscreen PDFs, 69, 76-77
file formats
    Illustrator, 297
    Job Definition Format (JDF), 380
    Photoshop PDF format, 304
file size, 53
    converting screenshots to black and white to reduce, 62
    Smallest File Size, 46, 49-53
financial reports, 86
fonts
    checking for problems, 38-39
    CID (Character ID) font technology, 198
    Distiller can't find fonts, 286
    double-byte, 198
    embedded, 38, 59-60
    fixing phantom font problems, 286-288
    no longer included with Acrobat or Adobe Reader, 47
    OpenType, 198
    single-byte, 198
    subsetting, 59-60
    system administration, 285-288
    terminology, 197-198
    TrueType, 60, 198
    Unicode, 198, 199
    in Ventura, 334-336
    working with, 58-59
footers, 23
Form Designer, 9
form toolbar, 16, 227-228
forms. *See* PDF Forms
FrameMaker. *See* Adobe FrameMaker

G

Gemini, 124
Generic PDFs, 304
graphics
    bitmap art, 60, 61, *62*
    clicking and dragging to resize, 62-63
    converting screenshots to black and white, 62
    in Microsoft Word, 100, *101*
    preparing for PDF, 60-61
    TIFF images, 61-63
    vector art, 60

H

Hand tool, 13
headers, 23
help, improvements in Acrobat 6, 19
High Quality, 46, 53-54
Honey, I Shrunk the Kids PDF, 36
    checking for problems, 41
    in onscreen PDFs, 69, 79-82
hyperlinks
    in Adobe InDesign, 317, 318
    creating, 72-73
    inserting a JavaScript, 254
    preserving, 75-76

I

IBM Tivoli, 289
Illustrator. *See* Adobe Illustrator CS
Image Solutions DocComposer, 58, 85, 222
imposition, 380-381
InDesign. *See* Adobe InDesign
Info tab, 13
Initial View, 80-82
Ink Manager, 376
installation
    Custom Setup options, 276-278
    incorrect, 274-278
    installing Acrobat across the enterprise, 288-289
    order of, 275
    what to install, 275-276
InstallShield Tuner, 288-289
Instant PDF, 55
interactive brochures, 86-88
interface
    improvements in Acrobat 6, 17-21
    similarity to MS Office applications, 20
Internet Explorer
    support on the Mac, 28
    Web capture, 111-113

J

Jade, 124
Japanese. *See also* languages
    accessibility support, 27, 93
    new features for, 196

JavaScript. *See* Acrobat JavaScript
Jaws PDF Creator, 55
JetForm, 7
Job Definition Format (JDF), 380
Job Options, changing, 47
JPEG, 61

K

keyboard shortcuts, 93

L

Labyrinth PDF, 34, *35*
    checking for problems, 40
    in onscreen PDFs, 68, 73-75
languages
    bookmarks in non-Western languages, 196-197
    different languages on separate layers, 196
    Japanese, 27, 196
    multilingual PDFs, 194-196
    new features in Acrobat 6, 194-197
    supported by PDF, 194
layers, 22
    different languages on separate layers, 196
    and Photoshop CS, 304
    printing, 378
links. *See* hyperlinks
Logical PDFs, 24, 26
logical reading order, 95, 96
Lost in Space PDF, 34
    checking for problems, 39
    in onscreen PDFs, 68, 69-73
Loupe tool, 12-13

M

Mac
    browser support, 28
    exporting comments into Word, 28
    PostScript driver setup, 288
    PostScript Printer Driver installation and configuration, 344-345
    Win vs. Mac differences, 27-28
mainframe computers, PDFs from, 212
marks, 376-377
measuring tools, 13, 378-379
menus, reorganization of items, 17-18
Microsoft Excel, 127
Microsoft Office, integrating Acrobat with, 110-111, 114-115
Microsoft Outlook, integration with, 113
Microsoft PowerPoint, 127-128
Microsoft Publisher, 113-114
Microsoft System Management Server, 289
Microsoft Visio, 129-130
Microsoft Word. *See also* PDFMaker
    bookmarks, 119-120, *121*
    creating a table of contents, 118-119
    creating Tagged PDFs, 99-100, *101*
    enabling Tagged PDFs, 115
    graphics, 100, *101*
    importing comments into, 150-152
    integrating Acrobat with Word XP, 15-16
    prepping documents for conversion to PDF, 117
    Settings tab, 120
    styles and fields, 117-118
    troubleshooting PDFs, 122-123
Microsoft Word XP, integration with, 15-16
Missing Pieces PDF, 36
    checking for problems, 41
Mo' Money PDF, 34
 See also Labyrinth PDF
movies, adding in Adobe InDesign, 320-321
multilingual PDFs, 194-196
    creating, 197-199
multimedia
    support in Professional, 12
    triggers, 252-253
Multiple Master technology, 198

N

navigation, buttons, 19
non-Adobe PDF products, 210-211

O

onscreen PDFs
    books in PDF, 89-90
    common problems, 68-69
    financial reports, 86
    fixing problem PDFs, 69-82
    good examples, 85-90
    interactive brochures, 86-88
onscreen reviewing, 132-133
    with Acrobat, 140-142
    browser-based reviews, 146-150
    commenting tools, 134-135
    Compare Documents feature, 153-154

duplicating a paper-based review cycle, 141-142
editor's marks, 136-137
e-mail-based, 142-146
importing comments into Word, 150-152
inserting a new Acrobat note, 136
Review & Comment button, 133
Review Tracker, 152-153
working with comments, 138-140
OpenOffice 1.1, 130
operating systems, Win vs. Mac differences, 27-28

P

page numbers, fixing in a Labyrinth PDF, 73-75
page orientation, 77-79
PageMaker. *See* Adobe PageMaker
Pages tab, 73-75
Pan & Zoom tool, 13
paper to PDF, 55-58
passwords. *See also* security
Document Open Password, 172
password-protected PDFs, 171-175
permissions passwords, 173
PDF Forms, 224-225
adding text fields, 229-230, *231*
benefits of, 225-226
Business Forms Management Association, 246
combo boxes, 234-239
creating a simple form, 228-245
e-mailing form data, 270-271
field calculation, 238-239
field signing, 242
formatting special numbers, 230-232
Forms toolbar, 227-228
vs. HTML forms, 226-227
layers, 228
list boxes, 234-239
from other applications, 245-246
radio buttons, 232-233
receiving form data, 242-245
Reset button, 233-234
restricting data entry in a field, 236-238
securing, 243
signing, 244-245
starting with an image, 228-229
Submit button, 241
submitting data, 239-241
tabbing order, 234, *235*
PDF Optimizer, 63-65
PDF Tweaker, 162
PDF Zone, 45
PDF2Word, 124
PDFMaker, 114-115, 278-279
bookmarks, 119-120, *121*
creating a table of contents, 118-119
options for Word, 116
running, 121-123
setting up for Microsoft Word, 116-121
Settings tab, 120
system administration, 278-279
See also Microsoft Word
PDFs
Certified, 21
combined, 23
creating, 32-33, 44-45
creating accessible PDFs, 26-27
creating settings for high quality, 53-54
as a file format, 30-32
Generic, 304
Logical, 24, 26
multilingual, 194-196
onscreen, 68-90
supported languages, 194
types of problem PDFs, 33-36
from Web-based products, 212
See also Tagged PDFs
PDFWriter, 54
PDF/X, 11-12, 358-360
advantages of, 361-362
resources, 362
PDF/X-1, 334, *335*
PDF/X-1a, 46-47
creating, 360-361
PDF/X-1a Sets option, 365
Save As PDF/X-1a, 363-364
PDF/X-3, 47
Perimeter tool, 378
Photoshop CS
automating PDF to PSD creation, 307-308
creating a PDF presentation, 308-309
importing and exporting PDF text and audio comments, 309-310
importing images from PDFs, 306-307
Layer Comps, 309
layers, 304
opening PDFs in, 306
PDF format, 304
placing PDFs in, 305-306
Save As PDF, 304-305
transferring metadata to PDF, 310
PitStop Professional, 370
PDF Profile Control Panel, 370-372

plaintext metadata, enabling, 174
Planet PDF, 45
pop-up menus, 266-267
PostScript driver setup, 279-280
  Adobe PDF Settings, 283-285
  Device Settings, 281-282
  fine-tuning in Windows 2000/XP/2003, 280-285
  Mac OS X issues, 288
  properties of the Adobe PDF Converter, 282-283
PowerPoint. *See* Microsoft PowerPoint
preflighting, 10-11
  in Acrobat 6 Professional, 363-365
  creating profiles, 368-369
  exporting and importing profiles, 369-370
  Extract ICC Profile option, 365
  PDF/X-1a Sets option, 365
  previewing color separations, 365-366
  previewing transparency flattening, 367
  profiles, 367-370
  Remove PDF/X option, 365
  software, 363
  Verify option, 364
  See also PitStop Professional
presets
  in Adobe Illustrator CS, 297-301
  in Adobe InDesign, 312-313
Press Quality, 46
printing
  from Acrobat, 372-378
  advanced settings, 374-375
  color, 358, 365-366
  with comments, 373-374
  imposition, 380-381
  Ink Manager, 376
  layers, 378
  marks and bleeds, 376-377
  output settings, 375-376
  PostScript options, 377
  print options, 372-374
  Printing Allowed option, 173
  transparency flattening, 377
  See also preflighting
problem PDFs, 33-36
  checking for problems, 38-42
  diagnosing, 36-38
product comparison, 5
Professional, Acrobat, 6
  components of, 276-278
  editor's marks, 13-15
  engineering drawings, 16-17
  enhanced user aids, 13
  form toolbar, 16
  integration with Word XP, 15-16
  multimedia support, 12
  PDF/X, 11-12
  preflighting, 10-11
  review process, 15
  tools for print and creative professionals, 9-10
  viewing options, 12-13
proofing, soft, 9

Q

QuarkXPress, 342
  creating the PDF, 347-348
  exporting the PDF, 351, *352*, 354-356
  installing an Adobe PostScript printer driver, 343
  installing and configuring the PPD for Windows, 343-344
  Jaws PDF Creator, 351-352
  PDF Filter QuarkXTension, 342, 348-350
  PostScript Printer Driver installation and configuration, 353-354
  printing to Adobe PDF from, 345-347
  versions 4 and 5, 342-351
Quick Check, 25, 164
Quite Imposing, 381

R

radio buttons, 232-233
Rapid PDF, 55
Read Aloud technology, 25
Read Out Loud, 93, 94
Reader. *See* Adobe Reader
reflow, 25, *26*, *27*, 93, 95-96
Rehabilitation Act of 1988, 92
repurposing PDFs, 123-127
restricted documents, 171-175
  See also security
reviewing, 15, 132-133
  with Acrobat, 140-142
  browser-based reviews, 146-150
  commenting tools, 134-135
  Compare Documents feature, 153-154
  duplicating a paper-based review cycle, 141-142
  editor's marks, 136-137
  e-mail-based, 142-146
  importing comments into Word, 150-152
  inserting a new Acrobat note, 136

Review & Comment button, 133
Review Tracker, 152-153
working with comments, 138-140
right-click combine, 24
RoboPDF, 55
rollovers, in Adobe InDesign, 316-317
rulers, 13

S

Safari, 28
scanning
converting paper to PDFs, 216-222
to create PDFs, 45, 55-58
documents into Acrobat, 82-83
screen readers, 24
scrolling, Auto Scroll, 25, 93
Searchable Image, 57, 217, 219
Searching for Bobby Fischer PDF, 36
checking for problems, 41-42
in onscreen PDFs, 69, 82-85
Section 508, 92
security
Adobe Policy Server, 175
Certified PDFs, 21
certifying documents, 186-189
digital identities, 175-181
digital signatures, 181-186
displaying settings, 170, *171*
eBooks, 170-171
improvements in Acrobat 6, 20-21
password-protected PDFs, 171-175
reasons for, 168-169
restricted documents, 171-175
securing PDF Forms, 243
types, 170-171
Select Table tool, 127
server solutions. *See also* server-side PDFs
examples of server-based PDF creation, 213-216
non-Adobe PDF products, 210-211
PDFs from Big Iron and UNIX and Windows servers, 212
PDFs from Web-based products, 212
server-side PDFs, 55, 211-212
single-byte fonts, 198
Smallest File Size, 46
modifying, 49-53
sniffing, 271
soft proofing, 9
Software Development Kit (SDK), 272
sound, adding in Adobe InDesign, 320-321
Standard, 6
Standard settings, 45-46
modifying, 48-49
system administration, 274
checklist, 291-292
font issues, 285-288
IBM Tivoli, 289
incorrect Acrobat installations, 274-278
installing Acrobat across the enterprise, 288-289
InstallShield Tuner, 288-289
Microsoft System Management Server, 289
PDFMaker, 278-279
PostScript driver setup, 279-285
updates, 289-291

T

table of contents
creating in Microsoft Word, 118-119
creating in WordPerfect, 159-162
tabular data, 127
Tagged PDFs, 24, 26, 38
accessibility and, 94-96
Adobe FrameMaker, 323, *324*
creating, 99-105
creating in Adobe FrameMaker, 102-103
creating in Adobe InDesign, 103-105, 321
creating in Microsoft Word, 99-100, *101*
editing tags, 105
enabling for accessibility in Word, 115
and WordPerfect, 163
task buttons, 17
terminology, 156-157, 197-198, 254-255
testing for accessibility, 106
third-party tools
creating PDFs from, 45, 54-55
desktop alternatives, 55
server-side PDFs, 55
thumbnails, 41
TIFF images, 61-63
See also graphics
toolbars
Commenting, 135
docking, 18
form toolbar, 16
Touchup Text tool, 169
transparency flattening, 377
previewing, 367

triggers, 250-251
On Focus, 252
On Lose Focus, 252
Mouse Down, 252
Mouse Enter, 252
Mouse Exit, 252
Mouse Up, 251-252
multimedia, 252-253
troubleshooting PDFs
created from Excel, 127
created from Word, 122-123

U

Unicode, 198
application support for, 199
UNIX, PDFs from UNIX servers, 212
updates, 289-291

V

vector art, 60
See also Adobe Illustrator CS; graphics
Ventura
bookmarks, 330-331
creating PDFs for specific uses, 331-332
fonts, 334-336
online PDFs, 329-331
PDFs for document distribution, 332
PDFs for editing, 332
PDFs for prepress, 333
PDFs for the Web, 333
PDF/X-1, 334, *335*
Publish to PDF feature, 328-336
version 10, 328
Verify option, 364
version 6, 4-5
version sniffing, 271
View Adobe PDF option, 276-277
viewing options, 12-13
Fast Web View, 35, 38, 77, 332
Initial View, 80-82
Visio. *See* Microsoft Visio
vision impairment, 92-93
See also accessibility

W

Waiting Game PDF, 35
checking for problems, 41
in onscreen PDFs, 69, 77
watched folders, 216
watermarks, 23-24
Web browsers
browser-based reviews, 146-150
viewing PDFs in, 111-113
Web capture, 111-113
WebDAV, setting up for browser-based reviews, 148-150
Windows
vs. Mac differences, 27-28
PDFs from Windows servers, 212
PostScript driver setup, 280-285
PostScript Printer Driver installation and configuration, 343-344
Word. *See* Microsoft Word
WordPerfect
creating a table of contents, 159-162
Define Table of Contents screen, 161
graphics, 164-165
making WordPerfect PDFs accessible, 163-165
PDF Tweaker, 162
Publish to PDF feature, 156, 157-158, 162-163
Reference Tools screen, 160
setting up your document to create a PDF, 158-162
terminology, 156-157
workflow, strategies, 58-63
Wrong Turn PDF, 35
checking for problems, 41
in onscreen PDFs, 69, 77-79

Z

ZIP compression, 61
See also compression
Zombie PDF, 33, *34*
in onscreen PDFs, 68, 69
and Standard settings, 45-46
zooming
Dynamic Zoom tool, 13
Pan & Zoom tool, 13

INTERNATIONAL CONTACT INFORMATION

AUSTRALIA
McGraw-Hill Book Company
Australia Pty. Ltd.
TEL +61-2-9900-1800
FAX +61-2-9878-8881
http://www.mcgraw-hill.com.au
books-it_sydney@mcgraw-hill.com

CANADA
McGraw-Hill Ryerson Ltd.
TEL +905-430-5000
FAX +905-430-5020
http://www.mcgraw-hill.ca

GREECE, MIDDLE EAST, & AFRICA (Excluding South Africa)
McGraw-Hill Hellas
TEL +30-210-6560-990
TEL +30-210-6560-993
TEL +30-210-6560-994
FAX +30-210-6545-525

MEXICO (Also serving Latin America)
McGraw-Hill Interamericana Editores
S.A. de C.V.
TEL +525-1500-5108
FAX +525-117-1589
http://www.mcgraw-hill.com.mx
carlos_ruiz@mcgraw-hill.com

SINGAPORE (Serving Asia)
McGraw-Hill Book Company
TEL +65-6863-1580
FAX +65-6862-3354
http://www.mcgraw-hill.com.sg
mghasia@mcgraw-hill.com

SOUTH AFRICA
McGraw-Hill South Africa
TEL +27-11-622-7512
FAX +27-11-622-9045
robyn_swanepoel@mcgraw-hill.com

SPAIN
McGraw-Hill/
Interamericana de España, S.A.U.
TEL +34-91-180-3000
FAX +34-91-372-8513
http://www.mcgraw-hill.es
professional@mcgraw-hill.es

UNITED KINGDOM, NORTHERN, EASTERN, & CENTRAL EUROPE
McGraw-Hill Education Europe
TEL +44-1-628-502500
FAX +44-1-628-770224
http://www.mcgraw-hill.co.uk
emea_queries@mcgraw-hill.com

ALL OTHER INQUIRIES Contact:
McGraw-Hill/Osborne
TEL +1-510-420-7700
FAX +1-510-420-7703
http://www.osborne.com
omg_international@mcgraw-hill.com